Frustrated Nationalism

SUNY series in Comparative Politics
―――――――
Gregory S. Mahler, editor

Frustrated Nationalism

Nationalism and National Identity
in the Twenty-First Century

Edited by
GREGORY S. MAHLER

Published by State University of New York Press, Albany

© 2024 State University of New York

All rights reserved

Printed in the United States of America

No part of this book may be used or reproduced in any manner without written permission. No part of this book may be stored in a retrieval system or transmitted in any form or by any means including electronic, electrostatic, magnetic tape, mechanical, photocopying, recording, or otherwise without the prior permission in writing of the publisher.

For information, contact State University of New York Press, Albany, NY
www.sunypress.edu

Library of Congress Cataloging-in-Publication Data

Name: Mahler, Gregory S., editor.
Title: Frustrated nationalism : nationalism and national identity in the twenty-first century / edited by Gregory S. Mahler.
Description: Albany : State University of New York Press, [2024] | Series: SUNY series in Comparative Politics | Includes bibliographical references and index.
Identifiers: ISBN 9781438496184 (hardcover : alk. paper) | ISBN 9781438496207 (ebook) | ISBN 9781438496191 (pbk. : alk. paper)
Further information is available at the Library of Congress.

10 9 8 7 6 5 4 3 2 1

Contents

Chapter 1
Frustrated Nationalism in the Twenty-First Century   1
  Gregory Mahler

Part I. Nationalism and Some Western Democratic States

Chapter 2
Frustrating Nationalism: U.S. Foreign Policy and Self-Determination   27
  David Ryan

Chapter 3
A Secular Turn: The Place of Culture in Quebec's Self-Conception   57
  Raffaele Iacovino

Chapter 4
Nation-Building within a Union State: Scotland's
Frustrated Nationalism   79
  Christopher A. Whatley

Part II. Nationalism and Minority Groups

Chapter 5
Contextual Nationhood: The Multiple Dimensions of Nationality
in the Mi'kmaw People's Nation-Building Strategies   105
  Simone Poliandri

Chapter 6
Rethinking Mexican Nationalism: Mestizaje, Indigenous Peoples, and Zapatismo   135
Neil Harvey and Dolores Trevizo

Chapter 7
Māori Struggle for Indigenous Rights: Contesting Sovereignty in New Zealand   163
Toon van Meijl

Part III. Nationalism and Ethnic Survival

Chapter 8
Virtual Tibet: Representation, Legitimacy, and Struggles for Democracy   185
Åshild Kolås and Tashi Nyima

Chapter 9
Self-Determination and National Liberation in Kurdistan in the Twentieth and Twenty-First Centuries   207
Joost Jongerden

Chapter 10
The Biafra Separatist Movement and Resurgence of Igbo Nationalism in Nigeria   231
Bernard Ugochukwu Nwosu and Kenneth Omeje

Chapter 11
Beyond a Militia: Notes on the History and Ideology of the Huthi (Ansar Allah) Movement in Yemen   259
Felipe Medina Gutiérrez

Part IV. Afterword

Chapter 12
Nationalism and National Identity in the Twenty-First Century   291
Gregory Mahler

About the Contributors	301
Index	307

1

Frustrated Nationalism in the Twenty-First Century

GREGORY MAHLER

Introduction

A modern nation "is a population that purportedly has a right to a state of its own."[1] Philip Roeder points out that "a piece of folk wisdom often repeated in academic and policy communities" suggests that today there "may be as many as six to eight hundred active nation-state projects, and another seven to eight thousand potential projects," yet only a few more than 190 nation-states have achieved the status of sovereignty.[2] Here the term "nation-state project" refers to an instance in which a specific population claims it should be self-governing within a sovereign state of its own, although that self-governing territory may not yet exist.[3]

Nationalism, it has been said, has been "one of the determining forces in modern history."[4] An understanding of the implications of nationalism for modern history and for our time appears to be a fundamental one. Ernest Gellner has written that nationalism "is primarily a political principle," one "which holds that the political and the national unit should be congruent,"[5] although Anthony Smith has defined nationalism as "an ideological movement for the attainment and maintenance of autonomy, cohesion and individuality for a social group deemed by some of its members to constitute an actual or potential nation." Smith emphasizes, therefore, that nationalism "is both an ideology and a movement, usually a minority one, which aspires to nationhood for the chosen group."[6] Nationalism has many forms, and it behooves us to understand its demands in order to understand the possible impact of nationalism today. As noted elsewhere, "on all continents there are competing projects to unite some states into larger states, such as a European Union . . . [or] to make others smaller by granting independence to such substate entities as the Basque Country or Somaliland."

Nationalism is a state of mind in which the supreme loyalty of the individual is felt to be due the nation-state. A deep attachment to one's native soil, to local traditions, and to established territorial authority has existed in varying strength throughout history. But not until the end of the eighteenth century did nationalism in the modern sense become a generally recognized sentiment increasingly molding all public and private life.[7]

Conflicts in the name of nationalism are unfortunately common and have been sources of social tension within and between nations for as long as individuals have been writing. Conflicts based on "national consciousness" and "patriotism" have long been with us.[8] In modern times social scientists have been more analytical about nationalism-inspired conflicts, trying to measure the factors that inspire them.[9] These are the issues addressed in this volume.

Many people use the word "nation" to signify a place, or a people, or a set of institutions. As commonly employed today, the term "nation" has two distinct meanings. The first refers to a country with a sovereign government. The second refers to a community of people, typically with a shared language, religion, culture, and territory. A related term, "nationality," also refers to a community of people with a shared language, religion, and culture, but not necessarily a fixed territory.

"Nation," of course, is a problematic term because of the "often-encountered failure in the vast literature of nationalism to find clearer distinctions between nationalism, nations, the nation-state, and national unity," as well as a divide between "those who view the nation as a political association and those who see it as a cultural community."[10] Not all nations correspond with their own nation-states, and many nation-states include more than one nation.[11] Fred Riggs of the University of Hawaii, working under the auspices of the International Social Science Council's Committee on Conceptual and Terminological Analysis, has defined a nation as "a group of people who feel themselves to be a community bound together by ties of history, culture, and common ancestry."[12] Although "nation" is used independently of "state" and "ethnic group," sometimes these terms overlap and provide compound nouns such as "ethnic nation," "social nation," or "official nation."

As Anthony Smith has noted, nationalism "provides perhaps the most compelling identity myth in the modern world." Myths of national identity typically refer to territory or ancestry (or both) as the basis of political community, and these differences furnish important, if often neglected, sources of instability and conflict in many parts of the world. It is no accident that many of the most bitter and protracted "inter-national" conflicts derive from competing claims and conceptions of national identity. An understanding of these ideas and claims is vital if we are ever to ameliorate, let alone resolve, some of these conflicts and create a genuine international community.[13]

Smith has suggested that a number of conditions can foster the formation of powerful nationalist movements, as identified in Table 1.1, although he notes that some of these can be more vital than others. His view is that bureaucratic authority, the myth of common history, and a historical outlook "appear to be prerequisites for an effective nationalism."[14]

One of the most widely cited modern analyses of the distinction between "nation" and "state" was offered by Hannah Arendt. She sought to understand the idea of "statelessness," perhaps because of her personal challenges as a German Jewish refugee in the Second World War. She distinguished between nations and states. A *nation* referred to a dominant group "with its culture, language, and shared history living in a bounded territory," whereas a *state* referred to "the legal status of persons living in a territory, that is those who are considered citizens with legal rights." Arendt

Table 1.1. Conditions Fostering the Formation of Nationalist Movements

I. Frameworks
   1. An easily identifiable territory and location
   2. A single political authority and bureaucracy, able to level and homogenize the population

II. Bases
   1. A myth and cult of common origins and history
   2. Other cultural differences like language or color
   3. Partial secularization of urban elites' traditions

III. Bearers
   1. Growth and exclusion of an urban intelligentsia
   2. An alliance between intelligentsia and one or more classes or status groups, usually urban
   3. Commercial penetration and mercantile assent

Source: Based on Anthony Smith, *Nationalist Movements* (1976, 915).

argues that a tension between "nation" and "state" has persisted since the late eighteenth century, suggesting that a special problem exists for people who are "denationalized," which was the fate of German Jews before the "final solution" of extermination was developed.[15]

In 1908, Friedrich Meinecke offered a distinction between the *Kulturnation* and the *Staatsnation*, the former referring to a largely passive cultural community and the latter referring to an active, self-determining political nation. Although many have indicated some unhappiness at basing nationalism upon a cultural dimension, this is an important distinction: cultural identities can and do exist without a corresponding national label. This means, then, that a "national" label must include some cultural dimension. As Smith has argued, "a political community . . . implies at least some common institutions and a single code of rights and duties for all the members of the community."[16] Smith has suggested five key characteristics of what he believes are included in a Western conception of the nation:

1. Nations have an historic territory, or homeland.
2. Nations have common myths and historical memories.
3. Nations possess a common, mass public culture.
4. Nations offer common legal rights and duties for all members.
5. Nations have a common economy with territorial mobility for members.

Thus a nation is defined as "a named human population sharing an historic territory, common myths and historical memories, a mass, public culture, a common economy and common legal rights and duties for all members."[17]

According to Max Weber's famous definition, "a state is that human community which (successfully) lays claim to the *monopoly of legitimate physical violence* within a certain territory . . . [T]he state is a relationship of *rule* (*Herrschaft*) by human beings over other human beings, and one that rests on the legitimate use of violence (that is, violence that is held to be legitimate)."[18]

Thus to make fully explicit the nature of today's common confusion, some self-perceived nations are not states (e.g. today's Québecois living in Canada); some self-perceived states are not nations (e.g., the former Russian empire, or the former Yugoslavia); and relatively few contemporary states are "pure" nation-states (e.g., Iceland).[19]

One challenge in this discussion is that there is more than one type of nationalism. As Jaakko Heiskanen has written: "[N]ationalism may manifest itself as part of official state ideology or as a popular non-state movement and may be expressed along civic, ethnic, cultural, language, religious, or ideological lines."[20] These self-definitions of the nation are used to classify types of nationalism. However, such categories are not mutually exclusive and many nationalist movements combine some or all of these elements to varying degrees.[21] Nationalist movements can also be classified by other criteria, such as scale and location."[22] In Smith's view, "nationhood" comprises three basic ideals: (1) autonomy and self-government for the group; (2) solidarity and fraternity of the group in a recognized territory of "home"; and (3) a distinctive and preferably unique culture and history peculiar to the group in question.[23]

The Ethics of Nation-building

Nationalism, as one scholar has noted, "is a confusing historical phenomenon."[24] It is "confusing" because observers of nationalist movements may or may not support nationalism *in principle*, independent of the specific case being discussed. Several of the chapters included in this book discuss nationalist movements that have strong emotional linkages for their observers. The Houthi in Yemen range from being seen as terrorists supported by outside agitators to being seen as saviors of local culture, religion, and society. Although Charles De Gaulle voiced his support for Québec in his "vive le Québec libre" speech in July of 1967 while giving a speech at the *Expo '67 World's Fair*, especially with his emphasis on the word "libre" (free), many Canadians saw Québec nationalism as a distinct threat to the nation, and Canadian Prime Minister Lester Pearson responded by saying that "Canadians do not need to be liberated."[25]

As Baum notes, some observers think of nationalism as a political movement associated with fascism, coming from history's experience with the actions of Nazi Germany and Italy and Japan in World War II, but at the same time, some observers have a great deal of sympathy for anti-imperialist nationalism of former colonies in Asia and Africa that have struggled—some successfully, others unsuccessfully—to become independent states.[26] It is difficult to judge a nationalist movement from the outside, but it is often also difficult to evaluate it from the inside, to completely understand its goals and motivations. Many nationalist groups have "official" doctrines and goals that appear to be laudable, but in fact have some subtext that is not so laudable. That is, we must be cautious when we look at nationalist movements to try to determine which are "good" and which are not. For many Canadians, the concept of nationalism was a good thing when it was being used to create Canadian institutions and culture and work toward independence from Britain, but it was not a good thing when Québec tried to use the same arguments to work toward independence from the rest of Canada.

Nationalism can be seen as both an ideology and a form of behavior. As an ideology, it is built on people's awareness of a nation "to give a set of attitudes and programme of action." As a form of behavior, it is linked to ethnocentrism and sometimes "shows itself in prejudice relating to foreigners, stereotyping of other nations, and solidarity with co-nationals."[27]

Nation-Building and National Sovereignty

Nation-building, relatedly, thus refers to the development and strengthening of a set of shared values and a common identity among the inhabitants of a country with a sovereign government. Some have referred to this kind of activity as "the production of conceptions of peoplehood. Sometimes, the peoplehood conceived by a particular nationalist ideology requires an independent state or autonomous territory for its realization."[28] This common identity and these common values promote the development of legitimate state institutions. When people have problems agreeing on a national identity, domestic unrest and even civil war may follow. Similarly, *state-building* refers to the creation and strengthening of the civil and military institutions that make up a government.

It is not only the existence (or lack thereof) of "nationhood" that is the focus of this collection of essays. National *sovereignty* is the subject of most of the essays here. Sovereignty, in brief, is the quality or state of being sovereign, of having supreme power or authority. Groups want to be able to control their own futures, within their own territories, and sovereignty in these instances means that the group will control territory with recognized and stable boundaries, that the group will have the ability to enter into relations with other sovereign states and govern foreign and domestic trade, that the group will be able to live there on an ongoing basis, and that the group will have the ability to regulate policy that affects that group.[29] No other set of actors will be able to set or regulate such policy. These tensions are exacerbated if the rulers of a political unit belong to a nation other than that of the majority of the ruled. In Gellner's words, "nationalism is a theory of political legitimacy" in which "ethnic boundaries should not cut across political ones, and, in particular, that ethnic boundaries within a given state . . . should not separate the power-holders from the rest."[30] In strictly legal terms, sovereignty describes the power of a state to govern itself and its subjects. Sovereignty is a concept that a state has the right and power to govern itself without outside interference; the state is free from external control.[31]

This type of debate over *national sovereignty* has a long and—from the perspective of those who have unsuccessfully sought such a condition—sad history. The unsuccessful side in a quest for national sovereignty often suffers dramatically at the hands of the group that is dominant and in power, as we shall see in many of the essays in this volume. Those *in* control often do not want to accede to the requests of nationalist movements because that would mean *giving up* control of some of the territory they control.

Nationhood and Ethnic Identity

Fox argues that "distinguishing between nationalisms, ethnicity, and racial identities has always been difficult because the categories are too loose." He argues that "an ethnic identity may easily become an ethnic nationalism; a nationalism that has failed to achieve an independent state may continue as an ethnic identity. Scottish and Welsh identities have moved back and forth over this range several times in the last century."[32]

> It is the case, however, that ethnicity has been a basis for nationalistic motivations over time. Smith points out that the "standard, Western model of the nation" has been based on historic territory, legal-political community, legal-political equality of members, and common civic culture and ideology, but that "a rather different model of the nation" emerged outside of Western Europe, "notably in Eastern Europe and Asia," and could be called "an 'ethnic' conception of the nation."[33] The key characteristic of this was that whereas the Western concept laid down that an individual had to belong to some nation but could choose to which he or she belonged, the non-Western or ethnic concept allowed no such latitude. Whether you stayed in your

community or emigrated to another, you remained ineluctably, organically, a member of the community of your birth and were forever stamped by it. A nation, in other words, was first and foremost a community of common descent.[34]

Many of the nations and national movements described in this volume correspond well to this latter approach to the definition of a nation: they are based on ethnic identity, and even with an absence of a defining territory they endure.

Smith identifies six attributes of ethnic community that are crucial to a national identity, including (a) a collective proper name, (b) a myth of common ancestry, (c) shared historical memories, (d) one or more differentiating elements of common culture, (e) an association with a specific "homeland," and (f) a sense of solidarity for significant sectors of the population.[35]

Sources of New Nations

Indeed, according to one study, decolonization is the single greatest source of new nations. One study has found that 62 percent of the total number of new states since 1815 come from this source.[36] Table 1.2 shows the sources of new and reconstructed nations between 1816 and 2000.

Table 1.2. Where Do States Come From?

Origin of state	Examples	Major States	Micro States	Total
Division of states	Argentina, 1816; Romania, 1878; Russia, 1991, North/South Korea, 1948	159	21	180
Unification of existing states	Germany, 1990; Vietnam, 1975	5		5
Newly incorporated territories	Liberia, 1847	6		6
Total		170	21	191

Source: Table derived from data in Roeder, Table 1.1, "Numbers of New and Reconstituted States Worldwide, 1816–2000" (Roeder 2007, 8).

One of the classic arguments among historians is whether nations can exist before nationalism. Many would argue that *nations* have existed from time immemorial, and that national*ism* is a much more modern phenomenon, often being dated to the French Revolution. Indeed, Kamenka suggests that "the history of Europe since the French Revolution has been the history of the rise and development of political nationalism. . . . Nationalism not only holds together the histories of the nineteenth and twentieth centuries . . . it has also brought the histories of Asia, Africa and the Pacific into relation with European history, making them part of a universal history."[37]

Before the period leading up to the French Revolution, we have only fleeting expressions of a national sentiment, and vague intimations of the central ideas of nationalism, with its emphasis on the autonomy of culturally distinctive nations. Even the nation is a purely modern construct, though here there is considerable disagreement among "modernists" as to the period of its emergence in Europe, with some favoring the eighteenth century or earlier and others backing the late nineteenth and early twentieth century, when the masses were finally "nationalized" and women enfranchised.[38]

Kamenka argues that nationalism "is a modern and initially a European phenomenon, best understood in relation to the developments that produced, and were symbolized by, the French Revolution of 1797."[39]

It is not enough, however, to say that "Asian nationalism" is simply a reaction to Western power and dominance, or that there was no idea of nation or national consciousness in Asia before conflict developed with the West.

Some of these peoples had also achieved national consciousness before modern times, most notably the Koreans sandwiched between the Chinese and the Japanese, the Vietnamese in their attitudes toward China, and the Burmans and the Thais in their attitudes toward each other. We can also include the Japanese in their attitudes toward Korea and China, the Chinese during the Sung and Ming dynasties in their attitudes toward the Mongols and various Manchurian military federations, and, less convincingly, various peoples living on the periphery of the Indian heartland, such as the Bengalis, the Tamils, and the Singhalese.[40]

While the British led the way to Western supremacy in Asia, followed by the Dutch and the French, the Asian response tended to be futile efforts at armed resistance in order to defend traditional rights and traditional dynasties, rather than to establish modern nation-states. It was only later that the "modern" concept of nationhood was established in Asia and Asian nationalist movements appeared

Disputed Nations

The issue of being "free from external control" is a challenge to which many groups are very sensitive. The Consortium of European Social Science Data Archives[41] has a substantial collection of data sets that focus on topics of national identity and national conflict. How ethnic minorities are counted in national surveys is important and can influence the kinds of results that surveys will produce.[42] It is the case, of course, that not *every* ethnic minority can have its own nation-state in which it is "free from external control." Such a situation would result in thousands of members in the United Nations, not nearly two hundred, as is the case today. The challenge, though, is to find a balance point where *significant* ethnic minorities become, in fact, majorities in their own nations, and no longer must live as minorities being ruled by other ethnic, religious, cultural, or some other majority group.

The challenge has always been deciding what the bases of nationalism should be. Language isn't a good option, as there often is "no inevitable or natural correspondence between language and territory in the claims of aspiring nationality groups."[43] Ethnic identities often spill over borders. Religion has been similarly inaccurate.

Of all the collective identities in which human beings share today, national identity is perhaps the most fundamental and inclusive. Not only has national*ism*, the ideological movement, penetrated every corner of the globe, but the world is divided, first and foremost, into nation-states—states claiming to be nations—and national identity ever underpins the recurrent drive for popular sovereignty and democracy, as well as the exclusive tyranny that it sometimes breeds. Other types of collective identity—class, gender, race, religion—may overlap or combine with national identity, but they rarely succeed in undermining its hold, though they may influence its direction.[44]

According to the World Population Review, a sovereign nation is "a nation that has one centralized government that has the power to govern a specific geographic area. Under the definition set by international law, a sovereign nation has a defined territory with just one government. These nations have a permanent population and can enter into relations with other sovereign countries. While most major sovereign nations are well known throughout the world, many smaller or less prominent nations are relatively *unknown countries*."[45] The number of sovereign nations in the world today is not agreed upon. The United Nations currently recognizes 206 states—193 member nations, two observer states, and eleven "other" states—but there are a large number of other regions that are considered sovereign nations by

Table 1.3. 15 United Nations States Whose Sovereignty Is Disputed

1. **Abkhazia**—is claimed by Georgia.
2. **Artsakh**—is claimed by Azerbaijan.
3. **China** (the People's Republic of China)—is partially unrecognized and is claimed by Taiwan (the Republic of China).
4. **Cyprus** (Republic of Cyprus)—is not recognized by Turkey.
5. **Israel**—is partially unrecognized. As of December 2019, 162 UN nations have recognized Israel as a sovereign nation [the United Nations currently has 193 members].
6. **Kosovo**—is claimed by Serbia. As of March 2020, 115 UN nations have recognized Kosovo as a sovereign state. However, some have also retracted or declined to confirm their recognition due to political pressure.
7. **North Korea** (The Democratic People's Republic of Korea)—is claimed by South Korea.
8. **Northern Cyprus** (Turkish Republic of Northern Cyprus)—is claimed by the Cyprus (Republic of Cyprus).
9. **Palestine**—is partially recognized and is disputed by Israel. As of 2019, 138 UN nations have recognized Palestine as a sovereign state.
10. **Sahrawi Arab Democratic Republic**—is claimed by Morocco.
11. **Somaliland**—is claimed by Somalia.
12. **South Korea** (The Republic of Korea)—is claimed by North Korea.
13. **South Ossetia**—is claimed by Georgia.
14. **Taiwan** (Republic of China)—is claimed by mainland China (the People's Republic of China). As of 2019, only fourteen UN nations have recognized Taiwan as a sovereign nation, largely due to China's interference.
15. **Transnistria**—is claimed by Moldova.

Source: World Population Review, "Sovereign Nation 2022." https://worldpopulationreview.com/country-rankings/sovereign-nation

some sources and not by others. Of the United Nations' 206 states, fifteen have disputed sovereignty.

Sovereignty expresses the fundamentally important notion of political independence. In this sense, sovereignty is an exercise of power by a state.

Peter Calvert has written that "one of the first tasks of most governments, when they have won independence, is to take it away from someone else . . . I would refer to them generally as 'minorities.' "[46] The goal of seeking power, after all, is to control power, and power invariably tends to be exercised *over others*. Calvert notes that "the vast majority of independent states which have achieved their independence through force tend to fall into the hands of those who will seek to make them as 'oppositionless' as possible."[47]

Are there sovereign states with no minorities to become the "other" in the exercise of power by the state? Not likely. When a new state is created based on a significant variable, such as religion or ethnic identity, citizens may look around and find that everyone is alike in the key variable. However, in short order, other variables will likely appear to create a social chasm, whether those variables are social characteristics, income, education, language, geography, or something else. This leads to what Calvert refers to as the *reductio ad absurdum* of a nationalist movement being victorious, leading to independence, and subsequently growing *its own* nationalist movements within its population that will seek to win *their own* independence.[48]

Plamenatz has suggested that nationalism "is a reaction of peoples who feel culturally at a disadvantage . . . Where there are several peoples in close contact with one another and yet conscious of their separateness, and these peoples share the same ideals and the same conception of progress, and some of them are, or feel themselves to be, less well placed than others to achieve these ideals and make progress, nationalism is apt to flourish."[49]

The Era of the Nation-State

The key to nationalism is the nation-state.[50] While not all nationalist groups *have* a nation-state, the nation-state is almost invariably the *goal* of nationalist movements. As the Pew Research Center has noted,

> Even as the world grows more comfortable with globalization, people continue to feel the strong pull of nationalism. This enduring sense of national identity is seen in a number of ways. There is a widespread belief among people in most nations that their culture is superior to others and that it needs protection from outside forces. Significant numbers of people assert that parts of neighboring countries rightfully belong to their country. And most would like to tighten controls on the flow of immigrants into their countries.[51]

Some have said that the era of the nation-state has come and gone, and that the challenge to state sovereignty comes from the inability of modern states to deal with multinational organizations and behaviors, including ethno-political conflict, multinational corporations, global terrorism, and other structures that do not recognize the sovereignty of contemporary nation-states.[52] Globalization may be the functional opponent of the nation-state, as multinational corporations and foreign direct investments undermine the practical dimensions of state sovereignty; states have proven to be incapable of protecting their citizens from external forces such as these. Similarly, the growing force of what are seen as universal human rights can also be seen to weaken state sovereignty.[53]

The study of nationalism in international relations is confusing because of the confounding of all of these terms. It is confusing because "it deals at times with *states* and at other times with *nations, nationalities* and *ethnic groups*, none of which are states."[54] Others, though, maintain that neither nationalism nor ethnicity is vanishing as part of "an obsolete traditional order." Craig Calhoun has argued that

> Both are part of a modern set of categorical identities invoked by elites and other participants in political and social struggles. . . . Numerous dimensions of modern social and cultural change, notably state building (along with war and colonialism), individualism, and the integration of large-scale webs of indirect relationships also serve to make both nationalism and ethnicity salient. Nationalism, in particular, remains the pre-eminent rhetoric for attempts to demarcate political communities, claim rights of self-determination and legitimate role by reference to "the people" of a country. Ethnic solidarities and identities are claimed most often where groups do not seek "national" autonomy but rather a recognition internal to or cross-cutting national or state boundaries.[55]

Nationalism and Conflict

Debate over nationalism has long been associated with war and intergroup violence. Woodrow Wilson once described World War I has having "its roots in the disregard of the rights of small nations and of nationalities," and he argued that future peace would have to rely on "the wishes, the natural connections, the racial aspirations, the security and the peace of mind of the peoples involved." His view was that out of World War I would emerge "a new international order based upon broad and universal principles of right and justice," including "self-determination," which was intimately tied in with national aspirations.[56]

Indeed, the peacemakers at the end of World War I saw the role of the nation as being central to the idea of peace in the future. Lloyd George wrote in March of 1919 that nationality was a guiding principle of future peace "because of its status as a 'human criterion.'"

> There will never . . . be peace in South-Eastern Europe if every little state now coming into being is to have a large Magyar *irredenta* within its borders. I would therefore take as a guiding principle of the peace that as far as is humanly possible the different races should be allocated to their motherlands, and that this human criterion should have preference over considerations of strategy or economics or communications, which can usually be adjusted by other means.[57]

"Conventional wisdom" will tell us that nationalism is dangerous, and that while nationalism is a relatively modern phenomenon it has already made its mark in the history of violent conflict. While Napoleon and Hitler are often cited in discussions of the dysfunction of nationalism, more modern examples of civil wars fought for that end—the Algerians against the French, the Biafrans against the Nigerians, Basques against Spaniards, Tibetans against Chinese, and so on—are easy to come by. David Laitin disagrees with this conventional wisdom, naming four routes that can lead ethnic and national groups to violence: (1) irredentism, (2) secession, (3) "sons-of-the-soil," and (4) communalism.[58]

Irredentism ("unredeemed" in Italian) exists when a nation has a state of its own but wants to also take back territory occupied by fellow nationals living in a neighboring state. Secession can be characterized as the inverse of irredentism: "when a nation is not larger but rather smaller than the state, and its self-appointed representatives seek to have a state of their own." This is a common model, and the Irish separating from Britain, the Basques trying to separate from Spain, the Igbos (as Biafrans) trying to separate from Nigeria, and the Tamils seeking to separate from Sri Lanka are all examples of this phenomenon. "Sons-of-the-soil" refers to an Indigenous population resenting a central-government-induced population shift that occurs when a central government seeks to move population into areas (formerly) dominated by minority populations. The minority population resents the expansion of the majority population in their midst, and may resort to violence to restore the *status quo ante*. Communal warfare takes place "when (quasi-) organized militias of one ethnic group attack civilians from another ethnic group that is living in the same place . . . Pogroms against Jews in Russia's Pale of Settlement, against Armenians in the Ottoman Empire as a prelude to the genocide, against (then-called) Negroes in the American South, against Muslims in North India, and against Chinese in Indonesia are well-known examples of this form of ethnic/nationalist violence."[59]

Laitin suggests in his analysis that despite possible associations between nationalism and inter-national political violence, the data shows little causal relationship. He suggests that a bias in the literature dealing with nationalism "overemphasizes explanations for violence at the expense of explanations for peace,"[60] and that we would do well to look elsewhere for explanations of violence, including what he calls "the weak state," one "unable to provide basic services to its population, unable to police its peripheries, and unable to distinguish law abiders from lawbreakers."[61] He cites an economic motive for civil war—"collecting the revenues that ownership of the state avails"—and suggests that insurgents have taken advantage of state incompetence.

The International Crisis Group publishes an annual list of "Conflicts to Watch" around the world, indicating major local conflicts that "serve as mirrors for global trends. They highlight issues with which the international system is obsessed and those toward which it is indifferent." Their lists for recent years reflect the kind of nationalism-related conflicts described in this volume; in the words of Robert Malley, "these wars tell the story of a global system caught in the early swell of sweeping change, of regional leaders both emboldened and frightened by the opportunities such a transition presents." The list for 2023 includes, but is not limited to, the following:

- The EU's integrated approach in Mozambique
- The Sudan: rebooting an endangered transition
- Afghanistan: the Taliban restrict women's rights, worsening the humanitarian crisis
- Myanmar: post-coup crisis and a flawed election
- The pressing task of advancing peace talks in the South Caucasus
- Keeping the right balance in supporting Ukraine

- Brazil: can Latin America's divides be bridged?
- The Gulf: promoting collective security through regional dialogue
- Iraq: staving off instability in both the near and distant future[62]

The Contributions in this Volume

The questions of group identities and their relations with the states within which they live are central to most of the essays included here. Chapters in this volume focus on a wide range of settings of conflict, be it conflict currently in "active" status or conflict resolved in a way that the nationalist movement did not seek. This volume is titled "Frustrated Nationalism" because the groups *seeking* sovereignty have not *attained* the full sovereignty being sought, although we will see that some of the groups being examined, such as those in Québec or the Māori, have achieved *some* of what they originally sought, while falling short of full sovereignty. Other groups, such as the Tibetans, have been driven from their home territory and are currently simply trying to keep their national identity and aspirations alive.

David Ryan's chapter on U.S. foreign policy and self-determination opens the collection, and shows the overall inconsistency of U.S. policy over the years. Ryan notes that "the ideological content of a string of seminal American documents pivots on the concepts of self-determination, liberty, and democracy," but at the same time American expansionism and globalization "frustrated the self-determination and nationalist aspirations of many" while compromising the sovereignty of nations. The United States is *postcolonial*, Ryan argues, yet in many ways it has emulated European empires. To take one example, "while the traditional interpretation of the 1823 Monroe Doctrine is frequently understood as an American proposition to support the nascent nations of Latin America, it evolved into something quite different." Looking at American foreign policy from the nineteenth century through the Cold War and the time of the Vietnam War, Ryan shows us that America's national interest steered American support of, or lack of support of, nationalist movements in many settings around the world.

Nationalism has evolved in Quebec over the past few decades. Raffaele Iacovino shows us that "with the Quebec independence movement in a state of dormancy for some time now, and no longer an imminent threat to the Canadian political system, the Québécois have nevertheless continued to engage in a national conversation about terms of belonging." At one point in time, nationalism in Quebec "emerged as the primary agent of modernization and social emancipation for francophones"; Quebec's strategy of pursuing what was called "integrative pluralism" strengthened interculturalism and allowed Quebec to achieve many of its goals while avoiding the conflicts of earlier years. Modernization and "catching-up" in Quebec during the Quiet Revolution "produced a wholesale change to the main tenets of national identity, away from a defensive posture toward openness to newcomers and tolerance of differences."

The relationship of Scotland to the United Kingdom is the subject of Christopher Whatley's chapter "Nation-Building within a Union State." Scotland joined with England and Wales in a union in 1603, but Whatley shows that the Scots "have never been entirely comfortable with Scotland's relationship with England." Scotland's national characteristics are discussed, as well as the history of feelings of nationalism and the unique identity of the Scots. Whatley discusses why tensions have "deepened and widened" in the past half-century, and reflects on Scotland's current position in relation to the union with the rest of the United Kingdom. Whatley concludes by noting that while there is no doubt that Scotland could survive as an independent nation, areas of uncertainty remain about what an independent Scotland might look like. Such uncertainties need to be resolved before Scottish voters feel ready to "sever the ties that for well over three centuries have, often uneasily, bound the peoples of Scotland and England together."

Simone Poliandri has contributed a chapter on the Mi'kmaq peoples of Canada and their pursuit of "contextual nationhood" in Canada. Following discussion of the First Nations of Canada, and the Mi'kma'ki and Mi'kmaw Nation more specifically, Poliandri offers historical analysis of the development of nationhood for the Mi'kmaq under British colonial rule. Today, over 30,000 Mi'kmaq are registered as members of twenty-nine recognized First Nations, all but one in Canada (one is in the U.S. state of Maine), and we see how they have been working on rebuilding and redefining their nation and sense of nationhood. Poliandri shows how certain legal cases became significant in the Mi'kmaw defense of their "commonly-held treaty rights," most recently in November 2021 with some commercial fishing issues, revealing the "dynamic nature of contemporary Mi'kmaw nationalist sentiments and the rapidity of their nation-rebuilding efforts."

Neil Harvey and Dolores Trevizo discuss Mexican nationalism and the challenges faced by Mestizaje, Indigenous peoples, and Zapatismo in the twentieth century. Mexico's "multi-layered national identity" left open the possibility for conflict, and full constitutional recognition of some key groups remained elusive, undermining Indigenous peoples' ability to pursue their own forms of development. While the reforms that followed the 1910 Revolution led to land reform for many, Harvey and Trevizo show that some groups were left out of the reforms and needed to act to seek a more inclusive and socially just nation. Land reform did "contribute to Mexico's relatively successful nation building," and reforms contributed to the ability of many Indigenous groups to "preserve their cultures, languages, and identities via control over land, water and other national resources." Nation-building worked, and even the armed movement in Chiapas in the 1990s took place *within* Mexican nationalism seeking more equality and inclusiveness, not seeking its own national independence.

Toon van Meijl presents a study of the Māori struggle for Indigenous rights with New Zealand, and how the Indigenous people of New Zealand have adapted their aspirations for nationalism in contemporary times. New Zealand has been more responsive to Māori demands than have been many other governments to ethnic nationalist movements, and the Indigenous groups have received land and other financial compensation for land that can no longer be returned to them. As van Meijl writes, "this process is still ongoing." The role of tribes has been important, as dispossessed lands have been returned to tribal ownership and thus tribes are "re-installing" their sovereignty. We see in this chapter that following the implementation of a settlement process that is trying to respond to and remove Indigenous grievances about wrongs done to them during the colonial era, much of the pressure behind Māori nationalism has decreased. In the settlement process of the 1990s, the goal of the government was to repair historical injustices done to the Māori by returning property to them and by recognizing Māori language and culture as an important part of New Zealand society. Māori cultural nationalism has been relatively successful in the twentieth century, van Meijl shows us, and it has re-introduced pride in Māori culture "that, in turn, also boosted Māori political confidence to never give up their struggle for justice and reconciliation."

The case of Tibet differs from several of the others in this volume because Tibet *was* an independent entity but is now occupied by the People's Republic of China, with little likelihood of regaining its sovereignty. In their chapter, "Virtual Tibet," Åshild Kolås and Tashi Nyima focus on Tibetans' challenge under China. A major concern, they note, is how to "keep the Tibetan heritage alive, or reconstruct the Tibetan nation in the diaspora, while also reinventing 'Tibet' in the attempt to define the

'Tibetan,'" This chapter describes the context of the struggle to democratize the Tibetan nation and the efforts to have the Tibetan nation *not* disappear through assimilation in other populations around the world through the creation of a government-in-exile with elected representation and virtual government. The role of the Dalai Lama in encouraging a split between secular government of the Tibetan community-in-exile and religious structures of Tibetan Buddhism is examined, even as the authors conclude that "religious and regional identities are fundamental to the very definition of 'Tibet' and 'Tibetaness,' embedded in the sense of belonging and 'home' of Tibetan refugees."

A chapter on self-determination and national liberation in Kurdistan is offered by Joost Jongerden, who offers a historical perspective of the Kurds' behavior beginning with the post–World War I context following the Ottoman collapse. The Kurds present a special challenge because they are found in several nation-states today, including Turkey, Iraq, Syria, and Iran. Jongerden focuses on the Kurdistan Workers Party in Turkey between 1971 and 1980, and discusses the relation between Kurdish political actors and the *ideas* of nation, state, and nation-state. He concludes that the Kurdistan Workers Party gave new direction to the idea of self-determination, and that direction is being pursued in political institutions today.

Bernard Nwosu and Kenneth Omeje have contributed a chapter on the Biafra separatist movement and Igbo nationalism in the fourth Nigerian republic. The current nationalist drive goes back to the 1967–1970 period when the Republic of Biafra attempted to secede from Nigeria, ultimately losing a violent and costly war. Nwosu and Omeje explain how in Nigeria nationalist movements do not operate in the same manner as Catalona, Quebec, or Scotland, but form their own organizations, and they describe the Igbo organizations that have formed and their behavior that is described as "new Igbo nationalism" or "neo-Biafran nationalism." This new nationalism is placed in the context of Nigeria's political landscape in which ethnic militias regularly make demands on the national state, and the state needs to respond. Ultimately, the use of military force by the state to suppress separatist agitation "tends to reinforce the resolve of campaigners and fuel their demand for a new state." The ultimate outcome of the current neo-Biafra movement remains unclear, but the authors offer several possible outcomes, including Nigeria "becoming a totally failed and ultimately dismembered state."

In the final chapter in this volume Felipe Medina Gutiérrez paints a complex and detailed picture of the Houthi movement in Yemen today. The

Houthi movement—also known as the Ansar Allah movement—emerged in the second half of the twentieth century in Yemen in response to political stresses of the time, including general Middle Eastern politics, the decline of Arab nationalism, the rise of the power of Saudi Arabia due to its petroleum industry, and the spread of religious conservatism and of Wahhabism, among other factors. The "Houthi movement" was known as both a religious and a political force, and its relationship with Iran has been a source of some uncertainty in the current tensions in the region. In recent years the conflict between the Houthi and the Saudi/United Arab Emirates coalition has been a humanitarian catastrophe, and the United Nations has stepped in on more than one occasion to help prevent even more bloodshed. The Houthi are not, strictly speaking, a religious group, but they are anchored in religious ideology, and their current challenge is to blend that ideology with a nationalist discourse to help them achieve their political goals.

∽

This volume seeks to make available to interested readers a number of portraits of contemporary challenges posed by nationalism and the desires of nationalist movements to achieve sovereign status. Nationalism is a state of mind, and "holds that each nation should govern itself, free from outside interference (self-determination), that a nation is a natural and ideal basis for a polity, and that the nation is the only rightful source of political power (popular sovereignty)."[63]

Notes

1. Philip G. Roeder, *Where Nation-States Come From: Institutional Change in the Age of Nationalism* (Princeton, NJ: Princeton University Press, 2007), 3.

2. Roeder, *Where Nation-States Come From*.

3. Roeder, *Where Nation-States Come From*, 12.

4. Hans Kohn, *Nationalism: Its Meaning and History* (revised edition) (Toronto: Van Nostrand Reinhold, 1971), 4.

5. Ernest Gellner, *Nations and Nationalism* (Ithaca, NY: Cornell University Press, 1983), 1.

6. Anthony Smith, ed., *Nationalist Movements* (New York: St. Martin's Press, 1976), 1.

7. Kohn, *Nationalism*, 9.

8. See Benedict Anderson, *Imagined Communities: Reflections on the Origin and Spread of Nationalism* (London: Verso, 1983).

9. See, for example, Michael Tierney, "Nationalism: A Survey," in *Studies: An Irish Quarterly Review* 34, no. 36 (1945): 474–482.

10. See Michael R. Lucas, "Nationalism, Sovereignty, and Supranational Organizations," 27. www.files.ethz.ch/isn/21128/hb114.pdf

11. For examples of this literature, see Anthony Smith, *Nationalism and Modernism* (London: Routledge, 1998), and John Breuilly, *Nationalism and the State* (Manchester: Manchester University Press, 1993). Atsuko Ichijo and Gordana Uzelac have edited a very interesting book that touches on this subject, *When Is the Nation? Towards an Understanding of Theories of Nationalism* (New York: Routledge, 2005).

12. James G. Kellas, *The Politics of Nationalism and Ethnicity* (New York: St. Martin's Press, 1991), 2.

13. Anthony D. Smith, *National Identity* (Reno: University of Nevada Press, 1991), viii.

14. Smith, *Nationalist Movements*, 10.

15. See Graham Scambler, "Hannah Arendt and the Nation-State." www.grahamscambler.com/hannah-arendt-and-the-nation-state

16. Smith, *National Identity*, 9.

17. Smith, *National Identity*, 14.

18. Max Weber, "The Profession and Vocation of Politics," in Weber, *Political Writings*, Peter Lassman and Ronald Speirs (Cambridge: Cambridge University Press, 1994), 310–311. Original emphasis.

19. For more discussion on the distinction between "state" and "nation," see, for example, Hugh Seton-Watson, *Nations and States: An Enquiry into the Origins of Nations and the Politics of Nationalism* (Boulder, CO: Westview Press, 1977), 1.

20. See Yael Tamir, *Liberal Nationalism* (Princeton, NJ: Princeton University Press, 1993), especially chapter 1, "The Idea of the Person."

21. See William Galston, "Twelve Theses on Nationalism," Monday, August 12, 2019. www.brookings.edu/opinions/twelve-theses-on-nationalism

22. Jaakko Heiskanen, "Spectra of Sovereignty: Nationalism and International Relations," *International Political Sociology* 13, no. 3 (2019): 315.

23. Smith, *Nationalist Movements*, 2.

24. Gregory Baum, *Nationalism, Religion, and Ethics* (Montreal: McGill-Queen's University Press, 2001), 3.

25. *"Prime Minister Pearson Stands up to de Gaulle."* CBC Digital Archives. www.cbc.ca/player/play/1753978144

26. Baum, *Nationalism, Religion, and Ethics*.

27. Kellas, *Politics of Nationalism and Ethnicity*, 4.

28. Richard G. Fox, "Introduction," in Nationalist Ideologies and the Production of National Cultures (Washington, DC: American Anthropological Association, 2001), 3.

29. See Umer Javaid Ghumman et al., "Nationalism in Indian Politics During PM Modi Regime (2014–19)," *Psychology and Education Journal* 58, no. 2 (2021). https://doi.org/10.17762/pae.v58i2.4030

30. Gellner, *Nations and Nationalism*, 1.

31. See Michael Hechter, *Containing Nationalism* (Oxford: Oxford University Press, 2000).

32. Fox, "Introduction," *op cit.*, 3.

33. Smith, *National Identity*, 11.

34. Smith, *National Identity*, 11. See also John Plamenatz, "Two Types of Nationalism," in Kamenka, *Nationalism: The Nature and Evolution of an Idea* (New York: St. Martin's Press, 1976), 23.

35. Smith, *National Identity*, 21

36. Roeder, *Where Nation-States Come From*, 6.

37. Eugene Kamenka, "Political Nationalism—The Evolution of the Idea," in Eugene Kamenka, ed., *Nationalism: The Nature and Evolution of an Idea* (New York: St. Martin's Press, 1976), 3.

38. Anthony Smith, *National Identity*, 44

39. Kamenka, *Political Nationalism*, 4.

40. Wang Gungwu, "Nationalism in Asia," in Kamenka, *Political Nationalism*, 83–84.

41. See the CESSDA web page. www.cessda.eu/About

42. See Dharmi Kapadia, "Represented Yet Excluded: How Ethnic Minority People Are Counted in National Surveys," published by the UK Data Service. https://blog.ukdataservice.ac.uk/represented-ethnic-minority-people

43. Glenda Sluga, *The Nation, Psychology, and International Politics, 1870–1919* (New York: Palgrave Macmillan, 2006), 13.

44. Smith, *National Identity*, 143.

45. World Population Review, "Sovereign Nation 2022." https://worldpopulationreview.com/country-rankings/sovereign-nation

46. Peter Calvert, "On Attaining Sovereignty," in Anthony Smith, *Nationalist Movements*, 135–136.

47. Calvert, "On Attaining Sovereignty," 137.

48. Calvert, "On Attaining Sovereignty," 139.

49. Plamenatz, "Two Types of Nationalism," 27.

50. Kim Holmes, "The Problem of Nationalism." The Heritage Foundation. www.heritage.org/conservatism/commentary/the-problem-nationalism

51. Pew Research Center, Views of A Changing World, 2003, Chapter 5: Nationalism, Sovereignty, and Views of Global Institutions." www.pewresearch.org/global/2003/06/03/chapter-5-nationalism-sovereignty-and-views-of-global-institutions

52. See Chris Gilligan, "Sovereignty and Natiionalism 2: 'The People' and Popular Sovereignty." https://networks.h-net.org/node/3911/blog/vistas/7609766/sovereignty-and-nationalism-2-%E2%80%98-people%E2%80%99-and-popular-sovereignty

53. The World Values Survey is an illustration of this kind of approach in which the nation-state is simply one variable included in a huge set of variables.

See *World Values Survey: Round Six—Country-Pooled Datafile*, ed. R. Inglehart, C. Haerpfer, A. Moreno, C. Welzel, K. Kizilova, J. Diez-Medrano, M. Lagos, P. Norris, E. Ponarin, B. Puranen, et al. (Madrid: JD Systems Institute, 2014). Version: www.worldvaluessurvey.org/WVSDocumentationWV6.jsp

54. Kellas, *Politics of Nationalism and Ethnicity*, 148.

55. Craig Calhoun, "Nationalism and Ethnicity," *Annual Review of Sociology* 19 (1993): 211–239, on 214.

56. Walter Lippmann, *Public Opinion* (New York: Macmillan, 1947), 24, 26.

57. Cited in A. Cobban, *National Self-Determination* (Oxford: Oxford University Press, 1945), 25.

58. This is a summary of a much longer discussion in David D. Laitin, *Nations, States, and Violence* (Oxford: Oxford University Press, 2007), 3–9.

59. Laitin, *Nations, States, and Violence*, 7.

60. Laitin, *Nations, States, and Violence*, 23.

61. Laitin, *Nations, States, and Violence*, 21.

62. Robert Malley, "Watch List, 2023," published online by the International Crisis Group. www.crisisgroup.org/global/watch-list-2023

63. Bernard Yack, "Popular Sovereignty and Nationalism," *Political Theory* 29, no. 4 (2001): 518.

References

Akzin, Benjamin. *State and Nation*. London: Hutchinson, 1964.

Anderson, Benedict. *Imagined Communities*. London: Verso, 1983.

Asiwaju, A. I., ed., *Partitioned Africans: Ethnic Relations Across Africa's International Boundaries*. London: Hurst and Col, 1985.

Baron, Salo. *Modern Nationalism and Religion*. New York: Meridian Books, 1960.

Baum, Gregory. *Nationalism, Religion, and Ethics*. Montreal: McGill-Queen's University Press, 2001.

Bendix, Reinhard. *Nation-Building and Citizenship: Studies of our Changing Social Order*. New York: Wiley, 1964.

Breuilly, John. *Nationalism and the State*. Manchester: Manchester University Press, 1982.

Connor, Walker. "A Nation is a Nation, Is a State, Is an Ethnic Group, Is a . . ." *Ethnic and Racial Studies* 1, no. 4 (1978): 378–400.

Deutsch, Karl. *Nationalism and Social Communication: An Inquiry into the Foundations of Nationalism*. 2nd ed. Cambridge, MA: MIT Press, 1966.

Doob, Leonard. *Patriotism and Nationalism: Their Psychological Foundations*. New Haven: Yale University Press, 1964.

Fox, Richard G. "Introduction," in *Nationalist Ideologies and the Production of National Cultures*. Washington, DC: American Anthropological Association, 2001.

Gellner, Ernest. *Nations and Nationalism.* Ithaca, NY: Cornell University Press, 1983.
Haim, Sylvia, ed. *Arab Nationalism: An Anthology.* Los Angeles: University of California Press, 1962.
Hayes, Carlton. *Nationalism: A Religion.* New York: Macmillan, 1960.
Hechter, Michael. *Internal Colonialism.* Berkeley: University of California Press, 1975.
Hechter, Michael. *Containing Nationalism.* Oxford: Oxford University Press, 2000.
Horowitz, Donald. *Ethnic Groups in Conflict.* Berkeley: University of California Press, 1985.
Ichijo, Atsuko, and Gordana Uzelac, eds. *When Is the Nation? Towards an Understanding of Theories of Nationalism.* New York: Routledge, 2005.
Kamenka, Eugene, ed. *Nationalism: The Nature and Evolution of an Idea.* New York: St. Martin's Press, 1976.
Kedourie, Elie. *Nationalism.* London: Hutchinson, 1960.
Kohn, Hans. *Nationalism: Its Meaning and History* (rev. ed.). Toronto: Van Nostrand Reinhold, 1971.
Laitin, David D. *Nations, States, and Violence.* Oxford: Oxford University Press, 2007.
Lewis, Ioann, ed. *Nationalism and Self-Determination in the Horn of Africa.* London: Ithaca Press, 1983.
Mayall, James. *Nationalism and International Society.* Cambridge: Cambridge University Press, 1990.
Minogue, K. R. *Nationalism.* London: Batsford, 1967.
Neuberger, Benjamin. *National Self-Determination in Post-Colonial Africa.* Boulder, CO: Lynne Rienner, 1986.
Plamenatz, John. "Two Types of Nationalism." In *Nationalism: The Nature and Evolution of an Idea*, ed. Eugene Kamenka. New York: St. Martin's Press, 1976.
Roeder, Philip G. *Where Nation-States Come From: Institutional Change in the Age of Nationalism.* Princeton, NJ: Princeton University Press, 2007.
Scambler, Graham. "Hannah Arendt and the Nation-State." www.grahamscambler.com/hannah-arendt-and-the-nation-state
Seton-Watson, Hugh. *Nations and States: An Enquiry into the Origins of Nations and the Politics of Nationalism.* Boulder, CO: Westview Press, 1977.
Shafer, Boyd. *Faces of Nationalism: New Realities and Old Myths.* New York: Harcourt Brace Jovanovich, 1972.
Sluga, Glenda. *The Nation, Psychology, and International Politics*, 1870–1919. New York: Palgrave Macmillan, 2006.
Smith, Anthony. *Theories of Nationalism.* New York: Harper and Row, 1971.
Smith, Anthony, ed., *Nationalist Movements.* New York: St. Martin's Press, 1976.
Smith, Anthony. *Nationalism and Modernism.* London: Routledge, 1998.
Tamir, Yael. *Liberal Nationalism.* Princeton, NJ: Princeton University Press, 1993.
Tivey, Leonard, ed. *The Nation-State.* Oxford: Martin Robertson, 1980.

I
Nationalism and Some Western Democratic States

2

Frustrating Nationalism

U.S. Foreign Policy and Self-Determination

David Ryan

Introduction

Born on the 4th of July, with the potent appeal of Jefferson's declaration on life, liberty, and the pursuit of happiness, the United States became a postcolonial empire. With its benign meta-narrative of justice and government, the hallowed document asserted that "Governments are instituted among Men, deriving their just powers from the consent of the governed," and that if government "becomes destructive of these ends, it is the Right of the People to alter or to abolish it, and to institute new Government," which was most likely "to effect their Safety and Happiness."[1] The ideological content of a string of seminal American documents pivots on the concepts of self-determination, liberty, and democracy. Yet American expansionism, territorially across the continent, through colonization in the Philippines and elsewhere, through informal empire in Central America and the Caribbean, and in pursuit of hegemony, frustrated the self-determination and nationalist aspirations of many. American nationalism emerged in an imperial setting.[2] Its assumptions on self-determination, race, and empire permeated its engagement with nationalists.[3]

The Open-Door policies, economic integration, and globalization also compromised the sovereignty of nations. The promotion of national self-determination in American rhetoric inconsistently advanced the process of European decolonization. Yet Washington focused on *decolonization*, economic integration, and American opportunity above the specific aspirations of nationalists. Often, local objectives could not be accommodated if they ran up against American interests. The pluralism associated with nationalism sometimes worked against the universalism of economic integration. The separate pursuits of life, liberty, and self-determination occasionally clashed.

Washington championed the right to self-determination in the "Second World"—the countries behind the Iron Curtain; as Soviet power was contained, the "captive nations" became the focus of American observance after 1953, even as it elided or denied rights to American Indians and African Americans.[4] The human rights of citizens of authoritarian American allies were not accorded significant attention. When nations in the "Third World" asserted their independence, from Iran to Guatemala, from Vietnam to Nicaragua, Washington frustrated their nationalist ambitions.

Nationalism presented a conundrum; certain forms of nationalism advanced American interests and chimed with their revolutionary experience of independence—other forms challenged American hegemony and its global aspirations.

American Ideology and Self-determination

The United States is a *postcolonial empire*.[5] The hybrid identity captures an incoherence in the American engagement with nationalism. After the American Revolution an exclusive understanding of a *nation* was forged, and that entity embarked on a history of expansion from continental border-colonization,[6] "manifest destiny," to overseas colonization, most famously in the Philippines. Bound by the 1898 Teller Amendment on Cuba that mandated "control of the island to its people,"[7] American formal colonization ceased even as informal empire advanced. In the Open-Door notes, Washington resisted colonial options to advance equal economic opportunity. Earlier, it participated in the 1884–1885 Berlin conference, advancing arguments on civilization and commerce, yet it overlooked aspects of European imperial intent.[8] From the outset, conceptual tensions prevailed between nationalist self-determination and American economic integration.

Nationalism was both progressive and regressive. It could be asserted as a positive force in the modernity within which the United States flourished. As such, the cultivation of nationalism, culminating in Woodrow

Wilson's influential message, worked against European empires. In the early twentieth century, many nationalists looked to Washington for assistance.[9] Famously, Wilson entered World War I with the powerful words, "We are glad . . . to fight for the ultimate peace of the world and for the liberation of its peoples . . . for the rights of nations great and small and for the privilege of men everywhere to choose their way of life and of obedience. The world must be made safe for democracy."[10] When nationalism worked against autarchic empires or the Soviet system, it benefitted the United States politically and economically. But when nationalism challenged the American-centered "world system," Washington reacted negatively, often working against aspirations that sometimes echoed its own experience of 1776.[11]

The tensions between political self-determination and economic integration vitiated American foreign policy. Later, the eloquent rhetoric of seminal documents, from the Declaration of Independence to the Monroe Doctrine, from Wilson's Fourteen Points to the Atlantic Charter, were invoked or cited in ironic indictment by some nationalists. In the Western hemisphere, nationalist sentiments frequently worked against American hegemony. Elsewhere, American ambivalence on postwar decolonization was compromised by its alliances with European empires. When revolutionary or moderate nationalists asserted their interests against Washington, from Guatemala to Cuba, Iran and Vietnam to Nicaragua, the United States sought to remove, or did remove, the regimes.

The United States' postcolonial identity can be considered in two ways. It is *post-colonial*, with the hyphen, to signify its emergence from the British Empire. And it is *postcolonial*, without the hyphen, because its seminal discourse spoke against empire, to the British specifically, and more broadly against imperialism. Yet long before the Anglo-American "special relationship," the United States also shared affinity with the British style of imperial rule,[12] even if the Declaration augmented by the writings of Thomas Paine implied a clear break with the past.[13] The Founding Fathers were revered and ritualized through various "invented traditions"; an exceptional identity was crafted based on its benign meta-narrative.[14] The American potential for both growth and disintegration advanced concurrently; Stephanson wrote, to avoid fragmentation a strong identity was crafted; "a set of simple symbols was required that would distil the past and at the same time proclaim the future. The extraordinary rapidity with which the Revolution was *monumentalized* actually showed the urgency: the revolutionary avant-garde turned into Founding Fathers, biblical patriarchs, Washington presiding as a near deity, all evoked with ritual solemnity every July 4."[15]

Of course, collective memory sanctifies a particular, exclusive and benign interpretation of the past.[16] Such memories cultivated in historical texts and a range of other sites are produced and bound by the limits of what Bourdieu called the field of cultural production; those powerful milieus centered on the media, publishing, communication, art, and so forth.[17] Societies and cultures forget.[18] The forgetting privileges the benign narratives until points of crisis necessitate re-readings of the past. Conflicts on race and empire are just two of several issues that prompted reinterpretation of American identity and nationalism.[19] The intersection on race and empire is interesting because despite the infamous call by Kaplan and Pease to reinject empire into the study of American culture,[20] and despite some advances, recent arguments identify an ongoing absence. Hōkūlani Aikau argued that cognitive gaps remain: "American studies' ongoing articulation of whiteness with national culture has resulted in the persistent marginalization of Native American and Indigenous studies (NAIS) within the field."[21] Such elision reinforces traditional conceptions of identity and the benign meta-narrative of American history.

Yet the concept of "empire" makes a perennial return in American historiography, during its colonialism, the Vietnam War, or after the 2003 American invasion of Iraq. The conjunction between empire and nationalism was observed in earlier historiographical debates, but earlier they were assumed by many "Founding Fathers" to go hand in hand. American nationalism was crafted in an imperial context.[22] Decades ago, Richard van Alstyne wrote on the "imperial republic" and "revolutionary conquest" emphasizing the assumptions about imperialism in the minds of George Washington, Benjamin Franklin, and Thomas Jefferson for instance.[23] William Appleman Williams extended and traced the "transformation of the expansionist outlook," capturing the seeming contradictions of "imperial anticolonialism" toward the end of the nineteenth century.[24] The transformation ignored continental conquest, as the United States advanced an identity associated with promotion of nationalism and self-determination.

Yet, until recent decades American exceptionalism in the historiography contrasted its identity with empires. Undoubtedly American historiography contributed to its nationalism.[25] Joyce Appleby, Jill Lepore, and David Thelen stressed the relationship between history and identity formation. Lepore wrote, "often, histories of nation states are little more than myths that hide the seams that stitch the nation to the state." Born into contradiction, Americans "will forever fight over the meaning of its history." She related that the influential histories of George Bancroft, who also served as

American Secretary of War, were closely associated with manifest destiny.[26] Epistemology mingled with westward expansion and conquest. The discordance between the benign histories and American expansion were often elided through informal ideologies, those symbols and beliefs that conflate contradiction yet provide inspiration and a sense of purpose.[27]

Over forty-five years ago, Arthur Gilbert wrote an essay on American Indians and American diplomatic history. He noted there that American Indians were largely confined to footnotes by domestic historians, secure in the knowledge that they would be treated as *"nations"* by foreign policy specialists. Yet those specialists ignored the American Indians because they were considered a *domestic* issue.[28] By the 1870s, Congress did not make new treaties with American Indians, and the Supreme Court obviated the old ones. A decade later, the Dawes Act (1887) redistributed tribal lands. Hunt observed, "Aside from sporadic outbreaks, the Indian now ceased to be a foreign problem and could be neglected as a domestic one."[29] Even in 2020, an article in *Diplomatic History* argued that the histories of "manifest destiny / internal expansion continues to write American Indian nationhood out of the nineteenth century."[30] Yet, building on this, George Herring's *From Colony to Superpower* drew a "direct line" between the handling of the American Indians and "the acquisition of overseas empire in the 1890s."[31] The partial recovery of that history is a comparatively recent phenomenon.[32] Despite Jefferson's initial intentions to gain consent on westward acquisition of land, that intention lapsed. In any case, government could not contain westward expansion even if it wanted to, Stephanson argued, so "there remained expulsion or extermination." His work *Manifest Destiny: American Expansion and the Empire of Right* charted the way "ethnic cleansing [could] be inserted into the overarching narrative of destiny."[33]

"Forgetting," Ernest Renan famously noted, "is a crucial factor in the creation of a nation," which is why historiographical evolution "often constitutes a danger for nationality." It is little wonder that the multitude of particular narratives are reduced to emphasize an essential identity marginalizing discordant voices.[34] Thomas Bender has noted that professional history assimilated the national ideology and advanced its central message: "the professional practice of history writing and teaching flourished as the handmaiden of nation-making; the nation provided both support and an appreciative audience." As a result, the United States isolated its history from the world. The United States' history is "here," while the international is "over there." His efforts to deprovincialize American history involve integrating the U.S. story with the larger stories of the world.[35]

The American empire grew into the "age of empires," and as such it also emulated European empires. Andrew Priest's *Designs on Empire*, exploring the coincidence of the United States' rise in the context of European imperialism, traced affinities between the United States and its contemporary colonial powers; there was much to assimilate and emulate.[36] It was not just about "civilization" and the "white man's burden" with the attendant assumptions on race, it was also about shared practices, policies, and power. The recent historiographical focus on empire draws attention to the similarities between the United States', British, and European empires that necessarily produces complex dispositions toward nationalism and nationalists challenging empire or economic imperialism.[37]

The definition of nationalism evolves constantly with the ebb and flow of the nationalist sentiment which is frequently associated with significant periods of economic downturn. Vastly influential, the works of Hobsbawm, Gellner, and Anderson have considered and advanced various ideas. Anderson's "imagined political community" not only helped to advance the notion of a shared [exclusive] community, but one that simultaneously absorbs a multitude of incoherence.[38] As such nations are essentially dominant narrations.

Beyond the elisions on American Indian, African American, Black, and Women's histories, the history of American foreign policy has been relatively exclusive until recently. Even still, at times of American expansion, whether in the late nineteenth century or the early Cold War, there has been what Louis Hartz referred to in the 1950s as an "ironic 'Americanist' outburst against imperialism, a nationalism consuming nationalism which could only occur in America" of those advocating the advance of American power set against those rekindling their sense of the imagined community centered on democracy, liberty, and self-determination.[39]

During the debate on imperialism, Senator George Hoar illustrated the contradictions: "The mighty figure of Thomas Jefferson comes down in history with the Declaration of Independence in one hand, and the title deed of Louisiana in the other," Hoar declared. He asked, "Do you think his left hand knew what his right hand did?"[40] Later, it was not just the obvious contradiction between the "consent" of the governed and the pursuit of happiness. Extending the sphere and integrating markets compromised self-determination and *consent* to the chagrin of certain nationalists. While nationalism spoke to the language of pluralism, economic integration aspired to the universal "end of History."[41]

So, while the traditional interpretation of the 1823 Monroe Doctrine is frequently understood as an American proposition to support the nascent nations of Latin America, it evolved into something quite different. It is also worth noting that a principal reason why the United States advanced that message unilaterally rather than with the British was that such multilateral accord would have limited American continental expansion.[42] About eighty years later, when the economies of Central America and the Caribbean were increasingly important to the United States, the Roosevelt Corollary warned nations to adhere to economic strictures. Theodore Roosevelt explained: "If a nation shows that it knows how to act with reasonable efficiency and decency in social and political matters, if it keeps order and pays its obligations, it need fear no interference from the United States." Yet, "Chronic wrongdoing . . . may . . . ultimately require intervention by some civilized nation, and in the Western Hemisphere the adherence of the United States to the Monroe Doctrine may force the United States, however reluctantly, in flagrant cases of such wrongdoing or impotence, to the exercise of an international police power."[43] Priest presciently concluded that "good government" was preferable over "self-government," "denying autonomy, reifying Western rule" even before Roosevelt uttered these words.[44] Yet this is the very period when nationalists across the region were trying to assert their agendas against American regional aspirations. American military intervention and prolonged occupation of several countries ensued.[45]

The evolution and conflations in the history of United States' foreign policy between its support for nationalism and self-determination on the one hand and internationalism and economic integration on the other endlessly complicated and compromised its identity. At times, international *order* was a basic premise, especially in Woodrow Wilson's thinking, whereas the pursuit of opportunity, under McKinley, dislodged older orders from which the United States was excluded.[46]

There are fine studies of American liberal internationalism—among them, G. John Ikenberry's *A World Safe for Democracy*, Tony Smith's *Pact with the Devil*, and David Milne's *Worldmaking*—that explain American thinking on these issues.[47] Yet, despite Woodrow Wilson's exclusive "universalism," William Pfaff observed that the quickening pace of internationalism coincided with the rise of European nationalism, and that "Nationalism's rival" was *internationalism*. There were the Marxist and Nazi variations, but the third rival to nationalism was "liberal internationalism."[48] Transcending the rise of nationalism from the mid–nineteenth century, liberal internationalism gradually replaced the "cultural internationalism" that had been lost.[49] American engagement was usually ambiguous.

The United States, Nations, and Empires

Point five of Wilson's famous Fourteen Points called for a "free, open-minded, and absolutely impartial adjustment of all colonial claims," based on popular sovereignty balanced "with the equitable claims of the government." Simultaneously, point three requested "removal, so far as possible, of all economic barriers and the establishment of an equality of trade conditions among all the nations" who consented to the peace and its maintenance.[50] Wilson's ideas were not original. Variations had evolved over the century.[51] The inherent contradictions of combining democratic self-determination with liberal doctrines on international trade, did not grapple directly with the fact that "transnational economic interests" could undermine "the sovereign rights of nation-states or the democratic rights of those within the boundaries."[52] Still, Wilson combined a deep sense of American benevolence, paternalism, exceptionalism, and racism. According to Lloyd Ambrosius, American identity was crafted in opposition to the British Empire, fusing nationalism with an ideological and geographical content. Still, Wilson's universalism was "Anglo-Saxon." He omitted reference to Asian and African Americans [or American Indians]; "his liberal inclusiveness excluded people of color. Nonwhite Americans did not fit his ideal of U.S. citizenship. . . . Wilson drew a sharp color line despite his apparently universal liberal rhetoric."[53]

These tensions were obvious in his rhetoric on Mexico. On August 27, 1913, he told a joint session of Congress that the Mexican revolution destabilized the country, disrupted the economy, and endangered American citizens. Wilson stressed that Mexican "peace and prosperity" meant much more than "an enlarged field for our commerce and enterprise." Their self-government and the "rights of a nation" with which the United States sympathized were being "disappointed." Wilson's emissary could not convince the Mexicans of his position. He seemed surprised that they rejected gestures of American "friendship," even though they had lost vast areas to the United States in the war of 1846–1848. Wilson observed: "Mexico lies at last where all the world looks on. Central America is about to be touched by the great routes of the world's trade and intercourse running free from ocean to ocean at the Isthmus."[54]

Wilson's internationalism, Ikenberry wrote, was "both breathtakingly ambitious and surprisingly limited," a mixture of principle and "moral blindness." He simultaneously promoted the rights of individuals and nations, yet did not inquire into the imperial or racial implications. He supported the United States' post–Civil War racial order. He did not hear W. E. B. Du Bois, who tried to see him at Versailles after the war; he similarly rebuffed attempts by Nguyễn Ái Quốc [Ho Chi Minh] to see him. Adam Tooze emphasized that Wilson was not interested in race and did not directly envisage the elimination of the European empires; he simply sought to curtail the imperialism that contributed to divisive aggression and a segmented world closed to the United States.[55] Still, the Wilsonian message appealed to nationalists around the world. Yet, self-determination was applied only to the collapsed European empires, whereas Ottoman lands were divided into Mandates of the League of Nations.

Other nationalists were initially inspired and hopeful. The United States emerged from the war a powerful influence in world history. John Meynard Keynes wrote that Wilson enjoyed "a prestige and a moral influence throughout the world unequalled in history." Nationalists from Ireland, Egypt, India, Indochina, and Ottoman Turkey saw the opportunity to challenge European empires. Key phrases of the Fourteen Points held out great hope for American collaboration, or at least political support. In *From the Ruins of Empire*, a book about Asian intellectuals who attempted to remake the world, Pankaj Mishra cited numerous nationalists who wrote to, appealed to, or sent delegations to Wilson—all to be disappointed. It was not only racial exclusion or territorial occupation; by advancing the Open-Door in the Fourteen Points, Wilson "did not see that free trade, the third of his Fourteen Points, could be seen as equally oppressive by economically disadvantaged peoples."[56] Yet such trade was also a source of poverty, disgruntlement, and oppression, and a contributor to anticolonial nationalism. Gandhi's *khadi* movement against British textiles began at this time. After Paris, many lamented the American failures and its stance on nationalism. Egyptian journalist Muhammad Haykal wrote that "the man of the Fourteen Points, among them the right to self-determination, [is] denying the Egyptian people its right to self-determination." He inquired if this was not "the ugliest of treacheries?" In India, Jawaharlal Nehru noted that the Wilsonian moment "ha[d] passed," it was time to focus on a longer term "distant hope," not the "immediate breathless looking for the deliverance."[57]

Despite Wilson's political failures in Paris and Washington, Wilsonian internationalism lived on and resurfaced in Franklin D. Roosevelt's internationalism. Again, the central ideas on self-determination and the Open-Door found their way into the 1941 Atlantic Charter, a principal statement of American war aims. First, the United States and the United Kingdom sought no territorial aggrandizement. Second, no territorial changes would take place without the "freely expressed wishes of the peoples concerned." Third, they agreed on the "right of all peoples to choose the form of government under which they will live; and they wish to see sovereign rights and self government restored to those who have been forcibly deprived of them." And fourth, with a clause that allowed Britain to sidestep the dissolution of their empire, they sought "all States, great or small, victor or vanquished, of access, on equal terms, to the trade and to the raw materials of the world which are needed for their economic prosperity."[58]

Warren Kimball affirmed that "[h]istorical memory is part of what nations are all about, and a visceral dislike of colonialism is part of the American self-image." American political self-determination went hand in hand with American economic freedom. They "condemned colonialism for its closed economic systems, since those doors threatened 'freedom' for the United States to grow and prosper in a world of empires."[59] Dismantle the political control, take down the imperial flags, remove the Governors and the troops, *but* "Support the preservation of the economic and political ties." Kimball argued to maintain the bases, the intelligence assets, but "keep the ex-colony in the 'system.' "[60]

European political decolonization was welcome if it did not undermine the war effort or, later, the Cold War balance of power. Yet, economic assertions of self-determination were problematical. In the eyes of various nationalists, American identity was significantly compromised. Washington was an allied power in war and the leader of the Western alliance in the Cold War, with messages on freedom at the heart of both.

Pollock and Kimball wrote: "[T]here was nothing unique about Roosevelt's general distaste for colonialism—it came with being an American"; his ideas were derived from Wilson and the Fourteen Points. Though FDR broached the issue of colonialism with the British and French, his beliefs were imbued with "ethnocentrism and distasteful racial notions," with paternalism and a "belief in white and Western superiority."[61] FDR's position was inconsistent. Paul Orders argued that even though he frequently compromised, he knew he was on the right side of history and that one day, eventually, the nations of Asia and Africa would gain their political independence.[62] On India, United States' support for decolonization was less than fulsome. Both wartime and Cold War contexts constrained Washington despite the American and Indian shared history as colonies in the British Empire. By the mid–twentieth century, Indian nationalism worked against American interests. Dennis Merrill wrote they were "separated by unbridgeable gaps in wealth, power, security interests and culture." Some in Washington sympathized with Indian nationalist aspirations, "but in the last analysis, the ironies of history prevented Washington from fully making the Indian struggle for national independence a part of its own crusade for human freedom."[63]

Despite Ho Chi Minh's 1945 ironic adaptation of Jefferson in the Vietnamese Declaration of Independence, Truman abandoned the United States' commitment to postwar independence. On September 2, 1945, the short-lived Vietnamese independence began with the declaration that "All men are created equal. The creator has given us certain inviolable Rights; the right to Life, the right to be Free, and the right to achieve Happiness." An OSS (U.S. Office of Strategic Services) team had assisted him, not only through the war against Japanese occupation but with these political ceremonies. Ho had invited the OSS team to dinner the night before, and spoke of hope for "fraternal collaboration" in the future.[64] Again, French interests took precedence over Vietnamese national aspirations. Later, a debate took place on whether Ho might be another Tito, a communist who acted independently, apart from the Soviet system. Some in the State Department recognized the inevitability of Vietnamese independence and wondered why the United States would "tie ourselves to the tail of their [French] battered kite?" Dean Acheson was skeptical. Infamously, he argued that all communists in colonial areas invoked nationalism. Washington sided with France against Vietnamese independence. The Cold War frame dominated; containment was essential. Besides, as Lloyd Gardner wrote, "while one Tito demonstrated that even communists could not tolerate Stalin's heavy-fisted rule, two Titos would suggest that the idea of a world communist conspiracy needed serious re-examination."[65]

Further, Ho preferred an autarchic Indochina, and Washington worried both about its "loss" to the world system and the example it might set; Gardner concluded: "Not only would it change economic patterns in those areas, it would cause instability in Europe, struggling already with the dollar gap, as traditional markets and dollar earnings disappeared."[66] Vietnam could not assert full independence precisely because it was an organic part of the world system; its economy was crucial to the postwar European order and recovery.[67]

State Department specialists on Asia anticipated the awkward position as Washington tried to reconcile nationalist demands with American allegiance to European colonial powers. Robert McMahon emphasized that American "policy makers were almost completely unprepared for the depth and intensity of the nationalist rebellions that erupted in Southeast Asia in the wake of the Japanese surrender." They assumed that reassertions of French power would be relatively smooth. Despite Ho's personal appeals to Truman, there was a "manifest tilt toward the colonial nations [that] reflected the sober calculation at the upper reaches of the Truman administration that European interests rated a distinctly higher priority than Asian ones."[68] Famously, in 1995, former U.S. Secretary of Defense Robert McNamara apologized to the American people for misunderstanding Vietnamese nationalism and confusing it with international communism.[69]

American interests in World War II and then the Cold War frustrated nationalist ambitions across Asia. Even if Washington saw itself as the champion of self-determination and an "honest broker" between the imperial powers and the nationalists, by mid-century neither London, Paris, and other "metropolitan" capitals nor the leaders of independence movements regarded the United States as such. American wartime alliances postponed the logical implications of its ideological traditions, if not its practice; the Cold War and economic imperatives delayed them further.[70] The dilemma was illustrated well in a 1957 National Security Council document (NSC 5719):

> Premature independence would be as harmful to our interests in Africa as would be a continuation of nineteenth century colonialism, and we must tailor our policies to the capabilities and needs of each particular area as well as to our over-all relations with the metropolitan power concerned. It should be noted that all the metropolitan powers are associated with us in the NATO alliance or in military base agreements.

Washington continued to assert support for self-determination but frequently used old paternalistic and racist notions on responsibilities and capability. The document cautioned they should "avoid U.S. identification with those policies of the metropolitan powers, which are stagnant or repressive, and, to the extent practicable, seek effective means of influencing the metropolitan powers to abandon or modify such policies," emphasizing the expansion of the "Soviet colonial empire" when "Western colonialism has been contracting."[71]

Nevertheless, it was not just about the political or security issues. Decolonization threatened global economic fragmentation and the links with the Europeans, and consequently American ambitions on integration. Nationalists throughout Asia and Africa, not to mention national revolutionaries in Latin America, threatened American vital interests and the cohesion of the "West." As Robert Wood argued, "the European Recovery Program was not simply about either Europe or recovery; it was much more ambitious than that."[72] The Marshall Plan gave the United States deeper access to colonial economies. In his tome on Truman's foreign policy, Melvyn Leffler observed, "As circumstances changed and threats mounted, U.S. tactics shifted but the overall goal remained the same. The periphery had to be held or the Eurasian industrial core would be weakened. To simplify, Japan needed Southeast Asia; Western Europe needed the Middle East; and the American rearmament effort required raw materials from throughout the Third World." Leffler, citing a Policy Planning Paper under Dean Acheson's State Department, said there was "a struggle for preponderant power . . . Preponderance must be the objective of U.S. policy."[73]

It would be mistaken to exclusively explain the frustrated nationalism through wartime or Cold War contexts. In 1914, when Robert Lansing, future Secretary of State to Woodrow Wilson, reconsidered the Monroe Doctrine, cutting across the traditional narratives of protection, and promotion of republican governance, he wrote that the doctrine was based on "selfishness alone," the "integrity of the other American nations is an incident, not an end."[74]

Washington shared much in common with European empires; it also learned from them, emulated certain aspects,[75] and obviously competed with them. Preponderance might have been the strategy Truman pursued, but American expansionist policies had long antecedents going back to continental conquest. When Lansing wrote that national integrity was an incident and not an end, nationalists in Central America and the Caribbean clashed with American economic interests.[76]

Despite the recurrence of universalist language in the Atlantic Charter and the United Nations Charter with its twin pillars of human rights and national equality, anticolonial nationalists attempted, but ultimately failed, to "reinvent" self-determination. Their efforts were *both* against political imperialism *and* the impact of the world economy, even after decolonization. Fifteen years after independence, Ghana's President Kwame Nkrumah argued that the United Nations should address imperialism, suggesting the exclusion of obstinate imperial powers, wrote Adom Getachew. The United Nations passed Resolution 1514 on self-determination, noting "the subjection of peoples to alien subjugation, domination and exploitation constitutes a denial of fundamental human rights."[77]

Crucially, Getachew argued that the history of anticolonial nationalists set within the Western frame implied that decolonization extended Western ideals of independence and self-determination. It disregards "anticolonial nationalism as a site of conceptual and political innovation."[78] The Western model was advanced as the expense of nationalist innovations on self-determination.

That discussion involved consideration of the impact of the international economy on the fundamental human rights at the center of national self-determination. Such demands on economic sovereignty were considered a threat to both liberal internationalism and the world system. For instance, Getachew related, Clyde Eagleton, a delegate to Dumbarton Oaks, argued that "invocations of a right to self-determination in the UN were abusing the principle by unsustainably extending it to mean economic as well as political sovereignty and claiming that it should apply to all colonized peoples." While Resolution 1514 succeeded, it did so without the more radical economic ideas; yet it still shifted self-determination from a principle to a right.[79]

In a different context, Nkrumah labeled the "independent" African condition, "neo-colonialism"—"the last stage of imperialism" . . . the "economic system and thus its internal policy is directed from outside." He identified a fundamental incoherence between economic integration and political fragmentation advanced by anticolonial nationalists; the former compromised the autonomy of the latter. An integrated global economy combined with political independence was, at times, untenable as far as democratic rights and self-determination were concerned. The former compromised notions of constituency and consent. If *consent, constituency,* and *legitimacy* are fundamental to democratic theory (and key themes in Jefferson's declaration), inequality in the international economy undermined those conditions.[80] Democracy theorist David Held observed that capitalism was rarely bound by the nation-state; it sought opportunity. In doing so it frequently undermined concepts of self-determination to the fury and frustration of revolutionary and moderate nationalists struggling against that system.[81] Emily Rosenberg observed that as American power grew, the "promotional state" backed private enterprise. Washington actively supported corporations, believing their objectives would enhance American grand strategy. Cordell Hull and Herbert Hoover wrote extensively on the association of "free" trade, liberty, and peace—it was axiomatic to liberal internationalism. Yet it was not just about peace, liberty, and trade, Rosenberg wrote: "In powerless states, archconservative regimes catering to domineering American private interests or agencies often directly resulted from America's expansion within a liberal international order; they were not unfortunate accidents brought about by America's insufficient attention to 'human rights' abroad."[82]

The growth of American power and the pursuit of economic integration elided nationalist aspirations through the period of decolonization. McCormick observed that "nation-states have tended to pursue policies of economic autarky—capitalism in one country or one self-contained trading bloc—and such approaches limit the options of capital in pursuit of maximum rewards." American hegemony, that combination of ideological, political, military, and cultural power, sought to induce nationalists into the United States–centered system.[83] "Ironically," Hunt observed, "the more actively Americans have devoted themselves too destroying spheres of influence, the further we have gone towards creating our own."[84]

Frustrating Nationalism

U.S. engagement with Cold War nationalism worked for and against American interests. In an anti-Soviet setting, nationalist aspirations coincided with United States' interests; elsewhere, liberation movements often threatened those interests. In Vietnam and to a lesser extent in Nehru's India, protectionist nationalism caused concern. Further, American policies on race, its association with European colonial powers in the transatlantic alliance, and the failures of the U.S. economy in the 1930s Depression compromised its attraction.[85]

As Third World nationalists opted for socialist or protectionist variations, they were frequently associated with "Soviet designs"; the exogenous influences were purported to undermine indigenous aspiration. That outlook—at times sincerely held, at others opportunistically deployed—extended misunderstanding and compromised American identification with national self-determination.

Such demands were often subsumed into a global calculus that both facilitated American military or covert intervention and obscured demands of local nationalists. In Guatemala, Juan José Arévalo, building on his inspiration—ironically, FDR—advanced *Vitalismo*, which sought to guarantee basic minimums for the people, including standards on "housing, nutrition, education, health, work, justice, and rest."[86] Arévalo's successor Jacobo Árbenz moved further, expropriating thousands of acres from the United Fruit Company. His nationalism was depicted as international communism. The 1953 top-secret National Security Council document NSC 144/1 noted that the "trend in Latin America toward nationalistic regimes maintained in large part by appeals to the masses of the population." Behind it lay the "demand for immediate improvement in the low living standards of the masses," leaving "most Latin American governments . . . under intense domestic political pressures to increase production and to diversify their economies." The document added that improved conditions are "essential to arrest the drift in the area toward radical and nationalistic regimes," and finally, that "the growth of nationalism is facilitated by historic anti-U.S. prejudices and exploited by Communists."[87]

Despite this, the "communist" frame was advanced over the nationalist one. Eisenhower committed to remove the regime. U.S. Ambassador John Peurifoy met with Arbenz and concluded that even if he were not a communist "he will certainly do until one comes along."[88]

As the CIA prepared operations, Louis Halle in the State Department wrote in dissent to Robert Bowie, Director for Policy Planning at the State Department, "that the widespread impression abroad is: (a) that the U.S. has become hysterical about the communist menace so that it is losing its head in dealing with it; and (b) that this is leading the U.S. to commit acts of international lawlessness."[89] He noted there was "no present military danger to us at all." There was potential for "communist infection," and that danger involved an *example* of independence that "Guatemala might offer to nationalists throughout Latin America." Halle read Arbenz's social reform through a nationalist frame.[90]

Outlining various economic considerations, Halle argued that "revolution is an expression of the impulse to achieve equality of status (a) for individuals and groups within the national society, and (b) for the nation-state within the international community. Social reform and nationalism are its two principal manifestations." Guatemalan history fueled the revolution; "Foreign ownership of the elements of Guatemala's economic life, together with the pattern of its international trade, gives the Guatemalans a vivid and unwelcome sense of dependence on foreigners." He concluded: "The revolution in Guatemala is nationalist and anti-Yanqui in its own right. It is, in its own right, a movement for 'social justice' and reform."[91]

The American intervention was not exclusively a Cold War conflict, nor an aberration in history, but rather, as Gleijeses argued, "it fit within a deeply held tradition, shared by Democrats and Republicans alike and centered on the intransigent assertion of U.S. hegemony over Central America and the Caribbean."[92]

Later, Fidel Castro's nationalization of American business in Cuba was read through a Cold War lens. Obviously, the trade agreement with Moscow reinforced such views. Yet even after the United States backed intervention at the Bay of Pigs in 1961, Kennedy's "fiasco," there was a lack of clarity on Castro. In an illustrative document, Walt Rostow, Deputy National Security Advisor to Robert Kennedy and Chair of the Policy Planning Staff, wrote *after* the invasion: "The roots of Castroism lie in Latin American poverty, social inequality, and that form of xenophobic nationalism which goes with *a prior* history of inferiority on the world scene." Latin American populations were vulnerable to such appeals. Economic growth was essential, and social inequality had to be reduced. There was wide-spread desire for a more "dignified partnership with the U.S." Rostow's antidote was the Alliance for Progress,[93] which deepened nationalist demands of a generation in the face of harsh and repressive regimes. Rostow lamented: "We do not know what Castro's policy towards the U.S. will be; nor do we know what Soviet policy towards Cuba will be." Yet, it might be necessary to eliminate the regime by force.[94]

On Nicaragua, the 1979 Sandinista revolution was read very differently in the Carter and Reagan administrations. U.S. Ambassador Lawrence Pezzullo reported that it was "very much a Nicaraguan phenomenon. There is no question about that. Sandanismo . . . is a Nicaraguan, home-grown movement. Sandino predates Castro . . . There is no reason to believe they are going to go out and borrow from elsewhere when they really have something at home." Crucially, Carter's Assistant Secretary of State, Viron Vaky, did not want the Sandinistas turning to Havana or Moscow if the United States isolated them; it was "essential to supply aid to keep the monetary/economic system viable and enmeshed in the international economy." Carter appropriated $75 million, with conditions, to co-opt the "revolution of revulsion," as the journalist Christopher Hitchens called it.[95] The inter-American dynamic and United States' occupation of Nicaragua stimulated nationalist resistance in the early twentieth century; Sandinista nationalism opposed the American-backed system of oppression and economic inequality under Anastasio Somoza Debayle. Later, the Reagan administration emphasized the Soviet east–west dimension, brushing Nicaraguan nationalism aside.[96]

Although the language had changed, there was an echo of Theodore Roosevelt's words on civilization, conformity, and obedience at play. The Sandinistas, and others before them, had challenged contemporary economic integration through revolutionary nationalism.[97]

Conclusion

Famously, George Kennan advocated a *realistic* pursuit of the United States' national interest unencumbered by "idealistic slogans."[98] Such realism is crucial to understanding U.S. power and its engagement with nationalism beyond and within its sphere of influence.

That "national interest" evolved and changed; it was moderated and modified to each contingent period and place, which speaks to the adaptability of a growing and ambitious power.[99] Where nationalism augmented American power, the example of the American revolution and the language of self-determination, democracy, and liberty was emphasized. Yet when nationalists viewed the United States as imperial, especially Latin Americans, the discourse of "civilization," Soviet threats, and modernization were frequently invoked. They too represented other forms of self-determination in Washington.

In some ways, little was revolutionary about the American revolution; most of it was conducted by the disgruntled in an expression of local interest against a distant metropole that famously injured American freedoms and exercised forms of tyranny.

Yet the story told in the *traditional* history of the United States built a nation with preconceptions of its position on a range of issues, including nationalism and self-determination. Much of that history has been deeply contested over recent decades but remains influential in American culture and presidential rhetoric, if no longer being as tenable in United States' and other academia. These histories weave together the benign meta-narrative that frequently belies the complex American engagement with its own understanding of nationalism, and the nationalism of others. Nationalists frequently echoed American messages: Castro, Nehru, and Arevalo were all early admirers of the United States until later encounters. Most ironically, Ho Chi Minh echoed Jefferson on Vietnamese independence.

The American Revolution advanced the principle of self-government in an expression of nationalism, even if the *nation* still needed definition. Independence, decolonization, and self-determination were crucial to that identity. Yet, continental expansion also informed the American conception of nationhood, which rested on the elision of the American Indian nations. Later, LaFeber wrote, "they also repeatedly supported decolonization so they could acquire territory. They established informal and formal colonies themselves. Unlike most other powers, Americans professed decolonization, and like all other nations, the United States followed its self-interest."[100]

Such a history might not be that surprising given the settler colonization in Canada, Australia, and elsewhere, but the United States created an exceptional identity that emphasized self-determination and liberty. Those stories widely inspired and frustrated nationalists.

Notes

1. Thomas Jefferson, "The Unanimous Declaration of the Thirteen United States of America," in *Documents of American History*, ed. Henry Steele Commager (New York: Appleton Century Crofts, 1963), 100.

2. David Waldetreicher, "Reinventing the Wheel of Early U.S. Nationalism," *Diplomatic History* 44, no. 4 (September 2020): 699.

3. Michael H. Hunt, *Ideology and U.S. Foreign Policy* (New Haven, CT: Yale University Press, 1987); David Ryan, *US Foreign Policy in World History* (London: Routledge, 2000); Brad Simpson, "The United States and the Curious History of Self-Determination," *Diplomatic History* 36, no. 4 (September 2012): 675–694.

4. Simpson, "Curious History," 684–692.

5. David Ryan, "The Postcolonial e/Empire The Case of the Missing Upper Case," in *Anglo-American Relations and the Transmission of Ideas*, ed. Alan Dobson and Steve Marsh (New York: Berghahn, 2022), 179–214.

6. Jurgen Osterhammel, *Colonialism: A Theoretical Overview* (Princeton, NJ: Markus Wiener, 1997), 5, 11.

7. Henry M. Teller, "H.J. Res. 233, Teller Amendment" (US Capitol, April 16, 1898). www.visitthecapitol.gov/exhibitions/artifact/hj-res-233-teller-amendment-april-16-1898

8. Andrew Priest, *Designs on Empire: America's Rise to Power in the Age of European Imperialism* (New York: Columbia University Press, 2021), 164, 154–189.

9. Pankaj Mishra, *From the Ruins of Empire: The Intellectuals Who Remade Asia* (New York: Farrar, Straus and Giroux, 2012), 187–215.

10. Woodrow Wilson, "Address Recommending the Declaration of a State of War between the United States and the Imperial German Government, Delivered at a Joint Session of the Two Houses of Congress," in *President Wilson's Foreign Policy: Messages, Addresses, Papers*, ed. James Brown Scott (New York: Oxford University Press, 1918), 284–285.

11. Ryan, *World History*, 16.

12. Priest, *Designs on Empire*, 191, 199.

13. Thomas Paine, *Common Sense [1776]* (London: Penguin Classics, 1986); A. J. Ayer, *Thomas Paine* (London: Faber and Faber, 1988).

14. Hobsbawm and Ranger, eds. *The Invention of Tradition* (Cambridge: Cambridge University Press, 1983); Benedict Anderson, *Imagined Communities: Reflections on the Origins and Spread of Nationalism* (London: Verso, 1983).

15. Anders Stephanson, *Manifest Destiny: American Expansion and the Empire of Right* (New York: Hill and Wang, 1995), 20.

16. Michael Kammen, *Mystic Chords of Memory: The Transformation of Tradition in American Culture* (New York: Vintage, 1993).

17. Pierre Bourdieu, *The Field of Cultural Production: Essays on Art and Literature* (Cambridge: Polity Press, 1993).

18. Paul Connerton, *How Modernity Forgets* (Cambridge: Cambridge University Press, 2009).

19. Sean Wilentz, "The Paradox of the American Revolution," *The New York Review of Books* 69, no. 1 (January 13, 2022): 26–28; Clive Webb, "More Colours than Red, White and Blue: Race, Ethnicity and Anglo-American Relations," *Journal of Transatlantic Studies* 18, no. 4 (December 2020): 434–454.

20. Amy Kaplan, "'Left Alone with America' The Absence of Empire in the Study of American Culture,'" in *Cultures of United States Imperialism* (Durham, NC: Duke University Press, 1993).

21. Hokulani K. Aikau, "Centering Hawai'i: Lessons on and Beyond United States Empire," *American Quarterly* 73, no. 4 (December 2021): 867.

22. Waldetreicher, "Reinventing," 699.

23. Richard W. Van Alstyne, "The American Empire: Its Historical Pattern and Evolution" (London: Historical Association, 1960), 3.

24. William Appleman Williams, *The Tragedy of American Diplomacy* (New York: Delta, 1962), 18–57.

25. Prasenjit Duara, "Transnationalism and the Challenge to National Histories," in *Rethinking American History in a Global Age*, ed. Thomas Bender (Berkeley: University of California Press, 2002).

26. Jill Lepore, "A New Americanism: Why a Nation Needs a National Story," *Foreign Affairs* 98, no. 2 (April 2019): 12–13, 19; David Thelen, "Making History and Making the United States," *Journal of American Studies* 32, no. 3 (December 1998): 373–397; Joyce Appleby, Lynn Hunt, and Margaret Jacob, *Telling the Truth about History* (New York: W. W. Norton & Company, 1994), 91–125.

27. Hunt, *Ideology*, 12.

28. Paul C. Rosier, "Crossing New Boundaries: American Indians and Twentieth Century U.S. Foreign Policy," *Diplomatic History* 39, no. 5 (November 2015): 955.

29. Hunt, *Ideology*, 55.

30. Rosier, "Crossing New Boundaries," 957.

31. George C. Herring, *From Colony to Superpower: U.S. Foreign Relations since 1776* (Oxford: Oxford University Press, 2008), 270.

32. Walter L. Hixon, "'No Savage Shall Inherit the Land': The Indian Enemy Other, Indiscriminate Warfare, and American National Identity, 1607–1783," in *U.S. Foreign Policy and the Other*, ed. Michael Patrick Cullinane and David Ryan (New York: Berghahn, 2017).

33. Stephanson, *Manifest Destiny*, 25–26; Walter L. Hixon, "'No Savage Shall Inherit the Land.'"

34. Thomas Bender, "Historians, the Nation, and the Plenitude of Narratives," in *Rethinking American History in a Global Age*, ed. Thomas Bender (Berkeley: University of California Press, 2002), 1.

35. Bender, 2–5; Ian Tyrrell, *Transnational Nation: United States History in Global Perspective since 1789* (Basingstoke: Palgrave Macmillan, 2007).

36. Priest, *Designs on Empire*.

37. Julian Go, *Patterns of Empire: The British and American Empires, 1688 to the Present* (Cambridge: Cambridge University Press, 2011); Dane Kennedy, *The Imperial History Wars: Debating the British Empire* (London: Bloomsbury, 2018); Bernard Porter, *Empire and Superempire: Britain, America and the World* (New Haven, CT: Yale University Press, 2006); A. G. Hopkins, *American Empire: A Global History* (Princeton, NJ & Oxford: Princeton University Press, 2018).

38. Anderson, *Imagined Communities*; Eric Hobsbawm, *Nations and Nationalism since 1780: Programme, Myth, Reality* (Cambridge: Canto, 1990); Ernest Gellner, *Nations and Nationalism* (Oxford: Blackwell, 1983).

39. Louis Hartz, *The Liberal Tradition in America: An Interpretation of American Political Thought since the Revolution* (New York: Harcourt Brace, 1955), 289.

40. Merrill D. Peterson, *The Jefferson Image in the American Mind* (New York: Oxford University Press, 1962), 266; Ryan, *World History*, 62.

41. Francis Fukuyama, "The End of History?" *The National Interest*, no. 16 (Summer 1989).

42. Ryan, *World History*, 43–50.

43. Theodore Roosevelt, "Message of the President, Papers, with the Annual Message of the President Transmitted to Congress, Foreign Relations of the United States" (Office of the Historian, December 6, 1904). https://history.state.gov/historicaldocuments/frus1904/message-of-the-president

44. Priest, *Designs on Empire*, 202.

45. Walter LaFeber, *Inevitable Revolutions: The United States in Central America* (New York: W. W. Norton & Company, 1983).

46. Walter LaFeber, *The American Search for Opportunity, 1865–1913* (Cambridge: Cambridge University Press, 1993).

47. G. John Ikenberry, *A World Safe for Democracy: Liberal Internationalism and the Crisis of Global Order* (New Haven, CT: Yale University Press, 2020); Tony Smith, *A Pact with the Devil: Washington's Bid for World Supremacy and the Betrayal of the American Promise* (New York: Routledge, 2007); David Milne, *Worldmaking: The Art and Science of American Diplomacy* (New York: Farrar, Straus and Giroux, 2015), 69–122.

48. William Pfaff, *The Wrath of Nations: Civilization and the Furies of Nationalism* (New York: Simon & Schuster, 1993), 201–202.

49. Pfaff, 202; Derek Hastings, *Nationalism in Modern Europe: Politics, Identity, and Belonging since the French Revolution* (London: Bloomsbury, 2018).

50. Woodrow Wilson, "Address on the Conditions of Peace Delivered at a Joint Session of the Two Houses of Congress," in *President Wilson's Foreign Policy: Messages, Addresses, Papers* (New York: Oxford University Press, 1918), 359–360.

51. Ikenberry, *Safe for Democracy*, 103.

52. Ryan, *World History*, 85.

53. Lloyd Ambrosius, "The Others in Wilsonianism," in *U.S. Foreign Policy and the Other*, 124–135.

54. Woodrow Wilson, "Address on Mexican Affairs Delivered at a Joint Session of the Two Houses of Congress," in *President Wilson's Foreign Policy: Messages, Addresses, Papers*, ed. James Brown Scott (New York: Oxford University Press, 1918), 1–10.

55. Ikenberry, *Safe for Democracy*, 133–135.

56. Mishra, *Ruins of Empire*, 187–197.

57. Mishra, 201–203.

58. Franklin Roosevelt and Winston Churchill, "Joint Statement by President Roosevelt and Prime Minister Churchill," Foreign Relations of the United States Diplomatic Papers, 1941, General, The Soviet Union, Volume 1 (Office of the Historian, US Department of State, August 14, 1941), https://history.state.gov/historicaldocuments/frus1941v01/d372; Lloyd C. Gardner, *Spheres of Influence: The Partition of Europe, from Munich to Yalta* (London: John Murray, 1993), 91–116.

59. Warren Kimball, "Foreword," in *The United States and Decolonization: Power and Freedom*, ed. David Ryan and Victor Pungong (London: Macmillan, 2000), xiii.

60. Kimball, xvi.

61. Fred E. Pollock and Warren Kimball, "In Search of Monsters to Destroy: Roosevelt and Colonialism," in *The Juggler: Franklin Roosevelt as Wartime Statesman* (Princeton, NJ: Princeton University Press, 1991), 127–130.

62. Paul Orders, " 'Adjusting to a New Period in World History': Franklin Roosevelt and European Colonialism," in *The United States and Decolonization*, 63–84.

63. Dennis Merrill, "The Ironies of History: The United States and the Decolonization of India," in *The United States and Decolonization*, 102–17.

64. Lloyd C. Gardner, *Approaching Vietnam: From World War II through Dienbienphu* (New York: W. W. Norton & Company, 1988), 64–65.

65. Lloyd C. Gardner, "How We 'Lost' Vietnam, 1940–54," in *The United States and Decolonization*, 133–134; Gardner, *Approaching Vietnam*, 91.

66. Gardner, "Lost Vietnam," 134.

67. William Appleman Williams et al., eds., *America in Vietnam: A Documentary History* (New York: W. W. Norton & Company, 1989), 45–46.

68. Robert J. McMahon, "Toward a Post-Colonial Order: Truman Administration Policies toward South and Southeast Asia," in *The Truman Presidency*, ed. Michael J. Lacey (Cambridge: Cambridge University Press, 1989), 342–345.

69. Robert S. McNamara, *In Retrospect: The Tragedy and Lessons of Vietnam* (New York: Random House, 1995).

70. David Ryan, "By Way of Introduction: The United States, Decolonization and the World System," in *The United States and Decolonization*, 16; David Ryan, *The United States and Europe in the Twentieth Century* (London: Longman, 2003), 65.

71. National Security Council, "National Security Council, U.S. Policy Toward Africa South of the Sahara Prior to Calendar Year 1960, NSC 5719, Record Group 273," 31 July 1957, NARA.

72. Robert E. Wood, "From the Marshall Plan to the Third World," in *Origins of the Cold War: An International History*, ed. Melvyn P. Leffler and David S. Painter (London: Routledge, 1994), 202–205.

73. Melvyn P. Leffler, *A Preponderance of Power: National Security, the Truman Administration, and the Cold War* (Stanford, CA: Stanford University Press, 1992), 18–19.

74. Robert Lansing, Memorandum, 11 June 1914, *Foreign Relations of the United States: The Lansing Papers 1914–1920*, Vol. 2 (GPO, Washington DC, 1940), 462.

75. Go, *Patterns of Empire*; Kennedy, *Imperial History Wars*; Ryan, "Postcolonial e/Empire"; Priest, *Designs on Empire*.

76. David Ryan, "Introduction," in *The United States and Decolonization*, 7.

77. Adom Getachew, *Worldmaking after Empire: The Rise and Fall of Self-Determination* (Princeton & Oxford: Princeton University Press, 2019), 73.

78. Getachew, 75.

79. Getachew, 75–79.

80. Ryan, *World History*, 5, 96, 202; Andre Gunder Frank, *Capitalism and Underdevelopment in Latin America: Historical Studies of Chile and Brazil* (London: Penguin, 1971); Ankie Hoogvelt, *Globalization and the Postcolonial World: The New Political Economy of Development* (London: Macmillan, 1997).

81. Getachew, 101; Ryan, *US Foreign Policy*, 4–5; David Held, ed., *Prospects for Democracy: North, South, East, West* (Cambridge: Polity Press, 1993), 13–52, esp. 27; LaFeber, *Search for Opportunity*.

82. Emily S. Rosenberg, *Spreading the American Dream: American Economic and Cultural Expansion, 1890–1945* (New York: Hill and Wang, 1982), 39, 234.

83. Thomas J. McCormick, *America's Half Century* (Baltimore, MD: Johns Hopkins Press, 1989), 4–5.

84. Hunt, *Ideology*, 174.

85. Eric Hobsbawm, *Age of Extremes: The Short Twentieth Century, 1914–1991* (London: Michael Joseph, 1994), 357.

86. Sheldon B. Liss, *Radical Thought in Central America* (Boulder: Westview, 1991), 36–44.

87. National Security Council, "NSC 144/1 United States Objectives and Courses of Action with Respect to Latin America, Foreign Relations of the United States, 1952–1954, The American Republics, Vol. 4" (Office of the Historian, US Department of State, March 18, 1953), https://history.state.gov/historicaldocuments/frus1952-54v04/d3

88. John Peurifoy, "Telegram to the Department of State, Foreign Relations of the United States 1952–1954, Vol. 4" (Office of the Historian, US Department of State, December 17, 1953), 1093.

89. Louis J. Halle to Robert Bowie, Policy Planning Staff, Department of State, 23 June 1954, Records of the Policy Planning Staff, RG 59 Lot 65 D101, box 79, NARA.

90. David Ryan, "U.S. Foreign Policy and the Guatemalan Revolution in World History,' conference paper on Guatemala, 1952–1954, in *Retrospective FRUS Volume, Guatemala, 1952–1954* (State Department, Washington, D.C., USA, May 15, 2003), https://2001-2009.state.gov/r/pa/ho/19799.htm.

91. Louise J. Halle to Bowie, Policy Planning Staff, 28 May 1954, RG 59, Lot 65 D101, box 79, NARA.

92. Gleijeses, *Shattered Hope*, 366; Ryan, "Guatemala."

93. W. W. Rostow, "Notes on Cuba Policy, Memorandum to the Secretary of State, Secretary of Defense, Director of Central Intelligence," in *The Cuban Missile Crisis, 1962*, ed. Laurence Chang and Peter Kornbluh, A National Security Archive Documents Reader (New York: The New Press, 1992), 18.

94. Rostow, 18.

95. Ryan, *World History*, 174–175; David Ryan, *US-Sandinista Diplomatic Relations: Voice of Intolerance* (London: Macmillan, 1995), 2–5.

96. David Ryan, "The Peripheral Center: Nicaragua in US Policy and the US Imagination at the End of the Cold War," in *Foreign Policy at the Periphery: The Shifting Margins off US International Relations since World War II*, ed. Bevan Sewell and Maria Ryan (Lexington: University of Kentucky, 2017).

97. Elizabeth Dore and John Weeks, *The Red and the Black: The Sandinistas and the Nicaraguan Revolution*, vol. 28, Institute of Latin American Studies, University of London (London: Institute of Latin American Studies, 1992); Dennis Gilbert, *Sandinistas: The Party and the Revolution* (Cambridge: Basil Blackwell, 1988); LaFeber, *Inevitable Revolutions*.

98. Policy Planning Staff, "Report, Review of Current Trends in U.S. Foreign Policy, PPS 23," in *Foreign Relations of the United States Vol. 1 1948*, 1948, 510–529.

99. H. W. Brands, "The Idea of the National Interest," *Diplomatic History* 23, no. 2 (April 1999): 239–261.

100. Walter LaFeber, "The American View of Decolonization, 1776–1920: An Ironic Legacy," in *The United States and Decolonization*, 38.

References

Aikau, Hokulani K. 2021. "Centering Hawaiʻi: Lessons on and Beyond United States Empire," *American Quarterly* 73, no. 4 (December).

Anderson, Benedict. 1983. *Imagined Communities: Reflections on the Origins and Spread of Nationalism*. London: Verso.

Appleby, Joyce, Lynn Hunt, and Margaret Jacob. 1994. *Telling the Truth about History*. New York: W. W. Norton & Company.

Ayer, A. J. 1988. *Thomas Paine*. London: Faber and Faber.

Bender, Thomas. 2002. "Historians, the Nation, and the Plenitude of Narratives," in *Rethinking American History in a Global Age*, ed. Thomas Bender. Berkeley: University of California Press.

Bourdieu, Pierre. 1993. *The Field of Cultural Production: Essays on Art and Literature.* Cambridge: Polity Press.

Brands, H. W. 1999. "The Idea of the National Interest," *Diplomatic History* 23, no. 2 (April).

Commager, Henry Steele ed. 1963. *Documents of American History.* New York: Appleton Century Crofts.

Connerton, Paul. 2009. *How Modernity Forgets.* Cambridge: Cambridge University Press.

Cullinane, Michael Patrick, and David Ryan, eds. 2015. *U.S. Foreign Policy and the Other.* New York: Berghahn.

Dore, Elizabeth, and John Weeks. 1992. *The Red and the Black: The Sandinistas and the Nicaraguan Revolution*, vol. 28. Institute of Latin American Studies. London: Institute of Latin American Studies.

Duara, Prasenjit. 2002. "Transnationalism and the Challenge to National Histories," in *Rethinking American History in a Global Age*, ed. Thomas Bender. Berkeley: University of California Press.

Frank, Andre Gunder. 1971. *Capitalism and Underdevelopment in Latin America: Historical Studies of Chile and Brazil.* London: Penguin.

Fukuyama, Francis. 1989. "The End of History?" *The National Interest*, no. 16 (Summer).

Gardner, Lloyd C. 1988. *Approaching Vietnam: From World War II through Dienbienphu.* New York: W. W. Norton & Company.

Gardner, Lloyd C. 1993. *Spheres of Influence: The Partition of Europe, from Munich to Yalta.* London: John Murray.

Gardner, Lloyd C. 2000. "How We 'Lost' Vietnam, 1940–54," in *The United States and Decolonization*, ed. Ryan and Pungong. London: Macmillan.

Gellner, Ernest. 1983. *Nations and Nationalism.* Oxford: Blackwell.

Getachew, Adom. 2019. *Worldmaking after Empire: The Rise and Fall of Self-Determination.* Princeton, NJ & Oxford: Princeton University Press.

Gilbert, Dennis. 1988. *Sandinistas: The Party and the Revolution.* Cambridge: Basil Blackwell.

Go, Julian. 2011. *Patterns of Empire: The British and American Empires, 1688 to the Present.* Cambridge: Cambridge University Press.

Hartz, Louis. 1955. *The Liberal Tradition in America: An Interpretation of American Political Thought since the Revolution.* New York: Harcourt Brace.

Hastings, Derek. 2018. *Nationalism in Modern Europe: Politics, Identity, and Belonging since the French Revolution.* London: Bloomsbury.

Held, David, ed. 1993. *Prospects for Democracy: North, South, East, West.* Cambridge: Polity Press.

Herring, George C. 2008. *From Colony to Superpower: U.S. Foreign Relations since 1776*. Oxford: Oxford University Press.

Hixon, Walter L. 2017. "'No Savage Shall Inherit the Land': The Indian Enemy Other, Indiscriminate Warfare, and American National Identity, 1607–1783," in *U.S. Foreign Policy and the Other*, ed. Michael Patrick Cullinane and David Ryan. New York: Berghahn.

Hobsbawm, Eric, and Terence Ranger, eds. 1983. *The Invention of Tradition*. Cambridge: Cambridge University Press.

Hobsbawm, Eric. 1990. *Nations and Nationalism since 1780: Programme, Myth, Reality*. Cambridge: Canto.

Hobsbawm, Eric. 1994. *Age of Extremes: The Short Twentieth Century, 1914–1991*. London: Michael Joseph.

Hoogvelt, Ankie. 1997. *Globalization and the Postcolonial World: The New Political Economy of Development*. London: Macmillan, 1997.

Hopkins, A. G. 2018. *American Empire: A Global History*. Princeton, NJ & Oxford: Princeton University Press.

Hunt, Michael H. 1987. *Ideology and U.S. Foreign Policy*. New Haven, CT: Yale University Press.

Ikenberry, G. John. 2020. *A World Safe for Democracy: Liberal Internationalism and the Crisis of Global Order*. New Haven, CT: Yale University Press.

Kammen, Michael. 1993. *Mystic Chords of Memory: The Transformation of Tradition in American Culture*. New York: Vintage.

Kaplan, Amy. 1993. "'Left Alone with America' The Absence of Empire in the Study of American Culture," in *Cultures of United States Imperialism*. Durham, NC: Duke University Press.

Kennedy, Dane. 2018. *The Imperial History Wars: Debating the British Empire*. London: Bloomsbury.

Kimball, Warren. 2000. "Foreword," in *The United States and Decolonization: Power and Freedom*, ed. David Ryan and Victor Pungong. London: Macmillan.

LaFeber, Walter. 1983. *Inevitable Revolutions: The United States in Central America*. New York: W. W. Norton & Company.

LaFeber, Walter. 1993. *The American Search for Opportunity, 1865–1913*. Cambridge: Cambridge University Press.

Lansing, Robert. 1940. Memorandum, 11 June 1914, *Foreign Relations of the United States: The Lansing Papers 1914–1920*, Vol. 2. Washington D.C.: GPO.

Leffler, Melvyn P. 1992. *A Preponderance of Power: National Security, the Truman Administration, and the Cold War*. Stanford, CA: Stanford University Press.

Lepore, Jill. 2019. "A New Americanism: Why a Nation Needs a National Story," *Foreign Affairs* 98, no. 2 (April).

Liss, Sheldon B. 1991. *Radical Thought in Central America*. Boulder, CO: Westview.

McCormick, Thomas J. 1989. *America's Half Century*. Baltimore, MD: Johns Hopkins Press.

McMahon, Robert J. 1989. "Toward a Post-Colonial Order: Truman Administration Policies toward South and Southeast Asia," in *The Truman Presidency*, ed. Michael J. Lacey. Cambridge: Cambridge University Press.

McNamara, Robert S. 1995. *In Retrospect: The Tragedy and Lessons of Vietnam*. New York: Random House.

Merrill, Dennis. 2000. "The Ironies of History: The United States and the Decolonization of India," in *The United States and Decolonization*, ed. Ryan and Pungong.

Milne, David. 2015. *Worldmaking: The Art and Science of American Diplomacy*. New York: Farrar, Straus and Giroux.

Mishra, Pankaj. 2012. *From the Ruins of Empire: The Intellectuals Who Remade Asia*. New York: Farrar, Straus and Giroux.

Orders, Paul. 2000. "'Adjusting to a New Period in World History': Franklin Roosevelt and European Colonialism," in *The United States and Decolonization*, ed. Ryan and Pungong.

Osterhammel, Jurgen. 1997. *Colonialism: A Theoretical Overview*. Princeton, NJ: Markus Wiener.

Paine, Thomas. 1776. *Common Sense*. London: Penguin Classics, 1986.

Peterson, Merrill D. 1962. *The Jefferson Image in the American Mind*. New York: Oxford University Press.

Pfaff, William. 1993. *The Wrath of Nations: Civilization and the Furies of Nationalism*. New York: Simon & Schuster.

Pollock, Fred E., and Warren Kimball. 1991. "In Search of Monsters to Destroy: Roosevelt and Colonialism," in *The Juggler: Franklin Roosevelt as Wartime Statesman*. Princeton, NJ: Princeton University Press.

Porter, Bernard. 2006. *Empire and Superempire: Britain, America and the World*. New Haven, CT: Yale University Press.

Priest, Andrew. 2021. *Designs on Empire: America's Rise to Power in the Age of European Imperialism*. New York: Columbia University Press.

Roosevelt, Franklin, and Winston Churchill. 1941. "Joint Statement by President Roosevelt and Prime Minister Churchill," *Foreign Relations of the United States Diplomatic Papers*, 1941, General, The Soviet Union, Volume 1. Office of the Historian, US Department of State, August 14). https://history.state.gov/historicaldocuments/frus1941v01/d372

Roosevelt, Theodore. 1904. "Message of the President, Papers, with the Annual Message of the President Transmitted to Congress, Foreign Relations of the United States" (Office of the Historian, December 6). https://history.state.gov/historicaldocuments/frus1904/message-of-the-president.

Rosenberg, Emily S. 1982. *Spreading the American Dream: American Economic and Cultural Expansion 1890–1945*. New York: Hill and Wang.

Rosier, Paul C. 2015. "Crossing New Boundaries: American Indians and Twentieth Century U.S. Foreign Policy," *Diplomatic History* 39, no. 5 (November).

Ryan, David. 1995. *US-Sandinista Diplomatic Relations: Voice of Intolerance*. London: Macmillan.
Ryan, David, and Victor Pungong eds. 2000. *The United States and Decolonization: Power and Freedom*. London: Macmillan.
Ryan, David. 2000. *US Foreign Policy in World History*. London: Routledge.
Ryan, David. 2003. *The United States and Europe in the Twentieth Century*. London: Longman.
Ryan, David. 2003. "U.S. Foreign Policy and the Guatemalan Revolution in World History," conference paper on Guatemala, 1952–1954, in Retrospective FRUS Volume, Guatemala, 1952–1954. State Department, Washington, D.C., USA, May 15, 2003. https://2001-2009.state.gov/r/pa/ho/19799.htm
Ryan, David. 2017. "The Peripheral Center: Nicaragua in US Policy and the US Imagination at the End of the Cold War," in *Foreign Policy at the Periphery: The Shifting Margins off US International Relations since World War II*. ed. Bevan Sewell and Maria Ryan. Lexington: University of Kentucky.
Ryan, David. 2022. "The Postcolonial e/Empire The Case of the Missing Upper Case," in Anglo-American Relations and the Transmission of Ideas, ed. Alan Dobson and Steve Marsh. New York: Berghahn.
Simpson, Brad. 2012. "The United States and the Curious History of Self-Determination," *Diplomatic History* 36, no. 4 (September).
Smith, Tony. 2007. *A Pact with the Devil: Washington's Bid for World Supremacy and the Betrayal of the American Promise*. New York: Routledge.
Stephanson, Anders. 1995. *Manifest Destiny: American Expansion and the Empire of Right*. New York: Hill and Wang.
Teller, Henry M. 1898. "H.J. Res. 233, Teller Amendment" (US Capitol, April 16), www.visitthecapitol.gov/exhibitions/artifact/hj-res-233-teller-amendment-april-16-1898.
Thelen, David. 1998. "Making History and Making the United States," *Journal of American Studies* 32, no. 3 (December).
Tyrrell, Ian. 2007. *Transnational Nation: United States History in Global Perspective since 1789*. Basingstoke: Palgrave Macmillan.
Van Alstyne, Richard W. 1960. "The American Empire: Its Historical Pattern and Evolution." London: Historical Association.
Waldetreicher, David. 2020. "Reinventing the Wheel of Early U.S. Nationalism," *Diplomatic History* 44, no. 4 (September).
Webb, Clive. 2020. "More Colours than Red, White and Blue: Race, Ethnicity and Anglo-American Relations," *Journal of Transatlantic Studies* 18, no. 4 (December).
Wilentz, Sean. 2022. "The Paradox of the American Revolution," *The New York Review of Books* 69, no. 1 (January 13).
Williams, William Appleman. 1962. *The Tragedy of American Diplomacy*. New York: Delta.

Williams, William Appleman et al. eds. 1989. *America in Vietnam: A Documentary History*. New York: W. W. Norton & Company.
Wilson, Woodrow. 1918. *President Wilson's Foreign Policy: Messages, Addresses, Papers*, ed. James Brown Scott. New York: Oxford University Press.
Wood, Robert E. 1994. "From the Marshall Plan to the Third World," in *Origins of the Cold War: An International History*, ed. Melvyn P. Leffler and David S. Painter. London: Routledge.

3

A Secular Turn

The Place of Culture in Quebec's Self-Conception

RAFFAELE IACOVINO

In the past twenty years or so, the Quebec nation has undergone a veritable transformation that has culminated in the adoption of a new kind of secularism meant to provide some clarity and closure to the practice of accommodations for religious and cultural minorities. With the Quebec independence movement in a state of dormancy for some time now,[1] and no longer an imminent threat to the Canadian political system,[2] the Québécois have nevertheless continued to engage in a national conversation about the terms of belonging. Indeed, the sentiment that the Québécois constitute a self-determining people free to forge its future as an autonomous collective political subject remains as robust as ever.[3] As Lecours has shown, when freed from the shackles of injecting some legitimacy to secession in the face of international observers and opponents of independence, the strategic imperative of establishing more inclusive markers of membership in the boundaries of the nation wanes.[4]

In other words, the decline of the independence movement in Quebec has paradoxically opened the floodgates to a (re)examination of what Michel Seymour has termed the "character" of Quebec identity,[5] its internal negotiations around the place of culture, religion, language, and other substantive identifiers, which he contrasts with the "structure" of culture, in which culture as the basis for nationalist mobilization is approached through the conceptual lens of the recognition of some form of collective affirmation in relation to other such movements or constituted political communities. This structural approach serves as an analytical tool with which to position and compare a variety of distinct, context-specific institutional frameworks for national affirmation. In Canada, the conventional story has been to characterize national integration as a dual process consisting of competing yet equally legitimate expressions of liberal-pluralist national spaces,[6] or as two distinct citizenship regimes,[7] or as the expression of colliding models of integration,[8] to highlight a few studies based respectively on fields as wide-ranging as political philosophy, political economy, and political sociology. Indeed, with the relative decline of considerations of Quebec's "place" in Canada and the world, much of the debate in Quebec in the post-referendum era has centered on finding the appropriate balance between the recognition of the majority culture as a lynchpin of the nationalist movement, and the place of minority cultural groups within that project. Otherwise stated, how can the majority culture serve as a vehicle for political self-determination, or as the basis of national identity, while embracing the sort of liberal-pluralist markers of belonging that tend to dilute the role of culture in order to broaden the reach of the nationalist project and signal a greater inclusiveness?

As the following discussion will make clear, however, the structural aspects of the Quebec question are never far away. The articulation of a particular brand of nationalism in Quebec cannot be examined in a silo, outside of its status as an internal nation that is nested within a larger Canadian national integration project that enjoys the imprimatur of a recognized nation-state. In other words, any evaluation of Quebec's attempts to frame the character and boundaries of its collective identity must account not only for normative guideposts rooted in political thought, but against a ready-made alternative, which enjoys the legitimating stamp of universalistic liberal-pluralist credentials.[9] This structural bind always serves to condition debates about the regulation of culture in Quebec.

This chapter will look at one specific dilemma that has confronted Quebec throughout its history, but particularly since the Quiet Revolution of the 1960s—the notion that Quebec nationalism, both in the formal political sphere and in the wider public realm, has been forced to formulate the terms of belonging while accounting for the existence of a cultural majority. Fiona Barker[10] has called this fine balancing act "learning to be a majority," and Blad and Couton[11] have termed the process of forging a nation through the choices made for integration "intercultural Nationalism." It is this introspection about the appropriate place of the cultural majority in defining the contours of the nation that has come to dominate the identity landscape in Quebec.

This discussion will examine recent developments in Quebec, in which the character of the national identity has gone from a cross-partisan consensus on the primacy of pluralism to its most recent secular turn that is without precedent in Canadian and Quebec history. This adoption of a new and contentious form of secularism cannot be taken as a legitimate response to an identifiable social crisis, or even a cynical instance of performative politicking. Rather, it is the result of a longstanding and ongoing debate which has, for the time being, been won by those seeking to finger pluralism as the main culprit for a perceived loss of Quebec's collective sense of self and thus its failure to achieve national affirmation. In short, contemporary Quebec has now officially signaled its desire to alienate minority communities in the name of some project to assume control of the social space, through an ill-conceived conception of regulation that claims to be grounded in neutrality.

A New Nationalism: Toward a Liberal-Pluralist Conception

The conventional approach in describing the transformation of the markers of Quebec national identity points to the effects of the Quiet Revolution in the 1960s in which the Quebec state emerged as the primary agent of modernization and social emancipation for francophones.[12] In simple terms, the idea was to bring the nation from its "ethnic" character, with an emphasis on lineage, and exclusive cultural-religious terms of membership that crossed the boundaries of Quebec's territory, to a more "civic" conception that leaned on language, territoriality, and a sort of liberal-pluralism meant to be more inclusive of a diversity of cultural and religious influences. Mathieu and Laforest describe this shift along four dimensions:

> Briefly, we can present that liberal-pluralist historiographical project as a quadripartite movement evolving away from the traditional French-Canadian national scheme: 1) from ethnicity to a more legal dimension; 2) from a French organic community to a new Francophonie mostly defined by reference to the language itself; 3) from a French-Canadian culture to a Quebecer's culture as the national one; and 4) from a strictly culturally oriented nationalism to a nationalism seen as widely open and as a collective work in progress.[13]

Without getting bogged down in debates about the intellectual veracity of this basic dichotomy,[14] for our purposes the salience of this particular sociopolitical transformation is that it spearheaded a seemingly all-consuming debate among Quebec nationalists that henceforth centered on the place and the role of the majority culture in defining the nation.[15] Stated bluntly, while some welcomed the turn toward liberal-pluralism as an injection of a sort of legitimacy to the nation in its quest to affirm and mobilize itself around the collective right of self-determination, others wondered if this transformation constituted a wholesale "de-nationalization" of the project—a mere facsimile of an already existing pluralist and post-cultural space forged by a competing national integration project in Canada. What demarcates the Quebec nation as a majoritarian project if not the existence of French-Canadian culture, history, and memory?

Interculturalism

While the Quebec state does not control the levers of citizenship, one area in which these debates have emerged quite explicitly is in the policy field of immigrant integration, an area for which the Quebec state does possess substantive policy instruments. Beginning with the establishment of its own Ministry of Immigration in 1968, and subsequently gaining control through successive bilateral agreements with the federal government of much of the responsibilities of recruitment, selection, and integration of newcomers, Quebec has welcomed the responsibility of constructing its own national model of integration that serves as somewhat of a counterweight to Canada's emphasis on multiculturalism within a bilingual framework. It is here that the boundaries of the Quebec nation are debated and articulated through the structural backdrop of simultaneous and competing nation-building projects.

Following the defeat of the first referendum on sovereignty-association in 1980, the governing Parti Québécois (PQ) sought to formulate a conception of the national project that would appeal to minority cultural communities by more systematically developing an indigenous variant of cultural pluralism to serve as an alternative to Canadian multiculturalism. In 1981, the PQ government published *Autant de façons d'être Québécois*,[16] which introduced "Interculturalism" as Quebec's national model of integration. The momentum of the neo-nationalism of the Quiet Revolution, with its orientations toward more open and inclusive terms of belonging, culminated in an official policy blueprint that outlined Quebec's version of cultural pluralism.

The first salient aspect of this initiative is that it was limited to a policy statement, not a body of legislation. Nevertheless, it was a pioneering endeavor in that through a series of consultations the government in effect recognized minority "cultural communities" as interlocutors. The idea was to create fertile ground for ongoing dialogue between the majority culture, heavily represented as agents of the state, and representatives from ethnocultural groups. Indeed, this majority-minority dynamic would come to define the main thrust of this version of interculturalism.

The statement highlighted three primary objectives:

- ensuring the preservation, specificity, and development of cultural communities;
- sensitizing francophone Quebecers to the place of cultural communities in developing a common heritage; and
- promoting the integration of the cultural communities in Quebec society, especially in the sectors where they were under-represented, particularly in the public service.

In essence, the novelty of this policy orientation was an acknowledgment that the francophone majority had a moral responsibility to recognize the contributions of diverse cultural groups, and even encourages cultural exchanges with countries of origin. The model explicitly accepts cultural pluralism as a defining aspect of Quebec's national identity, and commits the state to providing active measures in support of the flourishing of minority cultures, such as the establishment of the *Centre d'orientation et de formation des immigrants* and the *Programme d'enseignement des langues d'origines (PELO)*.[17] The statement also recommends increasing allophones'[18] accessibility to public service jobs, committing the state to service delivery that is better adapted to the specific needs of members of minority communities, and for financial assistance to minority cultural community associations. The Ministry of Immigration was even renamed the Ministry of Cultural Communities and Immigration, injecting its mandate with a greater responsibility for integration.

While the statement does signal a genuine acceptance of cultural pluralism by acknowledging the public contributions of diverse cultural groups, committing to ongoing dialogue, providing support for cultural preservation, and sensitizing the majority francophone community, its main thrust is nevertheless one that conceptualizes the majority culture as the "principle motor" toward which minorities will converge.[19] It emphasizes that this newfound openness is aimed at greater integration into the majority community without advocating outright assimilation. In other words, the identity markers of the majority culture will continue to serve as a pole of convergence. This serves two purposes: it allows for the acknowledgment that the majority culture, history, and memory continue to lie at the base of the Quebec national identity, and it defines the public sphere as a terrain for dialogue and interaction between cultures in an attempt to differentiate the model from Canadian multiculturalism, which had been widely criticized for promoting cultural silos and for denying the existence of Quebec as a proper host society.[20] The French language in this view serves as a vehicle for integration—a non-negotiable pillar of the political community that will allow newcomers access to the national story. As such, this early formulation of interculturalism still rested on a hierarchy of cultures, yet with an acknowledgment that the majority culture is open to new influences. In short, while representing a threshold of sorts into the terrain of cultural pluralism, this initiative nevertheless represented a modest pluralist turn. The goal was still to establish the bases for unity around an established core group. It did, however, signal Quebec's first formal foray into a pluralist normative terrain.

In 1991, the Quebec Liberal Party (PLQ) released *Au Quebec pour bâtir ensemble*, which remains to this day the most comprehensive and authoritative statement on Quebec interculturalism.[21] The basic change here, in contrast to the initial formulation of the model, is a move away from convergence to the majority toward a synthesis model, where the conception of cultural groups in the public sphere are recognized on an equal plane. In other words, interaction and exchanges between cultures in the public sphere, in French, will create a sort of dynamic and evolving cultural hybrid and this will constitute the basis for Quebec's national identity. Rather than aiming to integrate newcomers into the culture of the majority, this version emphasizes that majority–minority relations be guided by a *moral contract*, each accepting responsibilities for integration, with the objective of creating a *common public culture* that evolves over time and does not pre-suppose a cultural core. The key here is that the onus on integration is based on reciprocity—newcomers commit to integration into the francophone political community and the host society commits the necessary resources, both material and symbolic. Again, the defining characteristic here is an acceptance of the French language as the key identity marker for the Quebec nation, while also encouraging the flourishing of languages of origin in the private sphere.

This new approach based on a "fusion of horizons" nevertheless distinguished itself from multiculturalism due to its insistence that the objective is to foster participation as a prerequisite to recognition. The idea is to avoid cultural silos, discourage cultural enclosure and isolation, and through democratic deliberation to construct a public sphere open to all influences. In this sense, it looks very much like Canadian multiculturalism except that it outlines a key role for the French language, makes recognition conditional on intercultural exchange and participation, and broadly defines Quebec as the relevant national space for debating the terms and demarcating the actors through which membership will be negotiated.

Despite their differences, these consecutive initiatives to provide substance to a proper model of integration signaled a clear orientation for Quebec—they were based on a liberal-pluralist consensus that crossed party lines. At the very least, despite observations that highlight both basic ambiguities associated with conceptualizations of the models and their application,[22] the underlying normative framework remains clear—Quebec's journey in delimiting the boundaries of its national identity was moving toward an acknowledgment of the primacy of pluralism. These attempts to construct interculturalism as a specific "made in Quebec" alternative shared a spirit, or tone, that sought at the very least to recognize that the contributions of minority cultural communities were valued.

By the early 2000s, however, with the decline of the independence option and the global backlash against multiculturalism, Quebec began to traverse its own version of the culture wars, expressed through the prism of "reasonable accommodations." Essentially, increasing political currency came to be attached to the notion that accommodations for religious and ethnocultural groups had gone too far and that "Quebec values," or some form of return to a majoritarian conception of collective identity, ought to be more present in informing efforts at integration. Buttressed by a seemingly endless stream of highly sensationalized media stories[23] around minority groups supposedly subverting established values of Quebeckers, refusing to integrate or demonstrating outright hostility to the majority, the right-leaning *Action Démocratique du Québec* (ADQ) and the PQ began to capitalize on a general feeling that Quebec identity was under attack.

The Liberal government headed by Jean Charest thus called for the establishment of a Commission of Inquiry, to be led by Charles Taylor and Gérard Bouchard, two longstanding and established Quebec scholars on the questions of culture, diversity, and identity. The Commission represented a watershed of sorts since subsequent debates would in part coalesce around the

Commission's recommendations. The question of collective identity was now front and center—in what became somewhat of a mass therapy session—and this dominated the public conversation in Quebec. Debates about Quebec's national identity were no longer mobilized around a referendum campaign for independence, or constitutional battles with the rest of Canada. They had turned inward, in a remarkable display of introspection, and a wider array of voices entered the fray.

Without diving into a deep analysis of the Commission's findings, two recommendations require further examination. Essentially, the general tenor of the report was that Quebec's path to integration was relatively successful, and that it should strengthen its commitment to liberal-pluralist principles rather than point to them as the source of this societal malaise around cultural and religious accommodations. The Commission argued that this should be undertaken on two fronts.

First, Quebec should continue along the path of what the commissioners called "integrative pluralism" by strengthening interculturalism through actual legislation rather than limiting its impact to policy statements and framework documents. Indeed, the variant of the model explicitly adopted by the final report was one of cultural hybridization or synthesis rather than majoritarian convergence—Quebec collective identity would come to rest on the well-established parameters of a common public culture. There was no need for a radical transformation of the Quebec model, and Quebeckers ought to continue to rely on participation and deliberation between non-hierarchical cultural groups as the basis for collective purpose and social cohesion. They emphasized that this elusive set of "common values," the source of such malaise among critics of Quebec's liberal-pluralist turn, would be the result of a national conversation, through a process of "historization," not the product of a sort of imposed universalism or a forced neutrality. In this view, Quebec national identity is not the result of a pre-defined sociohistorical cultural fulcrum but the product of open cultural exchange over time.

Second, in the specific area of religious accommodations, the Commission also emphasized continuity by advocating for "open secularism" rather than a more restrictive version.[24] Open secularism was deemed to be more compatible with liberal-pluralism because state neutrality in the face of religious expression did not threaten to infringe on freedom of conscience—since all religious faiths had a place in the public sphere equally. Absolutist or restrictive secularism, on the other hand, was taken to encroach on the private lives and choices of individuals and was not aligned with the sorts of recognition practices established in Quebec. Open secularism, in other words, fit more comfortably with the sort of integrative pluralism of a strengthened and codified interculturalism policy.[25]

The Commission thus sought to assure Quebeckers that there was no "crisis," and to continue along a liberal-pluralist path in a spirit of tolerance, yet its main recommendations served only to mobilize opponents. The Commissioners were taken as either apologists for a Canadian-style version of multiculturalism, the reflection of a certain elitism that failed to take seriously the concerns of the majority, or the outright continuation of a process of "de-nationalization" of collective identity in Quebec.[26] Maclure noted that the final report ended up forging an unlikely alliance between absolute secularists and conservatives that promulgated a return to a Catholic cultural nationalism,[27] and this would usher in a new era for Quebec that shifted the terrain of nationalist discourse away from the hegemony of interculturalism as an integrative framework. In other words, if debates to this point had been structured around the predominance of convergence versus synthesis models, subsequent proposals for the accommodation of minority cultures would no longer be constrained by these boundaries.

The Commission's recommendations were for the most part ignored by the political classes, and the next phase of the battle would revolve around the idea of achieving closure, or to once and for all define terms of belonging in Quebec. The Québec Liberal Party (QLP) soon followed up with performative initiatives, including a law that sought to ban face-coverings in interactions with public officials (Bill 94), conveniently justified through the triad of security, communication, and identification and saying little about wider normative concerns about cultural accommodation.[28] This was followed by a requirement for newcomers to sign a "values pledge" affirming their commitment to the "common values of Quebec society." While in opposition, the PQ had even proposed a more comprehensive *Quebec Identity Act* (Bill 195),[29] which sought to amend the Quebec Charter of Rights and Freedoms through a preamble that would assert the equality between the sexes; explicitly acknowledge the secular character of public institutions; and simultaneously affirm the predominance of the French language with a vague allusion to the protection of Quebec culture. It also introduced Quebec's own citizenship certificate, to be granted to newcomers after a demonstration of proof of French proficiency and knowledge of the main tenets of Quebec culture. This certificate would be necessary for the exercise of political rights, including running for office in provincial, municipal, or schoolboard elections.

The slow and steady chipping away at a model based in reciprocity and tolerance inherent in the development of interculturalism proceeded incrementally. The majority in Quebec would assert itself, and the "moral contract" would be supplanted by a sort of hegemonic discourse in which the onus of adapting would be placed on minority cultural communities. The next phase, however, would not be so incremental.

From Bill 60 to Bill 21: The Secular Nation Takes Hold

The PQ's attempts to reinforce Quebec's majoritarian identity culminated in its proposal of the short-lived Charter of Quebec Values (Bill 60), which died with the defeat of the minority PQ government in April 2014. The Act sought to instill a new absolutist conception of secularism in Quebec while simultaneously providing a framework with which to adjudicate accommodation requests. It stipulated that "personnel members of public bodies" would henceforth be prohibited from expressing themselves through conspicuous religious symbols such as clothing, headgear, and jewelry. At the same time, in what was perhaps indicative of the desire to placate both secular republicans and conservative Catholics, the Act was replete with interpretive clauses that allowed for exemptions relating to Quebec's cultural heritage. The Act also provided a series of guideposts with regards to interpreting accommodation requests, including human rights considerations, gender equality, cost, health and safety, and so on, yet tacked on to this list a wide-ranging provision that allowed for much discretion for authorities to deny accommodation requests based only on the prerogative of the "public body" in question to determine whether "the separation of religions and State or the religious neutrality and secular nature of the State" was compromised.[30]

The PQ's election defeat, however, did not result in the disappearance of this secular strain in Quebec's nationalist circles. Following a period of PLQ rule,[31] the conservative Coalition Avenir Québec (CAQ) would win a majority in October 2018 under the leadership of former PQ cabinet minister François Legault, and the re-emergence of this desire to settle the question of religious accommodations resulted in Bill 21, *An Act respecting the laicity of the State*, which was adopted in June 2019.[32] Unlike its predecessor, this initiative did not seek to impose absolutist secularism throughout the public service. Rather, its reach was limited to a restriction of religious symbols and garments for those occupying positions of authority, such as teachers and police officers, with exemptions for those already employed. Moreover, it was presented as a more moderate endeavor since the Act does not aim to serve as a comprehensive guide for all accommodation requests, nor does it introduce a series of exceptions for the Catholic majority, whether or not framed in terms of "cultural heritage." One particularly novel aspect of Bill 21, however, was that it anticipated legal challenges based on the Canadian Charter of Rights and Freedoms, and therefore appended the Notwithstanding Clause (Section 33) to the legislation, which allows the National Assembly to override judicial interventions based on Charter infringements. The legislation also amended Quebec's own Charter of Human Rights, including a clause that the charter should henceforth be interpreted in a manner that respects "state laicity," again in order to shield it from challenges associated with freedom of religion or conscience.

For our purposes, a protracted debate about the merits of variants of secularism is not relevant and cannot be properly examined here. What this brief overview of Quebec's recent shift with regards to cultural and religious accommodation does demonstrate, however, is that secularism has come to be formulated as a proxy for the re-establishment of a majoritarian hegemony, the rejection of the primacy of pluralism. It signals a reclaiming of sorts of a majoritarian identitive space in Quebec at the expense of the recognition of minority groups and their diverse contributions to the public conversation. Otherwise stated, the actual terms of the debate have shifted altogether away from the legitimating language of liberal-pluralism and toward this perceived imperative to protect, shield, or immunize the collective identity from difference in the name of some ambiguous desire for neutrality. Rather than a majority conceived as sensitized to the vulnerability of minority groups, available in a spirit of reciprocity to engage in the enterprise of integration on an equal plane, the new emphasis on imposing secularism as a cure-all signals a retreat of sorts to a model that assumes minority groups are potential threats to the collective aspirations of the majority and must be overseen or supervised in some capacity. The majority has imposed its terms whether minorities like it or not. This view is effectively conveyed by Eisenberg, and merits quotation in full:

> this legislation is an exercise in establishing the terms by which the majority is willing to extend public services to minorities in the province. Essential public services, such as schooling and legal services, are displaced as "rights" of citizenship and instead presented as discretionary privileges that majorities extend to minorities on terms they see fit, and withhold when these

terms are not met. In this case, the majority's terms restrict religious freedom and remove any further consideration of the restriction from the purview of courts. If the aim of the bill is to protect what many consider to be a legitimate entitlement, namely the right of people to be treated equally and without prejudice by public officials, then this aim could be legislated by requiring public officials to act with equal consideration and to be accountable for their actions. Bill 21 goes much further and signifies the actions of an entitled majority that seeks to revoke the "privilege" of minorities to access public services, as is their right.[33]

Eisenberg's identification of a new nativism underpinning the ascent of majority rights is part of a broader global backlash against cultural pluralism as a basis for integration. One can concede, however, that Quebec's precarious position as a vulnerable minority nation requires an approach to cultural pluralism that is sensitive to its collective anxieties. In other words, the Quebec case has always been imbued with certain nuances associated with its constant need for national affirmation. This feature, however, is precisely what we see animating Taylor's defense of interculturalism.[34] For Taylor, the very act of Quebec formulating a model that responds to its own history and circumstances, or its "story," implied that a commitment to integrative pluralism did not inevitably reflect a shedding of its cultural core. It is through a particular collective history, culture, and shared memories that this French-speaking nation in North America has embarked on a societal project that chose, without external imposition, a model of pluralism to attain the ends of successful integration. Interculturalism is thus not just a rhetorical play on Canadian multiculturalism, it is Quebec's own policy and it is for Quebec. Rather than threatening the collective identity, as some critics contend, interculturalism is in fact implicitly grounded in a particular national story.

The idea that secularism can save the day as a necessary guarantor of Quebec's 'values' should not detract from the fact that Quebec has already affirmed its capacity to engage in a national conversation around the nature and scope of values in an open, tolerant, and respectful dialogue. Rather than add certainty to the matter of accommodations, and affirm collective boundaries, the secular turn in effect does the opposite—it closes off the public sphere to minority contributions, signals to them they have no place in crafting the societal project, and adds to a feeling of alienation and suspicion among minority groups. Hardly a recipe for integration. Jocelyn Maclure echoed this sentiment in defining the nation through its capacity to open up the dialogue to a diversity of cultural groups:

> This attachment to popular sovereignty or collective self-determination, rather than definitive agreement on a set of rights or on a shared identity, is the main facet of this new imaginary of belonging. In some of its variants, minority nationalism would thus be less a static quest for cultural survival than a struggle for the capacity to decide collectively which aspects of culture should be reproduced.[35]

This is precisely what is missing in conceptions of the national space that insist on reifying either a robust cultural core or imposing universalist or neutral "values," veiled as secularism. For Maclure, our era is characterized by an openness to allowing for constituted groups to engage in a conversation, and the site of that conversation is what demarcates the national community—having the debate about the place of constituent collective identities is, in itself, an act of self-determination.

Along these lines, for Gérard Bouchard, interculturalism exists as one pluralist option among many potential institutional responses to diversity along a continuum, which can be perfectly adaptable to Quebec's particular status as a minority nation with a majority culture.[36] Again, like Taylor, there's no attempt to erase the existence of a cultural core. Indeed, Bouchard recognizes that the sociological basis for interculturalism, relative to multiculturalism, is that it operates on a particular sociopolitical paradigm in which negotiations take place in a dualist framework, as opposed to a diversity paradigm that characterizes Canadian multiculturalism. Indeed, there are two key aspects of Bouchard's conceptualization of interculturalism that entail a rejection of Quebec's turn toward secularism.

First, Bouchard actually anticipated the appeal of a secular form of republicanism in Quebec and rejected it based on its propensity to generate mistrust rather than achieve its stated aims of certainty and closure. The basic normative thrust of interculturalism is not to further fragment Quebec society as such but to inject the practice of cultural regulation with a "pluralist mindset"—a spirit of reciprocity and a commitment to continue to deliberate, with the establishment of a legal framework for the protection of minorities. In this view, all participants, whether in the majority or minority group, are sensitized to the requirement for harmonious relations, and there is no ambiguity regarding the recognized interlocutors. This does not mean that the majority must erase itself, or that the normative force of Canadian multiculturalism will inevitably take hold, or even that the majority in some cases should not substantively impose some of its cultural preferences in the public sphere. It simply means that the majority should avoid taking measures that signal to minorities that they have little say in how their particular sources of meaning are recognized in the public sphere.

Second, having established that interculturalism is compatible with embracing the existence of a majority cultural core, Bouchard opted for the use of a more realist lens based on a certain sociological empiricism, and claimed that philosophically stringent models can never truly account for the precarious position of the majority group in Quebec. As such, he invoked a particular contextual variable in which he circumscribed situations where "ad hoc precedence" for the majority culture ought to prevail. He did not, however, contend that the majority should impose a sort of preferential status, as a condition of membership, through formal mechanisms. It is this realist concession to the majority that really distinguished Bouchard's contribution. It was simply impossible to bypass the very real condition that the majority group in Quebec must also act as the carrier of a minoritarian collective identity in North America.

Bouchard did not introduce this framework lightly, however, and conceded that it may be vulnerable to abuses. He thus introduced a series of qualifications that might temper the temptation to elevate the status of the majority and create two classes of citizens, and these qualifications must proceed from the "pluralist mindset" nourished by a strengthened and codified model of interculturalism. First, Bouchard insisted that any initiative that elevates the majority must pass muster with the Quebec Charter of Human Rights as well as undergo a transparent democratic debate through regular institutional channels. Second, Bouchard reminded us that even in established liberal democracies that seek to abide by strict universalist markers of belonging and cultural pluralism, liberal theorists have indeed coalesced around the notion that pure liberal neutrality is impossible, and that some customs and values of the majority will always be present in any constituted society. It thus follows that the same standard should apply to Quebec, and that the scope and impact of these practices should be acknowledged openly rather than denied in any model of integration or framework for accommodation practices. Third, if reciprocity is to serve as the overriding norm in deliberations between interlocutors, then this concession to the majority in certain cases can be seen as a sort of accommodation in itself—

an acknowledgment that the majority has a right to exist and lies at the heart of a legitimate and particular societal project. Fourth, in the context of globalization and the homogenization of collective identities, majority cultures have a role to play in global debates around the protection of cultural diversity on an international scale.

Like other small nations, majority cultures serve as the core of national cultures, and the promotion of symbolic reference points rooted in history, language, and memory in some cases cannot be represented by a civic legal architecture alone. This is a sort of acknowledgment that, with regards to its international status, the Quebec nation cannot forgo its past, and ought to be allowed to make the case for distinct status based on some robust cultural markers. Moreover, on a related note, Bouchard also invoked the argument that the collective mobilization of a majority cultural community can also benefit the whole of society as a source of social cohesion, in the pursuit of the common good. The instrumental force of culture in this view has some positive implications that ought to be recognized. Finally, Bouchard wrapped up his case for ad hoc precedence by highlighting that threatened majority groups have historically been prone to act out against minorities in a sort of backlash, and thus an open and honest conversation about the anxieties of the majority might serve to dampen a resort to power as a means through which these contests get resolved. In a sense, then, conceding that majorities exist and sometimes must be accounted for can result in a sort of ongoing mediation.

Regardless of whether one believes a model of cultural pluralism ought to be more sensitive to the plight of the cultural majority, either through a convergence model or Bouchard's appeal to sociological realism, the fact remains that Quebec's new approach represents a rupture from Quebec's pluralist path on all counts. It is simply a repudiation of the liberal-pluralist consensus described above. Again, Bill 21 is shielded from judicial oversight, required an amendment to Quebec's own Charter of Human Rights to be justified, and basically was enacted against the wishes of minority groups. The majority has staked its place on a conception of Quebec that is a little more hostile to integration, and it's still too early to predict where that will take us.

Conclusion

For those of us who were politically socialized in Quebec in the 1980s and '90s, it seemed as though the development of the main tenets of national identity in Quebec would progress in an almost deterministic fashion toward a greater acceptance of openness to diversity. There existed a sense that Quebec had begun to enter a sort of collective maturity, no longer threatened by different ways of belonging. Recent events remind us, as always, that political and social currents do not flow in a straight line. Students of Quebec Studies are taught that modernization and "catching up" in Quebec during the Quiet Revolution produced a wholesale change to the main tenets of national identity, away from a defensive posture toward openness to newcomers and tolerant of differences. The main political parties fought to establish their pluralist *bona fides*.

Following their defeat of the "yes" campaign in the 1995 referendum, Premier Jacques Parizeau's contention that "we" lost due to money and the ethnic vote resulted in near universal condemnation, and his own party ousted him from the position. In academic circles, the Quebec case was seen as a pioneer among those minority nations within larger liberal-democratic associative communities in its capacity to establish the contours of a liberal nation, enact comprehensive language legislation as the lynchpin of a territorial conception of belonging, respect minority language rights, recognize Indigenous nations, and develop a freestanding model of integration without recourse to the levers of citizenship. In isolation, this turn toward absolutist secularism may seem like a small concession to a more populist age. In context, however, it signals much more than that.

Notes

1. Valérie-Anne Maheo and Eric Bélanger, "Is the Parti Québécois Bound to Disappear? A Study of the Current Generational Dynamics of Electoral Behaviour in Québec," *Canadian Journal of Political Science* 51, no. 2 (2018): 335–356. https://doi.org/10.1017/S0008423917001147

2. François Rocher, "The Life and Death of an Issue: Canadian Political Science and Quebec Politics," *Canadian Journal of Political Science* 52, no. 4 (2019): 631–655. http://dx.doi.org/10.1017/S0008423919000672

3. Jean-François Daoust and A. Jabbour, "An Extraordinary Election? A Longitudinal Perspective of the Québec 2018 Election," *French Politics* 18, no. 3 (2020): 253–272. http://dx.doi.org/10.1057/s41253-020-00120-y

4. André Lecours, "Ethnic and Civic Nationalism: Towards a New Dimension," *Space & Polity* 4 (2000): 153–166. https://doi.org/10.1080/13562570020013672

5. Michel Seymour, "La nation et l'identité publique commune" in Stéphan Gervais et al. (eds.), *Du tricoté serré au métissé serré? la culture publique commune au Québec en débats* (Quebec City: Presses de l'Université Laval, 2008), 61–86.

6. Charles Taylor, "Shared and Divergent Values," in Guy Laforest (ed.), *Reconciling the Solitudes: Essays on Canadian Federalism and Nationalism* (Montreal: McGill-Queen's University Press, 1993), 155–186.

7. Jane Jenson, "Recognising Difference: Distinct Societies, Citizens Regimes and Partnership," in *Beyond the Impasse: Toward Reconciliation*, Roger Gibbins and Guy Laforest (eds.) (Montreal: Institute for Research on Public Policy, 1998)

8. Micheline Labelle and François Rocher, "Debating Citizenship in Canada: The Collide of Two Nation-Building Projects," in P. Boyer, L. Cardinal, and D. Headon (eds.), *From Subjects to Citizens: A Hundred Years of Citizenship in Australia and Canada* (Ottawa: University of Ottawa Press, 2004) 263–286.

9. Alain-G. Gagnon and Raffaele Iacovino, *Federalism, Citizenship, and Quebec: Debating Multinationalism* (Toronto: University of Toronto Press, 2007).

10. Fiona Barker, "Learning to Be a Majority: Negotiating Immigration, Integration and National Membership in Quebec," *Political Science* 62, no. 1 (June 1, 2010): 11–36.

11. Cory Blad and Philippe Couton, "The Rise of an Intercultural Nation: Immigration, Diversity and Nationhood in Quebec," *Journal of Ethnic and Migration Studies*, 35, no. 4 (2009): 645–667.

12. Louis Balthazar, *Nouveau bilan du nationalisme au Québec* (Montréal: VLB éditeur, 2013).

13. Félix Mathieu and Guy Laforest, "Uncovering National Nexus's Representations: The Case of Québec," *Studies in Ethnicity and Nationalism* 16, no. 3 (2016): 384. https://doi.org/10.1111/sena.12204

14. See Michel Seymour, "Quebec and Canada at the Crossroads: A Nation within a Nation," in *Nations and Nationalism* 6, no. 2 (2000): 227–255.

15. For a more detailed treatment of this longstanding debate around the limits of pluralism in the construction of Quebec's self-understanding, see Raffaele Iacovino, "Culture and National Identity in Quebec," in David McGrane and Neil Hibbert (eds.), *Applied Political Theory and Canadian Politics* (Toronto: University of Toronto Press: 2019), 383–408. doi:https://doi.org/10.3138/9781442623873-018

16. Québec, *Autant de façons d'être Québécois. Plan d'action à l'intention des communautés culturelles* (Quebec: Ministry of Communications, Direction générale des publications gouvernementales, 1981).

17. The first program sought to provide French language instruction as well as to provide basic transitional services for newcomers, while the second supported the maintenance of languages of origin, through educational programs specific to particular cultural groups and generally targeted to children.

18. Allophones are defined in Quebec as individuals whose first language is neither French, English, or an Indigenous language.

19. Micheline Labelle, "De la culture publique commune à la citoyenneté: Ancrages historiques et enjeux actuels." In *Du tricoté serré au métissé serré: La culture poublique commune au Québec en débats*, in Stéphan Gervais et al. (eds.), *Du tricoté*

serré au métissé serré? la culture publique commune au Québec en débats (Quebec City: Presses de l'Université Laval, 2008), 19–43.

20. See Guy Rocher, "Les ambiguïtés d'un Canada bilingue et multiculturel," in *Le Québec en mutation* (Montréal, Hurtubise HMH, 1973).

21. Québec, *Au Quebec pour bâtir ensemble. Énoncé de politique en matière d'immigration et d'intégration.* Quebec: Direction des communications du ministère des Communautés culturelles et de l'Immigration du Quebec, 1991. www.micc.gouv.qc.ca/publications/fr/ministere/Enonce-politique-immigration-integration-Quebec1991.pdf

22. François Rocher, Micheline Labelle, Ann-Marie Field, and Jean-Claude Icart, "Le concept d'interculturalisme en contexte Québécois: généalogie d'un néologisme," Rapport présenté à la Commission de consultation sur les pratiques d'accommodement reliées aux différences culturelles. Quebec City. https://numerique.banq.qc.ca/patrimoine/details/52327/66310?docref=z1mjd6gRq1BZb5Z-eIG2-A

23. Indeed, the Commission spent a considerable portion of its final report debunking many of the media stories that had been circulating in Quebec, making the case there was no crisis of accommodation in Quebec. As such, the commissioners argued that this burgeoning concern for a perceived attack on Quebec values by minority groups was overblown, and that Quebec in effect had been very successful in applying its integration policies. See Gérard Bouchard and Charles Taylor, *Building the Future: A Time for Reconciliation*, Report presented to the Consultation Commission on Accommodation Practices Related to Cultural Differences (Québec: Bibliothèque et Archives nationales du Québec, 2008).

24. For more on these divergent conceptions of secularism, see Jocelyn Maclure and Charles Taylor, *Secularism and Freedom of Conscience.* Trans. Jane Marie Todd (Cambridge, MA & London: Harvard University Press, 2011).

25. The Commission did indeed add a proviso to open secularism by sanctioning some restrictions on religious expression for public servants that were deemed to represent "coercive" positions, such as judges, police officers, and prison guards (not teachers). The CAQ referred to the report when enacting Bill 21. Both Commissioners, however, have been highly critical of the law. Taylor disavowed that section of the report altogether, while Bouchard continued to defend the recommendations of the Commission's final report, yet objected to Bill 21 because the government widened the scope of restrictions to other professions, failed to show why a ban was needed in the first place, and used the Notwithstanding Clause to shield the ban from legal challenges. See Philip Authier, *Bill 21 Feeds Intolerance, Gérard Bouchard Tells hearings? Montreal Gazette* (8 May 2019). https://montrealgazette.com/news/quebec/gerard-bouchard-challenges-legitimacy-of-bill-21-at-hearings

26. Mathieu and Laforest (2016) provide a useful overview of the intellectuals that came to be representative of these opposing positions, what they have labeled the "liberal-pluralists" versus the "conservative-republicans." The main protagonists in the former camp include the authors of the Commission's final report, Gérard

Bouchard, Charles Taylor, and Jocelyn Maclure, while the latter position was led by Jacques Beauchemin (2015), Joseph Yvon Thériault (2010), and Mathieu Bock-Côté (2012). For a sample, see Jacques Beauchemin, *La souveraineté en héritage* (Montréal: Boréal, 2015); Joseph Yvon Thériault, "Entre républicanisme et multiculturalisme: la Commission Bouchard-Taylor, une synthèse ratée," in Bernard Gagnon (ed.), *La diversité québécoise en débat* (Montréal: Québec Amérique, 2010); and Mathieu Bock-Côté, *Fin de cycle. Aux origines du malaise politique québécois* (Montréal: Boréal, 2012).

27. Jocelyn Maclure and François Boucher, "Quebec's Culture War: Two Conceptions of Quebec Identity," in S. Gervais, C. Kirkey, and J. Rudy (eds.), *Quebec Questions* (Toronto: Oxford University Press, 2016).

28. Québec, projet de loi no. 94, *An Act to establish guidelines governing accommodation requests within the Administration and certain institutions*, Première Session, Trente-Neuvième Législature (Éditeur officiel, 2010). www.assnat.qc.ca/en/travaux-parlementaires/projets-loi/projet-loi-94-39-l.html

29. Québec, projet de loi no. 195, *Loi sur l'identité québécoise*, Première Session, Trente-Huitième Législature (Éditeur officiel, 2007). www.assnat.qc.ca/fr/travaux-parlementaires/projets-loi/projets-loi-381 1

30. Québec, projet de loi no. 60, *Charter affirming the values of State secularism and religious neutrality and of equality between women and men, and providing a framework for accommodation requests*, Première Session, Quarantième Législature (Éditeur official, 2013). www.assnat.qc.ca/en/travaux-par-lementaires/projets-loi/projet-loi-60-40-1.html

31. The PLQ did attempt to enact Bill 62, which again limited restrictions of religious accommodation to face coverings, but this was held up in the courts until the Government was defeated in the 2018 election. See Carissima Mathen, "The Tenuous Constitutionality of Bill 62" in *Policy Options Politiques*, 23 October 2017.

32. Québec, projet de loi no. 21, *An act respecting the laicity of the state*, First session, 42nd Legislature (Éditeur official, 2019). assnat.qc.ca/en/travaux-parlementaires/projets-loi/projet-loi-21-42-1.html

33. Avigail Eisenberg, "The Rights of National Majorities: Toxic Discourse or Democratic Catharsis?" *Ethnicities* 20, no. 2 (2020): 325.

34. Charles Taylor, "Interculturalism or Multiculturalism?" *Philosophy & Social Criticism*, 38, no. 4–5 (2012): 413–423.

35. Jocelyn Maclure, "Between Nation and Dissemination: Revisiting the Tension between National Identity and Diversity," in Alain-G. Gagnon, Montserrat Guibernau, and François Rocher (eds.), *The Conditions of Diversity in Multinational Democracies* (Montreal: Institute for Research on Public Policy, 2002), 48.

36. Gérard Bouchard, "What Is Interculturalism?" *McGill Law Journal* 56, no. 2 (2010): 435–468.

References

Authier, P. (2019, May 8). Bill 21 Feeds Intolerance, Gérard Bouchard Tells Hearings? *Montreal Gazette*. https://montrealgazette.com/news/quebec/gerard-bouchard-challenges-legitimacy-of-bill-21-at-hearings

Balthazar, Louis. 2013. *Nouveau bilan du nationalisme au Québec*. Montréal: VLB éditeur.

Barker, Fiona. 2010. "Learning to Be a Majority: Negotiating Immigration, Integration and National Membership in Quebec." *Political Science* 62, no. 1 (June 2010): 11–36. doi:10.1177/0032318710370585

Beauchemin, Jacques. 2015. *La souveraineté en héritage*. Montréal: Boréal.

Bock-Côté, Mathieu. 2012. *Fin de cycle. Aux origines du malaise politique québécois*. Montréal: Boréal.

Bouchard, Gérard. 2010. "What Is Interculturalism?" *McGill Law Journal* 56, no. 2: 435–468.

Bouchard, Gérard, and Charles Taylor. 2008. *Building the Future: A Time for Reconciliation. Report presented to the Consultation Commission on Accommodation Practices Related to Cultural Differences*. Québec: Bibliothèque et Archives nationales du Québec.

Daoust, Jean-François, and A. Jabbour. 2020. "An Extraordinary Election? A Longitudinal Perspective of the Québec 2018 Election." *French Politics* 18, no. 3: 253–272. doi:http://dx.doi.org/10.1057/s41253-020-00120-y

Eisenberg A. 2020. "The Rights of National Majorities: Toxic Discourse or Democratic Catharsis?" *Ethnicities* 20, no. 2: 312–330. doi:10.1177/1468796819866488

Gagnon, A-G., and Raffaele Iacovino. 2007. *Federalism, Citizenship, and Quebec: Debating Multinationalism*. Toronto: University of Toronto Press.

Iacovino, R. 2019. "Culture and National Identity in Quebec." In D. McGrane and N. Hibbert (eds.), *Applied Political Theory and Canadian Politics* (383–408). Toronto: University of Toronto Press. https://doi.org/10.3138/9781442623873-018

Jenson, Jane. 1998. "Recognising Difference: Distinct Societies, Citizens Regimes and Partnership." In Roger Gibbins and Guy Laforest (eds.), *Beyond the Impasse: Toward Reconciliation* (215–240). Montreal: Institute for Research on Public Policy.

Labelle, Micheline, and François Rocher. 2004. "Debating Citizenship in Canada: The Collide of Two Nation-Building Projects." In P. Boyer, L. Cardinal, and D. Headon (eds.), *From Subjects to Citizens: A Hundred Years of Citizenship in Australia and Canada* (263–286). Ottawa: University of Ottawa Press.

Labelle, Micheline. 2008. "De la culture publique commune à la citoyenneté: Ancrages historiques et enjeux actuels." In Stéphan Gervais, Dimitrios Karmis, and Diane Lamoureux (eds.), *Du tricoté serré au métissé serré: La culture poublique commune au Québec en débats* (19–43). Quebec City: Presses de l'Université Laval.

Lecours, André. 2000. "Ethnic and Civic Nationalism: Towards a New Dimension." *Space & Polity* 4: 153–166. https://doi.org/10.1080/13562570020013672
Maclure, J., and C. Taylor. 2011. *Secularism and Freedom of Conscience*. Trans. Jane Marie Todd. Cambridge, MA & London: Harvard University Press.
Maclure, Jocelyn. 2003. "Between Nation and Dissemination: Revisiting the Tension between National Identity and Diversity." In Alain-G. Gagnon, Montserrat Guibernau, and François Rocher (eds.), *The Conditions of Diversity in Multinational Democracies* (41–57). Montreal: Institute for Research on Public Policy.
Mahéo, Valérie-Anne, and Eric Bélanger. 2018. "Is the Parti Québécois Bound to Disappear? A Study of the Current Generational Dynamics of Electoral Behaviour in Québec." *Canadian Journal of Political Science* 51, no. 2: 335–356. https://doi.org/10.1017/S0008423917001147
Mathen, Carissima. 2017. "The Tenuous Constitutionality of Bill 62." *Policy Options Politiques* (October).
Mathieu, F., and Laforest, G. 2016. "Uncovering National Nexus's Representations: The Case of Québec." *Studies in Ethnicity and Nationalism*, 16, no. 3: 378–400. https://doi.org/10.1111/sena.12204
Québec 1981. *Autant de façons d'être Québécois. Plan d'action à l'intention des communautés culturelles* (Quebec: Ministry of Communications, Direction générale des publications gouvernementales).
Québec. 1991. *Au Quebec pour bâtir ensemble. Énoncé de politique en matière d'immigration et d'intégration* (Quebec: Direction des communications du ministère des Communautés culturelles et de l'Immigration du Quebec). www.micc.gouv.qc.ca/publications/fr/ministere/Enonce-politique-immigration-integration-Quebec1991.pdf
Québec, projet de loi no. 94, 2010. *An Act to establish guidelines governing accommodation requests within the Administration and certain institutions*, Première Session, Trente-Neuvième Législature, Éditeur officiel. www.assnat.qc.ca/en/travaux-parlementaires/projets-loi/projet-loi-94-39-l.html
Québec, projet de loi no. 60, 2013. *Charter affirming the values of State secularism and religious neutrality and of equality between women and men, and providing a framework for accommodation requests*, Première Session, Quarantième Législature, Éditeur officiel. www.assnat.qc.ca/en/travaux-par-lementaires/projets-loi/projet-loi-60-40-1.html
Québec, projet de loi no. 195. 2007. *Loi sur l'identité québécoise*, Première Session, Trente-Huitième Législature, Éditeur officiel. www.assnat.qc.ca/fr/travaux-parlementaires/projets-loi/projets-loi-381 1
Québec, projet de loi no. 21, 2019. *An act respecting the laicity of the state*. First session, 42nd Legislature, Éditeur official. www.assnat.qc.ca/en/travaux-parlementaires/projets-loi/projet-loi-21-42-1.html
Rocher, F. 2019. "The Life and Death of an Issue: Canadian Political Science and Quebec Politics." *Canadian Journal of Political Science* 52, no. 4: 631–655. doi:http://dx.doi.org/10.1017/S0008423919000672

Rocher, François, Micheline Labelle, Ann-Marie Field, and Jean-Claude Icart. 2007. Le concept d'interculturalisme en contexte Québécois: généalogie d'un néologisme. *Rapport présenté à la Commission de consultation sur les pratiques d'accommodement reliées aux différences culturelles.* Quebec City. https://numerique.banq.qc.ca/patrimoine/details/52327/66310?docref=z1mjd6gRq1BZb5Z-eIG2-A

Seymour, Michel. 2008. "La nation et l'identité publique commune." In Stéphan Gervais, Dimitrios Karmis, and Diane Lamoureux (eds.), *Du tricoté serré au métissé serré: La culture poublique commune au Québec en débats* (61–86). Quebec City: Presses de l'Université Laval.

Seymour, Michel. 2000. "Quebec and Canada at the Crossroads: A Nation within a Nation." *Nations and Nationalism* 6, no. 2: 227–255.

Seymour, Michel. 2010. "Nationalistes ou pluralistes? Faut-il vraiment choisir?" *Le Devoir* (February). www.ledevoir.com/opinion/idees/282682/nationalistes-ou-pluralistes-faut-il-vraiment-choisir

Taylor C. 2012. "Interculturalism or Multiculturalism?" *Philosophy & Social Criticism* 38, no. 4–5: 413–423. doi:10.1177/0191453711435656

Taylor, C. 1993. "Shared and Divergent Values." In Guy Laforest (ed.), *Reconciling the Solitudes: Essays on Canadian Federalism and Nationalism* (155–186). Montreal: McGill-Queen's University Press.

Thériault, Joseph Yvon. 2010. "Entre républicanisme et multiculturalisme: La Commission Bouchard-Taylor, une synthèse ratée." In Bernard Gagnon (ed.), *La diversité québécoise en débat* (143–155). Montréal: Québec Amérique.

4

Nation-Building within a Union State
Scotland's Frustrated Nationalism[1]

CHRISTOPHER A. WHATLEY

For more than three centuries Scotland has been an integral part of the United Kingdom of Great Britain—that is, the British state. In 1707, by means of a union that incorporated Scotland's parliament within that of Westminster in London, Scotland ceased to exist as an independent nation. Prior to that, in 1603, Scotland had joined with England and Wales in a dynastic union—a multiple or composite monarchy, at the head of which was King James VI of Scotland (James I of England). For four centuries, therefore, the two nations (three if we include Wales) have been united under royal rulers, although not through a single blood line. The British union has been one of the longest lasting in the world. Over the course of the same period, many other unions have broken up, while former nation-states have vanished; as Norman Davis has observed, "the lifespan of even the mightiest states is finite."[2] At the time of this writing, early 2023, it remains possible that this could apply too to the United Kingdom, until the early twentieth century the custodian of the world's largest and most powerful empire.

Yet as we will see, some Scots have never been entirely comfortable with Scotland's relationship with England. Discomfort and even anger have periodically led to demands for constitutional change of various magnitudes—

ranging from complete separation through federalism to limited forms of devolution. The degree of frustration in Scotland currently with London government stands at an unprecedented level, as does support for independence, although for a variety of reasons, including internal divisions and a growing dissatisfaction with the performance of the Scottish government, the ruling Scottish National Party has recently begun to slip in the opinion polls. The reasons it is only in the past half-century or so that support for independence has deepened and widened are the focus of this chapter. It will trace Scotland's history from the time it became a nation, noting key developments that gave rise to or at least underpin the modern nationalist movement, and conclude with some reflections on where Scotland stands currently in relation to the UK union.

It is important at the outset to establish that Scotland is a nation. Its origins, partly mythical (a characteristic shared with numerous other nations determined to assert their independent status), complex, and contested, "lie deep in the Scottish medieval past."[3] In the ninth century, Kenneth mac Alpin became ruler of Alba, as what would later become the larger nation of Scotland was then known. By the thirteenth century, Scotland had become a recognizable geographical reality (not unlike the present, stretching from the northern islands and those in the west, to the border with England on the river Tweed in the south) as well as a sovereign territory in which "the king of Scots was the ultimate secular authority."[4] Scotland's claim to independence, it has been argued, dates back to 1249 with the inauguration of Alexander III, who gave homage to God rather than the king of England for "my realm of Scotland." Then as now, the challenge for Scots was what was an acceptable relationship with their more powerful and often aggressive immediate neighbor on the same landmass to the south: England. Well before the unions of 1603 and 1707, resentment of English imperial ambitions continued in Scotland which, periodically, English rulers attempted to achieve by force. Throughout, a determination endured to resist England and retain Scotland's sovereign status. Indeed, Scots have been particularly eager to establish their ancient nationhood and the right to exist independently.[5]

Arguably the most telling assertion of what can justly be called the nationalist tradition was the letter signed at Arbroath Abbey in 1320 by some forty Scottish magnates to Pope John XXII in which they traced the nation's roots in antiquity, and declared that as long as "a hundred of us remain alive," the Scots would never be subject to the lordship of a king of England or the English.[6] This letter, commonly known as the Declaration of

Arbroath, has been hailed by some as one of the most eloquent manifestos of national independence produced in medieval Europe. It has even been credited with influencing the American Declaration of Independence of 1776, albeit tenuously.[7] The Arbroath letter has had a fluctuating presence in Scottish history over the past seven hundred years, disappearing for long periods, and then reappearing and galvanizing Scots at key moments. The Declaration found echoes in some of the many petitions presented in Parliament in 1706 opposing or demanding changes to the articles of the proposed union with England as these became public knowledge.[8] A common trope was the assertion that Scotland had been an independent nation for almost two thousand years, when "many others who were a greater people than we, have been scattered, ruined, and their memories extinct."[9] In the twentieth century, and now, with the nationalist cause in Scotland attracting greater support than in the past, the Declaration has probably been referenced more often than at any time in the preceding six centuries—usually but not always with caution, given the violence, anti-Englishness, and extremism of what otherwise is stirring rhetoric.[10] But it provides background noise only; save for a minority is it a manifesto for Scotland's future.[11]

Why then, given the profoundly felt opposition to the incorporating union, one of the twenty-five articles of which was to eradicate the term Scotland and replace it with "North Britain," did it happen? For one thing, it was clear by the end of the seventeenth century that the existing regnal union was not working well, and certainly not in Scotland's interest. Multiple monarchy favored England rather than Scotland, attention to which was paid only when the Scots threatened English security.[12] Tensions between Scotland and England had intensified over the Scots' attempt in the mid-1690s to establish a trading colony at Darien in central America, to the extent that as the eighteenth century commenced, hostilities between the two nations were such that open war was at least a possibility. The "Glorious" Revolution of 1688 had brought the Protestant William of Orange and his wife Mary to the throne in place of the Catholic James VII and II. Late in his reign, in 1701, England had passed the Act of Settlement, which nominated the Protestant House of Hanover as the source of a successor in the event of the death of the heir-less Queen Anne (who would succeed William). Anne and her ministers wanted the Scots to follow suit, lest James's supporters—the Jacobites—invite his son to take the Scottish crown and thereby restore what they believed was the divinely ordained, hereditary native Stuart dynasty.

On the English side, too, fears existed that Scotland might ally with Louis XIV's France, with which country England was then locked in an era-defining, global war—an "existential struggle" of the first order.[13] Consequently, London ministers sought Scottish acquiescence, initially by way of a treaty but eventually, as the Edinburgh parliament proved uncooperative, by means of incorporation. However, unlike the incorporation at the same time of Catalonia with Spain (the Nueva Planta of 1707–1716), which was imposed through military conquest by Philip V, the Anglo-Scottish union was arrived at after negotiations between commissioners from both countries.[14] Crucially too, there were economic advantages in the Anglo-Scottish case—including free trade with England and her colonies. Too often overlooked is the fact that from the sixteenth century some Scots had advocated closer union with England (but always on the basis of an equal partnership), while in the seventeenth century there were several calls for a union of trade (as in 1668 and 1670).[15] Secured too in the agreed articles of union were essential features of Scottish civic society—above all the Church of Scotland and the Scottish legal system, but also the Convention of Royal Burghs, the body representing Scotland's towns. Scotland was to be represented too in what was now (nominally at least) a British parliament.

Most of those Scottish politicians who supported the 1707 union were moderate Presbyterians who believed that the Revolution settlement—and Protestantism—would be best protected if the two nations were united; to varying degrees they abhorred Roman Catholicism and feared French military and naval might. Protestantism, in opposition to the Catholic "Other," that is, the French people and French ways, would continue to bind the inhabitants of the British archipelago together, albeit somewhat superficially given the extant differences between English Anglicans and Scottish Presbyterians—who from the later seventeenth century were riven with internal divisions. Pro-union politicians tended too to be committed to constitutional monarchy (or at least to the principle of the crown being accountable to parliament), as opposed to the absolutism of the later Stuarts, and were therefore in accord with the Hanoverian succession. Few were enthusiastic unionists, but they were convinced that Scotland had been falling behind other nations economically and was without the kind of commercial empire others were amassing.[16] Scotland therefore would benefit from unhindered access to English markets for Scottish exports and the protection on the high seas afforded by the Royal Navy in an age of muscular mercantilism. The fact that Scottish negotiators had managed to win English agreement that Scotland was to be compensated for the vast financial losses incurred with the failure of the Darien venture was sufficient to secure enough parliamentary votes for union. The £400,000 (around £60m today) obtained was a welcome panacea for Scotland's cash-strapped economy.[17] A strong pragmatic current ran through the union treaty.

It is this union that modern-day nationalists are intent on ending if Scotland is to regain its independence. From the outset, and to varying degrees and at different times, the Union has been contested.

As what was being proposed became known in 1705 and more so in 1706, public opinion in Scotland turned overwhelmingly against incorporation, although not necessarily being opposed to a confederal arrangement of some kind.[18] Steps—not for the first time in recent memory—had to be taken by officers of state both north and south of the border to quell armed opposition as the treaty was being debated in Edinburgh, where the Scottish parliament was located. The resistance was led by the Jacobites, in all likelihood aided by France.[19] Critically, almost from the outset, the legitimacy of the measure was challenged by the allegation that the Scottish politicians responsible had betrayed the nation, that they had been bullied by their English counterparts who might have brought military force to bear had the union proposals not carried in the Scottish parliament. The most stinging denunciation, however, was that they had been bribed by promises of money, pensions, and promotions—"bought and sold for English gold." It is a charge that has stuck and has had real political purchase; it still informs attitudes to the union today, albeit at the margins. Indeed, since the commencement of the modern nationalist movement in the 1880s, and from the early 1920s under the auspices of the Scots National League, determined efforts have persisted on the part of nationalist writers, historians, and propagandists to discredit those Scottish parliamentarians who voted for the Union in 1706 and 1707. Even prior to this, the past was being politicized.[20] In order to "build up Scottish consciousness and awareness," nineteenth-century Whig interpretations of the Union were condemned as lies. Challenged was the oft-made assertion that Scotland had benefited enormously from it. It was also alleged that incorporation had undermined Scottish culture and identity.[21] Indeed union, it has been argued more recently by Tom Nairn, has been a secular wound, poisoning Scottish minds, which will be healed only with national autonomy.[22]

Unsurprisingly, the most vociferous condemnation of 1707 in the immediate post-Union decades came from the Jacobites. They and their allies had fought hard in the Scottish Parliament to resist the measure. Recognizing how unpopular the incorporating union was as efforts were made to implement it in Scotland, both the so-called "Pretenders"—James VII and II's son James Edward Stuart and his son, Charles Edward Stuart—

along with other Jacobite leaders committed themselves to reversing it. In aspiring to create a stronger and more fully sovereign Scottish Parliament, drawing on the idea of a native dynasty and employing powerful rhetoric from the Arbroath declaration and elsewhere, the Jacobites can fairly be described as proto-nationalists.[23] The Jacobite promise to break the Union did much to recruit Scots of all ranks to the Jacobite cause in 1715. It still carried weight by the time of the second major rising of 1745. In fact in the autumn of 1745, whilst in Scotland with the Jacobite army, Charles Edward Stuart pronounced the Union to be at and end, the British Parliament to be unlawful, and made clear his opposition to the 1701 Act of Settlement. The defeat of the Jacobite army at Culloden the following April, however, marked the last attempt by armed force in Scotland to regain independence, although its cultural legacy has endured to the present day.[24]

But it was not only Jacobites who aspired to abrogate the Union. Economic dislocation, new taxes on a wider range of commodities than before 1707, and the greater diligence in collecting customs and excise duties that followed Scotland's incorporation into the British fiscal-military state combined to cause even erstwhile supporters of the Union great unease. Within less than a decade, some—including the powerful second duke of Argyll and his brother the earl of Ilay—even demanded its abolition.[25] The issues Scottish members of parliament (MPs) raised on behalf of their constituents were treated disdainfully at Westminster, although the members themselves were reasonably well received. Even so they felt patronized and subject to the whims of their more powerful partner (a complaint recurring periodically to the present day), so that in 1713 the contingent of sixteen Scottish peers at Westminster, along with the country's forty-five MPs in the House of Commons, allied across party lines in an attempt to dissolve the Union, and came within a frustrating four votes of succeeding.

Even so, faced with the prospect of French invasion in both 1708 and 1715, and the restoration of a Catholic monarch, large numbers of those who had previously been lukewarm about the Union, above all extreme Presbyterians, declared for and even turned out in arms in defence of the status quo. Furthermore, and certainly by the 1740s, the economic benefits of union had begun to emerge. Partly these were the result of British state policy, which accepted that regardless of the Union treaty's principle that after a period of adjustment levels of taxation and support should be equal across the two countries, Scotland had to be treated more favorably if the danger that underemployed and penurious Scots would foment unrest and become disaffected was to be averted. (The British army, a constant presence repeatedly called on by local magistrates and others faced by serious outbreaks of civil disorder, could do only so much.)[26]

Opportunities that incorporation had opened up were seized by able and often hard-nosed Scottish merchants in the transatlantic tobacco and slave trades, while tens of thousands of relatively poor, money-hungry emigrants ventured to what were now British colonies in North America (until 1776) and the Caribbean, finding employment as governors, soldiers, doctors, plantation owners and overseers, and clerks.[27] Extensive government patronage as exercised by men such as the afore-mentioned Ilay helped secure Scots' loyalty to the new British state.[28] The British army did much the same, offering disproportionate openings for Scots as officers (who comprised around a quarter of the total for much of the eighteenth century) and ordinary soldiers who, particularly after 1746, played a critical part in Britain's imperial wars.[29]

War was arguably the premier agent that bound England, Scotland, and Wales together in the eighteenth century and far beyond, even until the end of World War II in 1945: over this period, an estimated three million men served in the Scottish regiments, half of whom were either killed or wounded.[30] Service in the East India Company and the prospect of untold riches (which many succeeded in acquiring) in India also lured many Scots, although the risk of an early death there or on the long seaward journey was 'ruinously high."[31]

Increasingly therefore, Scotland—North Britain—became enmeshed in the British imperial project. Toward the end of the eighteenth century and into the first decades of the nineteenth, Scottish industrialists not only closed the gap on their English counterparts but, in some sectors, overtook them to earn their place as major players in Britain's emergence as workshop of the world.[32] Those driving the transformation sought not only financial success and the consequent social rewards arising therefrom but also aspired to be part of what they saw as an imperial civilizing mission, taking religion (always Protestant and usually Presbyterian), shared values such as "the cult of superior and unique British liberty,"[33] and Scottish culture across the globe.[34]

Cross-border commitment to and belief in empire extended to sections of the working class. There was an identifiable Scottish dimension to the political radical movements of the 1790s and into the Chartist risings of the 1830s and 1840s. Yet also clear is the extent to which reformers in Scotland paid attention to what was going on in London and elsewhere in England and how closely they worked in unison with their counterparts in the south.[35] The cause of liberty was pan-British and promoted worldwide.

In short, such was the apparent depth of Scotland's involvement in Britain's global enterprise that the Union was hardly questioned: on the contrary, from the period immediately following Culloden until as recently as the 1970s, union has been described by Colin Kidd as "banal," like familiar wallpaper, the unremarked background to Scottish political life.[36]

Yet, as noted earlier, Scotland was never entirely at one with the consequences of incorporation. Some Scots seemed content to blend seamlessly into the new British state and to forget or even reject their Scottishness. It was a Scot, James Thomson, who in 1740 penned the words to Britain's national anthem, "Rule Britannia." Thomson's verse provided part of the inspiration for the Scottish capital Edinburgh's New Town plan, one version of which conceived the streets being laid out in the form of the national flag, the Union Jack.[37] Leading figures in the Scottish Enlightenment—David Hume, for example—made lists and tried hard to avoid the use of "Scotticisms." They wrote and (less often) spoke in standard English, one means of getting on, and respected, in Anglocentric Britain.[38] Being accepted could present something of a challenge, especially for Scots who migrated to London and other parts of England. They had long been portrayed as a beggarly race of people on the make. After the Union, other than the French, "no other nationality was so despised and derided" in the London press and public prints: Scots were commonly identified with rebellious Highland Jacobites.[39] The primary function of the many Scottish ethnic associations established in London and elsewhere in England (as well as across the globe) from the seventeenth century onward was provision for uprooted Scots in need, but their role in maintaining Scottish identity and celebrate Scottish traditions was equally sustaining at times when Scotophobia was particularly intense.[40]

Clearly, it should come as no surprise that from early in the post-Union era a distinctive Scottish agenda prevailed, with patriotic Scots consciously promoting Scottish culture—especially in literature—and articulating Scotland's interests. The Convention of Royal Burghs petitioned Parliament about specific Scottish concerns, while numerous national societies too were formed, often with the same objectives.[41] The Enlightenment itself as it manifested in Scotland was at core both practical and patriotic, notwithstanding the European context in which it flourished, the multiplicity of its interests, and the variety of views of its adherents.[42] Yet despite the vigor and impact of Enlightenment Scots—William Cullen, James Hutton, Adam Smith, and James Watt are good examples—and Scotland's very real contributions to the success of Hanoverian Britain, resentment persisted about the evident lack of respect that continued for Scotland and its people south of the border.

The ire of James Boswell—Scottish landowner, lawyer, frequenter of London society, and biographer of Samuel Johnson—was raised to boiling point in 1762 when at a performance at London's Covent Garden two Scottish Highlander soldiers present were insulted by a baying audience. Boswell, unable to contain his anger, roared in their defense, reflecting afterward that "I hated the English; I wished from my soul that the Union was broke and that we might give them another Bannockburn."[43]

This is a reference to perhaps the most famous military victory in Scottish history, when in 1314 a Scottish army led by Robert the Bruce defeated England's under Edward II. A key event during the thirteenth and fourteenth centuries' Wars of Independence, the triumph has long been celebrated in poetry and prose and was the subject of Robert Burns's "Scots wha hae.' Otherwise known as "Bruce to his Troops on the Eve of the Battle of Bannock-burn," in the nineteenth century the song was widely and enthusiastically sung by tens of thousands of Scots on all sorts of public occasions.[44] Yet like much of Burns's work it was appropriated for purposes other than as a martial anthem of Scottish independence in the face of tyranny, as for instance by political radicals throughout Britain in the early 1800s and as a marching song for Scottish regiments of the British army.[45] "Scots wha hae" began in the 1970s to be supplanted by another unofficial anthem—tellingly, on the same theme—"Flower of Scotland," although song in Scotland has not been as significant in uniting the nation as it was in Estonia from the time of the Song Festival in Tartu (1869) and more recently in the "singing revolution."[46] As with the contemporaneous Declaration of Arbroath, Bannockburn has flickered in and out of Scottish political consciousness for seven centuries, although without the galvanizing force of frequently re-memorialized battles that have played their part in the rise, for example, of Serbian nationalism.[47]

There were checks therefore to the force field of anglicization. Robert Burns, much of whose work was written in Scots, provided one of these. Dialect and language were viewed as genetic markers of Scottishness, without which, observed the lawyer Henry Cockburn, "we lose *ourselves*."[48] A collector and adaptor of Scottish song as well as a poet, Burns was credited in his own lifetime, as well as for the best part of a century after his death, with preserving and even saving the Scottish language—and, consequently, the nation.[49] Despite the plundering of his life and works by all kinds of interest groups, including those who wanted to secure him as a Briton, amongst sections of Scotland's political elite but more especially at the popular level, he was celebrated as a spokesman for the ideals and values that defined him as a Scot and, for some of the twentieth century, as a nationalist icon, albeit—and this is important—not universally.[50] Elsewhere in Europe, poets perceived as emerging from their native soil played similar roles in creating a collective sense of nationality—nineteenth-century Catalan peasant priest Jacinct Verdaguer, to name but one.[51]

Others too—novelists and poets James Hogg and Sir Walter Scott—embarked on similar projects. Scott, Scotland's other literary giant, whose life overlapped Burns's, generated a usable past by turning the "messiness and violence of [Scottish] history" into a romantic landscape.[52] Landscapes can play an important role in creating a seemingly persistent and ageless bond between nation and territory and are "a crucial element of national identity politics." The "ageless bond" was central to the celebrations in 2017–2018 that marked the independence of Finland, Estonia, and Latvia from the Russian Empire a century earlier.[53] Yet unlike romantic nationalism elsewhere in nineteenth-century Europe, Scott's Scotland seemed to be that of a former age, his recounting of it valedictory: old hostilities (not least those with England) were dead, and no guide, let alone an inspiration, for the future, which lay within the Union.[54]

On the other hand, and despite his unionism, Scott was conscious of and played a part in resisting England's influence on Scotland and the process of "dwindling into an English county."[55] In fact there were those who credited Scott with seeding a "national movement" that "burst forth throughout Scotland" in the early 1850s.[56] Frustration about the continuing disdain for the Scottish presumption that Scotland and England should enjoy equal status within the Union led to the first organized signs of challenge. The National Association for the Vindication of Scottish Rights (NAVSR) was active from 1853 until the outbreak of the Crimean War. Yet, in contrast to nationalist movements of the time elsewhere, the aim of the NAVSR was never independence but rather "Justice for Scotland" within the Union, by way of rectifying the neglect of Scottish interests at Westminster. Related issues were the paucity of state expenditure on Scotland, too few MPs representing Scottish constituencies, and other grievances relating to heraldic insignia. Called for too was a Secretary of State for Scotland.[57] The concept of unionist-nationalism has been used to capture this frame of mind.[58] Although internal contradictions hastened the demise of the NAVSR, what it partly reflected and perhaps channeled was the anger of some Scots about English attitudes to Scotland, which included denials of anything distinctive about Scotland. Indeed, in relation to the formation of the NAVSR, a journalist on the influential London *Times* had opined that, the "separate nationality of Scotland is . . . an anachronism"; the views of Lord Eglinton, a Tory, and one of the founders of the NAVSR were condemned as dangerous and his complaints likely to be redressed "by an outburst of national feeling and provincial indignation."[59]

Fierce rebuttals followed, such as lawyer, historian, and pioneer nationalist William Burns's widely read pamphlet "Scotland and Her Calumniators: A Reply to the English Press" (1858). "Impertinencies" such as the *Times* article and the mocking tone of the satirical London-based *Punch* magazine were one reason for the emergence of a campaign to erect a grand monument to William Wallace, Scotland's "GREAT NATIONAL DELIVERER" during the independence wars of the medieval period. Scotland, the colossal, Abbey Hill–mounted, highly visible (and not far from the Bannockburn battle site) edifice declared, as had many Scots beforehand and since, had never been conquered.[60] Equally, however, the Scottish nationality the Wallace memorial symbolized and asserted was moderate and deliberately designed not to be anti-English or to cause offense in England. Bound together in a harmonious union of equals, the two formerly independent nations had created a Britain that was truly great.[61] With Scottish nationality secured, the monument's silent voices declared, there was no need for independence.

But the nationalist genie was emerging from the unionist–nationalist bottle. Unfairly condemned as a lunatic fringe, what can be termed proto-nationalist voices began to be heard. To strengthen Scotland's position at Westminster, calls made earlier by the NAVSR became increasingly loud for the creation of a Scottish Office and the restoration of the office of Secretary for Scotland, which had been abolished in the wake of the last Jacobite rising. In 1885, the post was re-instated.[62] More significant, however, on the tail of the Highland Land League agitation and following the conversion of prime minister William Gladstone, leader of the hegemonic Liberal party in Scotland, to Irish Home Rule, was the formation in 1886 of the Scottish Home Rule Association (SHRA).[63] Although popular support for the SHRA was limited, it served as a means by which like-minded Scots could focus their efforts and as a vehicle that sponsored numerous hard-hitting pamphlet publications. Important too is that prominent Scots and even patriotic Tory aristocrats, such as the 3rd marquess of Bute who drew on his knowledge of Scottish history to bolster his argument for Home Rule,[64] were questioning the validity and utility of the Union itself.[65] Claims that it had contributed to the prosperity of the Scottish people were fiercely countered.[66] Scotland, it was argued, would be better governed by a Scottish parliament, sitting in Scotland and dealing with Scottish matters—but with an imperial parliament remaining at Westminster; Scotland's commitment to the British Empire remained unwavering well into the twentieth century.[67]

Strengthening too was the cultural dimension, energized by the so-called Celtic Revival, which captured a rise in nationalist sentiment.[68] Prominent too was the adoptee of a somewhat mythical Highland Scotland, the New Zealand–born neo-Jacobite Theodore Napier. Napier, it has been argued, "was one of the first to make Jacobitism and nationalism explicitly one cause," and without doubt he raised the profile of full-blown, unapologetic nationalism.[69] The thin Jacobite strand—representing now not a defunct dynasty but rather a call to arms for the future—was to run through into the nationalist movement of the twentieth century.

Like its predecessor body the NAVSR, the SHRA was a broad and ultimately unsustainable coalition of strong personalities with divergent views on how to achieve its goals. Hopes for these were dashed anyway with Gladstone and the Liberals' failure to promote Home Rule for Scotland, further proof for the SHRA that Scotland was in further danger of being provincialized.[70] Following World War I, the revived SRHA, boosted now by the involvement of the emergent Labour Party in Scotland, as well as other nationalist groups, including a cadre of writers associated with the Scottish "renaissance," continued to press the case for a Scottish parliament. As before the War, this was often but not always presented as a way of improving the governance not only of Scotland but for the British Empire as a whole.[71] Like the pre-war Liberals however, Labour in government (1923–1924) failed to match the rhetoric of its Home Rule–supporting MPs such as James Maxton, let alone Communist calls for a Scottish socialist republic. It was a "betrayal" that still has echoes in current Scottish politics.[72]

Even before this, nationalists frustrated by the lack of progress made when collaborating with British political parties had (in 1920) formed the Scots National League (SNL), the sole aim of which was to win Scottish independence. In 1928, the SNL was one of three associations to form the National Party of Scotland (NPS), which the following year began to contest elections, "something no overtly nationalist party had done since the days of the Jacobites."[73] Yet the NPS was an unlikely combination that included fiery Celtic nationalists much influenced by the Irish struggle to break with Britain, neo-fascists who wished Scotland had its Mussolini, and, at the other extreme, anti-Catholic, anti-Irish moderates in the Home Rule mold. Albeit strong on symbolism, like the rival more right-wing Scottish Party (1930), the NPS's aims were unclear. The major divide was between fundamentalists and devolutionists, strategy was underdeveloped, and critically, electoral organization was poor.[74] Personal rivalries were intense.[75] From such confusion arose the Scottish National Party (SNP), since then (1934) the vanguard movement of modern nationalism.

Despite attempts to win parliamentary seats in by-elections and at general elections, the party's success was limited until 1967 when Winifred Ewing sensationally won the Hamilton by-election for the SNP. Although electoral progress thereafter was slow and uneven, sympathy with nationalism as represented by votes for the SNP has increased. Concomitantly, support for the big two British, largely unionist parties that dominated in Scotland until the 1970s, Conservative (and Unionist) and Labour, has declined.[76] Pressure for constitutional change (as well as Labour's reluctant conversion to the cause of devolution) was such that in 1999, following a referendum in 1997, a Scottish parliament was established at Holyrood in Edinburgh.[77] It was the first time one had sat there since 1707. Within a decade the SNP became the largest party therein, and in 2007 formed a minority administration. Hitherto more successful in attracting votes in municipal elections and for Holyrood, in the UK general election in 2005 the SNP sent six MPs to Westminster. Ten years later, there were fifty-six, and at the last UK election, in 2019, with 45 percent of the vote, the SNP returned forty-eight MPs—that is, 81 percent of the total from Scotland.[78] Now firmly established in government at Holyrood, where they have been in power for fifteen years, they are far and away Scotland's largest political party.

Yet, in 1960—more than a half-century before the SNP began to make its mark at Westminster—one commentator wrote that "nearly every Scot is a nationalist at heart, and . . . will agree that the logical solution is in self-government."[79] It seems there was a disconnect between Scottish national sentiment and the SNP's becoming a mass membership party with substantial electoral support. A knot of factors provides the explanation. The galvanizing impact of World War II in heightening British national consciousness was one. Another was the conscious effort on the part of the British state to promote a British culture through institutions such as the British Broadcasting Corporation (BBC), although this was never uniform.[80] The BBC's Scottish station had resisted metropolitan pressures and played an important part in sustaining and even reinforcing Scottish national identity both before and after the war.[81] In fact, in 1951 over two million Scots signed the National Covenant that called, somewhat vaguely, for constitutional reform "in accordance with . . . Scottish traditions."[82] During the Depression of the 1930s, nationalists had been able to exploit the failure of British governments to tackle Scottish needs. Although not in power during World War II, Labour then and in government after 1945 did better, including implementing a program for Scotland.[83] Thereafter there was what has been described as a "strong 'British' feel" to postwar reconstruction, nationalization, and the creation of the National Health Service.[84] Meanwhile, the Scottish Unionists were never better supported; their response to Scottish needs—appalling housing conditions, especially—saw them rewarded electorally, based too on their association with Protestantism, unionism, and empire.[85]

Ominously, one of the principal foundations of Scotland's support for the Union—the British Empire—was rapidly disintegrating. Without what Spanish philosopher José Ortega y Gasset called a compelling "project of a life in common," former imperial states like Spain and the UK fall apart.[86] In part too, as the UK ceased to be the great power it had once been, pride in "Britishness" (which was a loose concept anyway) reduced as did the identification of Scots as British citizens as opposed to being Scottish.[87] (Disappointing from the nationalist perspective, however, the proportion of Scots feeling more Scottish than British has changed little into the present century, bolstered by solidarity-inducing events such as London's hosting of the Olympic Games in 2012 and valiant but ultimately doomed efforts to redefine Britishness for patriotic Scots in the twenty-first century.[88]) With the "cataclysmic" decline in membership of the Protestant churches from the 1960s another prop of the Union—the asymmetric commitment across the border to Protestantism and objection to Roman Catholicism that dated back to 1707—was kicked loose.[89] Westminster governments were becoming increasingly centralist—grist to the mill for nationalists who argued (with some justification) that Scotland was a mere satellite of England and, worse, as depicted in the nationalist-socialist Oliver Brown's hard-hitting *Scotlandshire—England's Worse-Governed Province* (1945). Scotland was no longer the industrial powerhouse it had been during the nineteenth century, and UK governments seemed incapable of dealing with the multiple and interlinked economic and social challenges created by de-industrialization, which were further exposed and exacerbated by the Conservative governments under Margaret Thatcher (1979–1990). Southern English values and free-market policies, which included a weakening of the welfare state (and the imposition of a violently opposed poll tax), were anathema in Scotland; in the UK election of 1997, the Scottish Unionists returned no MPs to Westminster.[90] With Labour now anxious not to follow the Conservatives' fate, a newfound urgency appeared in debates about and proposals for devolution.[91] But with British entry in the war against Iraq, the global financial crash in

2008, scandals related to Westminster MPs expenses, not to mention falling real wages, the argument that Britain was broken was difficult to contest.[92]

Concurrently, however, and easier to identify in hindsight perhaps than at the time, in Scotland itself, from the 1970s, beyond the formal political arena, there was a resurgence of Scottish cultural autonomy—in the arts, literature, drama, film, music, language (both Scots and Gaelic), and history, although for the nationalist cause this last is an uncertain ally.[93] (Indeed, nationalist arguments rooted in history, it has been suggested, "have saddled the cause of independence with a disabling baggage of myths and heroes."[94]) This "political surrogate," or cultural nationalism, which had precursors in the late nineteenth century and between the two world wars, was interwoven with a stronger sense of Scottish identity, and greater confidence in the Scots' ability to govern themselves, which was palpable by the time the Scottish Parliament was established.[95] This nation-building from below probably added to the solid electoral support there has been for the SNP, although, ironically, the party has shown little genuine interest in Scottish language and culture. And the case for its importance as a basis for independence can be exaggerated.[96]

Support for the SNP, however, is not the same as independence—that is, leaving the UK. In 2014, a Westminster-approved referendum was held in which the Scots were given a "once in a generation opportunity" to take this step. But in a poll in which an impressive 85 percent of those able to do so voted, the Yes (to independence) vote was 44.7 percent, and that for favoring the status quo, 55.3 percent. In many ways, the size of the Yes vote was remarkable—and unexpected.[97] For decades, opinion polls had suggested that only around a third of the Scottish electorate favored independence.[98] The Yes/SNP campaign was based on civic as opposed to any form of ethnic nationalism, and so accommodated Scotland's diverse, multicultural population. It deliberately stepped away from the grievance agenda of earlier times. This, allied to the hefty, pragmatic (if also under-inspiring, and unconvincing on the economy, defense, and the costs of separation) manifesto for a more democratic, independent Scotland (*Scotland's Future*, published in 2013), had clearly persuaded many voters of the merits of a government in Scotland that "always puts the people of Scotland first."[99]

Current opinion polls suggest that the nation is even more narrowly divided now, with the "democratic deficit" argument strengthened by the disparity between Scottish and English attitudes to the European Union in the 2016 referendum.[100] Scotland voted to remain, England by a sizeable majority to leave.[101] Further alienation occurred in 2019 when the Conservatives won again at Westminster, despite only six Conservative MPs being returned from Scotland, compared to forty-five for the SNP. The Conservative government under Prime Minister Boris Johnson (2019–2022) was with much justification perceived as heavy-handed and often dismissive in its attitude to Scotland, thereby adding to the sense of injustice that galvanizes support both for the SNP and independence.[102] As had happened in the Thatcher era when the prevailing individualist ideology ran counter to Scottish collective mores, Scots had not voted for the policies that they had to tolerate.[103] In 1823, novelist John Galt, the acutest of observers of Scottish society, commented "Scotch are a wrong-resenting race, according to right and feeling."[104] The characteristic applies equally aptly today.

Yet whilst evidence persists of widespread disenchantment with the Union, unlike other nations that have sought independence since World War II, in Scotland there is not the same sense of oppression. There is not the crushing reality of big neighbor domination that have inspired independence struggles, for example, in the Baltic states (in the USSR until 1991) or Catalonia. Despite the exaggerated claims made by some nationalists of the deleterious effects of the Union on Scottish life and culture, the fact is that within the UK union, important Scottish institutions, and a palpable sense of Scottish distinctiveness—and national identity—have by and large flourished in what has been an unusually pluralistic state.[105] Unlike Madrid in the case of Catalonia, or Moscow and the Baltic states, London has never outlawed the carriers of nationhood—flags, anthems, historic anniversaries, cultural life—or poets. Despite the common cause supporters of independence in Scotland have made with their Catalonian counterparts, in general there appears to be less unified popular commitment to and thirst for independence than has been witnessed in these other smaller nations.[106] Comparison with another small north European country—Finland—is instructive. There the concept of "one people, one language, one mind," had a purchase in the nineteenth and twentieth centuries that was crucial in building resistance to Russia in both 1918 and 1939.[107] In Scotland there are only faint parallels. The "iconic wounds" that have inspired other nationalisms are to be found in Scotland's past. Dark deeds were indeed done by England, but some of the harm has been self-inflicted (e.g., the assault on the Gaelic language from 1609 and the Highland Clearances of the eighteenth and nineteenth centuries).[108] Since the demise of the Jacobite movement in its martial form in the mid–eighteenth century the English "other" has been relatively benign.[109]

Just as expediency played its part in taking Scotland into the Union in 1707, currently, Scottish "identity matters less . . . than effective government."[110] Reputable opinion poll evidence suggests that most Scots feel that UK government listens less to Scots and works less well than it might in their interest.[111] Until very recently, Holyrood was seen to be listening, and to be making better, fairer decisions on matters affecting Scotland. However, while the demand continues for further powers for the Scottish Parliament, as yet no clear and sustained majority has arisen for Scotland leaving the UK. Scotland's future is in the balance, although public support for a further independence referendum has waned, in part due to concerns about the Scottish Government's policy record. The decision late in 2022 by the UK Supreme Court that the Scottish Parliament doesn't have the power to hold such a referendum has been a significant setback, and has further frustrated SNP ambitions. There is no doubt that Scotland can survive as an independent nation. It might even thrive. The past is not necessarily a reliable guide to the future.[112] However weaknesses in the case made for independence in 2014 remain.[113] Critics identify these as uncertainty about what Scotland's post-independence currency would be, as well as the position as regards EU membership and other trading partnerships. Equally pressing issues are fiscal sustainability, likely interest rates, including for mortgages, pension payments, and the likelihood that an independent Scotland would require higher taxes and lower public expenditure to deal with what is likely to be an unsustainable GDP deficit.[114] The frustration for Scottish nationalists is that such concerns mean that insufficient numbers of the voting public—more so males, older people, those who identify primarily as British, and Conservatives—are prepared to finally sever the ties that for well over three centuries have, often uneasily, bound the peoples of Scotland and England together.

Notes

1. Dr. Catriona M. M. Macdonald (University of Glasgow) kindly provided helpful comments on an earlier draft of this paper.
2. Norman Davies, *Vanished Kingdoms* (London: Allen Lane, 2011), 2–3.
3. Colin Kidd, *British Identities before Nationalism* (Cambridge: Cambridge University Press, 1999), 123.
4. Dauvit Broun, *Scottish Independence and the Idea of Britain* (Edinburgh: Edinburgh University Press, 2013 ed.), 2.
5. William Ferguson, *The Identity of the Scottish Nation* (Edinburgh: Edinburgh University Press, 1998), 6; Murray G. H. Pittock, *Scottish Nationality* (Houndmills: Palgrave, 2001), 20–21.
6. H. J. Hanham, *Scottish Nationalism* (London: Faber and Faber, 1969), 65.

7. Edward J. Cowan, *"For Freedom Alone": The Declaration of Arbroath, 1320* (East Linton: Tuckwell Press, 2003), 113–138.

8. Murray Pittock, "The Declaration of Arbroath in Scottish Political Thought, 1689–1789," in Klaus Peter Müller (ed.), *Scotland and Arbroath 1320–2020* (Peter Lang: Berlin, 2020), 165–180.

9. See Karin Bowie (ed.), *Addresses Against Incorporating Union, 1706–1707* (Boydell Press: Woodbridge, 2018).

10. Richard J. Finlay, "The Declaration of Arbroath and Scottish Nationalist Constitutional Thought in the Twentieth Century," in Müller (ed.), *Scotland and Arbroath*, 307–324, as well as, in the same volume, Robert Crawford, "Afterword: A Public Declaration," 535–558.

11. Catriona M. M. Macdonald, "Framing Thoughts of Scottish Independence During the Interregnum," *The Drouth*, 45 (Spring 2013), 12.

12. Roger Mason, "Debating Britain in Seventeenth-Century Scotland: Multiple Monarchy and Scottish Sovereignty," *Journal of Scottish Historical Studies*, 35, no. 1 (2015), 10.

13. Brendan Simms, *Europe: The Struggle for Supremacy, 1453 to the Present* (London: Penguin Books, 2014), 69–70.

14. J. H. Elliott, *Scots & Catalans: Union & Disunion* (New Haven & London: Yale University Press, 2018), 83–93.

15. Colin Kidd, *Union and Unionisms: Political Thought in Scotland, 1500–2000* (Cambridge: Cambridge University Press, 2008), 39–66; Mason, "Debating Britain," 7–8, 18–20.

16. Murray Pittock, *Enlightenment in a Smart City: Edinburgh's Civic Development, 1660–1760* (Edinburgh: Edinburgh University Press, 2019), chapter 2.

17. Christopher A. Whatley, "The making of the Union of 1707: History with a History," in T. M. Devine (ed.), *Scotland and the Union, 1707–2007* (Edinburgh: Edinburgh University Press, 2008), 32–34.

18. Pittock, *Scottish Nationality*, 53.

19. Daniel Szechi, *Britain's Lost Revolution? Jacobite Scotland and French Grand Strategy, 1701–8* (Manchester University Press: Manchester, 2015, 175–180.

20. James J. Coleman, *Remembering the Past in Nineteenth-Century Scotland* (Edinburgh: Edinburgh University Press, 2014), 180–184.

21. Richard Finlay, *Independent and Free: Scottish Politics and the Origins of the Scottish National Party* (Edinburgh: John Donald, 1994), 35–39.

22. Tom Nairn, "The Three Dreams of Scottish Nationalism," in Jamie Maxwell and Pete Ramand (eds.), *Tom Nairn: Old Nations, Auld Enemies, New Times* (Edinburgh: Luath Press, 2014), 38.

23. Daniel Szechi, *1715: The Great Jacobite Rebellion* (New Haven & London: Yale University Press, 2006), 61.

24. Murray Pittock, *Culloden* (Oxford: Oxford University Press, 2016), 4, 26, 158.

25. Roger L. Emerson, *An Enlightened Duke* (Kilkerran: humming earth, 2013), 50–51.

26. Christopher A. Whatley, *Scottish Society 1707–1830* (Manchester: Manchester University Press, 2000), 105–109.

27. Linda Colley, *Britons* (New Haven & London: Yale University Press, 1992), 128–132; Douglas Hamilton, "Scotland and the Eighteenth-Century Empire," in T. M. Devine and Jenny Wormald (eds.), *The Oxford Handbook of Modern Scottish History* (Oxford: Oxford University Press, 2012), 426.

28. Emerson, *Enlightened Duke*, 349.

29. See, for example, "The Scottish Military Experience in North America, 1756–83," in Edward J. Speirs, Jeremy A. Crang, and Matthew J. Strickland (eds.), *A Military History of Scotland* (Edinburgh: Edinburgh University Press, 2012), 383–406 and, in the same volume, Edward M. Speirs, "Scots and the Wars of Empire," 458–484.

30. Pittock, *Scottish Nationality*, 83–84.

31. Hamilton, "Scotland," 431.

32. Christopher A. Whatley, *The Industrial Revolution in Scotland* (Cambridge: Cambridge University Press, 1997), 34–37.

33. Linda Colley, *Acts of Union and Disunion* (London: Profile Books, 2014), 39.

34. Graeme Morton, *Ourselves and Others: Scotland 1832–1914* (Edinburgh: Edinburgh University Press, 2012), 259–260; Graham Walker, "Varieties of Scottish Protestant Identity," in T. M. Devine and R. J. Finlay (eds.), *Scotland in the Twentieth Century* (Edinburgh: Edinburgh University Press, 1996), 250–251.

35. Bob Harris, "Scottish-English Connections in British Radicalism in the 1790s," in T. C. Smout (ed.), *Anglo-Scottish Relations from 1603 to 1900* (Oxford: Oxford University Press, 2005), 189–212.

36. Kidd, *Union*, 24–25.

37. Whatley, *Scottish Society*, 118; for guidance on this I owe thanks to Anthony Lewis of Glasgow Life.

38. Robert Crawford, *Scotland's Books: The Penguin History of Scottish Literature* (London: Penguin Books, 2009), 277.

39. Paul Langford, "South Britons' Reception of North Britons, 1707–1820," Smout (ed.), *Anglo-Scottish Relations*, 148.

40. See Tanja Bueltmann, *Clubbing Together* (Liverpool: Liverpool University Press, 2914), 36.

41. Pittock, *Enlightenment*, chapters 4 and 5; Bob Harris, "The Scots, the Westminster Parliament, and the British state in the eighteenth century," in Julian Hoppit (ed.), *Parliaments, Nations and Identities in Britain and Ireland, 1660–1850* (Manchester: Manchester University Press, 2003), 124–145.

42. Whatley, *Scottish Society*, 118–120; for fuller discussion see Christopher J. Berry, *Social Theory of the Scottish Enlightenment* (Edinburgh: Edinburgh University

Press, 1997), especially chapter 8; and Alexander Broadie, "The Rise (and Fall?) of the Scottish Enlightenment," in Devine and Wormald (eds.), *Oxford Handbook*, 370–385.

43. Frederick A. Pottle (ed.), *Boswell's London Journal 1762–1763* (London & Sydney: Macdonald & Co., 1950), 78.

44. Hugh MacDiarmid, *Burns Today and Tomorrow*, in Alan Riach (ed.), *Hugh MacDiarmid: Albyn, Shorter Books and Monographs* (Manchester: Carcanet, 1996), 281.

45. Christopher A. Whatley, *Immortal Memory: Burns and the Scottish People* (Edinburgh: John Donald, 2016), 58, 75, 131–132.

46. Jörg Hackmann, "Narrating the Building of a Small Nation: Divergence and Convergence in the History of Estonian 'National Awakening,'" in Stefan Berger and Chris Lorenz (eds.), *Narrating the Past: Historians as Nation Builders in Modern Europe* (Houndmills: Macmillan, 2010), 177–189.

47. Robert Crawford, *Bannockburns: Scottish Independence and Literary Imagination 1314–2014* (Edinburgh: Edinburgh University Press, 2014), 2–3, 233.

48. Christopher A. Whatley, "Robert Burns, Memorialisation, and the "Heart-beatings" of Victorian Scotland," in Murray Pittock (ed.), *Robert Burns in Global Culture* (Lewisburg: Bucknell University Press, 2011), 213.

49. Richard Finlay, "The Burns Cult and Scottish Identity in the Nineteenth and Twentieth Centuries," in Kenneth Simpson (ed.), *Love & Liberty: Robert Burns, A Centenary Celebration* (East Linton: Tuckwell Press, 1997), 71.

50. Christopher A. Whatley, "Contested Commemoration: Robert Burns, Urban Scotland and Scottish Nationality in the Nineteenth Century," in Gerard Carruthers and Colin Kidd (eds.), *Literature and Union* (Oxford: Oxford University Press, 2018), 239–241.

51. M. Eaude, *Catalonia: A Cultural History* (Oxford: Signal Books, 2007), 61–71.

52. Ann Rigney, *The Afterlives of Walter Scott* (Oxford: Oxford University Press, 2012), 185.

53. Anu Printsmann et al., "Landscape 100: How Finland, Estonia and Latvia used Landscape in Celebrating their Centenary Anniversaries," *European Countryside* 11, no. 2 (2019): 187–210.

54. Hanham, *Scottish Nationalism*, 70; Tom Nairn, "Scotland and Europe," in Maxwell and Ramand (eds.), *Tom Nairn*, 125–127.

55. Hugh Scott, *The Progress of the Scottish National Movement* (Edinburgh: Alex Walker, 1853), 5

56. Paul Henderson Scott, "Independence is the Answer, in Paul Henderson Scott (ed.), *A Nation Again* (Edinburgh: Luath Press, 2008), 30.

57. Alex Tyrrell, "The Earl of Eglinton, Scottish Conservatism, and the National Association for the Vindication of Scottish Rights," *The Historical Journal* 53, no. 1 (2010): 87.

58. Graeme Morton, *Unionist Nationalism: Governing Urban Scotland, 1830–1860* (East Linton: Tuckwell Press, 1999).

59. Reprinted in the London *Evening Mail*, 7 November 1853, 2.

60. Murray Pittock, *The Road to Independence?* (London: Reaktion Books, 2013 ed.), 35.

61. Coleman, *Remembering the Past*, 50–58, 64–69.

62. Hanham, *Scottish Nationalism*, 82.

63. Graeme Morton, "The First Home Rule Movement in Scotland, 1886–1918," in H. T. Dickinson and Michael Lynch (eds.), *The Challenge to Westminster* (East Linton: Tuckwell Press, 2000), 115.

64. Marquess of Bute, *Parliament in Scotland* (Edinburgh: SRHA, 1892).

65. Hanham, *Scottish Nationalism*, 83–84.

66. Naomi Lloyd-Jones, "Liberalism, Scottish Nationalism and the Home Rule Crisis, c. 1886–93," *English Historical Review* 12, no. 539 (August 2014), 874–875.

67. Finlay, *Independent and Free*, 4–5.

68. Hanham, *Scottish Nationalism*, 133.

69. Murray G. H. Pittock, *The Invention of Scotland* (London: Routledge, 1991), 122, 132.

70. Lloyd-Jones, "Liberalism," 887.

71. Finlay, *Independent and Free*, 4.

72. Pittock, *Road to Independence?*, 72.

73. Pittock, *Scottish Nationality*, 106.

74. Catriona M. M. Macdonald, "Andrew Dewar Gibb," in James Mitchell and Gerry Hassan (eds.), *Scottish National Party Leaders* (London: Biteback Publishing, 2016), 111–113.

75. Finlay, *Independent and Free*, 104–125.

76. W. L. Miller, The Death of Unionism?," in Devine (ed.), *Scotland and the Union*, 175.

77. Catriona M. M. Macdonald, *Whaur Extremes Meet* (Edinburgh: Birlinn, 2009), 250–262.

78. Sam Pilling and Richard Cracknell, *UK Election Statistics: 1918–2021* (London: House of Commons Library, 2021), 11.

79. Robert Gayre of Gayre and Nigg, *The Imperative Need for a Solution of the Scottish Problem* (Edinburgh: Edinburgh University Press, 1960), 4.

80. R. Weight, "State, Intelligentsia and the Promotion of National Culture in Britain, 1939–45," *Historical Research* 69 (1996): 83–101.

81. See Thomas Hajkowski, *The BBC and National Identity in Britain, 1922–53* (Manchester: Manchester University Press, 2010).

82. Ewen A. Cameron, "The Politics of Union in an Age of Unionism," in Devine (ed.), *Scotland and the Union*, 133.

83. Ewen A. Cameron, "The Stateless Nation and the British State since 1918," in Devine and Wormald (eds.), *Oxford Handbook*, 629–630.

84. Cameron, "Politics of Union," 132.

85. T. M. Devine, "The Challenge of Nationalism," in Devine (ed.), *Scotland and the Union*, 151.

86. Harry Eyres, "Why Nations Fall Apart," *New Statesman* (January 2022): 38–39.

87. Devine, "Challenge," 147; Pittock, *Road to Independence*, 104–5.

88. Gordon Brown, *My Scotland: Our Britain* (London: Simon & Schuster, 2014), 169–199; Dennis Grube, "How Can "Britishness" Be Re-made?," *The Political Quarterly* 82, no. 4 (October–December 2011): 628–635.

89. Callum G. Brown, *Religion and Society in Scotland since 1707* (Edinburgh: Edinburgh University Press, 1997), 160, 190–191.

90. Macdonald, *Whaur Extremes Meet*, 223–224.

91. Pittock, *Road to Independence*, 98–102.

92. Peter Geoghegan, *The People's Referendum* (Edinburgh: Luath Press, 2015), 10–11.

93. Pittock, *Road to Independence*, 139–163.

94. Macdonald, "Framing Thoughts," 12.

95. David McCrone, "'Peeble Them wi' Stanes': Twenty Years of the Scottish Parliament," *Scottish Affairs* 28, no. 2 (2019): 146.

96. Scott Hames (ed.), *Unstated: Scottish Writers on Scottish Independence* (Edinburgh: Word Power Books, 2012), 1–15; Richard T. Ashcroft and Mark Bevir, "Liberal Democracy, Nationalism and Culture: Multiculturism and Scottish Independence," *Critical Review of International and Political Philosophy* 21, no. 1 (2018): 74–75.

97. *Enlightening the Constitutional Debate* (Edinburgh: Royal Society of Edinburgh, 2014), 236–237.

98. Iain McLean, "Challenging the Union," in Devine and Wormald (eds.), *Oxford Handbook*, 648–649.

99. *Scotland's Future: Your Guide to an Independent Scotland* (Edinburgh: Scottish Government, 2013), 7; Ben Jackson, *The Case for Scottish Independence* (Cambridge: Cambridge University Press, 2020), 162–167.

100. Ashcroft and Bevir, "Liberal democracy," 65–66.

101. Nicola McEwan, "Brexit and Scotland: between two unions," *British Politics* 13 (December 2017): 65–78.

102. Alex Massie, *The Times*, 15 February 2022, 22.

103. Jackson, *Case for Independence*, 172.

104. John Galt, *Ringan Gilhaize* (Edinburgh: Canongate, 1995 ed.), 449.

105. James Mitchell, "Contemporary Unionism," in Catriona M. M. Macdonald (ed.), *Unionist Scotland, 1800–1997* (Edinburgh: John Donald, 1998), 120.

106. See, for example, Geoghegan, *People's Referendum*, 81–99, 163.

107. Tujia Pulkinnen, "One Language, One Mind," in Thomas M. S. Lehtonen (ed.), *Europe's Northern Frontier: Perspectives on Finland's Western Identity* (Jyväskylä: Pekka Santalahti, 1999), 118–137. I am indebted to Professor John Blair (Cambridge) for this reference.

108. Neal Ascherson, *Stone Voices: The Search for Scotland* (London: Granta, 2002), 174–175.

109. Christopher A. Whatley, *The Scots and the Union: Then and Now* (Edinburgh: Edinburgh University Press, 2013), 426–429.

110. A. Brown, D. McCrone, L. Paterson, and P. Surridge, *The Scottish Electorate: the 1997 General Election and Beyond* (Houndmills; Macmillan, 1999), 162–163.

111. McCrone, "Peeble Them wi' Stanes," 135.

112. Robbie Mochrie, "The Essential Flaw in Gavin McCrone's New Book on Scottish Independence," *The National*, 26 February 2022.

113. Iain McLean, Jim Gallagher, and Guy Lodge, *Scotland's Choices: The Referendum and What Happens Afterwards* (Edinburgh: Edinburgh University Press, 2013).

114. Gavin McCrone, *The Economics of Independence* (Edinburgh: Birlinn, 2022).

References

Broun, Dauvit. 2013. *Scottish Independence and the Idea of Britain*. Edinburgh: Edinburgh University Press.
Ferguson, William. 1998. *The Identity of the Scottish Nation*. Edinburgh: Edinburgh University Press.
Finlay, Richard J. 1994. *Independent and Free: Scottish Politics and the Origins of the Scottish National Party, 1918–1945*. Edinburgh: John Donald.
Hanham, H. J. 1969. *Scottish Nationalism*. London: Faber and Faber.
Kidd, Colin. 2008. *Union and Unionisms: Political Thought in Scotland, 1500–2000*. Cambridge: Cambridge University Press.
McCrone, Gavin, 2022. *The Economics of Independence*. Edinburgh: Birlinn.
McLean, Iain, Jim Gallagher, and Guy Lodge. 2013. *Scotland's Choices: The Referendum and What Happens Afterwards*. Edinburgh: Edinburgh University Press.
Müller, Klaus Peter (ed.). 2020. *Scotland and Arbroath 1320–2020*. Peter Lang: Berlin.
Pittock, Murray. 2013 ed. *The Road to Independence?* London: Reaktion Books.
Whatley, Christopher A. 2014. *The Scots and the Union: Then and Now*. Edinburgh: Edinburgh University Press.

II
Nationalism and Minority Groups

5

Contextual Nationhood

The Multiple Dimensions of Nationality in the Mi'kmaw People's Nation-Building Strategies

SIMONE POLIANDRI

This chapter focuses on the nation-building "journey" and its different aspects that the Mi'kmaw[1] First Nation people of eastern Canada have undertaken in the last twenty to thirty years. It is not necessarily a failed one (re: "frustration" in this volume's topic) but rather one characterized by strategies that must necessarily take into account the deep legacies of colonialism. In particular, I illustrate and discuss the different forms in which the idea and reality of nation have recently developed among the Mi'kmaq of the Atlantic province of Nova Scotia.

First nationhood and First nationalism—the terms that I coined to define and highlight the peculiarity of Indigenous expressions of nationhood and nationalism—have increasingly become some of the strongest and most effective expressions, both ideological and practical, of sovereignty and self-determination for the Aboriginal people of North America, Mi'kmaw people included. They intersect with various aspects of indigenous experiences, among which the restoration and development of sound Indigenous governance, one of the key elements to achieve true decolonization of Indigenous–state relations.[2]

In the case of the Mi'kmaq, a central characteristic of this nation-building "journey" is that First nationhood and nationalistic sentiments have been concurrently developing in three separate social and political dimensions or contexts: at the tribal level, thus expressed by people from the whole Mi'kmaw territory (also known as *Mi'kma'ki*) about the entire territory; at the level of single bands (or reserve communities), which refer to themselves and are identified as First Nations; and at the provincial level, thus involving all the Mi'kmaw communities from single Canadian provinces, Nova Scotia in this case.

First nationalism and nation-building are thus grounded on territory. Yet, the extent of such territorial base differs according to whether nationhood and nation-building are expressed in social and cultural, economic, political, or administrative terms. I call this *contextual nationhood*.

For one, the development of these multiple dimensions of "nation" in different contexts—whether as a consequence of and reaction to external forces or the product of a conscious strategy to achieve visibility and voice in the local, provincial, and national sociopolitical arenas—has allowed the Mi'kmaq to cast their nation-building efforts in more prolific ways to pursue economic, political, and administrative agendas. By discussing the many forms that Mi'kmaw nationhood has recently assumed, I intend to highlight the mechanisms that have led to such a development and, at the same time, the rationales behind them. At the same time, by shedding light on the discrepancies inherent in such a process, I also wish to reveal the highly dynamic and, at the same time, complex nature of Mi'kmaw nationhood whose recent evolution, although indisputably powerful and important to the Mi'kmaq, has sometimes constituted a source of frustration.

To begin, a word of clarification about the term "First Nation" is in order here. Canadian tribal groups, or nations, call themselves and are called First Nations. Together with the Métis and Inuit, First Nations are the constitutionally recognized Aboriginal people of Canada. The term "First Nation" was introduced in 1982 by members of the National Indian Brotherhood (NIB), the institution created in 1968 to represent the status and treaty Indians of Canada, while participating in the discussions that led to the federal recognition of Treaty and Aboriginal Rights under section 35 of the Constitution Act in 1982. Shortly after achieving this historic victory for the Aboriginal people of Canada, the National Indian Brotherhood changed its name to Assembly of First Nations (AFN) and reorganized into its current structure. Today, the AFN represents the 634 First Nations communities across Canada.[3]

Mi'kma'ki and the Mi'kmaw Nation

Mi'kmaw territory spans across the Canadian Maritime provinces of Nova Scotia, New Brunswick, and Prince Edward Island, as well as parts of eastern Quebec, Newfoundland, and northern Maine in the United States. The Mi'kmaw people use the term *Mi'kma'ki* to refer to their traditional territory. Historically, Mi'kma'ki was divided into seven districts (see map 1): *Kespukwitk* (Land Ends), *Sipekne'katik* (Wild Potato Area), *Eskikewa'kik* (Skin Dressers Territory), *Unama'kik* (Land of Fog), *Epekwitk aq Piktuk* (Lying in the Water and The Explosive Place), *Siknikrewaq* (Drainage Area), and *Kespe'kewaq* (Last Land). These were governed autonomously by district chiefs and councils. A Grand Council, composed of all the district chiefs who elected one of them as the Grand Chief, addressed joint issues and fostered solidarity among all the Mi'kmaq.[4]

The Mi'kmaq conducted a migratory lifestyle throughout the year, setting seasonal camps as far as *Ktaqmkuk* (Land Across the Water), or

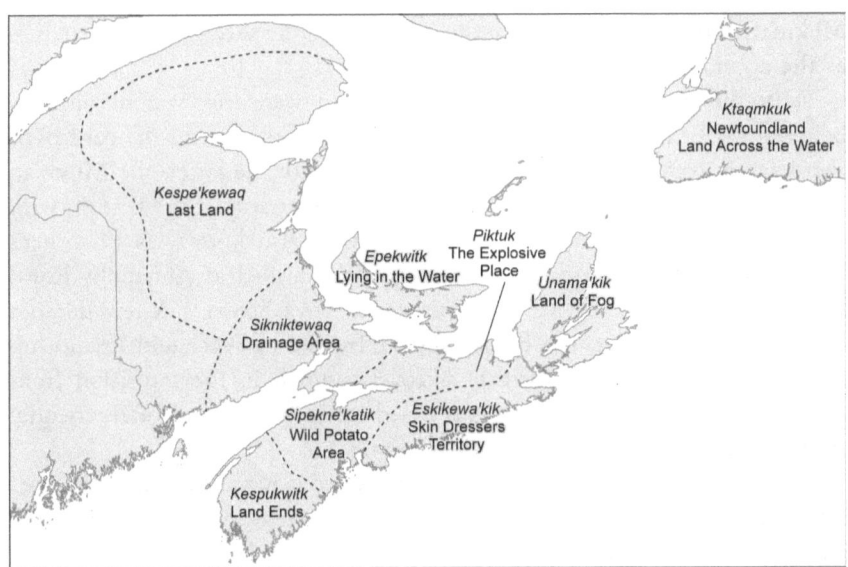

Map 5.1. The seven districts of Mi'kma'ki, the traditional territory of the Mi'kmaq, and the territory of Ktaqmkuk. Reproduced from *First Nations, Identity, and Reserve Life: The Mi'kmaq of Nova Scotia* by Simone Poliandri by permission of the University of Nebraska Press. Copyright 2011 by the Board of Regents of the University of Nebraska.

Newfoundland, which was not part of the traditional districts.[5] Today, Newfoundland is home to the Miawpukek First Nation (aka the Conne River band), which is registered under the Indian Act,[6] and the Qalipu First Nation, a landless Mi'kmaw First Nation legally established by a Canadian Order-of-Council in 2011.[7] The Mi'kmaw districts were also part of the broader Wabanaki Confederacy, an eastern Algonquian alliance that included the Abenaki, Maliseet, Passamaquoddy, and Penobscot peoples, and functioned until the mid–eighteenth century for the purpose of cooperation and mutual protection.[8]

Anthropologist and historian Harald Prins, among the academic experts in Mi'kmaw affairs, argued that evidence of such a chiefdom political system is unclear, while the idea of a national political structure may have stemmed from a recent revisiting of history. He stated, "relying primarily on 19th-century documentation, many Mi'kmaqs today accept the idea that Mi'kmaq country was originally divided into seven districts . . . even though some scholars suggest that it may not be older than the 18th century."[9] Yet, this issue is debated. The *Mi'kmaw Resource Guide*, most Mi'kmaw authors, including Mi'kmaw unofficial historian Daniel Paul,[10] and several Mi'kmaw Elders whom I have inquired consider the seven-district structure as the accurate one.

In the eighteenth century, the Mi'kmaq were involved in disputes between the British and the French settler colonial powers for the control of the Atlantic region, then called Acadia. Allied with the latter, the Mi'kmaq and their Wabanaki allies participated in many wars against the British, with whom they then signed the Treaty of Boston (also known as Dummer's Treaty) in 1725. This treaty was subsequently ratified at Annapolis Royal in June 1726 by all the Mi'kmaw tribes in Nova Scotia.[11] A few decades later, the Mi'kmaq and the British signed Treaties of Peace and Friendship in 1752 and 1760–1761. British takeover resulted in the transition from the French colonial rule, which was based on reciprocal and often friendly relations, to one of political subordination.[12]

In October 1763, the British crown issued a Royal Proclamation outlining the administration of its North American territories and defining the guidelines for the relationship with the Native populations.[13] The Atlantic region was placed under a single jurisdiction, under the name of Nova Scotia, and, as specified in the Royal Proclamation, would have portions of territory set aside for the Natives. However, local administrators were slow (if at all interested) in applying Royal instructions and rather focused on the rapid settlement of the region.[14] Notwithstanding its conciliatory language, the Royal Proclamation formally initiated a systematic process of land dispossession that would lead to the creation of the reserve system in the early 1800s.

References to the national body of the Mi'kmaq (or Micmacs or Mickmacks, as spelled in historical documents and scholarly publications until recently) do indeed emerge from early colonial and missionary reports from this region. One such reference, for instance, appears in the minutes from a colonial administrators' conference held at the house of Peregrine Thomas Hopson, the governor of Nova Scotia at the time, on September 14, 1752, when the convened council discussed plans to organize a meeting between the governor himself and the "tribes of the Mickmack nation."[15]

Another one appears in the written works of Roman Catholic Abbé Pierre Antoine Simon Maillard, a missionary among the Mi'kmaq between 1735 and 1762 (the year of his death) who also assisted them as counselor in their negotiations with the British authorities. Abbé Maillard recognized the national character of the tribes of Eastern Canada when he said, "[t]he original inhabitants of this country are the savages, who may be divided into three nations, the Mickmakis, the Maricheets, or Abenaquis (being scarcely different nations) and the Canibats."[16] Despite using the derogatory term "savages" to identify the Native peoples, which reflects the customary colonial language of the times, Maillard appears to recognize the national characteristics of the regional tribes. One may speculate that he acquired such a perspective during his long interaction with the Mi'kmaq, as he had the opportunity to observe their institutions and sociopolitical life.

Granted that the term "nation" in both these instances may arguably be used as a synonym or substitute for "collectivity" or "tribe," thus having a different significance from how it is intended in contemporary political discourse, it nonetheless hints at a perception of a national body including and binding all the people of Mi'kma'ki.

Such a national character by the Mi'kmaq would soon clash with the British settlers' nationalistic sentiments and model, which manifested in constant efforts to reproduce the architectural and landscaping patterns of England. In the second part of the 1700s and increasingly in the first half of the 1800s, the British settlers built houses and divided property to mirror the homeland model of the English countryside. The reproduction of this national character was also guaranteed by the founding of educational institutions employing curricula based on English models. Differently from the French, who had established trading and political alliances with the Aboriginal population of this region, the British made every effort to keep themselves separate from the Mi'kmaq by discouraging, when not denying, all relationships between Natives and non-Natives. What they mostly wanted was unobstructed access to and control of the land.[17]

The British settlers' drive to retain a sense of their own national identity and pride, which led to such profound transformations of the geographic and social landscapes of Mi'kma'ki, inevitably undermined the Mi'kmaw people's collective (or national) identity. Pressured by the colonial governmental policies and the ever-increasing number of settlers arriving from Europe, the Mi'kmaq faced a divide between, on the one hand, social and cultural (not to mention political) extinction and, on the other hand, assimilation.

Concurrently, the physical and sociopolitical state of the Mi'kmaq continued to deteriorate in the first half of the nineteenth century, when tuberculosis and other diseases ravaged the region claiming many victims and the reservation system created in the 1830s further compromised the Mi'kmaw people's relationship with their traditional territory. The creation of Canada as an independent country in 1867 did not reverse such a trend; rather, it paved the way for more transformations that further chipped away at the Mi'kmaw people's sense of nationhood. In 1876, the new Canadian government ratified the Indian Act, a comprehensive law to regulate Indian affairs, which strengthened the process of assimilation that, until then, had been mainly carried out by church personnel and Indian agents. Progressively divested from control over their own destiny, the Mi'kmaq remained socially and economically at the fringes of the Canadian society for the rest of the nineteenth century and much of the twentieth.[18]

The Indian Act, which was amended several times (most recently in 2017), also introduced the current system of elected band chiefs and councils in place of traditional governance, which was structured around a network of family and village leaders governing locally under the supervision and guidance of the Grand Council. Although still in existence, the Grand Council is devoid of political authority and serves in a ceremonial and cultural capacity.[19]

Among the most effective instruments in the assimilative process undergone by the Canadian Natives was the establishment of governmental residential schools. Operating between the mid-1800s until the late 1960s, these schools were administered by religious personnel, which strived to assimilate and Christianize the Aboriginal people. In Atlantic Canada, over 2000 Mi'kmaw children attended the Shubenacadie Indian Residential School between 1930 and 1967, when the school was finally closed. Run by Catholic personnel, residential schooling aimed at a more profound and transformative educational experience than the one offered by the day schools located within the Mi'kmaw reserves.[20] The stated goal was to transform the Mi'kmaw children into Euro-Canadian law-abiding, God-fearing productive citizens. Sadly, this model of education relied on coercive methods, both physical and psychological, to eradicate the children's language, religion, culture, values, and identities. In many cases, it succeeded; in others, it left emotional scars that compromised the life experiences of the former student for life and indirectly affected those of their family members as a result of "intergenerational trauma."[21]

The residential school program functioned alongside centralization, another governmental policy enacted between 1942 and 1950 to "improve" the lives of the Mi'kmaq and Maliseet peoples of the Maritime provinces. The federal government's goal was to optimize its administration of the dispersed Aboriginal population by moving it (mostly by intimidation or force) into four designated reserve communities, two in Nova Scotia and two in New Brunswick. The selected locations in Nova Scotia were Eskasoni, on Cape Breton Island, and Shubenacadie (then changed into Indian Brook and, most recently, Sipekne'katik) on the mainland. Centralization also fulfilled requests from the general population to remove Aboriginal people from their vicinity.

The then-called Department of Indian Affairs managed the program, promising new houses, employment, and better economic and educational opportunities. None of these was delivered. In the early 1950s, the Mi'kmaq started to oppose the centralization policy, which failed rapidly and was discontinued. Nonetheless, it contributed to disrupt reserve communities and the Mi'kmaw extended family system.[22] Rather than simplifying and improving things, this policy, grounded on geographic and social exclusion that Hanrahan termed "institutional racism,"[23] only ended up undermining yet again the Mi'kmaw people's relationship with their territory.[24]

Mi'kmaw acculturation also took place in non-coerced ways. Electronic media, for instance, promoted the rapid spread of Western lifestyle and values. Radio since the 1930, television since the 1950s, the internet since the mid-1990s, and social media in the last fifteen years have rapidly become part of Mi'kmaw people's daily experiences in and out of the reserves. In fact (and this is a topic outside the scope of this chapter worthy of deeper study), I argue the current use of social media by Mi'kmaw people in and out of the reserve communities generates a phenomenon comparable with that of print language in earlier centuries in forging an "imagined national community," which Benedict Anderson illustrated in his now classic theory of nationalism.²⁵ Yet, pushing Anderson's argument further, it may be contended that, given the large network of kinship and friendship relations existing throughout Mi'kma'ki, the electronic media have fostered greater interconnectedness and, arguably, cohesion among a Mi'kmaw national body that is not imagined, where it is assumed that a community of strangers finds a common sense of belonging, but real, as most Mi'kmaq know one another (and, in many cases, are related through kinship) across the Mi'kmaw communities.

Starting in the early 1950s, the Mi'kmaw people's relocation to urban areas, such as Boston and Toronto, increased. Several Mi'kmaw individuals and families moved permanently to the cities to pursue employment and better life conditions. In many cases, they spent part of the year in the cities and regularly returned to their home reserves,²⁶ a pattern that has remained in the twenty-first century. Many Mi'kmaq also traveled throughout the greater Northeast region in search for work, mostly in the form of apple, blueberry, and potato harvesting.²⁷ Although significantly reduced in recent years, this practice continues today.²⁸

Today, slightly over 30,000 Mi'kmaq are registered as members of twenty-nine federally recognized First Nations, all but one (in Maine) located on Canadian territory, specifically in Nova Scotia, New Brunswick, Prince Edward Island, southern Quebec, and Newfoundland. The Canadian government recognizes over sixty Mi'kmaw reserve areas. Some First Nations possess more than one reserve area. As of 2011, the Mi'kmaw population has increased by about 24,000, the registered members of the landless Qalipu First Nation, although this number and, more broadly, the criteria for membership in Qalipu have been topics of debate both among the Mi'kmaq and the Canadian government.²⁹

Contextual Nationhood

In the last three decades, the Mi'kmaq have been working on rebuilding and, as a corollary, redefining their nation and sense of nationhood, with the greater efforts taking place in the last twenty years.³⁰ Expectedly, multiple strategies, at times in discordance and some more successful than others, have been employed to achieve this.

Defining the nature and, as a corollary, the territorial extent of their national body has been among the peculiar challenges faced by the Mi'kmaq in such a rebuilding process. When discussing the current nature and characteristics of Mi'kmaw nationhood, Luke, an official in one of the Nova Scotia bands, recognized their high level of dynamicity, and illustrated them to me in these terms: "There are different levels to it. It is not stagnant nationhood. It is highly susceptible to change in accordance with the energy that exists within the nation. And that is a feature of nationhood. It can be as local as community. It can be as global as inter-communities, intertribal even. It has a way of suiting the specific circumstances. I don't see it as a stagnant sort of thing."[31] Such a statement provides a vivid illustration of what I call contextual nationhood, the concurrent existence of multiple dimensions of nationhood in different settings.

First, Mi'kmaw First nationhood and nationalism are a tribal concept and sentiment, respectively, thus expressed by people from the entire Mi'kmaw territory about the whole territory. This is mostly a social, cultural, and historical dimension of the Mi'kmaw nation. Mi'kmaw Elder, visionary leader, and Order of Canada Member Joe. B. Marshall expressed this in a succinct but clear statement: "Culturally we are one tribe: we speak the same language, and we practice the same traditions."[32] Such a unified perception of nationhood emerges in several contexts. Here I sample three: the Mi'kmaw powwow trail, the celebratory perception of late activist Annie Mae Aquash, and the legacies of the Shubenacadie Indian Residential School.

In the social and cultural contexts, the powwow circuit represents this tribal dimension of the Mi'kmaw nation. Powwows are gatherings, hosted either by single tribal communities or by larger intertribal organizations, ubiquitous across the United States and Canada. They take place particularly, but not exclusively, during weekends throughout the summer and feature drumming, various styles of dance (some competitive with money prizes and some open to the audience), food, Native craft vendors, and a general festive atmosphere.[33]

In line with this Native shared practice, the Mi'kmaw powwow season takes place every summer.[34] Almost each weekend of the season, the single communities take turns in hosting their powwows, which are attended by Mi'kmaw people from the whole Maritime region and occasional local non-Natives. A large number of Mi'kmaw individuals and families travel to provincial and extra-provincial locations to attend these events. Carpooling, short-term stay in the homes of family and friends residing in the hosting communities, and visits to relatives and acquaintances living afar are essential parts of the powwow routine. Although people travel to powwows for many reasons—including participating as dancers or drummers; visiting friends and family members living elsewhere; selling their crafts and food, such as the ubiquitous fry bread (a flattened round piece of dough which is deep fried and sometimes loaded with beans, cheese, lettuce, and tomatoes); or simply having fun—investing time and money in such long-distance trips is usually considered secondary to reconnecting with loved ones and supporting the hosting communities.[35]

The seasonal rejuvenation and strengthening of these ties among Mi'kmaq from all communities across Mi'kma'ki contributes to the maintenance of a larger Mi'kmaw community, one that extends beyond the boundaries of the single communities and the provinces. In addition, the need for material and emotional support while being away from home for long periods makes many Mi'kmaq dependent on specific people residing in other areas. Such a supportive network, which each Mi'kmaw individual visualizes differently on their mental social maps, is essential for the social and cultural survival of the Mi'kmaq. In this sense, the powwow trail constitutes a source of First national identification for the Mi'kmaw people.

Helen Ting has argued that national identity is produced and reproduced through social practices and interactions with others in tangible life experiences.[36] The Mi'kmaw powwow trail fits this perspective. As it extends the Mi'kmaw people's range of interaction across the whole Mi'kma'ki, it contributes to recreate and strengthen the Mi'kmaw Nation time and again.

Such a supra-territorial dimension of Mi'kmaw nationhood has also materialized in the form of national symbols, which are key elements for nation-building and the creation of a national identity.[37] One such symbol in Mi'kma'ki is the historical figure of late activist Annie Mae Aquash, a Mi'kmaw woman from Sipekne'katik (then the Shubenacadie reserve) who devoted much of her adult life to fighting for Aboriginal rights in North America, to raising public awareness of Native social problems, and to promoting the revitalization of Native values and cultures.[38]

Born in 1945, Annie Mae left Mi'kma'ki to join the American Indian Movement (AIM), the leading Native activist group in the United States in the 1970s. She participated in many landmark events in the recent history of Native American activism—including the Trail of Broken Treaties in 1972 and the seventy-one-day occupation of Wounded Knee in 1973—which drew national attention and put AIM in contrast with the U.S. government and the FBI. After years of struggles, Annie Mae was murdered by former AIM members in late 1975 or early 1976 in the Pine Ridge reservation in South Dakota and buried there.[39] In June 2004, her body was brought back to Sipekne'katik, her community of birth. A four-day ceremony, which culminated in a gathering and reburial ritual, completed a process to bring

Annie Mae back "into the arms of her nation," as written by Annie Mae's family in the event's official program.⁴⁰

Annie Mae has evolved into a positive symbol of Mi'kmaw First nationhood, representing a major source of collective identification and unity for the Mi'kmaw people of the twenty-first century, this contributing to the current Mi'kmaw nation-building process. However, this was not the case until a few decades ago, when many Mi'kmaq did not support her involvement in the radical, often violent, actions of AIM in the early 1970s. Some, as Annie Mae's family members have told me repeatedly in informal conversations, were also unaware of her militant lifestyle. For Annie Mae's figure to acquire validation it required the Mi'kmaw people to redress their perceptions of the Red Power Native American political activism of the 1960s and 1970s.

Today, AIM's actions and Annie Mae's radical times are distant and blurred enough to give way to celebrative discourses, which have shed their focus on the everyday episodes of violence of the late 1960s and 1970s while being recast to highlight her ideals of self-determination, the defense of Indigenous rights, and promoting the well-being of Native people. Today, the Mi'kmaq look at Annie Mae as a positive figure in their nation's recent history, one representing the Mi'kmaw people's strength and courage in surviving centuries of colonial aggression and injustice.

This unifying process of national identification has also resulted from a darker page in the recent history of the Mi'kmaq—namely, the collective experiences in and memories of the Shubenacadie Indian Residential School. By creating a sense of common impact, either direct or indirect, onto all the Mi'kmaq, past (since the establishment of the school) and present, these experiences and memories have resulted in the creation of an additional dimension, the "residential school survivor," in many Mi'kmaw people's individual and collective identities that has reached First national dimension in Mi'kma'ki.⁴¹

Although a minority of Mi'kmaq attended the residential school, which resulted in an identity distinction (or divide) between survivors and non-survivors, these traumatic experiences nonetheless tell a story of dispossession of language, culture, values, family relationships, self-esteem and, for many, emotional stability and mental sanity. Such a dispossession can be equated to the broader experiences of colonial dispossession that all Mi'kmaq (and, by extent, Aboriginal) people past and present have shared in one way or another. Associating residential schooling with colonial dispossession (particularly, but not exclusively, of land) allows survivors to readjust their individual experiences to the broader Aboriginal experiences and sense of destiny. I argue that the Shubenacadie Indian Residential School has also become part of the Mi'kmaw national narrative, thus representing a critical collective experience whose memory, regular mention in official and unofficial discourse, and the resulting ongoing healing process all contributed to shape the Mi'kmaw people's current representations of Mi'kmaw nationhood.

Once again, Luke provided a statement that captured perfectly such a unified perspective and sentiment. He said, "If one looks at the history of Mi'kmaw colonial relationships . . . or even now, when you look at legislation that comes down federally or provincially . . . or there are some key issues, like hydraulic fracturing, right? . . . There are certain things that hit a cord to our nation, almost like a string that is plucked, and there is a vibration that flows from it."[42] The history of the Mi'kmaw colonial relationships, which includes issues related to Aboriginal and treaty rights, is certainly a unified (read, tribal or national) experience for the Mi'kmaq. However, the current workings and negotiations around the right mostly take place at the single community or provincial level. Furthermore, economic development initiatives to improve the lives of Mi'kmaw people are mostly pursued independently and separately by single reserve communities.

In this perspective, Mi'kmaw First nationhood and First nationalism are also expressed distinctively by single bands (or communities), which are called individually and call themselves First Nations. This is mostly an economic and administrative dimension of Mi'kmaw and, more broadly, Aboriginal nationhood in Canada, a recent phenomenon that has added a further aspect to the Mi'kmaw people's expressions of nationality.

The single communities comprising an Aboriginal nation, the Mi'kmaw Nation in this case, now refer to themselves individually as First Nations, the Paq'tnkek First Nation and Millbrook First Nation, to cite two Mi'kmaw communities in Nova Scotia. The use of the term "nation" to refer to single reserves, some of which are the size of small villages, then reveals both a further layer in the Aboriginal people's perceptions of community and a foundation of sovereignty at the local level. Many years ago, Victor, a band leader at the time, provided confirmation to such a perception when he told me that for the Mi'kmaq "the band is a distinct layer of nationality."[43]

Incidentally, these two reserve communities are among the brightest examples of economic development carried out independently by single First Nations. Both reserves are cut through by Highway 104 and 102, respectively, the only two major corridors in Nova Scotia, an infrastructure development of the 1960s that they had to accept without any say. Faced with this challenge, though, both First Nations have recently been able to capitalize on the predictable high-volume traffic by establishing successful commercial districts, mostly leasing land to businesses, in the portions of their reserve lands cut through by the highways. Millbrook's Power Center, the name of its commercial district, opened in 2001, and Paq'tnkek's business park opened in 2019. The revenue generated in these locations belongs to and is invested in the betterment of the individual communities and their residents.

Such a single-band expression and dimension of nationhood is also exemplified by the recent disputes between the Mi'kmaq and the commercial lobster fishing operators in southwestern Nova Scotia. For decades, the Mi'kmaq have accessed and harvested natural resources including marine species, land animals, forest resources based on centuries-old treaty rights rather than governmental regulations. In the specific realm of fishing, the exercise of these harvesting rights has been based on a collective or tribal (read: national) initiative based on a shared interpretation of the Treaties of 1760–1761, signed between the governor of the British Colony of Nova Scotia and the Mi'kmaq, that guaranteed the latter access to resource harvesting in the region.[44]

The Marshall case—centered on the trial of late Donald Marshall Jr., a Nova Scotia Mi'kmaq accused of illegal fishing in 1993 and found guilty in the lower courts, only to see his sentence reverted in a historic Supreme Court decision in 1999—became a shared battleground for all Mi'kmaq, suggesting a unified Mi'kmaw national dimension in the defense of their commonly held treaty rights. In addition, the aggressive responses to Marshall from both the non-Native commercial fishing industry, fearing the potential damage to the lobster stock that the Supreme Court's decision would trigger by upholding the Mi'kmaq people's right to fish outside federal regulations, and the Department of Fisheries and Oceans (DFO), concerned with retaining control over access to marine resources, favored the consolidation of the Mi'kmaq into a unified body characterized by a sentiment of "national" solidarity.[45]

However, this unified effort to face the commercial fishing industry and the DFO as a single national entity gave way progressively to the concerns and interests of the single First Nations. All but two, Sipekne'katik and Burnt Church (in New Brunswick), negotiated separate interim agreements with the government that regulated their own fishing activity in exchange for cash, equipment, legal licenses, and training.[46] Albert, a former official of a Mi'kmaw band, illustrated this development in clear terms. "When the Marshall case happened," he stated, "all the chiefs said that we were going to stick together and do something about it. Then, one by one they all signed agreements."[47]

In late 2017, and then in October 2020 and November 2021, the latent resentment of the commercial fishermen erupted again in open confrontation that resulted in the destruction of Mi'kmaw equipment, storing facilities, and catch. These events involved only the Sipekne'katik First Nation, which, although receiving expressions of solidarity and moral support from all Mi'kmaq (as well as other Aboriginal nations in Canada), faced the challenges on its own.[48] In this regard, the Marshall case and its developments illustrate the difficulties that the Mi'kmaw leaders and communities have had in constituting a national front before external challenges.

Finally, the growth of a more insular dimension of Mi'kmaw nationhood surfaces from the Mi'kmaw people's perceptions of and relationship with their traditional territory. As a result of centuries of settler colonialism, the spatial continuity of the Mi'kmaw people's presence on the land has been compromised. Mike said, "When you read into the Indian Act, [Mi'kmaw] jurisdiction does not extend beyond a certain boundary, the community boundary."[49] Mi'kmaw reserve residents and the neighboring non-Native populations perceive these reserves as stand-alone communities, with fluctuating degrees of connections with and participation in the life of their surrounding region.

The reserves have gradually become the only place that many (if not most) Mi'kmaq feel as familiar. In the summer of 2015, during a research trip to Nova Scotia, I received confirmation of this during an informal discussion on this topic I had with a Mi'kmaw woman. I was intrigued and somewhat surprised to hear her say, "I wish we had one of those fast, elevated trains to move quickly from one reserve to the other, bypassing all that there is in between and below."[50] In such a brief but visually evocative statement, this person offered a territorial representation of Native political space in Mi'kma'ki in which the Mi'kmaw reserves, the exclusive space of the Natives, connect across an ocean of non–Native controlled land.

Similarly, another Mi'kmaw woman expressed such a compromised relationship with the territory by linking spatial boundaries with social community and the resulting relations among Native and Non-Native residents. She said, "I know so many people in every reserve, and I have relatives everywhere. I can go visit and stay. I am not too fond of going to a non-Native community and stay, but I feel comfortable going to a Native community. When you're Native and go to a non-Native community, they look at you funny, because you don't belong there."[51]

The Mi'kmaq have attempted to reacquire their connection to the (off-reserve) territory and they seemed to have had some success when promoting their interests within the legal and administrative realms of single provinces. In fact, First nationhood and the implementation of Mi'kmaw nation rebuilding strategies have recently become a provincial affair, thus involving all the bands from single provinces, Nova Scotia in this case. This is mostly a political and administrative dimension of Mi'kmaw nationhood.

Among the Nova Scotia Mi'kmaq, an embryonic attempt of this more recent nation-rebuilding initiative at the provincial level was made in 1969 as a response to the Trudeau administration's "White Paper" policy, a short-lived governmental initiative that intended to cancel Indian status, repeal the Indian Act, and end all federal responsibilities toward the Aboriginal population.[52] The Mi'kmaq of Nova Scotia joined in the Union of Nova Scotia Indians (now Union of Nova Scotia Mi'kmaq, UNSM), a tribal entity representing all thirteen bands of the province (see map 5.2), to form a unified political front.[53] In 1986, six Nova Scotia mainland Mi'kmaw bands left the Union to form the Confederacy of Mainland Mi'kmaq (CMM).

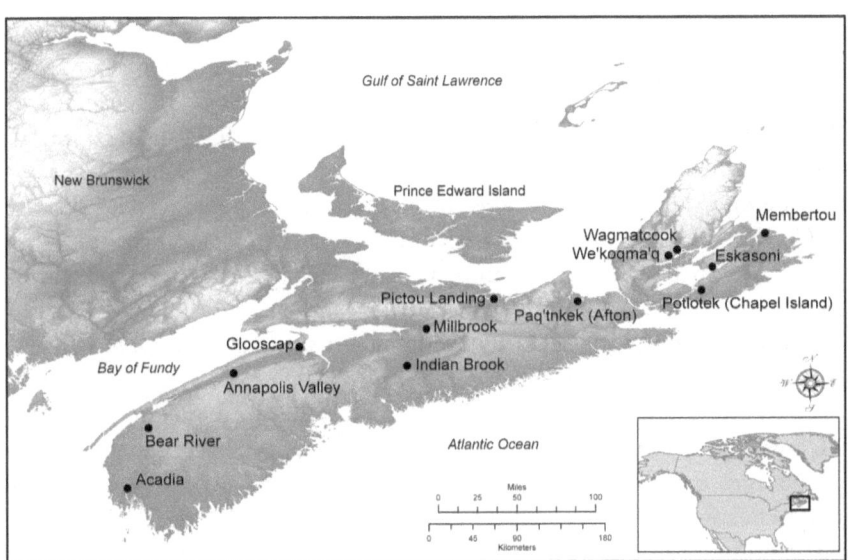

Map 5.2. The thirteen Mi'kmaw First Nations of Nova Scotia. Reproduced from *First Nations, Identity, and Reserve Life: The Mi'kmaq of Nova Scotia* by Simone Poliandri by permission of the University of Nebraska Press. Copyright 2011 by the Board of Regents of the University of Nebraska.

Today, as part of a recent restructuring, the Confederacy represents all eight First Nations in mainland Nova Scotia while the Union represents the five communities on Cape Breton Island. Since their inception, these tribal organizations mostly devoted their efforts to coordinate the administration of programs—including band membership and enrollment, health services, community services, aquatic-resource harvesting, education, legal services, and environment and natural resource programs—for the member communities.[54]

Nation-building efforts at the provincial level assumed a greater scope in more recent times. In June 2002, the Mi'kmaq of Nova Scotia approached both the governments of Nova Scotia and Canada to initiate formal discussions of treaty and Aboriginal rights. The three parties signed an Umbrella Agreement stating the willingness to work together in Nova Scotia. This officially started the Made in Nova Scotia Process, an ongoing table of negotiations for all rights related issues in the province. The Mi'kmaw people have been represented by the Assembly of Nova Scotia Mi'kmaw Chiefs, an organization that included the chiefs of all the thirteen Nova Scotia bands.

In 2004, the Made in Nova Scotia process was made into the Mi'kmaq Rights Initiative, or Kwilmu'kw Maw-klusuaqn (KMKNO), a tribal agency coordinating the negotiation efforts of all the Nova Scotia Mi'kmaw bands in the Tripartite Forum with the federal and provincial governments. In 2006, the Chiefs of the thirteen Mi'kmaw communities of Nova Scotia joined in the Assembly of Nova Scotia Mi'kmaq Chiefs (ANSMC), an organization created to make resolutions affecting all Nova Scotia Mi'kmaq as well as to provide direction and instructions to the KMKNO negotiators. In February 2007, the ANSMC signed a Framework Agreement on behalf of the Nova Scotia Mi'kmaq with the governments of Canada and Nova Scotia. This agreement set out a formal negotiations process on Treaty and Aboriginal rights and title related to Mi'kmaw land, resources, and governance. KMKNO has represented the ANSMC in this forum.[55]

When evaluating political and administrative efforts to implement Mi'kmaw governance and, more broadly, to improve the lives of the Mi'kmaw people and communities, First nationalism and nation-building seem to work more effectively at the provincial level. When discussing the operation of his community, Luke said, "We have to operate within the environment of provincial governments. We have to recognize those artificial divisions. You know, territorial, geographic. And when I say recognize them, I do not necessarily mean accept them, right? Just seeing them for what they are. Acknowledge their existence and trying to be highly pragmatic."[56] Similarly, when illustrating the negotiations on Aboriginal and Treaty rights that have taken place in Nova Scotia under the umbrella agreement, Elder Viola Robinson, former Lead Negotiator for KMKNO and one of the Commissioners in the 1996 Royal Commission on Aboriginal People, told me,

> One of the things that we want to pursue out of this whole process is to restore . . . or reinitiate the Mi'kmaw nation . . . A lot of people would conceive the Mi'kmaw nation, and they are correct, as covering a vast area [from Nova Scotia to eastern United States]. But because of the way in which Canada is divided now and the way that the governing structure of Canada works, divided into provinces and territories that have different governments . . . and we can't undo that . . . so, we are stuck within the parameters of provinces and federal government."[57]

The leadership of the Nova Scotia Mi'kmaq recognized this scenario and adjusted their strategy toward achieving empowerment and enhanced self-governance. To this purpose, on October 1, 2008, the Assembly of Nova Scotia Mi'kmaq Chiefs released the *Mi'kmaq of Nova Scotia Nationhood Proclamation*, a national declaration at the provincial level. A salient passage in this historic document reads, "The Chiefs of Nova Scotia hereby come together to proclaim and assert Nationhood of the Mi'kmaq of Nova Scotia over our traditional lands and waters. We, the Chiefs and Councils of Nova Scotia, as the elected representatives of the Mi'kmaq, agree to work together to develop a Mi'kmaw governance structure that unites and empowers our Nation to enhance the quality of life and well-being of our people."[58] Since 2008, the ANSMC (under the logistical coordination of KMKNO) has also been hosting annual Nationhood Conferences to assess the status of negotiations with the provincial and federal government, outline the accomplishments, and delineate objectives and strategies for the immediate future. More broadly, such gatherings have cemented the national character of the Nova Scotia Mi'kmaq.[59]

On August 31, 2010, another historic agreement among the Assembly of Nova Scotia Mi'kmaq Chiefs and the provincial and federal governments marked the Mi'kmaw nation-building process in the province. The parties met in the Millbrook First Nation to ratify the Mi'kmaq-Nova Scotia-Canada Consultation Terms of Reference, which instituted a consultation process to include the Nova Scotia Mi'kmaq in all legal discussion and government activities that have the potential to impact Mi'kmaw interests and rights.[60]

Such developments appear to be the result of a sound nation-building vision and strategy by the Nova Scotia Mi'kmaq. At the same time, this is also where the discrepancies started.

Successes and Roadblocks

In spring 2016, I was pleasantly surprised, not to say elated, when I opened the latest issue of *Native American and Indigenous Studies* to find Maura Hanrahan's article celebrating the incorporation of Mi'kmaw governance practices in their management of relationships with settler-colonial governments in Canada. In her timely paper, Hanrahan discussed the recent creation of KMKNO. In her analysis of this new provincial dimension of Mi'kmaw political relationships, despite acknowledging the colonial framework constraining the Mi'kmaw people's efforts to develop culturally-matched forms of governance, Hanrahan praised the ground-breaking work of KMKNO as "a new direction in Indigenous governance" and a successful model of governance linking Indigenous values, specifically commitment to political inclusion and consensus, and nation-building.[61]

I have been working with the Mi'kmaw people in Mi'kma'ki for over twenty years, devoting the last twelve to the study of nation-building and Indigenous governance. In spring 2016, I published an essay that illustrated this new Mi'kmaw institution as the newest expression of Mi'kmaw First Nationhood.[62] One can then understand my academic excitement, as Mi'kmaw issues, particularly those related to nation-building, seldom appear in academic literature. What are the odds that two publications on this very topic with a focus on the Mi'kmaq of Nova Scotia appear only weeks apart? Slim at best, one may think.

Yet, the changes that took place right when Hanrahan's article and my piece were going to press are testimony of the highly dynamic nature of Mi'kmaw nation-building. Despite some success, embodied by recent policy changes and economic growth, this provincial dimension of nationhood has already become a burden to some First Nations in the province. Until 2013 and arguably for another three years, it was mostly individual community members who voiced their skepticism toward the provincial "break-up" of the Mi'kmaw Nation. To these individuals, the short-term gains of this province-based strategy pose greater risks to the long-term cultural and political integrity of the Mi'kmaw Nation as a whole. Some of them fear that the negotiations over what they call "modern-day treaties," which entail the revisitations of rights acquired in colonial times, might compromise the force of the original treaties, particularly the 1752 and 1760–1761 ones. Others contend that, although united in the ANSMC under the administration of KMKNO to pursue collective goals in the province, all Chiefs have different agendas for their communities, which are dictated by distinct needs in different socioeconomic contexts. Finally, some individuals envision the Mi'kmaw values, lifestyle, culture, relations, and treaties as representative of one Mi'kmaw nation across Mi'kma'ki while rejecting an artificial vision of nationhood based on the colonial boundaries of the provinces.

One such individual, Mark, a middle-aged Mi'kmaw man, showed equal skepticism when discussing both the provincial dimension of Mi'kmaw nationhood and the political agenda of the Nova Scotia First Nations' chiefs. When I asked him about this new aspect of nationhood, he promptly replied, "When I think of Mi'kmaw nation, I think of the whole Mi'kma'ki. It is only in the past couple of decades that we started to think only about Nova Scotia. This is the work that the Chiefs are doing."[63]

Daniel, another middle-aged Mi'kmaw man, portrayed an even more skeptical and reductive picture of the state of Mi'kmaw nationhood when he answered the same question: "In my mind," he said, "I see us Mi'kmaw people as a nation, in unity, equality, and fairness. In reality, I only see groups of nationhoods, small clusters in each community. Each community has its own needs."[64]

Obviously, some leaders have been listening, as this individual skepticism rapidly assumed an institutional dimension. What changed since 2013, and then particularly in 2016 and 2020, has been the appearance of an official (read: Mi'kmaw elected leadership) skepticism toward this province-based approach to negotiation with the Nova Scotia and Canadian governments. As a result, three communities, Sipekne'katik, Millbrook, and Membertou, abandoned (in 2013, 2016, and 2020, respectively) the tribal alliance and have been pursuing negotiations independently.

Interestingly, the institutional perspective of Sipekne'katik and the reason why this First Nation left the tripartite forum in 2013 mirrors the skepticism that some individual Mi'kmaq display over the alleged tampering with the original treaties. A former member of the band's leadership expressed this clearly when he commented on Sipekne'katik's official exit from KMKNO. He said,

> We are hearing that KMKNO is trying to negotiate a modern-day treaty. They say that they're not, but I am not sure. The majority of our council voted to get out of KMKNO . . . We, Sipekne'katik, do our own consultation with the government.

> We have our consultation team . . . The reason we are strong with our treaty is that the 1752 treaty were signed by the chief of this community . . . We maintain our treaties very strong. Everything falls back to our treaties. That is our nationhood, I guess.[65]

Then, in 2016, I received copy of the Millbrook band's office communication of this from a Mi'kmaw friend right when I was reading Hanrahan's piece for the first time. Dated May 18, the communication reads,

> Effective immediately, the Chief and Council of the Millbrook First Nation has (sic) withdrawn its support and participation from the Kwilmu'kw Maw-klusuaqn KMK/Made in Nova Scotia Process and its governing body, the Assembly of Nova Scotia Chiefs. Millbrook is the second Mi'kmaw community to exit the KMK Process since 2013 . . . Concerns about the KMK Process and KMKNO work have grown amid wide-ranging criticisms from community members . . . As a Chief and Council, we owe it to our community to make decisions in good faith, and given our collective reflections on the KMK process, we decided to move forward in a new direction.[66]

Finally, in October 2020, the leadership of the Membertou First Nation, located within the town limits of Sydney on Cape Breton Island, announced its withdrawal from both KMKNO and the Assembly of Nova Scotia Chiefs because of disputes over the management and implementation of treaty rights, particularly related to fisheries. When asked about this important step, Membertou Chief Terry Paul stated, "My confidence in the operations of the organization have weakened over time. Supporting our Chiefs, our communities, and our rights has, and always will be my main priority. When the body that we meet under no longer allows for that support, it's important to adapt as necessary for our people."[67]

It is, therefore, interesting and, more importantly, revealing of the dynamic nature of contemporary Mi'kmaw nationalistic sentiments and the rapidity of their nation-rebuilding efforts that such a provincial dimension of nationhood has already generated multiple levels of discrepancy in less than ten years. Whereas individual community members' reservations were quick to arise only to be coupled with some institutional skepticism, now such different viewpoints within the Mi'kmaw leadership have solidified into a clear divide that necessarily results in contrasting political strategies for the purpose of conducting negotiations and maintain relations with federal and provincial governments.

Elder Viola Robinson captured such a sense of concurrent uncertainty and prospect arguably better than anybody when she said, "It would be much easier for administrative purposes to have 65 or 70 nations than the 635 or so bands that we have today in Canada. To begin, we'll start with the provinces. What we are hoping is gonna happen someday is that it will be restored to the larger [nation]. How it will happen we don't know."[68]

However contextually conceived and whatever shape it acquires in the future, Mi'kmaw nationhood will certainly be the foundation of great opportunities to such a resilient Aboriginal nation. At the same time, though, it seems that the path to get there will also require the Mi'kmaq to endure some inevitable frustration.

Notes

1. I utilize the Francis/Smith orthographic system according to which the variant form Mi'kmaw plays two grammatical roles: (1) it is the singular of Mi'kmaq (e.g., one Mi'kmaw, two Mi'kmaq) and (2) it is an adjective in circumstances where it precedes a noun (e.g., Mi'kmaw people). See Union of Nova Scotia Indians (UNSI), Confederacy of Mainland Mi'kmaq (CMM), and Native Council of Nova Scotia (NCNS), *The Mi'kmaw Resource Guide. Fourth Edition* (Truro, NS: Eastern Woodland Publishing, 2007), 2.

2. See, among others, Gerald R. (Taiaiake) Alfred, *First Nation Perspectives on Political Identity. First Nation Citizenship Research and Policy Series, Building Towards Change* (Ottawa, ON: Assembly of First Nations, 2009); Stephen Cornell, "Processes of Native Nationhood: The Indigenous Politics of Self-Government," *The International Indigenous Policy Journal* 6, no. 4 (2015): http://dx.doi.org/10.18584/iipj.2015.6.4.4; Stephen Cornell and Miriam Jorgensen, "What Are the Limits of Social Inclusion? Indigenous Peoples and Indigenous Governance in Canada and the United States," *American Review of Canadian Studies* 49, no. 2 (2019): 283–300, https://doi.org/10.1080/02722011.2019.1613790; Angela Riley, "Good (Native) Governance," *Columbia Law Review* 107, no. 5 (2007): 1049–1125; Jessica Shadian, "Navigating Political Borders Old and New: The Territoriality of Indigenous Inuit Governance," *Journal of Borderlands Studies* 33, no. 2 (2018): 273–288. https://doi.org/10.1080/08865655.2017.1300781

3. See the Assembly of First Nations website at www.afn.ca.

4. The boundaries among districts are traced according to one of the Mi'kmaw most popular representations, which is featured in UNSI, CMM, NCNS,

The Mi'kmaw Resource Guide, the joint informative publication of the three Nova Scotia Mi'kmaw tribal councils. Yet, these territorial divisions were not marked on the land and, therefore, must be considered approximate.

5. In the Mi'kmaw official representation of Mi'kma'ki, *Ktaqmkuk* (Newfoundland) does not appear as a separate traditional district. Yet, it is known that the Mi'kmaq traveled to *Ktaqmkuk* and established seasonal camps.

6. According to the Miawpukek First Nation's official website (www.mfngov.ca/about, accessed in May 2023), the community became a permanent settlement around 1822 and was then established as the Conne River Reserve in 1870. It was officially designated as an Indian Reserve under the Indian Act only in 1987.

7. See the official page of the Newfoundland government at www.gov.nl.ca/exec/iar/qalipu-first-nation. See also the Qalipu First Nation's official webpage at https://qalipu.ca. Both accessed in May 2023.

8. See Frank Speck, "The Eastern Algonkian Wabanaki Confederacy," *American Anthropologist* 17, no. 3 (1915): 492–508; Wilson D. Wallis, and Ruth Sawtell Wallis. "Culture Loss and Culture Change among the Micmac of the Canadian Maritime Provinces, 1912–1950," *Kroeber Anthropological Society Papers* 8 (1953): 100–129

9. Harald E. L. Prins, *The Mi'kmaq: Resistance, Accommodation, and Cultural Survival* (Fort Worth, TX: Harcourt Brace College Publishers, 1996), 177.

10. See Daniel N. Paul, *We Were not the Savages: Collision Between European and Native American Civilizations, Third Edition* (Halifax, NS: Fernwood, 2007 [1993]).)

11. See Harald E. L. Prins, "The Crooked Path of Dummer's Treaty: Anglo-Wabanaki Diplomacy and the Quest for Aboriginal Rights," in *Papers of the Thirty-Third Algonquian Conference*, ed. H. C. Wolfart (Winnipeg: University of Manitoba Press, 2002), 360–377, for an analysis of Dummer's Treaty and its consequences for the Mi'kmaq and their Wabanaki allies.

12. See Prins, *The Mi'kmaq*.

13. See Anthony J. Hall, *The American Empire and the Fourth World: The Bowl with One Spoon* (Montreal & Kingston: McGill-Queen's University Press, 2003).

14. See Margaret R. Conrad and James K. Hiller, *Atlantic Canada: A Region in the Making* (Don Mills, ON: Oxford University Press, 2001).

15. See Thomas B. Akins, *Selections from the Public Documents of the Province of Nova Scotia* (Halifax, NS: Charles Annand, 1869).

16. Pierre Antoine Simon Maillard, *An Account of the Customs and Manners of the Micmakis and Maricheets Savage Nations, Now Dependent on the Government of Cape-Breton* (London: S. Hooper and A. Morley, 1758), 24.

17. See Jennifer Reid, *Myth, Symbol, and Colonial Encounter: British and Mi'kmaq in Acadia, 1700–1867* (Ottawa: University of Ottawa Press, 1995).

18. See Paul, *We Were not the Savages*; Ruth H. Whitehead, *The Old Man Told Us: Excerpts from Mi'kmaw History 1500–1950* (Halifax, NS: Nimbus, 1991).

19. See Leslie Jane McMillan, "Mi'kmawey Mawio'mi: Changing Roles of the Mi'kmaq Grand Council from the Early Seventeenth Century to the Present" (MA thesis, Dalhousie University, 1996).

20. See Hamlet S. Philpot, *The Province of Nova Scotia, Canada: Resource and Development*, 4th Edition (Ottawa, ON: F. A. Acland, King's Printer for Department of the Interior, National Development Bureau, 1930).

21. See Isabelle Knockwood, *Out of the Depths: The Experiences of Mi'kmaw Children at the Indian Residential School at Shubenacadie, Nova Scotia, Fourth Edition* (Lockeport, NS: Roseway, 2015 [1992]); Simone Poliandri, "Surviving as Mi'kmaq and First Nations People: The Legacies of the Shubenacadie Indian Residential School in Nova Scotia" in *Power Through Testimony: Reframing Residential Schools in the Age of Reconciliation*, ed. Brieg Capitaine and Karine Vanthuyne (Vancouver: University of British Columbia Press, 2017), 113–134.

22. See Wallis and Wallis, "Culture Loss and Culture Change among the Micmac of the Canadian Maritime Provinces."

23. Maura Hanrahan, "Resisting Colonialism in Nova Scotia: The Kesukwitk Mi'kmaq, Centralization, and Residential Schooling," *Native Studies Review* 17, no. 1 (2008): 30.

24. See Paul, *We Were not the Savages*; Simone Poliandri, *First Nations, Identity, and Reserve Life: The Mi'kmaq of Nova Scotia* (Lincoln: University of Nebraska Press, 2011).

25. See Benedict Anderson, *Imagined Communities: Reflections on the Origin and Spread of Nationalism* (London: Verso, 1991 [1983]).

26. See Jeanne Guillemin, *Urban Renegades: The Cultural Strategy of American Indians* (New York: Columbia University Press, 1975).

27. See Harald E. L. Prins, "Tribal Networks and Migrant Labor: Mi'kmaq Indians as Seasonal Workers in Aroostook's Potato Fields, 1870–1980," in *Native Americans and Wage Labor: Ethnohistorical Perspectives*, eds. Alice Littlefield and Martha C. Knack (Norman: University of Oklahoma Press, 1996): 45–65, 274–276.

28. Since early 2020, though, the COVID-19 pandemic has heavily compromised the movements of people across the region and, even more, the U.S.-Canada border.

29. Population statistics are based on 2022 demographic data posted on the First Nations profiles page in the Government of Canada's Crown-Indigenous Relations and Northern Affairs Canada departments' website at https://fnp-ppn.aadnc-aandc.gc.ca/fnp/Main/index.aspx?lang=eng. The size of the Mi'kmaw population has been topic of debate since the creation of the Qalipu First Nation, as there have been more than 100,000 applications submitted by Newfoundland residents to acquire Qalipu membership as Mi'kmaw individuals. This was reflected in the recent 2016 Canada census, where the number of people checking the single Aboriginal ancestry box as Mi'kmaq rose to 152,145 (see "2016 Census Data on Aboriginal Ancestry Responses" at www12.statcan.gc.ca/census-recensement/2016/dp-pd/dt-td/Rp-eng.cfm?LANG=E&APATH=3&DETAIL=0&DIM=0&FL=A&FREE=0&GC=0&GID=0&GK=0&GRP=1&PID=110522&PRID=10&PTYPE=109445&S=0&SHOWALL=0&SUB=0&Temporal=2017&THEME=122&VID=0&VNAMEE=&VNAMEF=). Qalipu's membership application process was questioned by both the Mi'kmaq

Grand Council, which on 13 October 2013 sent a letter to the United Nations Special Rapporteur asking for assistance to redress what it perceives as a violation of Aboriginal status (copy of the letter is available at www.eskasoni.ca/uploads/newsletter/Sante-Mawiomi-Statement-to-UN-Special-Rapporteur.pdf), and the Canadian government, which in 2013 responded by rejecting many membership requests as part of its reevaluation of the Qalipu application process and, then, in 2021 suspended discussions with the Qalipu First Nations over the reopening of the application process (see "Qalipu First Nation 'In Shock' as Feds Suspend Talks to Include More Members," *CBC News*, April 6, 2021, www.cbc.ca/news/canada/newfoundland-labrador/qalipu-first-nation-membership-discussion-federal-government-1.5976650). All websites accessed in May 2023.

30. See Simone Poliandri, "The Mi'kmaw Path to First Nationhood: A Roadmap, Some Strategies, and a Few Effective Shortcuts," in *Native American Nationalism and Nation Re-building: Past and Present Cases*, ed. Simone Poliandri (Albany, NY: SUNY Press, 2016), 93–122.

31. Interview with Luke (pseudonym), 19 June 2015. Unless noted and granted permission to use a person's real name, all names have been changed to pseudonyms to respect the privacy of the interviewees.

32. Interview with Joe. B. Marshall, 2 July 2015.

33. See Clyde Ellis, Eric Luke Lassiter, and Gary H. Dunham, eds., *Powwow* (Lincoln: University of Nebraska Press, 2005).

34. The COVID-19 pandemic forced the cancellation of the 2020 and 2021 powwow seasons in Mi'kma'ki and throughout North America.

35. See Prins, *The Mi'kmaq*; Poliandri, *First Nations, Identity, and Reserve Life*.

36. Helen Ting, "Social Construction of Nation: A Theoretical Exploration," *Nationalism and Ethnic Politics* 14, no. 3 (2008): 453–482.

37. See David A. Butz, "National Symbols as Agents of Psychological and Social Change," *Political Psychology* 30, no. 5 (2009): 779–804; Gabriella Elgenius, *Symbols of Nations and Nationalism: Celebrating Nationhood* (London: Palgrave Macmillan, 2011).

38. See Devon A. Mihesuah, "Anna Mae Pictou-Aquash: An American Indian Activist," in *Sifters: Native American Women's Lives*, ed. Theda Perdue (New York: Oxford University Press, 2001): 204–222.

39. The exact date of death has never been established, as she disappeared in late 1975 and her partially decomposed body was found on February 24, 1976. See Johanna Brand, *The Life and Death of Anna Mae Aquash* (Toronto: Lorimer, 1993 [1978]); Steve Hendrix, *The Unquiet Grave: The FBI and the Struggle for the Soul of Indian Country* (New York: Thunder Mouth's Press, 2006).

40. The program was available to all community members and the public, which included me, participating in the events. (I hold a copy of this document.)

41. See Poliandri, *First Nations, Identity, and Reserve Life*, chapter 5; Poliandri, *Surviving as Mi'kmaq and First Nations People*.

42. Interview with Luke (pseudonym), 19 June 2015.

43. Interview with Victor (pseudonym), 27 October 2007.

44. See Thomas Isaac, *Aboriginal and Treaty Rights in the Maritimes: The Marshall Decision and Beyond* (Saskatoon, SK: Purich, 2001).

45. See See Ken Coates, *The Marshall Decision and Native Rights* (Montreal & Kingston: McGill-Queen's University Press, 2000); Leslie Jane McMillan, *Truth and Conviction: Donald Marshall Jr. and the Mi'kmaw Quest for Justice* (Vancouver: University of British Columbia Press, 2018); William C. Wicken, *Mi'kmaq Treaties on Trial: History, Land, and Donald Marshall Junior* (Toronto: University of Toronto Press, 2002).

46. See Simone Poliandri, "Mi'kmaw People and Tradition: Indian Brook Lobster Fishing in St. Mary's Bay, Nova Scotia," in *Papers of the Thirty-Fourth Algonquian Conference*, ed. H. C. Wolfart (Winnipeg: University of Manitoba Press, 2003): 303–310.

47. Interview with Albert (pseudonym), 10 April 2004.

48. See "Lobster Fishermen Accuse DFO Of Lax Enforcement of Indigenous Licenses," *CBC News*, September 14, 2017, www.cbc.ca/news/canada/nova-scotia/lobster-fishermen-accuse-dfo-of-lax-enforcement-of-indigenous-licences-1.4289759; "Fire Destroys Nova Scotia Lobster Facility, Leaving One Person In Hospital," *CBC News*, October 17, 2020, www.youtube.com/watch?v=JegOp4KRv0Q&ab_channel=CBCNews; "Fire Destroys New Edinburgh Lobster Pound Days Before Season Opens," *CBC News*, November 26, 2021, www.cbc.ca/news/canada/nova-scotia/fire-destroys-lobster-pound-1.6263458. All accessed in May 2023.

49. Interview with Mike (pseudonym), 26 June 2015.

50. Personal communication with the author, June 2015.

51. Interview with Jean (pseudonym), 24 June 2015.

52. See "Attempts to Reform or Repeal the Indian Act" in the Government of Canada's Crown-Indigenous Relations and Northern Affairs Canada departments' website at www.rcaanc-cirnac.gc.ca/eng/1323350306544/1544711580904. Accessed in May 2023.

53. See Tord Larsen, "Negotiating Identity: The Micmac of Nova Scotia," in *The Politics of Indianness: Case Studies of Native Ethnopolitics in Canada*, ed. Adrian Tanner (St. John's: Memorial University of Newfoundland, 1983): 37–136.

54. See the UNSM's website at www.unsi.ns.ca and the CMM's website at www.cmmns.com. Both accessed in May 2023.

55. See the KMKNO official webpage at https://mikmaqrights.com. Accessed in May 2023.

56. Interview with Luke (pseudonym), 19 June 2015.

57. Interview with Viola Robinson, 2 July 2015.

58. The full text of the Proclamation is available at https://mikmaqrights.com/wp-content/uploads/2020/10/NationhoodProclamation.pdf. Accessed in May 2023.

59. The COVID-19 pandemic disrupted these events in 2020 and 2021. The annual Nationhood Conferences resumed in November 2022.

60. See the details of the agreement on the Nova Scotia Government Office of L'Nu Affairs website at www.gov.ns.ca/abor/office/what-we-do/consultation. Accessed in May 2023.

61. Maura Hanrahan, "Making Indigenous Culture the Foundation of Indigenous Governance Today: The Mi'kmaq Rights Initiative of Nova Scotia, Canada," *Native American and Indigenous Studies* 3, no. 1 (2016): 87.

62. See Poliandri, "The Mi'kmaw Path to First Nationhood."

63. Interview with Mark (pseudonym), 18 June 2015.

64. Interview with Daniel (pseudonym), 16 June 2015.

65. Interview with Peter (pseudonym), 2 July 2015.

66. See "Millbrook First Nation Takes the Road Less Travelled, Walks Away from Kwilmu'kw Maw-klusuaqn KMK/Made in Nova Scotia Process." Millbrook First Nation Communication, 18 May 2016. (I hold a copy of this document.)

67. Quote in Angel Moore, "Respected Chief Leaves Two Mi'kmaw Political Organizations Because of 'Distrust' Over Moderate Livelihood Plans," *APTN National News*, October 28, 2020, www.aptnnews.ca/national-news/respected-chief-leaves-two-mikmaw-political-organizations-because-of-distrust-over-moderate-livelihood-plans. Accessed in May 2023.

68. Interview with Viola Robinson, 2 July 2015.

References

Akins, Thomas B. 1869. *Selections from the Public Documents of the Province of Nova Scotia*. Halifax, N.S.: Charles Annand.

Alfred, Gerald R. (Taiaiake). 2009. *First Nation Perspectives on Political Identity. First Nation Citizenship Research and Policy Series, Building Towards Change*. Ottawa, ON: Assembly of First Nations.

Anderson, Benedict. 1991 [1983]. *Imagined Communities: Reflections on the Origin and Spread of Nationalism*. London: Verso.

Brand, Johanna. 1993 [1978]. *The Life and Death of Anna Mae Aquash*. Toronto: Lorimer.

Butz, David A. 2009. "National Symbols as Agents of Psychological and Social Change." *Political Psychology* 30, no. 5: 779–804.

Coates, Ken. 2000. *The Marshall Decision and Native Rights*. Montreal & Kingston: McGill-Queen's University Press.

Conrad, Margaret R., and James K. Hiller. 2001. *Atlantic Canada: A Region in the Making*. Don Mills, ON: Oxford University Press.

Cornell, Stephen. 2015. "Processes of Native Nationhood: The Indigenous Politics of Self-Government." *The International Indigenous Policy Journal* 6, no. 4. http://dx.doi.org/10.18584/iipj.2015.6.4.4

Cornell, Stephen, and Miriam Jorgensen. 2019. "What are the Limits of Social Inclusion? Indigenous Peoples and Indigenous Governance in Canada and the United States." *American Review of Canadian Studies* 49, no. 2: 283–300.

Elgenius, Gabriella. 2011. *Symbols of Nations and Nationalism: Celebrating Nationhood*. London: Palgrave Macmillan.

Ellis, Clyde, Eric Luke Lassiter, and Gary H. Dunham, eds. 2005. *Powwow*. Lincoln: University of Nebraska Press.

Guillemin, Jeanne. 1975. *Urban Renegades: The Cultural Strategy of American Indians*. New York: Columbia University Press.

Hall, Anthony J. 2003. *The American Empire and the Fourth World: The Bowl with One Spoon*. Montreal & Kingston, McGill-Queen's University Press.

Hanrahan, Maura. 2016. "Making Indigenous Culture the Foundation of Indigenous Governance Today: The Mi'kmaq Rights Initiative of Nova Scotia, Canada." *Native American and Indigenous Studies* 3, no. 1: 75–95.

Hanrahan, Maura. 2008. "Resisting Colonialism in Nova Scotia: The Kesukwitk Mi'kmaq, Centralization, and Residential Schooling." *Native Studies Review* 17, no. 1: 25–44.

Hendrix, Steve. 2006. *The Unquiet Grave: The FBI and the Struggle for the Soul of Indian Country*. New York: Thunder Mouth's Press.

Isaac, Thomas. 2001. *Aboriginal and Treaty Rights in the Maritimes: The Marshall Decision and Beyond*. Saskatoon, SK: Purich.

Knockwood, Isabelle. 2015 [1992]. *Out of the Depths: The Experiences of Mi'kmaw Children at the Indian Residential School at Shubenacadie, Nova Scotia*, 4th edition. Lockeport, NS: Roseway.

Larsen, Tord. 1983. "Negotiating Identity: The Micmac of Nova Scotia." In *The Politics of Indianness: Case Studies of Native Ethnopolitics in Canada*, edited by Adrian Tanner, 37–136. St. John's: Memorial University of Newfoundland.

Maillard, Pierre Antoine Simon. 1758. *An Account of the Customs and Manners of the Micmakis and Maricheets Savage Nations, Now Dependent on the Government of Cape-Breton*. London: S. Hooper and A. Morley.

McMillan, Leslie Jane. 1996. *Mi'kmawey Mawio'mi: Changing Roles of the Mi'kmaq Grand Council from the Early Seventeenth Century to the Present*. MA Thesis, Dalhousie University.

McMillan, Leslie Jane. 2018. *Truth and Conviction: Donald Marshall Jr. and the Mi'kmaw Quest for Justice*. Vancouver: University of British Columbia Press.

Mihesuah, Devon A. 2001. "Anna Mae Pictou-Aquash: An American Indian Activist." In *Sifters: Native American Women's Lives*, edited by Theda Perdue, 204–222. New York: Oxford University Press.

Moore, Angel. 2020. "Respected Chief Leaves Two Mi'kmaw Political Organizations Because of 'Distrust' Over Moderate Livelihood Plans." APTN National News, October 28. www.aptnnews.ca/national-news/respected-chief-leaves-two-mikmaw-political-organizations-because-of-distrust-over-moderate-livelihood-plans

Paul, Daniel N. 2007 [1993]. *We Were not the Savages: Collision Between European and Native American Civilizations, 3rd edition*. Halifax, N.S.: Fernwood.

Philpot, Hamlet S. 1930. *The Province of Nova Scotia, Canada: Resource and Development, Fourth Edition*. Ottawa, ON: F. A. Acland, King's Printer (for Department of the Interior, National Development Bureau).

Poliandri, Simone. 2003. "Mi'kmaw People and Tradition: Indian Brook Lobster Fishing in St. Mary's Bay, Nova Scotia." In *Papers of the Thirty-Fourth Algonquian Conference*, edited by H. C. Wolfart, 303–310. Winnipeg: University of Manitoba.

Poliandri, Simone. 2011. *First Nations, Identity, and Reserve Life: The Mi'kmaq of Nova Scotia*. Lincoln: University of Nebraska Press.

Poliandri, Simone. 2016. "The Mi'kmaw Path to First Nationhood: A Roadmap, Some Strategies, and a Few Effective Shortcuts." In *Native American Nationalism and Nation Re-building: Past and Present Cases*, edited by Simone Poliandri, 93–122. Albany, NY: SUNY Press.

Poliandri, Simone. 2017. "Surviving as Mi'kmaq and First Nations People: The Legacies of the Shubenacadie Indian Residential School in Nova Scotia." In *Power Through Testimony: Reframing Residential Schools in the Age of Reconciliation*, edited by Brieg Capitaine and Karine Vanthuyne, 113–134. Vancouver: University of British Columbia Press.

Prins, Harald E. L. 1996. *The Mi'kmaq: Resistance, Accommodation, and Cultural Survival*. Fort Worth, TX: Harcourt Brace College Publishers.

Prins, Harald E. L. 1996a. "Tribal Networks and Migrant Labor: Mi'kmaq Indians as Seasonal Workers in Aroostook's Potato Fields, 1870–1980." In *Native Americans and Wage Labor: Ethnohistorical Perspectives*, edited by Alice Littlefield and Martha C. Knack, 45–65, 274–276. Norman: University of Oklahoma Press.

Prins, Harald E. L. 2002. "The Crooked Path of Dummer's Treaty: Anglo-Wabanaki Diplomacy and the Quest for Aboriginal Rights." In *Papers of the Thirty-Third Algonquian Conference*, edited by H. C. Wolfart, 360–377. Winnipeg: University of Manitoba Press.

Reid, Jennifer. 1995. *Myth, Symbol, and Colonial Encounter: British and Mi'kmaq in Acadia, 1700–1867*. Ottawa: University of Ottawa Press.

Riley, Angela R. 2007. "Good (Native) Governance." *Columbia Law Review* 107, no. 5: 1049–1125.

Shadian, Jessica M. 2018. "Navigating Political Borders Old and New: The Territoriality of Indigenous Inuit Governance." *Journal of Borderlands Studies* 33, no. 2: 273–288.

Speck, Frank. 1915. "The Eastern Algonkian Wabanaki Confederacy." *American Anthropologist* 17, no. 3: 492–508.

Ting, Helen. 2008. "Social Construction of Nation: A Theoretical Exploration." *Nationalism and Ethnic Politics* 14, no. 3: 453–482.

Union of Nova Scotia Indians (UNSI), Confederacy of Mainland Mi'kmaq (CMM), and Native Council of Nova Scotia (NCNS). 2007. *The Mi'kmaw Resource Guide. 4th Edition*. Truro, N.S.: Eastern Woodland Publishing.

Wallis, Wilson D., and Ruth Sawtell Wallis. 1953. "Culture Loss and Culture Change among the Micmac of the Canadian Maritime Provinces, 1912–1950." *Kroeber Anthropological Society Papers* 8: 100–129.

Whitehead, Ruth H. 1991. *The Old Man Told Us: Excerpts from Mi'kmaw History 1500–1950*. Halifax, N.S.: Nimbus.

Wicken, William C. 2002. *Mi'kmaq Treaties on Trial: History, Land, and Donald Marshall Junior*. Toronto: University of Toronto Press.

6

Rethinking Mexican Nationalism
Mestizaje, Indigenous Peoples, and Zapatismo

NEIL HARVEY AND DOLORES TREVIZO

This chapter argues that revolutionary nationalism in Mexico fashioned a multilayered national identity from post-colonial, post-revolutionary, anti-imperialist ideas linked to a positive re-interpretation of the *mestizo*, or mixed-race person. Mestizaje was celebrated in the twentieth century as the essence of Mexicanidad and the reinterpretation of racial mixing as synthesis symbolically embraced Indigenous identities in ways that were not meaningless. Symbols matter, and the recognition of indigeneity as a constitutive part of Mexicanidad over the course of time made possible significant public support for various indigenous autonomy movements in Chiapas and Guerrero, for example. Full constitutional recognition, however, has remained elusive, in large part due to the priority given by the federal government to the promotion of extractive industries and infrastructure projects which undermine Indigenous peoples' ability to pursue their own forms of development. These contradictions have become more politically salient due to the effects of neoliberal economic reforms since the 1980s, the impacts of the Zapatista uprising in Chiapas in 1994, and the current threats to Indigenous lands and cultures (posed by violent criminal organizations and large-scale development projects).

We begin with the historical context of the 1910 Revolution as well as a description of the way that the new official nationalist discourse of *mestizaje* (or racial mixing) informed social policy in the twentieth century. Subsequent sections explain the importance of land reform and state policy toward Indigenous peoples (*indigenismo*) for nation-building in the twentieth century, as well as the ruptures with *indigenismo* that emerged in the 1980s that led to the struggle for Indigenous rights best exemplified by the Zapatista uprising of 1994 and its subsequent development. We conclude that, while the Revolution's signature land reform program contributed to Mexico's relatively successful nation-building, its contradictions have been critiqued by Indigenous peoples seeking a more inclusive and socially just Mexico.

The Mexican Revolution and Revolutionary Nationalism

After ten years of civil war that began in 1910, Mexico's revolutionaries ushered a hegemonic variant of autocracy that, for all its failures, succeeded at nation-building during much of the twentieth century. This stands in contrast to the failure of nation-building in the period of political and economic instability that followed the wars of independence from Spain (1810–1821) a century earlier. The wars of independence resulted in the destruction of mines and agricultural fields and undermined the economy for many decades, while Catholicism, political differences over type of government, as well as racism against Indigenous people fueled conflict in the immediate post-colonial period.

The new political elites of the early nineteenth century—Mexico-born Spanish descendants called *criollos*—did little to integrate the thousands of small and linguistically distinct Indigenous *pueblos* into the nation. Further, for much of the nineteenth century, governance proved extremely unstable with various revolts, counter-revolts, a (failed) Spanish Reconquista effort, a short war with France, Texan independence, and the loss of roughly half of Mexico's territory to the United States following the war.[1] All of this before a new three-year civil war (1858–1861) that was almost immediately followed by a five-year French occupation replete with a new European monarch (an Austrian archduke, Ferdinand Maximilian of Hapsburg).[2] The perpetual conflict kept Mexico's treasury near bankruptcy throughout much of the nineteenth century, which meant that basic infrastructure—such as roads, railways, and schools[3]—would not be initiated until the last decades of the nineteenth century.

Consequently, few possibilities existed of connecting the geographically distant and linguistically diverse peoples of a rather large territory. Though Spanish was spoken in the larger rural towns and certainly in the urban centers, the language remained largely unknown in the Indigenous pueblos. Thus, by the end of a long dictatorship referred to as the Porfiriato (1911),[4] a national identity strong enough to displace the *patria chica* identification of villagers had yet to emerge in what was a rural, spatially dispersed, largely illiterate, and grossly unequal society.

Nation-building developed in the context of a social revolution that began in 1910. Given that violent flare-ups after 1920 were put down rather quickly, the civil war lasted about ten years and killed between 1.5 and two million people.[5] That most of the fighting was conducted by tens of thousands of landless peons, sharecroppers, dispossessed *serranos* (mountain folk), small peasant proprietors, rural villagers, as well as some urban workers, partly explains why the basic demands of the mostly rural masses would eventually be addressed. Put differently, reconstruction would require social policy that would demobilize the largely rural popular armies. We argue that some of Mexico's nation-building successes during the twentieth century were attributable to the 1917 Constitution that enshrined many social rights—some of them achieved through the redistribution of privately owned rural property—and laid the foundation for further meaningful social policy.

During Reconstruction, revolutionary leaders mythologized the civil war's martyrs and promised that their sacrifices would contribute to a more democratic and socially just Mexico. An emerging revolutionary nationalism also infused the goals of reconstruction and post-revolutionary state-building with a political vision informed by a three-hundred-year history of colonial subjugation, a short French occupation, as well as violent imperialist interventions by the United States, including one permitted by the dictator Porfirio Díaz against striking miners at the American owned Cananea Consolidated Copper Company in 1906. Liberal ideas calling for effective suffrage (for men) and no re-election; anti-clerical and/or socialist ideas favoring social reform, secular education, and the redistribution of resources; as well as a mix of agrarianist and indigenist ideas calling for land reform, all informed the reconstruction agenda. As did the memory of constant civil strife in the nineteenth century. The middle-class liberals who wrote the Constitution of 1917 understood they could not achieve democracy without social peace and that, in turn, required substantive social reforms. Thus, new laws enshrined economic and social rights by promising land to those who needed it, by codifying labor rights (with a living wage provision), educational and health rights, as well as by guaranteeing social welfare.

Mexico's Constitution also stipulated that land, water, and subsoil resources (e.g., mineral and oil deposits) belong to the nation. This led some presidents to use powerful eminent domain laws to expropriate land and oil concessions owned by foreign companies, including Americans. One of the most notable examples was President Lázaro Cárdenas's nationalization of the holdings of several foreign-owned oil companies in 1938 to establish what would become a state-owned petroleum company called PEMEX. This nationalization was widely perceived as an anti-imperialist reaction to foreigners who exploited Mexican workers with labor practices that violated Mexican law. Over time, the anti-imperialist motives of the expropriations led to richer arguments favoring economic independence from powerful countries, especially the United States, and the expropriation of land owned by foreigners continued intermittently through the 1970s.[6]

To end the country's dependency on foreign investors and trade, post-revolutionary governments also embraced Import Substitution Industrialization (ISI) for over forty years (1940s–1982). The ISI model of development sought to promote national industrial growth, generate employment, and improve the standard of living of Mexicans rather than serve the interests of foreigners. To this end, foreign ownership was limited to 49 percent of Mexican firms and foreign investment was subject to the approval of the Ministry of Foreign Relations. ISI policies also included import quotas, tariffs, and strict licensing procedures, and prohibited foreign oil and banking companies from investing in Mexico. To achieve national self-sufficiency, the state itself promoted industrial development by building roads, ports, dams, airports, railroads, and electric power and irrigation systems. Officials even experimented with mass communication through state-owned radio stations. The state also extended credit to both agricultural and industrial producers, and offered potential investors tax exemptions. Between 1940 and 1970, the state's role in the economy was estimated to be roughly "41 percent of [all] capital formation."[7] For about thirty years, ISI economic policies led to a robust annual average growth rate of close to 6 percent.

To be clear, economically powerful foreigners were not the main target of the revolutionaries of 1910. While it is true that during the military phase of the revolution the popular armies sometimes targeted shopkeeper or hacendado *gachupines* (Spanish immigrants), these actions reflected smoldering post-colonial ethnic resentments against Spaniards and their Mexico-born descendants, *criollos*.[8] While the wars for independence from Spain had been won in 1821, three hundred years of Spanish rule left a legacy of an ethnic-supremacist ideology that contributed to the political and economic inequalities that morally outraged the masses in 1910. To dismantle such inequalities, revolutionaries created a constitution that would, in theory, deliver a representative democracy. Regarding economic inequalities, President Lázaro Cárdenas (a former General) went so far as to exclude Mexico's businessmen from representation in the dominant party on the grounds that their interests were particularistic, thus defining business people as partly responsible for Mexico's stark inequalities.[9]

Land Reform, *Indigenismo*, *Mestizaje*, and Nation-Building in Twentieth-Century Mexico

Further, to prevent the re-emergence of the *latifundio*, the grossly unequal landed estates that had inspired the moral outrage of many revolutionaries, constitutional law targeted landed elites—most of whom were Mexico born—by limiting the extent of rural property. Land holdings that exceeded legal caps were vulnerable to expropriation by the state for redistribution to those who could prove they needed it. Put differently, while owners of most private property in Mexico would have the typical rights to sell, rent, mortgage, and bequeath, owners of rural property would be constrained by land cap rules designed for "small holders" (small proprietors called *pequeños propietarios*). Until the 1990s, the state had the power to expropriate land from proprietors who exceeded the legal caps in order to redistribute the excess land to proximate landless, or nearly landless, rural communities. By the end of his term in 1940, President Cárdenas redistributed forty-nine million acres of land, and roughly a third of all eligible Mexicans received land from the state during this period. Further, because constitutional law promised land to the landless, the law itself created incentives for rural people to invade large private proprieties in the hopes of triggering land reform. It was in response to such invasions that Luis Echeverría redistributed millions of hectares of expropriated land by the end of his term in 1976. If land reform waxed and waned according to presidential term, total land (and water) resources redistributions proved substantive over time and did not end until the last years of the twentieth century.

It is important to note that land redistributions typically came in the form of collective property that resembled pre-capitalist indigenous forms of landholding, and such property forms proved central to nation-building, including among Indigenous communities. Whether as the collective *ejido* or the Indigenous *comunidad*, these types of property were possessed, not owned, which means that for much of the twentieth century they remained inalienable. Until a constitutional reform in 1992, neither form of property could be legally sold, rented, or mortgaged. By the end of Luis Echeverria's presidency in 1976, nearly half of the country's arable land was redistributed to previously landless people, mostly as collective *ejidos* but also, if to a lesser degree, as Indigenous *comunidades*. Further, agrarian law (Article 199) gave Indigenous people legal preference in land redistribution through the restitution law.[10] It also allowed *comunidades* greater forms of political and economic autonomy from local and national authorities.[11] In practice, Indigenous folks received land under both legal forms, and the state gave peasants in both *ejidos* and *comunidades* green revolution technologies such as seeds and fertilizer. Similarly, in the 1970s, government passed new legislation that encouraged small producers to create cooperative unions that would be eligible for preferential credits, technical assistance, and marketing channels to overcome the lack of capital and the dependence on local usurers and corrupt merchants. The state also subsidized peasant consumption by creating a food company, Conasupo, which sold basic staples at subsidized prices during the 1970s (thus, the opposite of the *Tienda de Raya* that had kept peons in perpetual debt servitude in the late nineteenth century through the first decade of the twentieth).

The state's direct role in supporting agricultural production and peasant consumption may have been partly inspired by agrarianist and indigenist ideas about landholding, but it also facilitated the political control of rural folk. For example, peasants were also required to affiliate with the ruling party's corporatist peasant organization, the Confederación Nacional Campesina, (CNC) created in 1938. But even though the *ejidos* and the compulsory peasant association were tools for the state's political control, land redistribution and state subsidies led many communities to produce and, therefore, to reproduce themselves, including culturally. While many produced only for their family's subsistence, some communities could market a surplus. Rapid demographic growth eventually put pressure on the land, which led to a profound subsistence crisis by the late 1960s. This, in turn, led to rural out-migration, whether to urban centers within Mexico or to the United States. Still, many subsistence producers survived even in this context and, in so doing, also reproduced their languages and other cultural practices by virtue of their control of land. Land reform, along with the state's provision of fertilizer, seeds, and other benefits to peasants, are some of the reasons that rural people continuously voted for the party that ruled Mexico for seventy-one years.

Revolutionary and post-revolutionary governments not only sought social peace and political control through land redistribution, they also sought to forge a national community. To do so, they re-articulated a Mexican identity in a way that centered the popular classes. To center workers and especially peasants, officials and intellectuals reinterpreted the old colonial notion of mestizaje, or "racial" mixing, in a more positive light than during the colonial period. While the meanings associated with the mestizo category had never been static,[12] the hierarchical connotations that defined whites as civilized and superior did not disappear in the post-colonial context. But during Reconstruction, revolutionaries linked various intellectual trends (including eugenics) to produce a positive reinterpretation of "mestizaje" that explicitly excluded the association with mongrelization it had during Spanish rule. The new emphasis on synthesis as a form of "upbreeding" was advanced with the concept of a "cosmic race" famously articulated by Mexican philosopher and politician José Vasconcelos. In the revolutionary nationalist re-articulation, the people of the popular classes—the vast majority—were defined as mestizos who differed from the white colonial or post-colonial *gachupines* or *criollos*; they were also different from imperialist *"yanqui,"* or *"gringos,"*[13] as well as from Mexican *latifundistas and caciques* (strongmen).

Since roughly 29 percent of the population spoke an Indigenous language in 1921,[14] and since for a hundred years (since 1821) Afromexicans had been described as disappearing as a "racially" distinct group,[15] mestizaje was presumed to reflect a mixture of primarily European and Indigenous lineages. In other words, the nation-building project of the early twentieth century did not take into account Afromexicans in part because they were perceived to exemplify prior successful assimilation (or absorption) through racial mixing.[16] Afrodescendent people remained at the margins of the national consciousness by the time post-revolutionary governments officially repudiated racism when re-defining mestizaje nearly a hundred years later, in the early twentieth century.[17] In keeping with the ideal of non-racism in a post-racial society, their censuses did not count Afromexicans who, in turn, would remain demographically invisible until 2015. When ethnographers recognized actually existing Afromexican communities in the twentieth and twenty-first centuries (in Veracruz, Guerrero, and Oaxaca, for example), they were treated as regional "cultural" legacies of a distant Colonial past, or as foreign. Either label rendered Afromexicans anomalies to be explained.[18] Put differently, the post-racial claims of the official cosmic (mixed-)race ideology resulted in the exclusion of over two million Afrodescendent peoples in the twentieth century "from most local, regional and national expressions of race and nation."[19]

At the same time, as noted, the positive reinterpretation of the mestizo category in the "mestizophilia"[20] of the first half of the twentieth century innovated by celebrating indigeneity. It did so, for example, in the country's literature, muralist movement, and music of the 1920s and 1930s. The latter two genres are good examples of public art aimed at non-elites, including the non-literate. This celebration is also evident in Mexican anthropological studies, archeological excavations, and national museums. Indeed, the commitment to highlighting indigenism in mestizaje extended to state-building itself with the creation of the Instituto Nacional Indigenista (INI) in 1948. While it is true that the INI's original mission was assimilationist, its policies evolved over time. The twentieth-century revolutionary nationalist embrace of indigeneity did not, in short, lead to the disappearance of Indigenous communities. Instead, because indigeneity is declared a constitutive part of Mexican bodies, Indigenous communities are defined as members of the nation, at least symbolically. Such a portrayal made Mexico distinct in that national identity did not exclude indigeneity in the same way that was evident in Chile or Argentina. Still, the reinterpretation of mestizaje in Mexico itself could produce racist effects by eliding the fact that many Indigenous communities in the post-revolutionary period were neither mestizo nor interested in becoming quasi-Spanish, or Europeanized.

The anti-racist stance implied by the idea of mestizaje proved pernicious in other ways. Mexico's liberal rejection of race and racism during the nineteenth and early twentieth centuries[21] obscures the persistence of discrimination based on skin pigmentation up to the present. Colorism not only continues to privilege whites (in education, jobs, and marriage partners), but the incessant focus on pigmentation (described as a "prieta-o-metro" [or, dark-o-meter] by some) produces socially toxic distinctions about beauty, intelligence, and worth even within families.[22] If colorism overvalues Whiteness and devalues darker pigmentation, it also specifically denigrates blackness in many ways,[23] including the perception of black bodies as flawed.[24] Consequently, Afromexicans in Veracruz acknowledge African lineage by emphasizing mestizaje, referring to themselves as *moreno* (mixed but dark), rather than *negro* (black).[25] Afrodescendent people from (San Nicolás) Guerrero similarly refer to themselves as *moreno*, not *negro*, to signal the Mexican authenticity conferred by the Indian ancestry of their mixed-race status.[26] In sum, the prejudices experienced by many contradicts the Mexican ideal of a post-racial society. It shows that despite the "invested denial" of racism, prejudice exists in Mexico but is obscured by the "normative identity of mestizo as the national identity."[27] Since the topic of race is generally eschewed, colorism remains endemic and, like the specificity of antiblack bias, it is difficult to confront.

Yet despite the everyday degradations still produced by colorism and racism, many Afromexican communities identify with both mestizaje and *Mexicanidad* in ways that suggest not only ideological "contradictions"[28] but also a meaningful sense of national belonging. Indeed, we argue that the official nationalist emphasis on the mestizo "synthesis" was not only romantic, patronizing, white-washing, racist, and not always empirically correct—it also enabled multiculturalism over the long term,[29] and did so especially for Indigenous groups. As noted, Indigenous rights were codified in the constitution in ways that proved substantive, if incomplete. Since Mexico was a multilingual and mostly rural society until about 1960, officials worked to integrate geographically distant folk—including those living in Indigenous communities—into the nation through various educational and cultural outreach programs.

Beginning in the 1920s, for example, government officials distributed radios and loudspeakers to rural schools and in working-class neighborhoods.[30] Mestizo men were to provide for their families, while mestizo women were instructed over radio on how to clean their homes to raise healthy children that would develop into strong, productive, modern citizens and quasi-citizens (regional variation notwithstanding, women did not have the right to vote until 1953). Radio broadcasting expanded in the 1930s, and officials maintained their ability to influence the political and cultural content even of commercial radio for decades.[31] The government also sometimes aired their own state-run radio broadcasts to evoke the nation civically, politically, and, as Hayes observed, culturally. To create a national "panorama" view, for example, state-owned radio stations broadcast music from different parts of the country to redefine multiple local genres as "authentic" expressions of *Mexicanidad*.[32] In this way, the government manufactured a shared nostalgia.[33] The cultural revolution that Hayes argued culminated in a "radio nation" became a model for commercial radio, cinema, and television. All of these mass communication tools articulated a "national mythology" about Mexicanidad.[34] Even when they did not own radio and television stations, the government maintained strong regulatory control and the ability to influence the content of mass media, including in newspapers.

In addition to the indigenism observed in the mestizophilia of the twentieth century, Mexico's revolutionary nationalism was inspired by various socialist visions of progress. As noted, the constitution of 1917 stipulated that education would be free and secular, and José Vasconcelos indeed focused on creating rural schools when he became Minister of public education (in 1921). In just four years, the state built over one thousand rural schools between 1920 and 1924, and further resourced two thousand small libraries by 1924. Vasconcelos sent teachers (on horseback and mules) to hundreds of isolated and inaccessible hamlets that lacked potable water and electricity. His goal was to integrate Indigenous people into the nation by instructing them in Spanish as well as hygiene. Children would be taught writing, reading, mathematics, geography, history, agriculture, pedagogy, and hygiene. By the middle of the 1920s, the Ministry of Public Education used radio broadcasts for educational purposes. For his part, President Lázaro Cárdenas (1934–1940) similarly opened hundreds of rural schools, and his investment in rural education was double what it was in the urban centers. In addition to focusing on teachers' salaries, Cárdenas approved a curriculum that would include some socialist ideals. If future presidents would be less focused on rural education, many still promoted literacy.

Despite rapid demographic growth and the kind of grinding poverty that compels children to leave school to work (to help their parents), Mexico eventually saw some educational progress. However slowly and unevenly, Mexico's literacy rate among people fifteen years of age and older increased over time. Recent data show that the "percentage of illiterate people 15 years old and over, decreased from 26 percent to 7 percent between 1970 and 2010."[35] It is fair to conclude that real—albeit slow, spatially uneven, and still insufficient—educational gains have occurred in the country since the early twentieth century. While improved relative to the early twentieth century, the educational gaps that remain are especially large in the rural areas and even more so among Indigenous peoples who have remained at the bottom of Mexico's grossly unequal income distribution.

Notwithstanding Mexico's Constitution's claims about health "rights," access to health services remains limited, and especially so in the rural and indigenous areas. President Calles (1924–1928) created the Ministry of Public Health and initiated a mass vaccination campaign that inoculated over five million people against smallpox in 1926. Ongoing public health campaigns that emphasized hygiene in the schools and on daily radio broadcasts may very well have contributed to improving life expectancy over time. In addition, infant mortality rates dropped from 222 in 1920, to 125 in 1940, and to 36.2 in 1990 per thousand live births. Since Mexico's transition to democracy in 2000, access to health care improved by 37 percentage points by 2020.[36] And infant mortality rates continue to drop in the democracy period, from 23.6 in 2000, to 13.9 deaths per thousand live births in 2015, according to the World Bank. But as noted, access to basic medical care remains exceptionally challenging in the rural and especially Indigenous communities.

Such health gains contributed to the country's postwar demographic growth, one that was especially rapid during the 1960s. Industrial development could not keep pace with a growing labor force and, thus, the economic "miracle" created by ISI economic policies could not solve the country's enduring inequality. A worsening land-to-labor ratio led to growing landlessness in the countryside in the late 1960s and to high unemployment and underemployment in the urban centers by the early 1970s. President Luis Echeverría (1970–1976) responded with a return to statist policies that increased the state's involvement in production and redistribution of goods by fourteen-fold. While the state had previously owned and operated the national oil company (PEMEX), railroads, and electricity, state ownership of firms jumped to 1,155 companies. Notwithstanding the nationalist and populist rhetoric that justified increasing state intervention in the economy, the government's expenditures were paid for by borrowing from foreign commercial banks. Thus, Luis Echeverría not only gave full substantive meaning to the revolutionary idea of a mixed economy, but he also dramatically increased public foreign debt from $4.2 billion in 1970, to $20 billion in 1976.

The economy did not recover quickly from the debt default of 1982, and the ruling party's hegemony waned as the public coffers emptied. As importantly, the government's use of politically motivated repression to manage increasing levels of social unrest since the late 1960s further undermined the state's legitimacy. Over time, peasants, workers, and middle-class sectors—including women, business people, doctors, teachers, and especially students—would reject the state's political control of all groups in civil society. For their part, workers and peasants understood that some of their (limited) social rights were delivered through compulsory corporatist organizations affiliated with the ruling party that had been in power for most of the twentieth century. Further, the same party that had concentrated the power of the presidency began to privatize the economy, including by passing the constitutional reforms necessary to legally privatize collective rural property by the 1990s. The emerging neoliberal authoritarian state would be challenged by short, but armed, Indigenous peasant uprisings, first in Chiapas and later, on a smaller scale, in Guerrero. These two rural states have large numbers of extremely poor Indigenous peoples who rejected the state's turn to neoliberal policies.

The Decline of *Indigenismo* and the Struggle for Indigenous Rights

The state's adoption of neoliberal policies underscored that Mexican indigenism and discourse of *mestizaje* tended to reflect a top-down approach that helped build an increasingly authoritarian state led by the dominant Institutional Revolutionary Party (PRI). For Mexico's Indigenous peoples, PRI rule combined a particular mix of carrots and sticks in order to gain political control in the often remote, poor, and rural areas of southern states such as Chiapas, Oaxaca, and Guerrero. Recall that one of the PRI government's main "carrots" was land reform, or at least its promise.

Land reform itself was bitterly resisted by local landowners who also controlled to varying degrees the structures and occupants of municipal and state government. Thus, while artists and intellectuals were portraying a new nation based on pride in its indigenous past and its mestizo present, local *caciques* (strongmen) were busily blocking reform efforts and turning to violent means to suppress Indigenous community leaders who insisted on their rightful claims to the reforms promised by the very same revolution depicted in murals, novels, and speeches. Contradictions such as these gave rise to a series of ruptures with indigenismo as a form of statecraft, opening the way for other, post-indigenista projects to emerge in the following decade, to which the Zapatista uprising gave a major impetus. It is important to note, however, that none of the post-indigenista projects, not even the armed uprisings, sought national independence.

As peasants and Indigenous communities began to self-organize in response to local caciques or to their subsistence crisis, the state responded with either repression or with measures to co-opt peasant movements. For example, officials created a variety of new national level organizations such as the National Council of Indigenous Peoples (CNPI). The CNPI was created as the indigenous wing of the PRI-affiliated National Peasant Confederation (CNC) in 1975 as part of a new round of state-led indigenous assimilation policies or *indigenismo*.[37]

Such initiatives formed part of what we have already noted about Mexico's mestizo nationalism—they promised integration and equality without any formal or legal discrimination—but they also served the goals of a dominant party in an authoritarian state. As such, they were top-down measures designed to undermine potential support for more radical rural opposition while simultaneously co-opting a new generation of Indigenous community leaders who had been fighting against sub-national powerbrokers and corrupt local officials for many years. The opportunities provided by new state-run agencies in indigenous areas of Guerrero, Oaxaca, and Chiapas—for example, of the Mexican Coffee Institute, INMECAFE (founded in 1973), or the Rural Credit Bank (BANRURAL)—were important in that they did provide access to capital, technical assistance, and marketing channels for many rural and Indigenous communities, particularly those that were well organized and had support from advisers committed to social justice in Mexico in the post-1968 era.[38]

What is significant about this point is that, as noted earlier, the official emphasis on the mestizo "synthesis" was contradictory. On the one hand, its intent was to serve the goals of the PRI government and, through co-optation and repression, limit the potential for more independent rural social movements to grow. On the other hand, however, the creation of these new agencies, programs, and discourses of *indigenismo* limited the state's ability to counter demands for Indigenous rights and a recasting of Mexican national identity in a more democratic, inclusive, and multicultural way. For this recasting to happen, several moments of rupture had to occur—as they did in the 1980s and early 1990s.

The first of these ruptures was the creation of national networks of rural and Indigenous peoples outside of the control of the PRI and its official confederations (such as the CNC) or even the newer organizations such as the above-mentioned CNPI. Several independent organizations gathered strength and national presence in the late 1970s and until the early 1990s, including the mostly indigenous-based National Plan de Ayala Network (CNPA, formed in 1979 and grouping more than twenty regional organizations at its height in 1981). By "independent," we mean organizations that did not have ties to the PRI and the government; some, not all, had relations with leftists, or with the liberation theology wing of the Catholic Church, but they all tended to share the desire to demand rights rather than petition for favors in the traditionally clientelistic pattern of Mexican politics, especially in rural areas. The CNPA became one of the most combative networks of rural organizations in the 1980s, especially in Chiapas, Oaxaca, and Guerrero. Repression of its local members by state police, military, and rural bosses attracted the attention of human rights observers, including Amnesty International, whose 1986 report documented arbitrary arrests, torture, and extra-judicial killings of Indigenous community leaders in southern Mexico.

The second break came when many peasant and Indigenous communities had to mobilize against the austerity cuts that arose from the 1982 debt crisis. No sooner had the new agencies of rural development been established, it seemed, than their funding and ability to provide services were under threat. Structural Adjustment Programs designed by the World Bank and implemented by the Mexican government as part of the shift to neoliberal economic policy impacted small producers quite dramatically. For example, in 1989, in the face of collapse in global coffee prices, the Mexican government failed to intervene to uphold guaranteed prices to small producers and began instead to dismantle INMECAFE, cut back on technical assistance, and abandon such producers to the vagaries of the market.

Finally, a third rupture in the 1980s concerned the place of Indigenous cultures in the Mexican nation. We noted how the Mexican Revolution was vital for establishing a new set of values to support a process of nation-building based on the ideology of racial mixing, or *mestizaje*. Consolidation of *mestizaje* required a complex and often contradictory appeal to the presence of Indigenous cultures, and the state-led programs of integration known as *indigenismo* were central to this process. However, such efforts were subjected to criticism in the 1970s by a new generation of Mexican social scientists and anthropologists who, as participants in the broader struggle for democratization, rejected *indigenismo* as a legitimizing tool for continued domination by the PRI regime.[39] The critique of the assimilationist goals of *indigenismo* was particularly well expressed by Guillermo Bonfil Batalla in his 1987 book *México Profundo: La negación de una civilización*, in which he describes a cultural split between "imaginary Mexico" and "deep Mexico," the former referring to the urban-based, modern, and Westernized culture of the wealthier groups that dominate government, business, and universities, while the latter is rooted in Mexico's Indigenous cultures which, although central to the identity of millions of Mexicans, are subordinated and marked as inferior by the leaders of "imaginary Mexico." For Bonfil Batalla, such a societal division was unsustainable and called for reforms that would allow for greater recognition of Indigenous cultures, rather than conveniently celebrating their pre-Hispanic past while ignoring their ongoing presence and their future aspirations.[40]

Such challenges to *indigenismo* manifested themselves at the level of the main government agency responsible for assimilation—namely, the National *Indigenista* Institute. Within the INI's regional centers conflicts emerged between a new generation of employees, including activists imbued with theories of social change drawn from Marxism and anti-colonialism, and the older generation of leaders reluctant to question their intellectual assumptions or their relationship to the public officials of the PRI regime and the President of the Republic. Such conflicts arose at the same time as demands for recognition and promotion of Indigenous languages and cultures were being put forward by newly trained Indigenous, bilingual teachers. As agents of the state's modernizing efforts in education and health, Indigenous officials occupied the contradictory space between *indigenismo* and a more independent, community-based expression of aspirations and demands. The formation of the National Alliance of Bilingual Indigenous Professionals (ANPIBAC) in 1977 by officials within the INI and the Ministry of Public Education (SEP) set the stage for a series of demands to ensure education not only in Spanish but also in indigenous languages as part of the state's obligations in the realm of public education.

Multiculturalism, Neoliberalism, and the Zapatista Uprising of 1994

By the time the Mexican government began to grant legal recognition of the multi-ethnic composition of the nation, several of the processes noted above had also created the conditions to go beyond these official steps. In 1990, just two years after one of Mexico's most fraudulent elections, then President Carlos Salinas de Gortari announced the ratification of an important framework in international law known as the Convention 169 of the International Labor Organization (ILO), referred to as the Indigenous and Tribal Peoples' Convention. This convention had initially come into being in 1957 with an explicitly assimilationist goal in which nation-states gave themselves the right to paternalistically control and integrate Indigenous peoples to economic and social modernization projects that ignored the cultures and aspirations of those same peoples. Resistance to this model became more widespread internationally in the 1970s and 1980s. The reform of the ILO Convention 169 was, therefore, a product of a much broader movement for change and a recognition at the global level of the need to move beyond assimilationism and for states to uphold the rights of Indigenous peoples to choose their own paths of development within national frameworks. Mexico was one of the first countries to ratify the newly revised Convention, opening the way for reforming the relationship between the state and Indigenous peoples in ways that critics, like Bonfil Batalla and others, had been calling for in the previous two decades.

This action was followed in 1992 by the reform of Article 4 of the Mexican Constitution, which defined the nation in multicultural terms: "The Mexican nation has a multicultural composition whose origins are based on its indigenous peoples. The law will protect and promote the development of their languages, cultures, practices, customs, resources and specific forms of social organization and it will guarantee indigenous people effective access to the jurisdiction of the State. In those agrarian procedures and court hearings in which they participate, their juridical practices and customs will be taken into account in the terms established by the law." However, in the same year, 1992, another constitutional reform would have a more far-reaching impact. This refers to Article 27 which, since the close of the Mexican Revolution in 1917, had permitted landless peasants to organize and solicit from the state the redistribution of large, private landholdings to rural and Indigenous communities. The reform to Article 27 of the Constitution in 1992 made possible the privatization of communal property that we described earlier. The Mexican government also argued that land redistribution had reached its end and that those producers who had received communal lands should be given the freedom to sell their plots and enter into association with private investors. The reform came in the context of President Salinas's push to open up Mexico to foreign investment and to remove tariffs on trade by negotiating the North American Free Trade Agreement (NAFTA) with the United States and Canada. Salinas believed that Mexico could provide foreign investors with more confidence that the state would facilitate rather than constrain capitalist enterprises in the rural sector by ending land reform and communal property.

The official support for a multicultural Mexico was therefore accompanied by economic reforms that, by threatening the continuity of communally held lands, called into question the State's commitment to "protect and promote the development of [Indigenous peoples'] languages and cultures." The end of land redistribution was particularly controversial in areas where landlessness remained high and where a long backlog of petitions for land had not been resolved. Such was the case in Chiapas where the younger generation of Indigenous Mayans no longer had legal channels through which they could petition for land. In this context, many joined the indigenous-based and clandestinely organized Zapatista Army of National Liberation (EZLN) in the late 1980s and early 1990s. It was in response to the reforms to Article 27, as well as the collapse in coffee prices and the general dismantling of government support for the rural poor, that the EZLN, or Zapatistas, argued they had been left no choice but to rise up in arms against the Mexican government on January 1, 1994.[41]

Their uprising occurred on the same day that NAFTA came into effect. As the poorly armed Zapatistas seized six municipal seats in highland and eastern Chiapas, they shattered the dream of those at the top of "imaginary

Mexico" who were preparing to celebrate the country's entry into the First World but instead were awakened by a loud cry from *México profundo* calling for democracy, justice, and national independence in the face of the United States. It is indicative of how much had changed during the shift to neoliberalism that, for the Zapatistas and their civilian supporters, it was the Indigenous people who were most committed to ensuring that Mexico strengthen its independence as a nation, not the technocrats and president who were prepared to hand over the nation's public resources to foreign investors in the name of modernization and regional integration.

Neoliberal Multiculturalism and Indigenous Autonomy

The simultaneous shift to neoliberal economics and the recognition of the multicultural character of the Mexican nation raised the question of how a new relationship between the state and Indigenous peoples would be forged. Mexico was not unique in this regard. Similar trends were playing out across Latin America and led some scholars to use the term "neoliberal multiculturalism"[42] to denote how Indigenous rights were limited by the macro-economic priorities of states, multilateral financial institutions, and the need to attract foreign investment. The distinction between "authorized" and "radical" indigeneity, or *el indio permitido* and *el indio tajante*, reflects how elites who control the main institutions of the state have tended to approach the challenge of multiculturalism. Indigenous people in Mexico, however, had their own ideas about the new relationship they were to forge with the state. Their vision of Indigenous rights is captured by the slogan "Never again a Mexico without us." This slogan was articulated by the newly formed National Indigenous Congress in October 1996 as it announced its support for the rights of Indigenous peoples to autonomy within the framework of the Mexican nation.[43] These words echoed those of many Indigenous people throughout Mexico who seek a more equal relationship with the rest of society and state institutions.

Thus, the ongoing activism of Indigenous communities, the ideology of *mestizaje*, and the international multicultural turn of the 1990s allowed for greater recognition of Indigenous cultures in Mexico as compared to other places in Latin America. Although the Mexican military was deployed to violently put down the Zapatistas, the fighting lasted for only twelve days as hundreds of thousands of Mexicans peacefully protested and called for an end to hostilities. The possibility for peace negotiations was great due to the legitimacy of the Zapatistas' main demands for democracy and social justice in the country, particularly, but not solely, for Indigenous peoples. This opening led to a period of talks punctuated by the government's desire to capture the EZLN's mestizo leader, *Subcomandante* Marcos, in a military offensive against Zapatista communities in February 1995. Once again Mexicans rallied in large numbers in major cities, chanting "*todos somos Marcos*" ("we are all Marcos") or "*todos somos Ramona*" ("we are all Ramona," in reference to one of several important women leaders in the EZLN).

Although the government decided to not pursue an all-out campaign of violence, it did adopt a strategy of low-intensity conflict that has sought to gradually wear down the Zapatistas and encourage Indigenous people to join pro-government organizations through which they are promised land, housing, farming equipment, and other benefits. This is akin to Hale's notion[44] of dividing communities by enforcing compliance with government policies and subjecting those who resist to the constant harassment of a superior military force. Counterinsurgency in Chiapas has, therefore, limited the opportunity to build a more equal relationship of respect between the state and Indigenous peoples, despite the broad cultural acceptance of indigeneity among the majority of Mexicans.

Such low-intensity conflict also undermined the only advance achieved in peace negotiations—the San Andrés Accords on Indigenous Rights and Cultures, which the representatives of the Zapatistas and the federal government signed in February 1996. It is important to note that these accords include many similar measures to those outlined in the ILO Convention 169, with additional input from Indigenous advisers from Oaxaca and other parts of Mexico. The accords set the stage for a new level of unity of Indigenous organizations in Mexico, many of which formed the National Indigenous Congress (CNI) in October 1996, a network of local and regional organizations that continues to be the Zapatistas' main ally among Indigenous people to the present.

The signing of these accords presented a historic opportunity for the Mexican state to deepen the rights of Indigenous peoples so they could govern themselves rather than be subordinated to non-indigenous political and economic elites. Unfortunately, the opportunity was not taken and the administration of President Ernesto Zedillo (1994–2000) failed to send the accords to Congress for the purpose of enacting the constitutional reforms that would have allowed for implementation of its measures. Instead, Chiapas saw a rise in paramilitary groups—often backed by local PRI politicians—who used the lack of political solution as an opportunity to attack and threaten Zapatistas and even non-Zapatistas who refused to collaborate in such attacks.

The years 1997–1999 were marked with many acts of paramilitary violence, including the infamous massacre of forty-five members of a pacifist group in highland Chiapas known as Las Abejas who refused to support violent actions against their Zapatista neighbors.

Another opportunity to support Indigenous rights was lost in the spring of 2001 when the national Congress watered down a proposal, based on the San Andrés Accords, to introduce new constitutional reforms. A delegation of the Zapatistas had marched from Chiapas to Mexico City to show their support for this proposal, believing they could take advantage of the fact that the PRI had lost the presidency the previous year. Although skeptical of the administration of the center-right National Action Party (PAN) and the new president, Vicente Fox, the Zapatistas felt that the changes in national government represented a chance to achieve meaningful reforms through the political system. Despite their efforts, the proposed reforms were watered down by federal senators of all the major parties, and an unsatisfactory bill finally passed. The Zapatistas, the CNI, and regional indigenous organizations all rejected the reforms as insufficient because they retained many of the paternalistic relations according to which the state would provide social programs but without allowing Indigenous peoples to implement their own plans for development in their own regions.

A form of neoliberal multiculturalism, therefore, emerged in Mexico after 2001 that attempted to co-opt some Indigenous organizations and leaders into programs to promote greater integration into the new markets opened up by globalization. The Zapatistas resisted this trend and instead deepened efforts to build alternative models at the community and regional level in Chiapas. In 2003, the EZLN announced the creation of five autonomous regional centers, known as *Caracoles*, that would serve as the site for their Councils of Good Government (*Juntas de Buen Gobierno*, or JBG).[45] Each JBG encompassed several Rebel Autonomous Zapatista Municipalities and, since 2003, has seen the rotation of leaders selected in community assemblies. More women have participated in the running of the JBGs and the various projects that have allowed the Zapatistas to sustain their autonomy and refuse any programs from the Mexican government, which are seen as attempts to undermine the Zapatistas' struggle. Resistance requires a level of commitment that is not always easy to maintain and, over the years, there has been a fluctuation in membership as some seek to find better economic opportunities outside of Chiapas or in the United States. Despite these challenges, by 2019, the Zapatistas were still able to announce the creation of seven new *Caracoles* in the central highlands of Chiapas.

In the period since their 1994 uprising, the Zapatistas have transformed their organization in several ways that help illustrate the dynamism of indigenous political movements in Mexico today. First, the EZLN quickly adopted peaceful strategies of mobilization and resistance, subordinating armed struggle to the gradual construction of autonomous spaces of government that help coordinate projects in health, education, agroecology, and justice. Second, the increasing presence and role of Indigenous women in the Zapatista movement has demonstrated the potential for reforming gender relations and empowering female leadership.[46] Third, autonomy for the Zapatistas has never meant separation from Mexico as a nation but rather separation from the structures of mestizo-led government, political parties, corporations, and other agencies that have historically treated Indigenous people as second-class citizens.

Having tried and failed to win reforms through the political system that could have changed this reality, the Zapatistas have instead focused on building alternative models of community and regional governance outside of the official institutions. Moreover, as the Mexican state has abandoned rural areas overtaken by violent criminal organizations, or has engaged in collusion with such organizations, Indigenous people who have achieved some degree of local territorial control through their autonomous systems of governance have been more able to resist encroachments by drug traffickers and other criminals on their lands. The Zapatistas' model is unique in providing such resistance, but there are other examples in Oaxaca (San Juan Copala), Guerrero (La Montaña region), and Michoacán (Cherán). As Mariana Mora has argued (2021), indigenous autonomy is proving to be a flexible tool that has led to the creation of alternative forms of community and regional governance, but it is also a vital source of protection when such forms are threatened by state and non-state actors, such as the drug cartels that operate with impunity in areas with large Indigenous populations.

In contrast to the state's ongoing assimilationist efforts toward Indigenous peoples in postrevolutionary Mexico, the invisibility of blackness meant that no similar institutions as the INI were created or developed to manage relations with Afromexican communities. As a result, the legal-institutional terrain through which Indigenous organizations could resist, challenge, and transform the ideology of mestizaje was largely unavailable for Afrodescendent groups. It was only in the late 1980s and early 1990s that critical anthropologists and advocates for black identity opened up some new spaces for the recognition of what Bonfil Batalla and others termed Mexico's "Third Root."[47] In line with the constitutional reform of 1992 that officially declared

Mexico to be a multicultural nation, Afromexican communities began to demand an end to discrimination and appealed for recognition. In response to this growing activism, the state eventually allowed for people to identify as Afrodescendent in the 2015 national census for the first time in Mexico's history as an independent republic (that is, since 1821). Similar measures of official recognition had already been passed by state governments in Oaxaca and Guerrero in part due to the efforts of community groups and civil society organizations such as *Black Mexico* (*México Negro, A.C.*). Despite these steps, most Afrodescendent Mexicans continue to suffer from discrimination and poverty with very limited access to education.[48]

Similar to Indigenous peoples' struggles, efforts to make a black presence more visible in Mexico requires not only the recognition of the important history and contributions of Afromexicans but also improvements in current living conditions and an end to the kind of discrimination and socioeconomic inequalities that persist, and which stand in stark contrast to the idea that mestizaje created a society in which racial identities and racism are absent.

Conclusions

The Mexican revolution did not accomplish its main goals of democracy and social justice, but the land reform program that came in the form of collective ejidos and comunidades succeeded in ending both debt peonage as well as the hacienda system of centuries prior. Land reform also contributed to Mexico's relatively successful nation-building. It did so because neither the embrace of indigeneity nor the positive reinterpretation of the mestizo were merely symbolic gestures. Rather, they proved substantive in terms of land reform as both ejidos and comunidades contributed to the very ability of many—but certainly not all—Indigenous groups to preserve their cultures, languages, and identities via control over land, water, and other natural resources. To date, millions of people describe themselves as Indigenous even if the percent of the population that speaks an indigenous language has dropped from 16 percent in 1930, to 6.5 percent in 2015.[49] And many Indigenous groups continue to refer to land reform and water rights decreed by former President Cárdenas during the 1930s to control territory and water resources well into the twenty-first century (for example, the Yaqui in Sonora). They do so for their livelihoods but also to preserve cultural autonomy.

The Mexican revolution thus legitimated cultural diversity in ways that proved unimaginable at first and progressive over time. Nation-building worked as evidenced in the national pride of most Mexicans. Not even an armed movement in Chiapas in the 1990s sought national independence but, rather, integration into a new, more equal, and inclusive nation. Many Mexicans therefore responded positively to the goals, if not the methods, of the Zapatistas. Indeed, in the days following the uprising in January 1994, hundreds of thousands of Mexicans participated in demonstrations in major cities calling for peace talks and an end to the government's initial military response. Partly due to this pressure, President Salinas announced a ceasefire after twelve days of fighting in which approximately 145 Zapatistas had lost their lives.

By the end of February 1994, both sides were engaged in peaceful negotiations mediated by the Bishop of the Diocese of San Cristóbal de Las Casas, Samuel Ruiz, at the town's colonial Cathedral.[50] Although these talks did not produce lasting agreements, they did reveal widespread support among Mexicans for the Zapatistas' demands for democracy and an end to the poverty, injustice, and discrimination faced by Indigenous people. People from all over Mexico traveled to Chiapas and supported the negotiations in San Cristóbal in 1994 (as well as later rounds of talks in San Andrés in 1995–1996) by forming peace cordons to protect Zapatista delegates from potential attacks. Their physical presence was a powerful show of solidarity in support of political solutions. In addition, since 1994, social movement activists from around Mexico and the world, particularly youth, students, women, and Indigenous people, have participated in numerous meetings hosted by Zapatista communities.[51] Such international connections have helped to create a new network that calls for alternatives to neoliberal globalization and nationalist ideologies alike. Within Mexico, solidarity has also been possible due to both the inclusiveness of the Zapatistas' demands and the close affinity that many Mexicans feel toward Indigenous cultures as an inextricable part of their own sense of national identity.

Despite this cultural affinity, there are many challenges ahead for ending racism, extreme poverty, and gross income inequality, especially in the rural areas and among Indigenous and Afromexicans. Although the percentage of people in extreme poverty fell from 11 percent in 2008 to 7.4 percent in 2018, nearly half of Mexico's population lives in poverty; and those in extreme poverty are disproportionately rural folk, Indigenous, and/or Afromexican. These enduring problems now combine with the absence of the rule of law that has contributed to the extraordinary violence of the twenty-first century that—in numbers of deaths per 100,000—compares to civil war levels.

Neither the revolution nor Mexico's young electoral democracy (since 2000) have been able to fix the country's extreme inequalities. One hopes the increasing awareness and recognition of the country's multicultural character, as well as the ongoing need to ground that recognition in new political agreements, will help create a path forward to benefit all of its people.

Notes

1. The presidency changed hands thirty-six times between 1833 and 1855.
2. The French were expelled in 1867, the year that Maximilian was sentenced to death.
3. Less than 1 percent of the population was in school as of 1842.
4. Porfirio Díaz ruled Mexico with an iron fist from 1876 to 1880, and then from 1884 to 1911.
5. McCaa "Missing millions," 367–400.
6. Dolores Trevizo, *Rural Protest*, 102.
7. Levy and Bruhn, *Mexico*, 152.
8. Carlos Illades, *Conflict, Domination and Violence*.
9. Roderic Camp, *Entrepreneurs and Politics*, 39.
10. Gustavo Esteva *The Struggle for Rural Mexico*, 162.
11. Ibid., 2.
12. Medina, "El mestizaje." Also see Theodore Cohen, *Finding Afro-Mexico*.
13. U.S. troops invaded Mexico twice since 1910, once in Veracruz and once in pursuit of revolutionary Pancho Villa.
14. Christina Sue, *Land of the Cosmic Race*, endnote 91, 200.
15. Cohen, 2020.
16. Although they had once been more populous than whites during the early Colonial period (1521–1640), Afromexicans constituted roughly 10 percent of the population at the start of the War of Independence in 1810 (Cohen 2020, 8–9). Believing that the law should and would treat citizens equally, without racial distinction, post-colonial Mexican governments of the nineteenth century abolished the casta categories of the colonial period, stopped keeping demographic track of Afrodescendent Mexicans in the census, and banned slavery in 1837 (Cohen 2020). This nineteenth-century liberalism predicted that mestizaje, racial mixture, would promote a raceless society (Cohen 2020).
17. Cohen, 2020.
18. Cohen, 2020.
19. Cohen, 2020, 283.

20. Stern, "Responsible Mothers and Normal Children," 389.
21. Cohen, 2020.
22. Sue, 2013.
23. Sue, 2013.
24. Figueroa, 2010.
25. Sue, 2013.
26. Lewis 2000, 899.
27. Moreno Figueroa and Saldívar Tanaka 2016: 527–528; also see Sue 2013.
28. Sue, 2013.
29. In *Finding Afro-Mexico*, Theodore Cohen offers a history of Mexico's Third Root project.
30. Joy Elizabeth Hayes, *Radio Nation*, 40–44.
31. Hayes, *Radio Nation*, 40–44.
32. Hayes, *Radio Nation*, 40–44.
33. Hayes, *Radio Nation*, 62.
34. Hayes, *Radio Nation*, xvii–11.
35. CONEVAL 2012, 116.
36. CONEVAL (2021).
37. Aída Hernández Castillo, *Histories and Stories*, 108–110.
38. Dolores Trevizo, *Rural Protest*.
39. Hernández Castillo, *Histories and Stories*, 102–114.
40. Guillermo Bonfil Batalla, *México Profundo*.
41. Neil Harvey, *The Chiapas Rebellion*.
42. Hale, "Does Multiculturalism Menace?"
43. Congreso Nacional Indígena (CNI), "Never Again."
44. Hale, "Does Multiculturalism Menace?"
45. Baronnet et al. 2011; Cerda 2011; Stahler-Sholk 2008.
46. Teresa Ortiz *Never Again a Mexico without Us*; Harvey "Practicing Autonomy," 1–24.
47. Cohen 2020, 275–279.
48. Minority Rights Group, n.d.
49. INEGI, "Estadísticas" (9 de Agosto).
50. Ana Carrigan, "Afterword."
51. Neil Harvey, 2011, "Más allá de la hegemonía."

References

Amnesty International. 1986. *Mexico: Human Rights in Rural Areas. Exchange of Documents with the Mexican Government on Human Rights Violations in Oaxaca and Chiapas*. London: Amnesty International.

Baronnet, Bruno, M. Mora, and R. Stahler-Sholk (eds.) 2011. *Luchas "muy otras": Zapatismo y autonomía en las comunidades indígenas de Chiapas*. Mexico: Universidad Autónoma Metropolitana, CIESAS & Universidad Autónoma de Chiapas.
Bonfil Batalla, Guillermo. 1996. *México Profundo: Reclaiming a Civilization*. Austin: University of Texas Press.
Camp, Roderic. 1989. *Entrepreneurs and Politics in Twentieth Century Mexico*. New York: Oxford University Press.
Carrigan, Ana. 2001. "Afterword: Chiapas, the First Postmodern Revolution," in J. Ponce de León (ed.), *Our Word Is Our Weapon: Selected Writings of Subcomandante Insurgente Marcos*. San Francisco: Seven Stories Press. 17–443.
Cerda, Alejandro. 2011. *Imaginando Zapatismo: Multiculturalidad y autonomía indígena en Chiapas desde un municipio autónomo*. México: Universidad Autónoma Metropolitana/Porrúa
Cohen, Theodore W. 2020. *Finding Afro-Mexico: Race and Nation after the Revolution*. New York: Cambridge University Press.
Consejo Nacional de Evaluación de la Política de Desarrollo Social (CONEVAL). 2010. "Carencia por acceso a los servicios de salud" Mexico City: Mexico. www.coneval.org.mx/rw/resource/coneval/med_pobreza/Acceso_a_los_servicios_de_salud_Censo_2010/Carencia_a_los_servicios_de_salud_2010.pdf
Consejo Nacional de Evaluación de la Política de Desarrollo Social (CONEVAL). 2012: "Evaluation Report on the Social Development Policy in Mexico" Mexico City: Mexico www.coneval.gob.mex
Congreso Nacional Indígena (CNI). 1996. "Never Again a Mexico without Us." www.culturalsurvival.org/publications/cultural-survival-quarterly/declaration-never-again-mexico-without-us
Esteva, Gustavo. 1983. *The Struggle for Rural Mexico*. Boston, MA: Bergin and Garvey.
Hale, Charles. 2002. "Does Multiculturalism Menace? Governance, Cultural Rights, and the Politics of Identity in Guatemala." *Journal of Latin American Studies* 34, no. 3: 485–524
Harvey, Neil. 1998. *The Chiapas Rebellion: The Struggle for Land and Democracy*. Durham, NC: Duke University Press.
Harvey, Neil. 2011. "Más allá de la hegemonía: El zapatismo y la otra política," in B Baronnet, M. Mora, and R. Stahler-Sholk (Eds.), *Luchas "muy otras": Zapatismo y autonomía en las comunidades indígenas de Chiapas*. Mexico: Universidad Autónoma Metropolitana, CIESAS & Universidad Autónoma de Chiapas. 163–190.
Harvey, Neil. 2016. "Practicing Autonomy: Zapatismo and Decolonial Liberation." *Latin American and Caribbean Ethnic Studies* 11, no. 1: 1–24.
Hayes, Joy Elizabeth. 2000. *Radio Nation: Communication, Popular Culture, and Nationalism in Mexico, 1920–1950*. Tucson: University of Arizona Press.

Hernández Castillo, Aída Rosalva. 2010. *Histories and Stories from Chiapas: Border Identities in Southern Mexico*. Austin: University of Texas Press.
Illades, Carlos. 2017. *Conflict, Domination and Violence: Episodes in Mexican Social History* New York: Berghahn Books.
INEGI 2020. "Estadísticas a Propósito Del Día Internacional de los Pueblos Indígenas (9 de Agosto)" Comunicado de Presa Núm. 392/2020 (7 de Agosto de 2020, Página 1/1).
Levy, C. Daniel, and Kathleen Bruhn. 2006. *Mexico: The Struggle for Democratic Development*. 2nd edition. Berkeley: University of California Press.
Lewis, Laura. 2000. "Blacks, Black Indians, Afromexicans: The Dynamics of Race, Nation, and Identity in a Mexican Moreno Community (Guerrero)." *American Ethnologist* 27, no. 4: 898–926.
McCaa, Robert. 2003. "Missing Millions: The Demographic Costs of the Mexican Revolution." *Mexican Studies* 19, no. 2: 367–400.
Medina, Rubén 2009. "El mestizaje a través de la frontera: Vasconcelos y Anzaldúa. *Mexican Studies/Estudios Mexicanos* 25, no. 1 (Winter 2009): 101–123.
Minority Rights Group International. 2023. "Mexico: Afro-Mexicans," *World Directory of Minorities and Indigenous Peoples*. https://minorityrights.org/minorities/afro-mexicans
Mora, Mariana. 2021. "Entre la autonomía como ejercicio propositivo y la autonomía a la defensiva: Transformaciones de sentidos políticos indígenas frente a la violencia extrema en México," in M. González et al. (eds.) *Autonomías y autogobierno en la América diversa* (507–534). Cuenca, Ecuador: Abya Yala/ Universidad Politécnica Salesiana.
Moreno Figueroa, Mónica. 2010. "Distributed Intensities: Whiteness, Mestizaje and the Logics of Mexican Racism." *Ethnicities* 10, no. 3: 387–401.
Moreno Figueroa, Mónica, and Emiko Saldívar Tanaka. 2016. "'We Are Not Racists, We Are Mexicans': Privilege, Nationalism and Post-Race Ideology in Mexico." *Critical Sociology* 42, no. 4–5: 515–533.
Ortiz, Teresa. 2001. *Never Again a Mexico without Us: Voices of Mayan Women in Chiapas, Mexico*. New York: Epica Task Force.
Stahler-Sholk, Richard. 2008. "Resisting Neoliberal Homogenization: The Zapatista Autonomy Movement." In R. Stahler-Sholk, H. E. Vanden, and G. D. Kuecker (Eds.), *Latin American Social Movements in the Twenty-First Century*. New York: Rowman & Littlefield. 113–129.
Stern, Alexandra Minna. 1999. "Responsible Mothers and Normal Children: Eugenics, Nationalism, and Welfare in Post-Revolutionary Mexico, 1920–1940." *Journal of Historical Sociology* 12, no. 4: 369–397.
Sue, Christina A. 2013. *Land of the Cosmic Race: Race Mixture, Racism, and Blackness in Mexico*. Oxford: Oxford University Press.
Telles, Edward. 2014. *Pigmentocracies: Ethnicity, Race, and Color in Latin America*. Chapel Hill: University of North Carolina Press.

Trevizo, Dolores. 2011. *Rural Protest and the Making of Democracy in Mexico, 1968–2000*. University Park: Pennsylvania University Press.
World Bank data "Mortality rate, infant (per 1,000 live births)—Mexico. https://data.worldbank.org/indicator/SP.DYN.IMRT.IN?locations=MX

7

Māori Struggle for Indigenous Rights
Contesting Sovereignty in New Zealand

Toon van Meijl

Before the arrival of European explorers and voyagers, the society of the Indigenous population of New Zealand was made up of tribes. These had been founded and developed by the crew of a range of canoes that had arrived from eastern Polynesia at different moments in time since the thirteenth century. Indigenous people in New Zealand did not have a name for themselves as a people, only a multiplicity of tribal names. A nation in the strict sense of the term did not—yet—exist.

The awareness that the Indigenous people of New Zealand shared a similar identity and also a similar language that distinguished them from European visitors only emerged around the year 1800, when more and more Europeans were arriving. Increasing interactions between Indigenous people and Europeans in New Zealand soon led to the designation *maaori* for locals, which was initially recorded as an adjective of *taangata* ("person" or "people"), meaning "usual," "ordinary," or "normal." The use of the concept of Māori as a noun in reference to the Indigenous population of New Zealand was not common until after the 1850s (Williams 1971, 179). Around the same time, Europeans came to be referred to as Pākehā, which was derived from the adjective *paakehaa*, meaning "foreign" (252).

The etymology of the meaning of Māori is essential for understanding indigenous aspirations to nationalism in New Zealand, which are unquestionably of postcolonial origin. The goal to achieve pan-tribal unity and develop a national identity is, furthermore, inherently linked to the postcolonial struggle for "sovereignty" in New Zealand. Sovereignty is also the key concept in the debate about Indigenous rights in the settler colony of New Zealand, since a covenant was signed between the Māori and the British in a place called Waitangi in 1840, in which sovereignty was exchanged for the continuing possession of lands and other natural resources (Orange 1987). The Treaty of Waitangi was drawn up in both English and Māori, however, which soon generated a discussion about the translation and also a struggle about its political implications. Indeed, the Treaty of Waitangi continues to dominate contemporary discussions, which must be regarded against the backdrop of a colonial history of conquest and confiscations.

In the course of the nineteenth century, New Zealand came to be dominated by colonial settlers, mainly from the United Kingdom, but around 1900 the Indigenous population was left largely dispossessed, having lost 94.1 percent of their lands (Kawharu 1977, 35). At the same time, they were demographically on the brink of extinction, with only 40 percent of the original number of people remaining (Pool 1991, 76). Wars and epidemic diseases had wreaked havoc among the Māori, and also influenced their political strategies to restore the sovereignty that had been taken from them following the implementation of the Treaty of Waitangi (Belich 1996, King 2003). Various attempts to achieve pan-tribal unity in the struggle for justice were made, but throughout history Māori nationalism has been hampered by tribal rivalries (Van Meijl 2008). At the same time, Māori attempts to regain sovereignty have not been successful until rather recently.

Following a renaissance of Māori culture starting in the late 1960s, the political tide gradually changed in the 1970s. Eventually, this resulted in a—partial—recognition of the rights of the Māori as the Indigenous population of New Zealand in the 1980s (Kawharu 1989). Soon thereafter a so-called settlement process was initiated to redress Māori colonial grievances about violations of the Treaty of Waitangi. Some dispossessed lands are being returned to Indigenous ownership, and financial compensation is offered on top of that for lands that can no longer be returned since they are held in private ownership. This process is still ongoing (Wheen & Hayward 2012).

In the wake of the settlement process, however, tribes have re-emerged since as part of the compensation agreements dispossessed lands have been returned to tribal ownership (Belgrave 2014). At present, therefore, tribes are re-installing their sovereignty, at least to some extent, which in turn has led to the disintegration of nationalist movements. Simultaneously, a distinct tradition of Indigenous cultural expressions has emerged throughout New Zealand, with some regional variation.

In this chapter, I will offer a historical sketch of Māori nationalism, its emergence in the nineteenth century, and its demise in the twenty-first century following the implementation of the settlement process that aims at removing Indigenous grievances about their dispossession during the colonial era. I begin with a more detailed explanation of the Treaty of Waitangi.

The Treaty of Waitangi

As indicated above, the discourse about Māori nationalism centers on the concept of sovereignty and its implications for governance in the settler colony of New Zealand. This follows the principal position of the notion of sovereignty in the Treaty of Waitangi, a covenant between the British Crown and numerous Māori chiefs from both the South and the North Island. The Treaty was signed in 1840 when the Colonial Office in London, administering the territories of the British Empire, felt it had to intervene in the gradual extension of the imperial frontier from the penal colony of New South Wales (in Australia) to the islands of New Zealand (Adams 1977).

There are at least four versions of the Treaty of Waitangi, with significant differences between English and Māori translations, and it seems certain that each of the two signing parties had different understandings of their key aspects. Under the English version of the Treaty, the Māori chiefs ceded "all the rights and powers of Sovereignty" over their respective territories to the Queen of England. The Māori version, however, does not use the nearest equivalent to sovereignty, which is probably *mana*, but instead the term *kawanatanga* was introduced, a transliteration of "governorship" improvised by the missionaries. To the Māori chiefs who signed the Treaty, *kawanatanga* might not have meant more than the coming of the first governor. In addition, one can question whether a translation of sovereignty with *mana* would have made a difference, since in the Treaty of Waitangi the Māori people were also confirmed and guaranteed "the full exclusive and undisturbed possession of their Lands and Estates Forests Fisheries and other properties." In the Māori version, the concept of possession was translated as *rangatiratanga*, which in some sense was equivalent to a chief's *mana* (Orange 1987, 42).

In spite of this agreement between Māori and Europeans under the terms of the Treaty of Waitangi, the covenant legitimized the settlement of increasing numbers of Europeans in New Zealand which, in turn, accelerated the disastrous transfer of vast tracts of Māori land to European immigrants (Ward 1973). The alienation of Māori land under the impact of the Treaty of Waitangi caused Māori tribes to disavow inter-tribal rivalries and discuss their common interests. A movement for pan-tribal unity emerged in defense of Māori sovereignty.

In Search of Pan-Tribal Unity

Since the middle of the nineteenth century when the British began to outnumber the Indigenous population of New Zealand, the colonial history of the Māori has been characterized by a continuous search for pan-tribal unity on several levels and in many contexts, both in time and space (for a useful overview, see Cox 1993). In this chapter, I focus on what I consider the main attempts to reach pan-tribal unity that had a major impact beyond their regional origins.

The first major attempt to establish a pan-tribal organization began in the 1850s, when a more coherent type of organization was required to protect Māori from European interference and to make a ban on land sales effective. For that reason, Māori tribes united in inter-tribal councils or *rūnanga* to trace out a common strategy. Initially, the meetings of what became known as the movement for *kotahitanga* or "oneness," were geared to put a *tapu* on land sales within certain boundaries, but soon the idea of a Māori king occurred. Ultimately, the movement for pan-tribal unity eventuated in the crowning of the Waikato chief Potatau Te Wherowhero as first Māori King in 1858 (Van Meijl 1993).

Initially Potatau was supported by twenty-three tribes, but it goes without saying that the crowning of Potatau and the unfurling of the flag of the *Kīngitanga* or kingship could only reduce, rather than resolve, traditional tribal rivalries, which in the 1850s were compounded by different views on the Treaty of Waitangi and European settlement at large (Sinclair 1991, 39–48). However, tribes that declined to pledge their allegiance to the King were still supportive of the policy of the Kīngitanga to withhold land from the market. Thus, Potatau provided a focus of Māori discontent regarding the government's land purchase policies that were implemented to appease the disenchanted settlers who had migrated to New Zealand to settle there but encountered an increasingly unreceptive population of Indigenous people.

In 1860, the struggle over access to land and the control of sovereignty developed into a series of wars between the government and Māori tribes in various areas (Belich 1986). These lasted until the end of 1864, when the government moved to confiscate more than 1,200,000 hectares (3,000,000 acres), or 4.4 percent of land, most of which belonged to the tribal confederation of the Māori King. Thus, the *Kīngitanga* was punished for its central role in the resistance against the European invasion. The confiscation of the entire tribal territory of the Māori King entailed that subsequently he focused his activities after the wars predominantly on seeking redress for the confiscations. As a corollary, his tribal considerations soon became identified with the aim and objectives of the Kīngitanga. It confronted the Māori King with great difficulties in acquiring support for his attempt to make the kingship a politically effective institution (Van Meijl 1993, 682). His ultimate goal of centralizing his authority in order to strengthen his position in the negotiations for a settlement of the confiscations with the government was disputed by many tribes, which could not accept his self-constituted claim to rule over the entire North Island (Williams 1969, 47). As a consequence, the dissension among Māori tribes regarding pan-tribal unity in the form of the Kīngitanga sparked off a new movement to achieve Māori unity toward the end of the nineteenth century.

In the 1890s, it was commonly believed that the Māori as a people were doomed to extinction in the near future (Pool 1991). The size of the Māori population reached an absolute low, and some sort of anxiety about the possible waning of Māori society became widespread. Some form of cooperation between Māori tribes was required again to offset the threat of total assimilation, but nobody was prepared to unite behind the Māori King. The Māori members of Parliament[1] therefore revived the *kotahitanga* movement of the 1850s, and set up a Māori Parliament in June 1892 to present tribal and pan-tribal grievances to the government (Williams 1969, 48–67).

The story of the Māori Parliament, however, does not amount to one of the most successful episodes in Māori history. European society was now so well established that it could afford to neglect what it considered a separatist movement, but more interestingly, many Māori people were scarcely interested in the Māori Parliament either. The Kingites still argued for unity behind the Māori King, while others did not support the Māori Parliament because they accepted European society. Large sections of the Māori population refused to join because they were looking for other avenues to solve their problems of poverty than the protest meetings of the Māori Parliament that often stalled in bickering about tribal differences. Eventually, the division of Māoridom within the Māori Parliament proved fatal during the final five years of the nineteenth century. The Māori Parliament was finally disbanded in 1902 (Williams 1969, 98–112).

The Creation of a National Identity

In the beginning of the twentieth century, Māori political aspirations shifted from requests for legal recognition of Indigenous sovereignty under the umbrella of the Kīngitanga or a separate Māori Parliament toward equal rights of Māori people as New Zealand citizens. Since they had largely been dispossessed in the course of the nineteenth century, they had no option but to search for employment and integrate to the best of their ability into the European type of society that had been established and developed by colonial settlers in New Zealand.

The great advocates of the new political strategy emerging across Māoridom were the members of the students' association of a Māori Anglican Boys College in Hawke's Bay, the Te Aute College Students' Association. The organization is commonly referred to as the Young Māori Party, although it never formed a political party. It was more a group of educated individuals who operated politically, and of whom some took up parliamentary seats later (Fitzgerald 1977, 32).

The Young Māori Party pleaded, first and foremost, for socioeconomic equality. At the same time, however, it aspired to retaining a distinctive culture and identity within the boundaries of the society in which Māori and Europeans were to hold an equivalent status. Hence they simultaneously claimed the right to be excluded from some dimensions of New Zealand society in order to maintain their own culture and customs (Sigley 1974). The latter aim became later known as the policy of biculturalism. It involved a complementary—cultural—distinction between different nations within the same state. Thus, the Young Māori Party rephrased the previously political desire for a sovereign Māori nation, albeit each tribe was always meant to retain its own autonomy, into an aspiration toward a pan-tribal, predominantly cultural nation with a relatively autonomous status within the overarching European society. This new vision of Māoridom is most clearly exemplified by the innovative concept of Māoritanga.

In order to offset the negative impact European society could have on a Māori identity, the members of the Young Māori Party reconstituted and revalorized Māori cultural customs. Being Māori became very much a conscious precept, as a result of which a glorifying attitude was adopted in respect of a Māori identity. The Young Māori Party advocated a sense of pride in being Māori, and a stylized proto-culture was constructed to support that view, especially in the arts, dance, and music (Ramsden 1948). The term "Māoritanga," or "Māoriness," was coined to express the new creation of a Māori identity in the modern world.

Māoritanga

Initially, Māoritanga was interpreted as a call for separatism, but it was meant to be applied in a context of "biculturalism."[2] The most prominent leader of the Young Māori Party and later statesman Sir Apirana Ngata (1940, 176–177) defined the term as follows: "an emphasis on the continuing individuality of the Maori people, the maintenance of such Maori characteristics and such features of Maori culture as present day circumstances will permit, the inculcation of pride in Maori history and traditions, the retention so far as possible of old-time ceremonial, the continuous attempt to interpret the Maori point of view to the *pakeha* in power." This conception of a Māori way of life was initially constructed during the days of the Young Māori Party but was prevailing in nationalist discourses throughout the twentieth century. As such, it indicates the emergence of a second type of Māori nationalism. The conception of Māoritanga as constructed by the members of the Young Māori Party underlies a conception of Māori nationalism that differs from nineteenth-century tribal and inter-tribal initiatives to re-acquire Māori sovereignty in the sense that it is appealing exclusively to pan-tribal sentiments.[3] The semantics of the new concept of Māoritanga are particularly significant in this respect.

As indicated above, it is most significant that the concept of "Māori" is of postcolonial origin and emerged during the early years of colonial contact in reference to the Indigenous population of New Zealand as "normal" people who may be distinguished from the "strangers" or "foreigners," the

Pākehā. Over the course of the nineteenth century, the concepts of Māori and Pākehā became gradually accepted, but as a political category Māori was not adopted until after the Young Māori Party had advocated pride in "Māoritanga." The pan-tribal representation of Māori society underlying the neologism Māoritanga had far-reaching political implications for the emergence of a Māori nationalist movement. Indeed, the rise of modern Māori nationalism, in which tribal differences do not play a role of significance, can be traced to the days of the Young Māori Party (*cf.* Ngata 1898). For that reason, too, it is not surprising that the members of the Te Aute College Students' Association were referred to as the *Young* Māori Party.

Benedict Anderson (1983, 109), an influential scholar in studies of nationalism, has commented that in nationalist discourses, particularly in postcolonial situations, concepts of "young" and "youth" do not necessarily refer to age but instead signify "dynamism, progress, self-sacrificing idealism and revolutionary will." Although in emerging European nations "young" and "youth" could rarely be defined in terms of class, status, or use of language, in colonial circumstances "young" and "youth" invariably refer to "the *first* generation in any significant numbers to have acquired a European education, marking them off linguistically and culturally from their parents' generation, as well from the vast bulk of their colonized agemates" (109, my emphasis). Thus, concepts of "youth" in colonial situations draw attention to the role of education in promoting postcolonial nationalism. In New Zealand, too, the *Young* Māori Party consisted of individuals who without exception had been educated at a European school, which at the same time explains why their campaigns for the improvement of Māori welfare were initially far from successful.

The Young Māori Party campaigned for the Māori people to follow education and to embrace European technology in order to develop the land still held in communal ownership, while they also encouraged them to adopt better hygiene practices and other European norms and practices.[4] By doing so, they in fact advocated the enforcement of European, middle-class conventions of respectability (e.g., Prentice 1899), which were evidently associated with their European education. As a result, the political program of the Young Māori Party was widely contested, and some elders who wished their children to be educated to enable them to compete with their European peers on equal terms expressed grief that the boys at Te Aute College became lost for the Māori cause. For this reason, too, tribes tended to be careful in the selection of boys to be sent to college, in order to ensure they would, rather than simply introducing European mores, apply their knowledge and skills to the benefit of the Māori people at large (*cf.* Fitzgerald 1977, 30–31).

Tribal Reservations about Māoritanga

As the obvious impact of European education on the political objectives of the campaigns of the Young Māori Party was controversial, so has their innovation of a pan-tribal concept of Māoritanga raised suspicion about their European antecedents among tribal leaders. Forty years later, a well-known Tuhoe leader, the late John Rangihau (1977, 174–175), for example, suggested that

> there is no such thing as Maoritanga because Maoritanga is an all-inclusive term which embraces all Maoris. And there are so many different aspects about every tribal person. Each tribe has its own history. And it's not a history that can be shared among others . . . I have a faint suspicion that Maoritanga is a term coined by the Pakeha to bring the tribes together. Because if you cannot divide and rule, then for tribal people all you can do is unite them and rule. Because then they lose everything by losing their own tribal histories and traditions that give them their identity.

Although Rangihau's main aim with this provocative proposition was probably to criticize a tendency toward over-generalizing Māori "culture" in the 1970s, it is interesting to note that his suggestion that "Maoritanga is a term coined by the Pakeha" was not simply hypothesized. After all, the tribal status of the member of the Young Māori Party who coined the term, James Carroll (Ngata 1940, 176), was rather liminal. Carroll was of mixed Irish and Māori descent, but more importantly he served on the European side during the New Zealand Wars in the 1860s. Subsequently, he was a Member of Parliament for a non-Māori electorate for twenty-six years (Winiata 1967, 50).[5] His biography, as well as the European education of other members of the Young Māori Party, therefore illuminates the Western presuppositions of the Young Māori Party's policy of integration in the economic and political frameworks of European society, while it also makes apparent the postcolonial parameters of the movement's conception of a Māori nation.

The controversy surrounding the Young Māori Party's conception of Māoritanga, moving away from the tribal struggle for sovereignty to a vision of a predominantly cultural nation in pan-tribal form, directly proceeds from the postcolonial origin and character of their sociopolitical ideal. The notion of a Māori nation in which inter-tribal differences are transcended into a pan-tribal polity is based on a view of a united Māori community that only emerged in postcolonial circumstances characterized by the establishment of European control after a massive wave of colonial settlement in the nineteenth century. The imagined national community of Māori people regardless of their tribal background was constructed primarily in opposition to the success and completion of European domination (*cf.* Said 1993, 209–220). For that reason, too, the ideal of a pan-tribal nation was founded in a postcolonial discourse that emerged from the very structures of colonial power against which a vision of a Māori nation was constructed (Chatterjee 1986, 38). Moreover, Māori nationalism as expressed and espoused by the Young Māori Party invoked a discourse that seeks to differentiate a Māori nation within a context dominated by a nation aiming to assimilate Māori nationalist thought (38–39, 42). The aspiration toward a pan-tribal Māori nation is thus inherently contradictory.

The inherent contradiction in the pan-tribal conception of Māori nationalism as constructed by the Young Māori Party, however, also creates the possibility for multiple interpretations and representations (Dirks 1992, 15; Fox 1990). Its pan-tribal aspirations were rejected by tribal leaders who had not given up hope to regain the lands from which their ancestors had been dispossessed and continued to aim at re-establishing sovereignty on their tribal territories. At the same time, however, it did appeal to the increasing number of Māori who moved to urban environments, where pan-tribal sentiments reflected the solidarity among members from different tribal territories who had abandoned their homelands in search of employment (Metge 1964). As the nineteenth century may be characterized as the century of dispossession, so the twentieth century may be characterized as the century of urbanization. The proportion of Māori people living in cities and boroughs increased from 10 percent in the 1930s to more than 80 percent in the 1970s (Pool 1991). Maori began moving to urban environments in search of paid work during the Great Depression, but they qualified only for the lower-skilled jobs. Maori therefore became an urban proletariat, which was hit the hardest when New Zealand moved into a long-term recession in the early 1970s. For that reason, too, a protest movement emerged in the cities. In those days, it generated a tremendous cultural renaissance in the spirit of the Young Māori Party, but more importantly it called for a recognition of the Treaty of Waitangi.

The Waitangi Tribunal

Under the impact of global developments, such as the Black civil rights movement in the United States and mass demonstrations against the war in Vietnam in many countries, the political climate in New Zealand changed in the late 1960s. The Māori in the cities constituted an urban proletariat that was hit very hard when New Zealand moved into a long-term recession, especially after the United Kingdom joined the European Union in 1973. It reinforced Māori demands for a recognition of their rights as Indigenous people, which they saw protected by the Treaty of Waitangi. The government responded, first by declaring the day the Treaty was signed a national holiday, but in 1975 it also introduced the Treaty of Waitangi Act that established the Waitangi Tribunal. This act enabled Māori to submit claims to the Waitangi Tribunal on grounds of being "prejudicially affected" by any policy or practice of the Crown that was "inconsistent with the principles of the Treaty," although "anything done or omitted before the commencement of [the] Act" was excluded from the tribunal's jurisdiction. In spite of this limitation, the act vindicated Māori faith in the Treaty and encouraged them to reinforce their protests. In 1985, the jurisdiction of the Waitangi Tribunal was eventually back-dated from 1975 to 1840 when the Treaty was signed at Waitangi (Kawharu 1989). This amendment opened up an important avenue for Māori people to seek redress for their colonial grievances.

Soon after the expansion of its jurisdiction, the Waitangi Tribunal received some twelve hundred Māori claims, most of which were submitted by tribal organizations (Wheen & Hayward 2012). Although it is possible for any Māori, tribal or nontribal, to submit a claim to the Waitangi Tribunal, most claims concern lands, forests, and fisheries, the ownership of which is claimed exclusively by tribes. In consequence, tribes dominate the debate on redressing violations of the treaty. And since this issue has become more topical over the past twenty-five years, it may be argued that the pan-tribal protest movement that emerged in the cities in the 1960s and 1970s sparked the re-emergence of tribes in contemporary New Zealand.

After years of negotiations between different Māori tribes and the New Zealand government, the settlement process was finally started in the mid-1990s and has made great progress since. In 1995, the first major compensation agreement was signed with the Waikato-Tainui tribes, the groups upholding the Māori monarchy since the crowning of Potatau in 1858. The deal included a formal apology from the Crown, acknowledging it had acted unjustly in dealing with the Kingites (supporters of the Māori monarchy) in the 1860s, and provided for the return of 14,164 hectares (about 35,000 acres), or 3 percent of the lands originally confiscated, and a significant sum for compensation (Van Meijl 1999).

Since the mid-1990s, a large number of other compensation agreements have also been signed. All settlements have so far been reached with tribes. The returned lands, forests, and other natural resources are used for tribal development programs that aim at restoring sovereignty on tribal territories, mainly in rural areas (Bell et al. 2017). Notwithstanding the progress being made with redressing long-standing Māori grievances, the settlement process remains controversial because the government negotiates settlements only with tribal organizations, whereas 80 percent of the Māori population is currently living in urban environments in which tribal connections have lost a great deal of meaning. This has raised the question regarding the main aim of the settlement process.

Settling Colonial Grievances

When the settlement process began in the 1990s, the main aim of the government was to repair historical injustices by returning property to Māori ownership. At the same time, the Office of Treaty Settlements (1995, 5) stated that settlements would not relieve the government of its duties to provide services to all Māori, such as health services, and educational and welfare entitlements. Settlements were argued not to restrict the ability of any Māori to enjoy the rights to these services held by all New Zealanders. The distinction between these dimensions of government policy has been described as historical justice versus social justice (Lashley 2000). This distinction parallels the interpretation of the Treaty of Waitangi, which guarantees Māori proprietary interests in Article Two but also pledges to Māori "all the Rights and Privileges of British Subjects" in Article Three. Article Two applies to tribes as owners of territories dispossessed during the colonial era; Article Three applies to all Māori citizens, including urban Māori who have lost their tribal connections but are living on the periphery of New Zealand society. Indeed, the Indigenous population features negatively in all socioeconomic statistics, with unemployment rates twice as high as the national average and life expectancy some eight years lower (McIntosh and Mulholland 2011; see also www.stats.govt.nz). In view of the abominable socioeconomic indicators of the Māori population, it is beyond doubt that the government has violated both Article Two and Article Three. Against this background, criticisms of the settlement process have been increasing and intensifying in recent years. These are expressed both by tribal members and by pan-tribal communities in the cities.

Given the complex sociopolitical organization of Māori society and its transformation in the course of colonial history, the government decided it only wanted to negotiate about compensation for violations of the Treaty with so-called larger "claimant groups" (Office of Treaty Settlements 1995, 12). In practice, this concept refers to tribes, which are made up of lower-ranking subtribes, which in turn are made up of a number of extended families. The boundaries between these kinship units are inherently fuzzy because of the ambilineal descent practices, offering people the option to trace their descent in either the father's or the mother's genealogy. And they can revise their initial decision until two generations later, which in the nineteenth century resulted in a "crazy patchwork" of property rights at the grassroots (Ballara 1998, 195). In order to avoid discussion about property rights, the government opted to return the land and additional compensation funds not to the families or subtribes that used to own and work the land in the past but to their overarching tribes. Following the settlement process, these have in recent years developed into huge corporations managing significant amounts of land, other natural resources, and money but who fail to live up to the obligation to distribute funds among its members and invest in the well-being of their beneficiaries (Van Meijl 2013). Although the settlements signed so far are meant to be "full and final," the disenfranchisement of families and subtribes will no doubt have to be resolved in the future.

At the same time, criticisms of the settlement process expressed by pan-tribal communities in urban environments are increasing and intensifying as well. They are not included in negotiations about compensation, which focus exclusively on violations of Article Two of the Treaty of Waitangi and aim at returning land and natural resources to those from whom it was taken in the past. Yet the government also has obligations to meet Article

Three of the Treaty and offer the same services to all Māori people. Over the past two years, this issue manifested itself also in higher rates of infections with the Covid-19 virus among the Māori population as well as with lower vaccination rates. It is inevitable that these inequalities between Māori and non-Māori that are endemic in all dimensions of New Zealand society will also have to be addressed.

Although the discussion about Indigenous rights in New Zealand is dominated by the Treaty of Waitangi, it is also held in the context of international law. In recent years, this has revolved around the Declaration on the Rights of Indigenous Peoples, which was adopted by an overwhelming majority in the General Assembly of the United Nations in 2007. This declaration covers a broad range of rights and freedoms, including the right to self-determination, culture, and identity but also rights to land, education, economic development, religious customs, health, and language. New Zealand, however, voted against it, along with Australia, Canada, and the United States, the four countries with the largest Indigenous populations within their borders. These four countries shared a concern about the precise meaning of "self-determination," the implications of recognizing "land rights," and the lack of a clear definition of the term "indigenous." Over the years, however, it was recognized that these issues could be addressed by each country at the national level, so the four countries that initially voted against it have reversed their position since the declaration was adopted. At the same time, it continues to be an open question what political consequences the most comprehensive international instrument on the rights of Indigenous peoples may have in the respective countries.

New Zealand endorsed the declaration in 2010 and officially acknowledged that Māori hold a special status as "people of the land" (*tangata whēnua*) and as such have a special interest in all legislative and policy measures. The government also confirmed its commitment to the main objectives of the declaration. At the same time, it pointed out that the legal and constitutional frameworks of New Zealand define the country's bounds of engagement with the declaration. In 2019, a first rapport entitled *He Puapua* (meaning "a break") was released, with possible plans to realize and implement the declaration in New Zealand. Since then, however, there appears to be a political deadlock as the working group that compiled the report is advocating for separate service systems for Māori because the contemporary structure fails to deliver adequately to the Māori population. Needless to say, this debate will continue for some time to come.

The Māori Renaissance

The political changes that have taken place in New Zealand in recent decades and that have opened up the avenue for Māori to seek redress of their colonial grievances since the 1980s are paralleled with a widespread revival of Māori culture. It began during the first hearings of the Waitangi Tribunal in the 1970s, when the loss of land was consistently linked to a loss of cultural traditions, which in Indigenous cosmology are intimately connected to the land (Sorrenson 1989). It was argued compellingly and emotionally that not only the land would have to be returned, but in order to reshape New Zealand into a country in which the Indigenous population holds an equal position to that of settlers, their cultural values and traditions would have to be accepted and appreciated as well.

Māori campaigns for comprehensive change focused on all dimensions of society, although from the outset priority was given to education. This sector received a first impulse with the introduction of so-called *Kōhanga Reo* or "language nests," kindergartens in which preschool children are immersed in the Māori language and values. This program was important in view of decreasing numbers of fluent speakers of the Māori language. It was incredibly successful and soon seven hundred Kōhanga Reo had been set up, while at the same time bilingual schools and even colleges were established in order to raise a new generation that is truly bilingual. In 1987, the growing recognition of the Māori language culminated in the Māori Language Act, offering the language a legal status. This in turn entailed an obligation for the government to publish official documents both in English and in Māori, and also to facilitate the introduction of Māori radio channels and television stations.

In sum, then, it may be argued that in recent decades significant progress has been made with the recognition of Māori language and culture as an inherent part of New Zealand society, ranging from education and health to economics, politics, and justice. As a corollary, socioeconomic indicators of the Māori populations have also begun improving, although the gap between the Indigenous people and European New Zealanders is still a cause for concern. Yet optimism is generally prevailing since in contemporary New Zealand it has become unavoidable to take into account a so-called Māori perspective on a broad range of policy issues. Recognition of Māori cultural traditions is especially apparent in the public domain. Official meetings or even seminars at universities usually begin and end with a Māori *karakia*, often translated as "prayer," although "incantation" would be a better term since traditionally they call for the inspiration or blessings from ancestors. They indicate that the renaissance of Māori culture and traditions has gradually transformed New Zealand into a society that is aware and even proud of its location in the South Pacific, far removed from England, its original colonizer.

Concluding Remarks: Frustrated Nationalism?

The colonial history of the New Zealand Māori is characterized by a long-term struggle to regain sovereignty over their lands and natural resources taken from them by British settlers who invaded the country from the beginning of the nineteenth century. As Māori society was a tribal society in precolonial times, with the concept of Māori itself being a postcolonial construct, the struggle of the Indigenous population was predominantly designed and organized as a tribal struggle. Several attempts have been made to establish pan-tribal unity, but politically Māori nationalist movements have met limited success because national interests have been consistently checked and balanced against tribal interests.

The so-called frustration of nationalist movements could therefore not prevent the demise of the Maori population toward the end of the nineteenth century. This, in turn, generated a new movement that introduced a form of cultural nationalism, which has been relatively successful in the twentieth century, at least to the extent that it re-introduced pride in Māori culture that, in turn, boosted Māori political confidence to never give up their struggle for justice and reconciliation. In the 1970s, this eventually caused a turning of the political tide that enabled Māori tribes to seek redress of their colonial grievances and demand a return of their lost properties. In recent decades, New Zealand is making great strides with this so-called settlement process, although it is unlikely to resolve all remaining problems of Māori marginalization on the short term. This is partially related to the large-scale urbanization of the Māori in the twentieth century, whereas the government is prepared to negotiate compensation settlements only with tribal organizations from whom the lands and resources were taken in the nineteenth century. At the same time, however, the settlement process has gathered momentum since it started and is currently paralleled by a widespread revival of Māori culture and language in all domains of New Zealand society. Indeed, Māori people share a unique ethos as an Indigenous population whose nationalist aspirations may have been frustrated in the course of colonial history, but at present they are increasingly influential in their efforts to re-establish sovereignty, albeit on a tribal basis.

Notes

1. In 1867, the Māori Representation Act was passed, under which the Māori people were given "manhood suffrage" in four seats in Parliament (Ward 1973, 208–210).

2. It should be realized that the concept of "biculturalism" has only become vogue since the late 1960s (Schwimmer 1968).

3. Visions of a pan-tribal Maori nation have also been constructed by several Maori prophets, some of whom had a significant impact in many parts of New Zealand. A discussion of prophetic perspectives of Maori nationalism is, however, beyond the scope of this article. For an interesting discussion of Maori prophets leaders, see Binney (1990).

4. The evidence for this is contained in numerous papers and addresses that were read by members and associated members of the Young Maori Party at the annual conferences of the Te Aute College Students' Association held between 1897 and 1905—for example, Buck 1899; Ngata 1897; Prentice 1898.

5. For a brief biosketch of James Carroll, see *The Dictionary of New Zealand Biography, Volume Two* (Dept. of Internal Affairs, 1993), reference C-10.

References

Adams, Peter. 1977. *Fatal Necessity; British Intervention In New Zealand 1830–1847.* Auckland/Oxford: Auckland/Oxford University Press,

Anderson, Benedict. 1983. *Imagined Communities: Reflections on the Origin and Spread of Nationalism.* London & York: Verso.

Ballara, Angela. 1998. *Iwi: The Dynamics of Maaori Tribal Organisation from c.1769 to c.1945.* Wellington: Victoria University Press.

Belgrave, Michael. 2014. "Beyond the Treaty of Waitangi: Māori Tribal Aspirations in an Era of Reform, 1984–2014." *The Journal of Pacific History* 49, no. 2: 193–213.

Belich, James. 1986. *The New Zealand Wars, and the Victorian Interpretation of Racial Conflict.* Auckland: Auckland University Press.

Belich, James. 1996. *Making Peoples: A History of the New Zealanders, from Polynesian Settlement to the End of the Nineteenth Century.* Honolulu: University of Hawai'i Press.

Bell, Rachael, Margaret Kawharu, Kerry Taylor, Michael Belgrave, and Peter Meihana, eds. 2017. *The Treaty on the Ground: Where Are We Headed and Why It Matters*. Auckland: Massey University Press.

Binney, Judith. 1990. "Ancestral Voices: Māori Prophet Leaders," In *The Oxford Illustrated History of New Zealand*, ed. Keith Sinclair. Auckland: Oxford University Press. 153–184.

Buck, Peter. 1899. "The Decline of the Maori Race: The Causes and Remedies." In *Papers and Addresses Read before the Third Conference of the Te Aute College Students' Association, December 1898*, edited by Te Aute College Students' Association, 3–7. Southbridge: Ellesmere Guardian.

Chatterjee, Partha. 1986. *Nationalist Thought and the Colonial World: A Derivative Discourse?* Delhi: Oxford University Press.

Cox, Lindsay. 1993. *Kotahitanga; The Search for Maaori Political Unity*. Auckland: Oxford University Press.

Department of Internal Affairs, 1993. *The Dictionary of New Zealand Biography; Volume Two, 1870–1900*. Wellington: Dept. of Internal Affairs.

Dirks, Nicholas B. 1992. "Introduction: Colonialism and Culture." In *Colonialism and Culture*, ed. Nicholas B. Dirks. Comparative Studies in Society and History Book Series. Ann Arbor: University of Michigan Press. 1–25.

Fitzgerald, Thomas K. 1977. *Education and Identity: A Study of the New Zealand Maori Graduate*. Wellington: New Zealand Council for Educational Research.

Fox, Richard G. 1990. "Introduction." In *Nationalist Ideologies and the Production of Nationalist Cultures*, ed. Richard G. Fox. Washington DC: American Anthropological Association, American Ethnological Society Monograph Series, Number 2. 1–14.

Kawharu, I. H. 1977. *Māori Land Tenure: Studies of a Changing Institution*. Oxford: Oxford University Press.

Kawharu, I. H., ed. 1989. *Waitangi; Māori & Pākehā Perspectives of the Treaty of Waitangi*. Auckland: Oxford University Press.

King, Michael. 2003. *The Penguin History of New Zealand*. Auckland: Penguin.

Lashley, Marilyn E. 2000. "Implementing Treaty Settlements via Indigenous Institutions: Social Justice and Detribalization in New Zealand." *The Contemporary Pacific* 12, no. 1: 1–55.

McIntosh, Tracey, and Malcolm Mulholland, eds. 2011. *Māori and Social Issues*. Wellington: Huia.

Metge, Joan. 1964. *A New Maori Migration; Rural and Urban Relations in Northern New Zealand*. London & Melbourne: Athlone Press/Melbourne University Press.

Ngata, Apirana. 1897. "Sexual Immorality amongst the Maoris." In *Papers and Addresses Read before the First Conference of the Te Aute College Students' Association, February 1897*, edited by Te Aute College Students' Association. Gisborne: Poverty Bay Herald. 40–42.

Ngata, Apirana. 1898. "A Plea for the Unity of the Maori People." In *Papers and Addresses Read before the Second Conference of the Te Aute College Students' Association, December 1897*, edited by Te Aute College Students' Association. Napier: Daily Telegraph. 23–27.

Ngata, Apirana. 1940. "Tribal Organization." In *The Maori People Today: A General Survey*, edited by I.L.G. Sutherland. Wellington: Whitcombe & Tombs. 155–181.

Office of Treaty Settlements. 1995. *Crown Proposals for the Settlement of Treaty of Waitangi Claims: Detailed Proposals*. Wellington: Office of Treaty Settlements.

Orange, Claudia. 1987. *The Treaty of Waitangi*. Wellington: Allen & Unwin/Port Nicholson.

Pool, Ian, 1991. *Te Iwi Māori: A New Zealand Population—Past, Present and Projected*. Auckland: Auckland University Press.

Prentice, W. T. 1898. "Cleanliness." *Papers and Addresses Read before the Second Conference of the Te Aute College Students' Association, December 1897*, ed. Te Aute College Students' Association. Napier: Daily Telegraph. 12–15.

Prentice, W. T. 1899. "Punctuality." *Papers and Addresses Read before the Third Conference of the Te Aute College Students' Association, December 1898*, edited by Te Aute College Students' Association. Southbridge: Ellesmere Guardian. 22–25.

Ramsden, Eric. 1948. *Sir Apirana Ngata and Maori Culture*. Wellington: Reed.

Rangihau, John. 1977. "Being Maori." In *'Te Ao Hurihuri,' The World Moves On: Aspects of Maoritanga* (1975), ed. Michael King. Auckland: Longman Paul. 165–175.

Said, Edward W. 1993. *Culture and Imperialism*. New York: Knopf.

Schwimmer, Erik. 1968. "The Aspirations of the Contemporary Maori." In *The Maori People in the Nineteen-Sixties*, ed. Erik Schwimmer. Auckland: Blackwood & Janet Paul. 9–64.

Sigley, Dene. 1974. "The Young Maori Party." In *Te Aranga o Te Aute: Ta te Rangatira tana Kai he Korero ta te Ware he Muhukai*, edited by Mark Te Aranga Hakiwai, Dene Sigley, and Malcolm Sword. Pukehou: Te Aute College. 22–36.

Sinclair, Keith. 1991. *Kinds of Peace: Maori People after the Wars, 1870–1885*. Auckland: Auckland University Press.

Sorrenson, M.P.K. 1989. "Towards a Radical Reinterpretation of New Zealand History: The Role of the Waitangi Tribunal." In *Waitangi: Maori and Pakeha Perspectives of the Treaty of Waitangi*, ed. I. D. Kawharu. Auckland: Oxford University Press. 158–178.

Van Meijl, Toon. 1993. "The Maori King Movement: Unity and Diversity in Past and Present." *Bijdragen tot de taal-, land- en volkenkunde* 149, no. 4: 673–689.

Van Meijl, Toon. 1999. "Settling Maori Land Claims: Legal and Economic implications of Political and Ideological Contests." In *Property Rights and Economic Development: Land and Natural Resources in Southeast Asia and Oceania*, ed.

Toon van Meijl and Franz von Benda-Beckmann. London: Kegan Paul. 259–291.
Van Meijl, Toon. 2008. "Māori Nationalism." In *Nations and Nationalism: A Global Historical Overview*, Vol. 4., ed. Guntram H. Herb and David H. Kaplan. Santa Barbara: ABC-CLIO. 1855–1863.
Van Meijl, Toon. 2013. "Ownership and Distribution in the Settlement of Maori Grievances: Balancing Historical and Social Justice between Classes." In *Engaging with Capitalism: Cases from Oceania*, ed. Kate Barclay and Fiona McCormack. Melbourne: Emerald. 29–52.
Ward, Alan. 1973. *A Show of Justice: Racial "Amalgamation" in Nineteenth-Century New Zealand*. Auckland & Oxford: Auckland University Press / Oxford University Press.
Wheen, Nicola R., and Janine Hayward, eds. 2012. *Treaty of Waitangi Settlements*. Wellington: Bridget Williams.
Williams, John A. 1969. *Politics of the New Zealand Maori: Protest and Cooperation, 1891–1909*. Auckland & Oxford: Auckland University Press / Oxford University Press.
Williams, H. W. 1971. *A Dictionary of the Maori Language*. Wellington: Government Printer, 7th edition.
Winiata, Maharaia. 1967. *The Changing Role of the Leader in Maori Society: A Study in Social Change and Race Relations*. Auckland: Blackwood & Janet Paul.

III
Nationalism and Ethnic Survival

8

Virtual Tibet

Representation, Legitimacy, and Struggles for Democracy

ÅSHILD KOLÅS AND TASHI NYIMA

In the aftermath of the fourteenth Dalai Lama's historic flight from the Tibetan capital Lhasa in 1959, following a Tibetan uprising against Chinese rule, approximately one hundred thousand Tibetans went into exile in India and Nepal. Soon after settling in the picturesque hill town of Dharamsala in Himachal Pradesh, the fourteenth Dalai Lama Tenzin Gyatso and his followers started to articulate their vision of the Tibetan nation in the diaspora.

During his first conversation with then prime minister of India, Jawaharlal Nehru, the Dalai Lama and Nehru discussed the need to provide education for the Tibetan children.[1] This was barely a decade after India had freed itself from British colonial rule and gained independence. Nehru agreed to help the Tibetans set up separate educational institutions for Tibetan children outside the Indian school system. The purpose of this was to preserve the Tibetan language and identity, while also providing modern education to help young Tibetans work for the Tibetan cause internationally. For first-generation exile Tibetans, it was a Herculean task to start a new life from scratch, let alone think about the future of Tibet.[2]

Tibetan refugees initially settled in India, Nepal, and Bhutan, but gradually they moved further away from their homeland, to Europe, North America, and Australia. Over the following decades, Tibetans witnessed unprecedented changes in the diaspora Tibetan society, including democratization of political institutions, the Dalai Lama stepping down as their political leader, and a steadily growing digitalization of Tibetan cultural, social, and political life.³

With Dharamsala as their capital, diaspora Tibetans have become virtually connected. They communicate and organize Tibetan political and social activities online, using social media to discuss the performance of their representatives in the Tibetan Parliament-in-Exile and to support candidates running for office. Participating in this virtual Tibetan politics can be as easy as the click of a "like" button. It is this digitally mediated community, an imagined "Tibet away from Tibet" that we refer to as "virtual Tibet," borrowing a term used by Orville Schell in his book *Virtual Tibet: Searching for Shangri-La from the Himalayas to Hollywood*.⁴ In contrast to Schell, who used the term to describe popular Western conceptions of Tibet, we employ this term to describe the construction of "Tibet" in the Tibetan diaspora. We employ this term because it serves three important purposes in our description and analysis of the reassertion of the Tibetan nation outside the Tibetan plateau.

First, we use the term "virtual" to refer to efforts to define the "Tibetan" in places outside the physical Tibet, dislocated but essentially representing the Tibet of the past by appealing to past traditions and memories of social order to produce consensus on the meaning of the "Tibetan." This includes keeping Tibetan religious institutions and cultural traditions alive by reproducing and curating Tibetan material culture and performing arts and preserving and publishing Tibetan literature.⁵ Increasingly, this cultural production involves the use of digital applications and platforms.

Second, much of today's Tibetan cultural and political expression, communication, and social life, is digital. Social media platforms such as Whatsapp, Telegram, and Wechat have provided opportunities for Tibetans to share information and discuss with other Tibetans regardless of their physical location.⁶ Diaspora Tibetans use these platforms to discuss topics such as religion, science, technology, economics, traditional medicine, politics, philosophy, language, and literature, all in Tibetan, while Tibet Online TV airs sessions of the Tibetan Parliament-in-Exile. The Covid-19 pandemic has moved even more of these discussions online into the virtual world of cyberspace.

Finally, the Tibetan government-in-exile is set up to provide "equal" political representation for Tibetans from all three Tibetan regions (*cholkha gsum*), and adherents of all Tibetan religious traditions (four Tibetan Buddhist schools and the Indigenous religion Bon). The former type of representation is "equal" in the sense that it reflects the Tibetan geography, and to some extent, the demographic composition of Tibetans living in the three Tibetan regions, rather than the place of origin of members of the Tibetan exile community. Diaspora Tibetans thus elect an equal number of parliamentarians from each of the three regions of Tibet: Ü-tsang, Kham, and Amdo, while approximately 70 percent of exile Tibetans are from Ü-tsang (central Tibet). The objective of this election system is partly to create a democratic form of government, and partly to define the makeup of the "real" Tibetan nation.

Reconstructing "Tibet" in Exile

Refugees from Tibet started to settle in Northern India, Nepal, Bhutan, and Sikkim during the 1950s, as the Communist regime led by Chairman Mao Zedong started to dispossess Tibetan farmers and herders, close monasteries, and restrict trade and travel, especially in eastern Tibet. Beginning in 1952, thousands of Tibetan youths were educated in special schools for ethnic minorities (Chinese: *minzu xueyuan*) in China. Many of them were from the borderland regions, that is, Amdo and Kham. With no other opportunities for modern education, many young Tibetans welcomed this opening. In 1954, the Dalai Lama and Panchen Lama, the two most influential reincarnate lamas in Tibet, were both invited to attend the first People's Congress in Beijing to participate in the adoption of the constitution of the People's Republic of China (PRC).

In the People's Congress, Lhasa and Shigatse (headquarters of the Dalai Lama and Panchen Lama respectively), were assigned nine seats between them, while the Chamdo region in eastern Tibet was allotted three. The Tibetan delegation was also presented with plans for a Preparatory Committee for the formation of the Tibetan Autonomous Region. The Committee was to direct the work of the "Local Government of Tibet" in Lhasa, the Shigatse Council, and the Chamdo People's Liberation Committee. The Committee was comprised of ten members from each of the three areas, five from the Central Government of China, and seventeen from Tibetan organizations, to be approved by China's State Council.[7]

Tibet was traditionally divided into three regions called *cholkha gsum* (*cholkha* meaning "region," and *gsum* meaning "three"). The three regions were called Ü-tsang (དབུས་གཙང་), Amdo (ཨ་མདོ་), and Kham (ཁམས་). The term *cholkha* was used in the Yuan dynasty, when Mongols governed Tibet. What used to be a Mongolian administrative term was gradually adopted into the Tibetan language and became a term of self-identification.

Prior to the Chinese "liberation" of Tibet, the Lhasa government had jurisdiction over less than half the territory of the combined "greater Tibet" (the three historically and culturally Tibetan regions). The rest of this "greater Tibet" was either *de facto* independent or remained under the control of local warlords.[8] Most of the central and western region known as Ü-tsang was under the administration of the Dalai Lama and Panchen Lama. Most of Amdo was integrated into Qinghai, a province on the northern Silk Road with a long history of domination by Muslim warlords. Kham was split up between Chamdo District and the highlands of Sichuan, with smaller areas incorporated into Yunnan in the South, and Qinghai and Gansu in the North. These areas were not consolidated politically under a single national government of "Tibet."

As noted by Henrion-Dourcy: "The land that Tibetans imagine as theirs, approximately the expanse of the Tibetan empire (seventh to ninth centuries), is not coextensive with a bounded territory that existed politically and administratively in the recent past [. . .] But what the PRC considers to be "Tibet" covers only a half of that, in both space and population.[9] It corresponds roughly to the area under the rule of the Dalai Lamas (1642–1959), now labeled the Tibet Autonomous Region." However, "Buddhism has shaped much of the social, political, economic, and cultural makeup of all Tibetan societies, notably through integrated networks of monasteries."[10] Monasteries have played a vital sociopolitical role as cultural, educational, and religious institutions that have continued traditions, disseminated knowledge, and upheld the social order. Clerics were also involved in the discovery of reincarnated lamas (Tibetan: *spruls sku*).

The Tibetan Buddhist concept of "government of religion and politics" (Tibetan: *chos srid gnyis ldan*) describes the idea that Tibetan religious institutions and governance structures are inseparable.[11] Buddhist monks and reincarnate lamas in the large monasteries in Amdo and Kham were deeply involved in local governance and were often called on to mediate in conflicts between herders fighting over grasslands or farmers involved in disputes with neighbors or relatives. Well-off families would send at least one of their sons to the monastery to study and become associated with monastic elites. The monasteries were vital to Tibetan political as well as religious life. When the People's Liberation Army invaded Kham in the mid-1950s, major monasteries were also used as operative bases for armed and unarmed resistance.

The three areas represented in the Preparatory Committee for the Formation of the Tibetan Autonomous Region were located primarily in the region of Ü-tsang. The outcome of this committee was the founding of the "Tibet Autonomous Region." The Communist Party of China (CPC) sought to create a "People's Republic" by building alliances with local rulers when they were willing to collaborate. They recruited many prominent Tibetans, including the Dalai Lama and Panchen Lama, as representatives of "their" people in the People's Congress. The Communists continued to work with these figures while consolidating their power. In the longer term, however, their goal was to eradicate feudalism. They recognized the power of monasteries, temples, and mosques as key sociopolitical centers in the "old" society.[12] When the Communist regime was unable to control the Tibetan clergy, they dismantled the monasteries and confiscated their estates.

The Idea of a Democratic Tibet

When the Dalai Lama fled to India in 1959, the founding of a new Tibetan government-in-exile in Dharamsala was not only a daunting challenge but also a unique opportunity to reform the archaic system of government and reassert the existence of the Tibetan nation. Tibetan refugees flocked around the Dalai Lama, happy to be able to reaffirm their common cultural traditions and share the challenges they experienced under Communist Chinese rule. As the exile government launched their nation-building project, a vital objective was to preserve and curate Tibetan material culture, performing arts, and literature. Cultural institutions such as the Tibetan Institute of Performing Arts (TIPA) and Tibetan Medical Institute (TMI) were among the first institutions to be set up in Dharamsala. In addition to the public institutions, nongovernmental organizations such as the Tibetan Women's Association (TWA), Tibetan Freedom Movement, and Tibetan Youth Congress were set up as a civil society in exile. These organizations were active in garnering international support for the "Tibetan cause."[13]

In February 1960, the Dalai Lama visited the Indian pilgrimage site Bodh Gaya, the place where the Buddha achieved enlightenment. In front of a large crowd of Tibetan pilgrims who had gathered to see him, the Dalai Lama gave a speech where he introduced his followers to the idea of democracy. He suggested that exiled Tibetans should set up an elected body with three lay representatives, one from each of the three regions (Ü-tsang, Amdo, and Kham), and four monk representatives, one from each of the four schools of Tibetan Buddhism.[14]

The Dalai Lama and Panchen Lama both belong to the Gelugpa school. Historically, the different schools of Tibetan Buddhism engaged in rivalry, often vicious and sometimes violent. Religious institutions have continued to be a crucial political force in the Tibetan diaspora, as they have been throughout Tibetan history.[15] By including all three regions and four schools in the new assembly, the Dalai Lama was clearly trying to unify as well as reassert the Tibetan nation.

The first elections in the Tibetan diaspora were held in 1960. This was of course an entirely new experience for the refugees. There were no lists of candidates. The voters simply printed the name of whoever they wanted to vote for on a piece of paper.[16] The first members of the Commission of Tibetan People's Deputies took their oath of office on September 2, 1960. Two days later, the Dalai Lama lectured the deputies on the importance of a fully functioning polity, which should be rooted in traditional values but adapted to the widely accepted modern democratic system of governance.[17]

A week-long joint meeting was held to discuss the strengths and weaknesses of the existing Tibetan polity, the future course of action, expansion of the existing departments of the Central Tibetan Administration (CTA), and the appointment of civil servants.[18] The members proposed people to act as ministers (Tibetan: Kalon) of the councils for Religion, Home, Foreign Relations, and Education; the Office of Finance, Information and Security, and the Civil Service Commission. The newly elected parliamentarians decided to gain experience by working in the various councils of the CTA as deputy directors.[19]

The next important task was to prepare a draft constitution. After many consultations and lengthy discussions, the Dalai Lama promulgated a constitution on March 10, 1963. The term of elected deputies in the Assembly was to be three years. In 1964, rules were also framed concerning elections and terms of office for local assembly members in the larger settlements. The local assemblies (Tibetan: Gharthue) were to have one representative from each of the three regions elected directly by the people living in the settlement. Their main task was to assist the Settlement Officer in overseeing development activities.[20]

The total number of members of the Assembly of Tibetan People's Deputies (ATPD) was later increased from thirteen to seventeen, with one additional seat reserved for a woman from each of the three regions, while the Dalai Lama himself nominated one eminent Tibetan. In 1981, the Dalai Lama reduced the number of elected regional deputies to two each from the three regions, while keeping the five deputies representing the four Buddhist schools (Nyingmapa, Sakyapa, Kagyupa, and Gelugpa) and Bon, and directly appointing one eminent Tibetan. Moreover, due to disagreement on the voting process, the Dalai Lama was given the task of selecting the Deputies from a list determined by the primary election.[21]

Throughout the 1980s, the Dalai Lama stressed he would hold no responsibility as head of state when a new government was set up in a future free Tibet. However, in 1987, the Dalai Lama had to nominate all the members of the ninth ATPD, as an interim measure proposed by the National General Assembly. The ninth ATPD was dissolved after only one year, and a new election was held. On September 3, 1988, in an address to the tenth ATPD, the Dalai Lama emphasized the need for more democratic reforms, including the election of a head of government. He suggested setting up a constitution drafting committee for this purpose.

On May 11, 1990, a Special People's Congress was called. The Congress decided that the ministers (Tibetan: Kalon) would continue to be appointed by the Dalai Lama, but the elected Deputies would no longer be approved by him. The cabinet of ministers (Tibetan: Kashag) and Assembly of Tibetan People's Deputies were dissolved, and the Dalai Lama directed participants in the Special Congress to elect an interim Kashag to hold office while a Constitution Review Committee drafted a democratic charter for the Tibetans in exile and reviewed the existing draft constitution for the future Tibet. The Dalai Lama agreed to continue to act as head of state but again stressed he would no longer hold such a position when a truly democratic system was introduced.[22] Moreover, the Dalai Lama outlined a proposal to expand the membership of the Assembly, elect Kalons, give greater representation to women, and set up two Houses of the legislature. He also proposed to set up a judicial tribunal to investigate people's complaints.

On May 29, 1991, the Dalai Lama addressed the eleventh ATPD on the outcome of the process. The membership of the Assembly was to be increased from twelve to forty-six: ten members each from the three regions of Tibet (Ü-tsang, Amdo, and Kham), two each from the four Buddhist schools and Bon, two members from Europe, one from North America, and three nominated by the Dalai Lama himself.

A Supreme Justice Commission was set up as the apex tribunal for arbitrating civil cases within the Tibetan diaspora and for interpreting the

Tibetan laws. The main function of the Supreme Justice Commission (SJC) is to adjudicate civil disputes within the Tibetan diaspora, but parallel with the Indian legal system. The SJC is clear in its mission statement not to oversee disputes viewed to be in contravention of the laws of India. Further, all criminal cases are handled only in Indian courts. In this regard, the power of the SJC is rather limited in scope. Nonetheless, it has tried dozens of civil cases within the Tibetan diaspora.

With the founding of the Supreme Justice Commission, the three pillars of democracy were firmly established in the Tibetan diaspora, ensuring a fully functioning democratic polity with a system of checks and balances. An independent Audit Commission was set up to audit the accounts of all central and local offices. An independent Public Service Commission was set up to oversee recruitment and maintain records of all Tibetan public servants. Finally, an independent Election Commission was set up to oversee the election of Kalons, members of the ATPD, Settlement Officers, and members of local assemblies.

The ATPD was to approve and sanction the budget of the government-in-exile presented by the Minister of Finance. The Kalons were made accountable for the utilization of funds. The ATPD was given the power to impeach the ministers, the Supreme Justice Commissioners, and the heads of the three independent bodies: Audit, Public Service, and Election, by two-thirds majority. Even the Dalai Lama could be impeached by a three-fourths majority vote of the Assembly.[23]

The Central Tibetan Administration (CTA) consisted of seven departments. The Department of Religion and Culture (formerly the Council for Religious and Cultural Affairs) was established in 1959 to "preserve and promote understanding of Tibetan religion and culture." The Tibetan Institute of Performing Arts and the Library of Tibetan Works and Archives at Dharamsala, the Central Institute of Higher Tibetan Studies at Varanasi, and Tibet House at New Delhi operated under the supervision of the Department of Religion and Culture. The Department of Finance was responsible for the annual CTA budget and oversaw business operations that provided income for the CTA and employment for Tibetans in tourism, carpet weaving, and handicraft production. The Department of Education managed thirty-three schools and a major child sponsorship scheme, and oversaw another fifty-one schools in India, Nepal, and Bhutan.[24]

The Department of Security was set up in 1959 to ensure the personal security of the Dalai Lama. The Department also helped refugees renew their Refugee Residential Certificates. This was necessary for most Tibetans, who had yet to become Indian citizens. The CTA policy was to advise Tibetans not to apply for citizenship. The Department of Health was established in 1980. It was mandated to run health centers and hospitals in Tibetan settlements. The department also supervised the Tibetan Medical and Astrological Institute.[25]

The Department of Information and International Relations (DIIR) was responsible for collecting and distributing information on Tibetan affairs, monitoring Chinese language publications, interviewing recent arrivals from Tibet, publishing journals and books in Tibetan and English, and organizing exhibitions, video shows, and public talks. The Department of Home was responsible for rehabilitation schemes for Tibetan refugees. Each settlement had a Welfare Officer or Settlement Officer responsible for looking after the welfare of the settlement's residents. An elected camp leader for each village served as the chief coordinator between the Settlement Officer and the public.[26]

In 1998, the Dalai Lama proposed further reforms to the election of Kalons. These were achieved on March 15, 2001, when the Charter was amended to provide for direct election of the head of the executive (Tibetan: Kalon Tripa) and for the Kalon Tripa to nominate candidates for the election of ministers (Tibetan: Kalon).

In September 2003, the Dalai Lama insisted on giving up the last vestiges of his administrative power. He announced he would no longer make nominations to the Assembly, no longer appoint heads of the three independent institutions of Audit, Public Service, and Election Commission, and no longer nominate Supreme Justice Commissioners. Selection committees were to be formed for the appointment of the Supreme Justice Commissioners and the heads of the three independent institutions.[27]

In 2011, the Assembly formally changed its name from Assembly of Tibetan People's Deputies (ATPD) to the Tibetan Parliament in Exile (TPiE). The Chairman's title was changed to that of Speaker and the Vice Chairman to Deputy Speaker.

On March 10, 2011, the Dalai Lama announced his retirement from the position as head of state, suggesting that the necessary amendments be made to the Charter to devolve the authority of the Dalai Lama to the elected leader. The Parliament reluctantly agreed. On April 27, 2011, the Chief Election Commissioner announced the new members of Parliament and declared Dr. Lobsang Sangay as the Kalon Tripa.

All Tibetans twenty-five years of age or older can stand for election to the parliament, while the minimum age for voting is eighteen. Sessions are held twice every year. A standing committee of twelve members is in place when the Parliament is not in session, consisting of two members from each region, one from each religious denomination, and one directly nominated by the Dalai Lama.

Representation and Identities in the Making

Tibetan refugees have come from all three regions of Tibet, but the majority came from central Tibet (Ü-tsang). The initial wave of Tibetan refugees included followers of all four schools of Tibetan Buddhism and Bon, and the heads of these schools escaped into exile as well. For the young Dalai Lama, the immediate mission was to rebuild the Tibetan nation along with the introduction of new public institutions, including cultural and educational institutions that highlighted the common Tibetan culture and national identity.

As soon as they arrived in the diaspora, Tibetan refugees started to organize in welfare associations according to their region or place of origin (Tibetan: *skyidug*). These organizations operated independently of the institutions established by the Tibetan government-in-exile. The number of Tibetan settlements has grown steadily. As of 2009, about 130 Tibetan settlements and communities were located in various parts of India, Nepal, and Bhutan. Of the forty-seven large settlements, thirty-seven had elected local assemblies: "The local administration is accountable to the local assembly and the local assembly to the people. A settlement constitutes a cluster of camps or villages. Each village in the cluster elects a camp leader who keeps in touch with the Settlement Officers, thus forming a sort of democratic pyramid."[28] In smaller settlements established without support from the exile government, refugees tended to congregate according to their native area, such as Kham, Amdo, or Tsang. As noted by Dawa Norbu, a Tibetan political scientist, "sub-national identities" prevailed in Tibet long before the 1950s: "Regionally, Tibetans identified themselves as Khampa, Topa, Tsangpa, and Amdo-wa of Kham, Toi, Tsang (Shigatse), and Amdo regions. Sectarian identity is rooted in the different traditions of Tibetan Buddhism and is particularly powerful among the lamas. Regional identities and attachments to homelands (phayul) are more popular among the laity. In practice, of course, sectarian and territorial identities may overlap and reinforce each other."[29] The young fourteenth Dalai Lama was eager to introduce a democratic system of government in the early years of exile.[30] To accomplish this, he wanted the new Tibetan polity to represent all three regions of Tibet: Ü-tsang, Kham, and Amdo. The Dalai Lama also wanted all four schools of Tibetan Buddhism, and Bon, the indigenous religion of Tibet, to be equally represented. He saw the importance of equal political representation not just for the sake of equality but to unite all Tibetans in the diaspora, including religious minorities. This was the groundwork for a nation in exile, with democratic institutions based on a constitutional charter.[31]

Six decades after the 1959 exodus, diaspora Tibetans continue to identify strongly with their region (Tibetan: *cholkha*) as they define themselves as Tibetans. Every region maintains a regional organization with a main office and a Standing Committee, and branches in all the major Tibetan settlements. The headquarters of these committees are based in Dharamsala. A key purpose of these organizations is to act as *cholkha* representative bodies.

Since 1959, 164 monasteries and seven nunneries have been "re-established" in India and Nepal. Sera was "rebuilt" in Byllakuppe; Ganden and Drepung in Mundgod; and Nechung and Namgyal in Dharamsala. As of 1992, there were about thirteen thousand monks and five hundred nuns in these monasteries and nunneries, a third of whom had arrived since 1980 as new refugees.[32] The monasteries are still vital institutions of the exile community, but their role in society has undergone significant changes. Monasteries no longer control large estates, nor do they engage in moneylending. The largest Gelugpa monasteries depend on the Central Tibetan Administration for most of their funds.

The Dalai Lama's idea of a democratic Tibet is nowhere better reflected than in the organizational structure of the Tibetan parliament, where seats of both regional and religious representatives are allocated to form a representative body of the people of Tibet. Demographically, Tibetans from western and central Tibet (Ü-tsang) dominate the diaspora population by 70 percent, while Tibetans from Kham and Amdo constitute the remaining 30 percent of the population. As for the religious traditions, the great majority of Tibetans follow the Gelugpa school, while followers of the other schools and Bon are small minorities. Nevertheless, the parliamentary seats remain divided equally among religious schools and regions: two seats for each of the five religious schools and ten seats for each of the three regions. In addition, two seats are reserved for Tibetans living in North America, two seats are reserved for Tibetans living in Europe and Africa, and one seat is reserved for Tibetans living in Australasia, irrespective of the inequality in representation this setup produces.[33] Once elected, parliamentarians are expected to work in the interest of the Tibetan community as a whole. This is expressed in the official oath parliamentarians take when they accept their position. In practice, some parliamentarians adopt a divisive stance, based on their regional or religious affiliation, or personal interests.

In the early days of Tibetan democracy, the regional *cholkha* organizations were tasked with nominating candidates for parliamentary elections and for the position of head of the executive (Tibetan: Kalon Tripa, later Sikyong). This mandate was abolished in 2017, when Dr. Lobsang Sangay served as Sikyong. Sangay argued this was necessary to prevent identity politics from dominating electoral politics.

The Tibetan diaspora also has subregional welfare associations (Tibetan: *skyidug*) that are far less political in nature than the regional committees. These are grassroots, nongovernmental welfare organizations that function mainly as help centers for people who come from the same place in Tibet. Moreover, they also serve as an arena for socialization for second- or third-generation Tibetans whose parents were born in the same part of Tibet. Being displaced from their homeland and unable to return, place-based identity is reinforced in a combination of personal memories of lived experience and narratives of home that are retold across generations, as well as a national discourse of longing for Tibet as the homeland.

The main task of the welfare associations is to help the poor and needy individuals and families in the diaspora who come from a specific area of Tibet. There are dozens of such associations in the Tibetan diaspora. At present, these associations are particularly visible in the virtual world, as their members are scattered across the world. The primary objective of these organizations is to look after the socioeconomic well-being of its members, but because they are place-based, they can also be arenas for regional identity politics. During recent elections, many of these platforms have become sites of identity politics.

Parliamentary sessions are often live streamed on Tibet TV for viewers across the world.[34] This appears to exacerbate the tendency toward regionalism and factionalism. The number of viewers has been rising significantly in the last few years, as political disputes and disagreements have intensified. In the new virtual environment, subregional identities appear mainly to reinforce regional identities.

A Constitutional Crisis

In 2020, a constitutional crisis occurred in the Tibetan diaspora. The conflict started with a disagreement between the Supreme Justice Commission (SJC) and the Tibetan Parliament-in-Exile over the postponement of the parliament's winter session (September 2020–March 2021) "due to Covid-19."[35] The justices argued that the parliamentarians violated the Charter by failing to meet for their session and decided to punish the parliament's Standing Committee for their dereliction of duty by removing their voting rights during the preliminary Sikyong and parliamentary elections in 2021.[36] In response, the parliament proposed to dismiss all three judges from their positions, accusing them of interference in the work of legislative branch of government. According to the parliamentarians, the justice commissioners violated article 58 of the Constitutional Charter for Tibetans-in-Exile,[37] which states that the SCJ has no authority to interfere in the work of the Parliament.[38] The resolution was passed in March 2021 by more than a two-thirds majority in the Parliament.[39] All three judges publicly accepted the resolution and left their positions, while insisting they had done nothing wrong.[40] The parliamentary resolution led to a situation in which there was no functioning Supreme Justice Commission.

This all took place in the middle of an election season, with the election of a new Sikyong (executive head of government) and new members of the legislative body less than a month away. According to the constitution, the newly elected Sikyong and parliamentarians must take their oath of office in front of the Chief Justice Commissioner. However, due to the earlier parliamentary resolution, all the justices had been dismissed. Social media chatrooms were ablaze with debate about the parliament's resolution to fire the judges, as were Tibetan-language media. An interview with the former Kalon Tripa, Professor Samdhong Rinpoche, broadcast by Voice of Tibet, had significant influence on the dispute.[41] A highly respected authority in the Tibetan diaspora, Rinpoche was involved in drafting the Charter in the early 1990s. In the interview, Rinpoche maintained that the Parliament had no authority to dismiss the judges. He also questioned the method by which the Parliament passed the resolution. The interview sparked an intense reaction in the diaspora community, especially among former Kalons and judges, who appealed to the Standing Committee to withdraw the resolution. The outgoing cabinet under the leadership of Lobsang Sangay appointed a committee to find new candidates for the positions of the judges but failed to find willing candidates.

An extraordinary parliamentary session was proposed to settle the matter, but members failed to assemble. In the meantime, diaspora Tibetans had elected a new Sikyong and new parliamentary members, while the three ousted judges returned to their former positions, citing the interview with Rinpoche and the democratic crisis. According to the constitution, the newly elected Sikyong and parliamentarians must take an oath of office in front of the Chief Justice. Without the Chief Justice, the new Sikyong and representatives could not be inaugurated. Thus, the justices returned to let the new Sikyong take his oath in front of the Chief Justice. However, the problem reemerged when the newly elected members of parliament were to take their oath. Most of the parliamentarians refused to take their oath in front of the *pro tempore* Speaker, since he had taken his oath in front of the ousted Chief Justice. They argued that the commissioners had no authority to return without a parliamentary mandate. This further divided the parliament, which entered a stalemate until the Dalai Lama finally intervened, telling the members of parliament to take their oath in front of the pro tempore Speaker.

The conflict between the Supreme Justice Commission and the Tibetan exile legislature was deeply destructive to the democratic process.[42] Initially, the political crisis appeared to be a conflict over authority between the Supreme Justice Commission and the parliament, but as the controversy unfolded it took on a tone of factionalism, and even regionalism.

When the resolution to oust the justices was first passed, it was backed by representatives from all regions and religious schools, with a majority of more than two-thirds. However, identity politics, factionalism, and the intense use of social media messaging heightened the tension and contributed to the crisis spiraling out of control. When Tibetan politicians engaged in regional alliances, the constitutional crisis continued even after the elections were over and a new Sikyong and new members of parliament were inaugurated. While members of parliament were polarized, divided into supporters and opponents of the Justice Commission, regionalist discourses came to the forefront of the Tibetan social media, with both sides accusing each other of disrespecting or violating the Charter.

The parties in the conflict were thus divided along regional lines. Representatives from Ü-tsang and Amdo banded together as one group against representatives from Kham and the five religious traditions, together with a single Ü-tsang representative. The composition of the two parties to the conflict suggests that identity politics played a tacit role in this political drama. This has cast a shadow over the idea of a united diaspora Tibet as enshrined in the Charter.

Virtual Tibet Challenged

The Dalai Lama and the Tibetan government-in-exile have worked hard to create a representative and united "virtual" Tibet in the diaspora, and to not only survive but also give voice to Tibetans inside the "real" Tibet. The objective was to preserve Tibetan culture for posterity in the hopes that Tibetans will one day be able to return to a free Tibet, bringing the "virtual" and the "real" Tibetan nation together.

Regional and religious identities have been part and parcel of the reinvention of a Tibetan national identity in exile. In recent years, however, these identities have begun to play an increasingly prominent role in diaspora politics. On the one hand, regional identities have become the basis of constructing a government in exile based on a shared national identity, while on the other, political representation built on the basis of regional and religious identities appears to help perpetuate and even intensify regionalism in the diaspora. Removing the task of nominating regional candidates from the mandate of the Cholkha committees has done little to address the problem of regionalism. When political contestation heats up, as it did in the 2020–2021 crisis, diaspora Tibetans revert to alliances based on regional identities.

One of the original ideas of the Tibetan government-in-exile was to bring together all Tibetans from across the Tibetan plateau under a single, modern government. From this perspective, the Tibetan exodus to India presented a unique opportunity, as it provided a powerful incentive for Tibetans from across the "greater Tibet" to come together under the leadership of the Dalai Lama. However, decades of attempts to construct a strong national identity has not overcome regionalism and sectarianism in the diaspora polity. This is evident in both social media and exile political institutions, especially electoral politics. Many exile politicians play along with identity politics and intensify regionalist discourse. Importantly, regionalism remains an integral feature of the Tibetan parliamentary setup, as members of parliament continue to be elected by region.

In the immediate aftermath of the exodus to India, Tibetans guided by the Dalai Lama were eager to establish diaspora institutions to preserve and share expressions of Tibetan cultural identity, and to assert a national political identity based on the ideal of liberal democracy. The Dalai Lama had the ability to unite Tibetan refugees of all regions and religious denominations and convince them to work together for the good of the Tibetan nation. Under the Dalai Lama's leadership, Tibetans laid the foundation for what appeared to be a vibrant democracy with representation of all the Tibetan regions and religious denominations. However, a closer look into the political scene shows that regionalism and divisive identity politics is a constant challenge. While many diaspora Tibetans are dissatisfied with the current development, the Tibetan government-in-exile seems unable to bring Tibetans back to the sense of unity that existed in the early years of exile. On the contrary, many exile politicians highlight their regional identity and exploit regional networks to gain popularity with their voters. When electoral politics is dominated by regionalism, the discourse on the united Tibetan national identity suffers.

Conclusion

In 2011, the Dalai Lama relinquished his political position to the elected head of the government (Tibetan: Kalon Tripa). Despite decades of nation-building efforts and a smooth transfer of political power to an elected executive head, "virtual" Tibetan politics is marred by a strong appeal to regionalism and an increasing use of social media for minute political debate. In the absence of political parties, regional identity has become one of the major divisive elements creating "us" versus "them" within the Tibetan diaspora. Although these fault-lines existed prior to the Dalai Lama's resignation from his political position, and prior to the exodus from Tibet, they were not as prominent as they have been in the past decade, and especially during the latest election cycles. There are growing forces of disunity and divisiveness at play, primarily due to identity politics, especially since the 2016 election. This is detrimental to the development of a fully functioning Tibetan exile democracy in the years to come. The constitutional crisis in 2020–2021 was indicative of a trend in which regionalism is becoming increasingly prominent, while the vision of a common Tibetan nation deteriorates. Having experienced this unprecedented setback, the Tibetan Parliament-in-Exile is currently performing its duties as it should. Questions remain, however, as to how diaspora Tibetans will be able to overcome the hurdles of identity politics and regionalism.

Tibet-in-exile has persisted as a "virtual Tibet" since 1959, celebrating its sixtieth anniversary in 2019. At present, this "virtual Tibet" is at a juncture, fraught with rapid cultural encroachment inside Tibet and a lack of meaningful progress in the Dalai Lama's dialogue with Beijing. More importantly, "virtual Tibet" is also facing unprecedented challenges of continuity and survival in its nation-building endeavor. These challenges may appear insignificant at present, while the fourteenth Dalai Lama is still there to intervene in a constitutional crisis. In the future, however, such crises of political legitimacy may disrupt or derail the nation-building project and even lead to the demise of "virtual Tibet" in the Dalai Lama's absence. The recent crisis suggests that the deficit of political maturity and ineffectiveness of checks and balances in the political structure are key challenges that future leaders of the Tibetan diaspora will have to navigate.

Religious and regional identities are fundamental to the very definition of Tibet and "Tibetaness," embedded in the sense of belonging and "home" of Tibetan refugees. Regional identities are not controversial *per se*, but they are divisive when played into politics, fracturing the community into "us" versus "them." With the rapid digitalization of social life, local community- and faith-based identities can easily find new virtual spaces to be nurtured and thrive, just like the national identity. This sense of belonging coupled with composition of the exile Tibetan parliament based on religious denomination and regional identity provides opportunities for identity politics, discord, and division.

Notes

1. Gyatso, Tenzin, *14th Dalai Lama, My Land and My People: The Memoirs of His Holiness the Dalai Lama of Tibet*, 2nd edition (New Delhi: Srishti Publishers, 1997). See also Gyatso, Tenzin, 14th Dalai Lama, Freedom in Exile: The Autobiography of the Dalai Lama (Calcutta: Rupa & Co., 1990).

2. Ibid.

3. See, for instance, the Tibetan parliament website: https://tibetanparliament.org/ and Tibet Online TV: www.tibetonline.tv.

4. Orville Schell, *Virtual Tibet: Searching for Shangri-la from the Himalayas to Hollywood* (New York: Metropolitan Books, 2000).

5. Claes Corlin, "The Nation in Your Mind. Continuity and Change among Tibetan Refugees in Nepal," Doctoral dissertation, Department of Social Anthropology, Gothenburg University. 1975; Margaret Nowak, *Tibetan Refugees: Youth and the New Generation of Meaning* (New Brunswick, NJ: Rutgers, 1984), see also Åshild

Kolås, "The Struggle for an Independent Tibet," Cand. Polit. Thesis, Department and Museum of Anthropology, University of Oslo, 1994.

6. The Chinese-owned WeChat app used to be an important tool for diaspora Tibetans to communicate with relatives and friends inside Tibet. In 2020, the Indian government imposed a ban on Chinese apps, including WeChat, leading to a massive exodus from WeChat to other social media platforms such as WhatsApp and Telegram.

7. Kolås, Åshild. "The Struggle for an Independent Tibet," Cand. Polit. Thesis, Department and Museum of Anthropology, University of Oslo, 1994, 49. See also Tsering. Shakya, *The Dragon in the Land of Snows: A History of Modern Tibet since 1947* (London: Pimlico, 1999).

8. Warren W. Smith, *Tibetan Nation: A History of Tibetan Nationalism and Sino-Tibetan Relations* (Boulder, CO: Westview, 1996).

9. Isabelle Henrion-Dourcy, "Tibet" in *The Wiley-Blackwell Encyclopedia of Race, Ethnicity and Nationalism*, 2016, 1.

10. Ibid.

11. Bina Roy Burman, *Religion and Politics in Tibet* (New Delhi: Vikas, 1979); Corlin, "The Nation in Your Mind"; Fiona McConnell, "The Geopolitics of Buddhist Reincarnation: Contested Futures of Tibetan Leadership," *Area* 45, no. 2 (2013): 162–169; Phuntsog Wangyal, "The Influence of Religion on Tibetan Politics," *The Tibet Journal* 1, no. 1 (1975): 78–86.

12. Kolås, "The Struggle for an Independent Tibet"; Åshild Kolås, *Tourism and Tibetan Culture in Transition: A Place Called Shangrila* (London: Routledge, 2007).

13. Kolås, "The Struggle for an Independent Tibet," 90–93.

14. Tibetan Parliamentary and Policy Research Centre. Tibetan Parliament-in-exile. www.tpprc.org/tpie.html

15. Dongkar Thinly, "bod kyi chos srid zung 'brel lam lugs skor bshad pa" [The Merging of Religious and Secular Rule in Tibet]. Beijing: mi rigs dpe skrun khang (Beijing: Foreign Languages Press, 2004).

16. John F. Avedon, *In Exile from the Land of Snows* (London: Wisdom, 1985), 138.

17. Assembly of Tibetan People's Deputies. Booklet on the democratization of Tibet's parliament in exile (Dharamsala, 2009). www.tpprc.org/publication/tpie2009.pdf

18. Ibid., 19.

19. Avedon, *In Exile from the Land of Snows*.

20. Assembly of Tibetan People's Deputies. Booklet on the democratization of Tibet's parliament in exile (Dharamsala, 2009). www.tpprc.org/publication/tpie2009.pdf

21. Ibid.

22. Central Tibetan Administration (1990). Address of His Holiness the Dalai Lama at Special Congress. Dharamsala, 11 May 1990. https://tibet.net/address-of-his-holiness-the-dalai-lama-at-special-congress-dharamshala-11-may-1990

23. Assembly of Tibetan People's Deputies. Charter of the Tibetans-in-Exile (Dharamsala, 1991). https://tibet.net/wp-content/uploads/2011/06/Charter1.pdf

24. Kolås, "The Struggle for an Independent Tibet," 68.

25. Kolås, "The Struggle for an Independent Tibet."

26. Kolås, "The Struggle for an Independent Tibet," 68.

27. Assembly of Tibetan People's Deputies. Booklet on the democratization of Tibet's parliament in exile (Dharamsala, 2009). www.tpprc.org/publication/tpie 2009.pdf

28. Assembly of Tibetan People's Deputies. Booklet on the democratization of Tibet's parliament in exile (Dharamsala, 2009), 49.

29. Dawa Norbu, "'Otherness' and the Modern Tibetan Identity," *Himal*, May/June: 10–11 (1992), 10.

30. Tenzin Gyatso, *14th Dalai Lama, My Land and My People: The Memoirs of His Holiness the Dalai Lama of Tibet*, 2nd edition (New Delhi: Srishti Publishers, 1997); Gyatso, Tenzin, *14th Dalai Lama, Freedom in Exile: The Autobiography of the Dalai Lama* (Calcutta: Rupa & Co., 1990).

31. Assembly of Tibetan People's Deputies. Charter of the Tibetans-in-Exile (Dharamsala, 1991). https://tibet.net/wp-content/uploads/2011/06/Charter1.pdf

32. Planning Council. Tibetan Refugee Community Integrated Development Plan, 1992–97 (Dharamsala: Central Tibetan Administration, 1992), 183.

33. Tibetan Parliament-in-Exile: An Introduction and Insight, 6th edition (Dharamsala: Central Tibetan Administration, 2017).

34. For example, Central Tibetan Administration. Eighth Day of Budget Session of the 16th Tibetan Parliament-in-Exile. Dharamsala, 24 March 2021. https://tibet.net/the-eighth-day-of-the-budget-session-of-the-16th-tibetan-parliament-in-exile

35. Phayul Media. Tibetan Parliament votes out top judges of apex court (2021). www.youtube.com/watch?v=pf3f8kn55Pg, 03:48

36. Supreme Justice Commission. Notification to the Election Committee (31 December 2020).

37. Assembly of Tibetan People's Deputies. Charter of the Tibetans-in-Exile (Dharamsala, 1991). https://tibet.net/wp-content/uploads/2011/06/Charter1.pdf

38. Voice of Tibet. Exclusive Interview with Professor Samdhong Rinpoche (2020). www.youtube.com/watch?v=hpQMRJYSdt4, 44:24

39. Phayul Media. Tibetan Parliament votes out top judges of apex court (2021). www.youtube.com/watch?v=pf3f8kn55Pg, 03:48

40. Radio Free Asia. Members of Tibetan Supreme Justice commission said no one is "above the law" (2021). www.youtube.com/watch?v=qE1L8MFqi7Q, 5:17

41. Voice of Tibet. Exclusive Interview with Professor Samdhong Rinpoche (2020). www.youtube.com/watch?v=hpQMRJYSdt4, 44:24.

42. Phayul Media. Tibetan Parliament votes out top judges of apex court (2021), www.youtube.com/watch?v=pf3f8kn55Pg, 03:48; Radio Free Asia, Members of Tibetan Supreme Justice commission said no one is "above the law" (2021). www.youtube.com/watch?v=qE1L8MFqi7Q, 5:17.

References

Assembly of Tibetan People's Deputies. 2009. *Booklet on the Democratization of Tibet's Parliament in Exile*. Dharamsala. www.tpprc.org/publication/tpie2009.pdf

Assembly of Tibetan People's Deputies. 1991. *Charter of the Tibetans-in-Exile*. Dharamsala. https://tibet.net/wp-content/uploads/2011/06/Charter1.pdf

Avedon, John F. 1985. *In Exile from the Land of Snows*. London: Wisdom.

Burman, Bina Roy. 1979. *Religion and Politics in Tibet*. New Delhi: Vikas.

Central Tibetan Administration. 1990. *Address of His Holiness the Dalai Lama at Special Congress*. Dharamsala, May 11, 1990. https://tibet.net/address-of-his-holiness-the-dalai-lama-at-special-congress-dharamshala-11-may-1990

Central Tibetan Administration. 2021. *Eighth Day of Budget Session of the 16th Tibetan Parliament-in-Exile*. Dharamsala, March 24, 2021. https://tibet.net/the-eighth-day-of-the-budget-session-of-the-16th-tibetan-parliament-in-exile

Central Tibetan Administration. 2017. *Tibetan Parliament-in-Exile: An Introduction and Insight*. 6th edition. Dharamsala: Central Tibetan Administration.

Corlin, Claes. "The Nation in Your Mind. Continuity and Change among Tibetan Refugees in Nepal." Doctoral dissertation, Department of Social Anthropology, Gothenburg University, 1975.

Gyatso, Tenzin, 14th Dalai Lama. 1990. *Freedom in Exile: The Autobiography of the Dalai Lama*. Calcutta: Rupa & Co.

Gyatso, Tenzin, 14th Dalai Lama. 1997. *My Land and My People: The Memoirs of His Holiness the Dalai Lama of Tibet*. 2nd edition. New Delhi: Srishti Publishers.

Henrion-Dourcy, Isabelle. 2016. "Tibet" in *The Wiley-Blackwell Encyclopedia of Race, Ethnicity and Nationalism*.

Kolås, Åshild. 1994. "The Struggle for an Independent Tibet." Cand. Polit. Thesis, Department and Museum of Anthropology, University of Oslo.

Kolås, Åshild. 2007. *Tourism and Tibetan Culture in Transition: A Place Called Shangrila*. London: Routledge.

McConnell, Fiona. 2013. "The Geopolitics of Buddhist Reincarnation: Contested Futures of Tibetan Leadership," *Area* 45, no. 2: 162–169.

Norbu, Dawa. 1992. "'Otherness' and the Modern Tibetan Identity," *Himal* (May/June): 10–11.

Nowak, Margaret. 1984. *Tibetan Refugees: Youth and the New Generation of Meaning*. New Brunswick, NJ: Rutgers University Press.

Phayul Media. 2021. Tibetan Parliament votes out top judges of apex court. www.youtube.com/watch?v=pf3f8kn55Pg, 03:48

Planning Council. 1992. Tibetan Refugee Community Integrated Development Plan, 1992–97. Dharamsala: Central Tibetan Administration.

Radio Free Asia. 2021. Members of Tibetan Supreme Justice commission said no one is "above the law." www.youtube.com/watch?v=qE1L8MFqi7Q, 5:17

Schell, Orville. 2000. *Virtual Tibet: Searching for Shangri-la from the Himalayas to Hollywood.* New York: Metropolitan Books.

Shakya, Tsering. 1999. *The Dragon in the Land of Snows: A History of Modern Tibet since 1947.* London: Pimlico.

Smith, Warren W. 1996. *Tibetan Nation: A History of Tibetan Nationalism and Sino-Tibetan Relations.* Boulder, CO: Westview.

Supreme Justice Commission. 2020. Notification to the Election Committee, 31 December 2020.

Thinly, Dongkar. 2004. "bod kyi chos srid zung 'brel lam lugs skor bshad pa" [The Merging of Religious and Secular Rule in Tibet]. Beijing: mi rigs dpe skrun khang. Beijing: Foreign Languages Press.

Tibetan Parliamentary and Policy Research Centre. Undated. Tibetan Parliament-in-exile. www.tpprc.org/tpie.html

Voice of Tibet. 2020. Exclusive Interview with Professor Samdhong Rinpoche. www.youtube.com/watch?v=hpQMRJYSdt4, 44:24

Wangyal, Phuntsog. 1975. "The Influence of Religion on Tibetan Politics, *The Tibet Journal* 1, no. 1: 78–86.

9

Self-Determination and National Liberation in Kurdistan in the Twentieth and Twenty-First Centuries

JOOST JONGERDEN

Introduction

Located in the northern Middle East, Kurdistan includes southeastern Turkey, western Iran, northern Iraq, and parts of northern Syria. After Arabs, Persians, and Turks, Kurds comprise the largest ethnicity in western Asia, counting a population of some thirty to forty million people. The largest part of this population lives in Turkey, where an estimated ten to twenty million Kurds make up between 15 to 25 percent of the total population. The seven million Kurds in Iraq constitute approximately 25 percent of the population there, with the eight million Kurds in Iran and over two million Kurds in Syria accounting for around ten percent of the total populations of those countries. Today's division of the Kurds across different states is the result of the transformation of empires into nation-states. Although Kurdish national movements did emerge in the nineteenth century, they were weak actors, and in the post–World War I power play that followed the Ottoman collapse, the Kurds became divided by the new borders marking out Turkey, Iraq, Syria, and Iran.

The regimes that emerged in these new states equated nation-building with a standardization of the population. They considered the nation their garden, employing a metaphor coined by the sociologist Zygmunt Bauman,[1] determining some parts of the social habitat as belonging and others as its weeds: "Like all other weeds, they must be segregated, contained, prevented from spreading, removed, and kept outside society's boundaries; if all these means prove insufficient, they must be killed."[2] In the garden of the nation-state, the Kurds became a people to many.

One of the great ideologues of Turkish nationalism, Ziya Gökalp, formulated the gardener's job in a famous poem thus:[3]

> The people is like a garden
> We are supposed to be its gardeners!
> First the bad shoots are to be cut
> And then the scion is to be grafted.

The "cutting of the bad shoots" was enacted in several ways, including population exchanges between Turkey and its neighbors to the (north)west[4] and the destruction of the Armenian population.[5] The crafting of the scion in the Republic of Turkey involved a range of methods intended to "civilize" those who were considered to be "not-yet" Turks. It was in this context of assimilative efforts aimed at destroying the Kurdish identity that the Kurdish issue and Kurdish national movements emerged.[6]

Attempts to discuss the formation and development of Kurdish national movements run the risk of falling into two traps. The first risk concerns the trap of providing a chronology of the many political actors trying to found a state through which to animate a Kurdish nation. The second is the search for the origins of a Kurdish nation. This involves both an *ethnogenesis*, in which the nation is defined on the basis of an ancient ethnic identity, and *sitogenesis*, in which the nation is defined through its belonging to an ancient homeland.[7] These are traps that problematically conflate elaborate description with essentialist claims.

This chapter takes a different approach, discussing the relationship between Kurdish political actors and the *ideas* of nation, state, and nation-state. It first discusses the Kurdish issue as an effect of the disintegration and breakdown of empires and their transformation toward culturally restrictive political spaces in which the Kurdish identity became a target for destruction. Thus, it was in this context that Kurdish political actors started to develop the desire for a state of their own and claimed the right to self-determination. As will be discussed, however, frictions emerged among the Kurdish claims and definitions of the right to self-determination as racially exclusive (in the so-called "liberal" definition), geographically exclusive (in the UN decolonization definition), and politically restricted (in the Marxist definition). A critical assessment of the concept of self-determination is followed by the Kurdistan Workers Party's (*Partiya Karkêren Kurdistan*, PKK) redefinition of it as societal empowerment.

The Emergence of Kurdish Nationalism

Studies of nations and nationalism distinguish roughly between three different approaches. These can be categorized around the following analogies: the nation as organic, as an onion, or as an artichoke.[8] The organic view is rooted in German romanticism and sees the nation as given by nature. The nation is a human collectivity represented as an enduring feature of human society. Each nation bears a fundamental essence, which makes it distinct from other nations. As an ideology and political movement that emerged in the nineteenth and twentieth centuries, nationalism adds a new political feature to the idea of the nation: the nation-state. Based on the premise that the borders of the state as a political entity and the nation as a cultural entity[9] should be territorially congruent yet facing cultural difference on the ground,[10] the very idea of congruence gave rise to the politics of genocide (e.g., of the Armenians), expulsion (e.g., the Turkey–Greece population exchanges) and assimilation (e.g., the Turkification of Kurds).[11] This is the nation-state nationalism that became the dominant form that developed in much of the former Ottoman Empire.

Unlike the organic or primordial idea of the nation, the more recent "onion" analogy or modernist approach to nations and nationalism holds that these are essentially modern phenomena. The main proponent of this approach is Ernest Gellner,[12] who asserts that (1) nations and nationalism are the inevitable consequence of industrial society, and (2) it is nationalism that engenders nations, and not the other way around. Underlining the nation's invented character, Gellner argues that nationalism creates its "tradition" as a patchwork of bits and pieces made from an (invented) past: "The cultural shreds and patches used by nationalism are often arbitrary historical inventions," he writes. "Any old shred and patch would have served as well."[13]

Thus, the nation has no historical past (just a mythology), and hence the analogy with an onion, whose layers can be peeled away to reveal nothing.[14]

The third approach is the "artichoke" or ethno-symbolist approach, a response to the modernist. One of the main protagonists of this slant was Anthony Smith, a student of Ernest Gellner. Although the ethno-symbolists share with the modernists the idea that the nation is both a modern phenomenon and socially constructed, they also argue that the story of the nation does not begin there since it does have historical origins. The modern nation is influenced by premodern ethnic legacies, which implies the need for an analysis that considers differences and similarities between modern nations and the collective cultural units of previous eras.[15] The core of this ethnicity resides in myths and symbols that are transmitted through generations, creating group identities on the basis of cultural distinctions made and the maintenance of a boundary between "self" and "other" on the basis of these myths and symbols. Nations, in this view, are modern cultural complexes crafted and grafted upon an ethnic core passed down from generation to generation. Hence, the analogy of the artichoke, whose modern national leaves surround a perennial ethnic heart.[16]

While ethno-symbolists believe that modernists disregard the past, modernists hold that the world of nations was created around the end of the eighteenth century and nothing before is of relevant consequence.[17] A debate on the role of "history" has been a divisive issue in explications of Kurdish nationalism. Essentially, it asks whether nations have an origin, in the meaning of a lineage from which they evolve, or just a starting point before which there was nothing. Some have argued that origins are indispensable for an understanding of Kurdish nationalism. They regard it a mistake to ignore continuities between today's nationalism and nations, on the one hand, and ideas and societal formations located in the past, on the other. This de-historicizes both nations and nationalism, from the mapping of the nation and its territorial boundaries to the structures of political power in nationalist movements and the visions of past and current elites.[18]

Other authors, however, maintain that Kurdish nationalism has no past. They consider Kurdish nationalism an effect of the collapse of the Ottoman Empire with a link to the past engineered.[19] Since there is no past of contemporary Kurdish nationalism, it is argued, one need not look for the origins of Kurdish nationalism, only for its beginnings and how it creates the idea of a historical origin. Kurdish nationalism, like any nationalism, animates a past, which makes the Kurdish nation (like any other) a discursive construct of nationalism.[20]

A New Polity

Most authors agree to locate the emergence of Kurdish nationalism at the end of World War I.[21] A foundational moment for this politicization of Kurdish cultural identity was the collapse of the Ottoman Empire and creation of Turkey as a nation-state, which led to a shift from a decentralized polity that showed little concern for the ethnic or cultural identity of people to a centralized polity obsessed with the ethnic and cultural identity of its population.

Spread across Europe, North Africa, and Asia, the Ottoman Empire had been an assemblage of systems of direct and indirect rule. The main areas effectively centralized were parts of the Balkans and Egypt, along with key transportation routes; the remaining territories were mostly self-governed. In Kurdistan, a vassal system was constructed from the interactions between Ottomans and local fiefdoms.[22] These emirates or principalities had an ambiguous relationship with the central state,[23] characterized by submission to but also autonomy from. Their location, at a zone of conflict between the Ottoman and Persian Empires, created possibilities to negotiate further autonomy.[24] Moreover, the rulers of the Empire did not consider themselves the bearers of a national identity or representatives of a nation, nor did they express any urge to mold, shape, and create a population.

The status of the emirates started to change in the first half of the nineteenth century. The center began to enforce its authority as a way of bolstering the Empire. Central state administration started to gain control and replace indirect rule.[25] Looking at Kurdistan from the time frame of the fifteenth to twentieth centuries, Martin van Bruinessen[26] characterized the political developments in the region as a reverse state formation process since Kurdish society passed through the "stages" of (proto-)state to chiefdom and tribe. One could add that in the Republic's early, radical years, the Kemalist regime further targeted tribal and religious authority in order to create a country of subjects directly bound to the state.

The disintegration of the larger political institutions in Kurdistan and the aggressiveness of nascent Turkish and Arab as well as Persian nationalism threatened Kurdish political elites and the linguistic and cultural expressions of Kurdish identity in daily life. And it was in this context that Kurdish resistance emerged, first as elite responses to the erosion of their positions of authority, and then in the second half of the twentieth century as a popular movement advocating self-determination.

In the transition from Empire to Republic, the central state increasingly imposed its authority, and its marriage with an aggressive Turkish nationalism started to create new political fault lines around cultural identity, as Kurds had to self-define as Turks and become competent in the political vocabulary of the Kemalist elite to count as citizens.[27] The situation was similar in Iran under "Pahlavi absolutism," in which a centralized administration aimed to construct a uniform Iranian national identity. This eventually became a principal force behind the establishment of the Republic of Mahabad, the independent state of 1946 that, though short-lived, had an enormous impact on the political imagination of the Kurds.[28]

The Arab nationalists of the Ba'ath regime considered the cultural integration of the Kurds into a Syrian identity in the 1960s and 1970s to be "delicate," at best. The prevalent view was that the Kurds were a malignancy in the side of the Arab nation that had to be removed.[29] In the process of nation-state formation, the Kurds became the "other," whose identity required erasure to build the nation that paradoxically was claimed to already exist in the territory of these states.[30]

In response to the developing state-centralist nationalism in the nineteenth and early twentieth centuries, Kurdish elite groups waged several struggles, aiming to claim and maintain some form of autonomy. These rebellions were both brief and protracted but ultimately failed. They were geographically confined and politically mostly limited to the followers of religious and tribal leaders.[31] The approach of the Ottoman state toward rebellions in general was twofold. It would crush them with the means available, but it also viewed these uprisings as a bargaining strategy employed by subordinate or peripheral groups to address their concerns and improve their status within the Empire.[32] The Kurdish elites were experienced in negotiating since many of them also occupied significant posts within the Ottoman state.[33] Similar to the Ottoman state, the Republican regime repressed rebellions, but this was not followed by a revised "contract" with subordinate Kurdish groups at its periphery. For the Republic, state power rested not on delegation and alliances but on the linkage of Turkish identity to territory. The Kurdish identity itself became a target to be destroyed.[34]

Kurdish nationalism emerged as a response to the disintegration and breakdown of the Ottoman state.[35] Yet "it was not just the downfall of the Ottoman Empire that encouraged Kurdish ethnonationalism, but also the conscious transformation of the Empire from an ethnically tolerant to an ethically defined, restrictive political space."[36] It is in this context that Kurdish political actors started to claim the right to a state.

Self-Determination and National Liberation

Only a few years before Turkey became established as a nation-state, President Wilson[37] heralded "national aspirations" as something that "must be respected" since "peoples may now be dominated and governed only by their own consent"; indeed, " 'self-determination' is not a mere phrase," he stated, but "an imperative principle of actions." Referring to the political principle Wilson had introduced, Kurdish elites made claim to their right to statehood. References to the Treaty of Sèvres, which had developed the possibility of a separate state of Kurdistan, were to no avail as this agreement became void following the Cairo Conference in 1921 when it was decided that Southern Kurdistan (Mosul province) would be included in the new state of Iraq, and the Lausanne Treaty in 1923[38] that formalized the division of Ottoman Kurdistan between Turkey, Iraq, and Syria.[39] Coming from a devastating war, Britain and France had no intentions of standing up against the assertive new regime in Turkey. Thus, a new state system was born in the Middle East.

After Sèvres and the establishment of the principle of self-determination in international politics, Kurds began to express their wish for self-determination as an inalienable right of nations. Martin Strohmeier[40] argues that this came with a different attitude toward the would-be population of their state on the part of the Kurdish elite active in nationalist movements. Where these elites had previously seen backwardness and ignorance as their main enemies and civilization an ideal aspired to, now they argued for the high level of civilization of Kurds, a moral superiority over the savage Turks and thus qualification for membership of the elite club of independent states. Such claims fell on deaf ears.[41]

Next to the new political realities on the ground, it is important to consider the context of Wilson's "Fourteen Points," in which his principle of self-determination was formulated.[42] Set against the background of the rebuilding of Europe after World War I, these were not intended to reverse the international order of colonialism. As Getachew argues, the Wilsonian principle was "racially differentiated" and "fully compatible with imperial rule."[43] It did not assume non-Western populations as citizens but rather as subjects since they failed to meet the standards of civilization.[44] This was a self-determination of which conditions and unequal membership became a key feature—facilitating tutelage and mandates over so-called "colored races." Those not considered civilized were to "be governed with some minimal consent."[45]

Neither did Kurdish claims for self-determination and the right to a state find an audience when the right to self-determination was propelled into international politics through the anticolonial liberation struggle after World War II. Adopted on December 14, 1960, UN General Assembly Resolution 1514 (XV) declared that "the subjection of peoples to alien subjugation, domination, and exploitation constitutes a denial of fundamental human rights, is contrary to the Charter of the United Nations, and is an impediment to the promotion of world peace and cooperation."[46] However, the principle and practices in this post–World War declaration were mainly directed toward the freeing of territories occupied by the Powers, primarily the dismantling of the British and French Empires and decolonization of the "Third World." Kurdistan, of course, did not fall into this category. Although delegations of Kurds raised their case at the UN at various times in the 1960s and 1970s, it was without effect.[47]

This international deafness has extended into the new millennium. The organization of the 2017 independence referendum in southern Kurdistan, informed by a powerplay of the ruling Barzani family against a loss of legitimacy and reputation,[48] was opposed by the West defending the unity of Iraq against the right of Kurdish self-determination. The denial of a place at the Geneva talks on the future of Syria to the Autonomous Administration of North and East Syria (AANES) echoes the reluctance of international powers and the UN to recognize the Kurds' quest for self-determination. In this context, the Kurdish cause has generally become subsumed under the broader considerations of international rivalries, mostly established by the Cold War, where relations with the regional powers—states—are maintained for their utilitarian value.

Both the Wilson and United Nations' principles of self-determination were restricted in scope and had only a limited appeal to Kurds. However, there was an alternative narrative on self-determination that offered opportunities for state-claiming. Preceding Wilson and the UN, the Bolsheviks had provided a definition of self-determination that "has had great importance to the Kurdish movement."[49] Stalin, the expert on the national question among the Bolsheviks and whose text on the subject became seminal among communists worldwide, had argued in chapter 7 of *Marxism and the National Question* that "the right of self-determination is an essential element in the solution of the national question"[50]—while Lenin[51] had specified in the opening chapter of *The Right of Nations to Self-Determination* that this right meant "the political separation of these nations from alien national bodies and the formation of an independent national state."

The Bolshevik definition of self-determination did not place geopolitical limitations on the principle. Self-determination and thus the right to a state could be claimed as part of a revolutionary struggle by any "stable community of people, formed on the basis of a common language, territory, economic life, and psychological make-up manifested in a common culture."[52] Moreover, while the emphasis of the UN definition was on ending alien rule, conceiving self-determination in the context of bilateral relations between colonizer and colonized, the Bolshevik approach to self-determination came with a radical re-imagination of a world free of domination. Lenin (1916) had argued that "Just as mankind can achieve the abolition of classes only by passing through the transition period of the dictatorship of the oppressed class, so mankind can achieve the inevitable merging of nations only by passing through the transition period of complete liberation of all the oppressed nations, i.e., their freedom to secede."

Most Kurdish national liberation movements emerging after World War II were to claim the Bolshevik terminology of self-determination.[53] Their revolutionary discourse provided a double legitimation of the struggle: first, applying the principle of national self-determination to the Kurdish case and, second, making the Kurdish case part of an international revolutionary struggle. Thus, in the 1970s, Kurdish liberation movements and political parties linked their situation to universalizing principles.[54] This helped the Kurds to imagine an inversion of their position, from that of the object of state-building by the states in which they found themselves to that of the subject or agent of state-building and thence as part of a movement to change the international order.

National Liberation and the Struggle with Marxist Orthodoxy

The emergence of political actors inspired by Marxist ideas coincided with a transformation of societal relationships. In Turkey, industrialization and urbanization undermined the previously hegemonic authority of traditional bonds, such as those between peasant and landlord. Under the influence of urban migration, the formation of a working class (and working-class neighborhoods), and the growth of a student population (facilitated by a scholarship system and accommodation in dormitories), new forms of radical politics emerged.

When Kurds in Turkey took to the streets in the 1960s and 1970s and started to organize, they did so within or in alliance with the Left in

Turkey.[55] In the same period, the Kurdish nationalist movement in Iraq, and its main political party, the Kurdistan Democratic Party (*Partîya Demokrata Kurdistanê*, KDP), had begun to lose part of its appeal to Kurds in Turkey because of infighting and Turkish (state) tutelage. Instead, the revolutionary Left and socialism became an important ideological point of reference and political practice.

Despite supplying the Kurdish movement with renewed vigor and energy, however, Marxist orthodoxy also introduced new problems. First, while, in the 1970s, Kurdish political activists discussed the colonial status of Kurdistan and the Turkish sociologist Ismail Beşikçi[56] introduced the concept of "international colony" for the status of Kurdistan (i.e., as a single entity divided among different colonizing states), the status of colony was denied by most of the parties on the Left.[57] Rather, they argued that colonialism was a feature of the historical stage of imperialism. Turkey could not be an imperialist country since it was itself in the situation of a (semi)-colony to the United States. Relatedly, colonialism was defined as a relationship between a capitalist country and a dependent country, and Turkey was not a capitalist country, its relation with Kurdistan could not be one of colonizer and colony, and nor could the struggle of the Kurdish masses be defined in terms of self-determination.

Second, if the Kurds did not form a nation, what then? Most of the socialist parties at the time, from Iran to Turkey, considered the Kurds an oppressed national or ethnic minority.[58] According to the Stalinist tropes, nations had the right to self-determination, yet the rights of national minorities could only be guaranteed by the democratization of a country. Workers of all nationalities should be organized in one single party and not "isolate themselves within their national shells, fenced off from each other by organizational barriers."[59] Since the Left argued that the political struggle of the Kurds could not be characterized as an anticolonial one, it had to be defined in terms of class struggle. Neither nationality nor a colonial identity but only class was recognized. This was regarded as a signifier of revolutionary meaning and parameter for struggle and organization. All suppressed classes, without differentiating between nations, had to struggle against the ruling class, which had control over the state.[60]

In the Marxist orthodoxy, ethnic nationalism was identified with aspirations of the bourgeoisie wherein the Kurdish bourgeoisie was its regional faction; the Iranian proletariat, with the Kurdish proletariat as its faction, was identified as the agent of a historical process in which a socialist revolution would be followed by the recognition of national (minority) rights.[61] Thus, the struggle for Kurdish rights was perceived as a struggle of a Kurdish proletariat as part of the working class. There was no political autonomy of a Kurdish struggle but rather its subsumption to that of the class struggle.

This Marxist orthodoxy came with a heavy price. In the Iranian case, part of the cadre of the Kurdistan Democratic Party of Iran (*Hîzbî Dêmukratî Kurdistanî Êran*, KDPI), whose history dates back to the establishment of the independent Republic of Mahabad, accepted the Stalinist thesis of a national minority, whereby rights could be secured only through a socialist transformation of Iran. This faction joined the ranks of the pro-Soviet *Tudeh* party or the revolutionary *Fedaiyan*, while *Komala*, emerging from the KDPI at the end of the 1960s, merged with the Maoist Union of Communist Militants.[62]

In Turkey, Marxist theoretical orthodoxy took a different toll. Competition and sectarian conflicts among those following Moscow and those following Peking (Beijing) and theoretical discussions about the character of Turkey—as feudal or with an Asiatic mode of production or capitalist—had an important impact on the definition of objectives for political struggle. The Maoist Three Worlds Theory and its identification of primary and secondary contradictions led *KAWA*, a main Kurdish nationalist party in the 1970s, to consider an "anti-imperialist coalition" with the very same Kemalist regime responsible for a denialist and repressive politics toward the Kurds in Turkey.[63] Other Kurdish nationalist parties, like *Rizgarî*, again turned their backs on rural struggles just when they were growing in intensity. They had declared that the advance of capitalism meant economic progress would render the contradiction between peasant and landlord obsolete when the rural struggle with feudal landlords started to gain traction.[64]

Emerging in the 1970s, the PKK was not so concerned with models and abstract theorems. By declaring revolutions and struggles elsewhere part of a common heritage of the oppressed, the PKK transcended Marxist orthodoxy, referring here by "orthodoxy" to the adherence to a "correct" socialist ideology (i.e., organized in accordance with the emerging international divisions between the Soviet Union and China, as well as Albania and, to a lesser extent, Cuba). The PKK concern was less with the "right" model than with understanding the nature of the oppression of Kurds and the organization of a struggle for liberation Referring to Turkey, from where it emerged, the PKK presented an analysis of the process of colonization to which the Kurds were subjected that distinguished three phases during the Kemalist (Republican) period.

First, there was military occupation, taking rebellions as a pretext, starting with the Sheik Said rebellion and completed after the suppression of the 1938 Dersim rebellion. Second, there was the cultural assimilation process, symbolized by boarding schools, which aimed at culturicide. And third, from the 1960s onward, there was a period of economic colonization, symbolized by a (state-led) agricultural modernization that functioned to break up the traditional (tribal-based) structures of Kurdish society.[65] The organization gained a foothold in Kurdistan already in the early years of its formation, the second half of the 1970s.

The Fall and Rise of Self-determination

When the PKK was established in 1978 as the outcome of a process of group formations that had first begun around 1973, independence was defined in terms of self-determination, envisaged and fought for through the establishment of an independent state. The construction of a state was to be followed by a social revolution, which had to put an end to the traditional, exploitative feudalistic, land ownership–based relationships of Kurdish society. Moreover, the consolidation of Kurdistan was supposed to take place in some form of unity with neighboring peoples, friendships with socialist countries, and an alliance with national liberation movements. Thus, in the 1960s and 1970s, the PKK did not perceive self-determination as state-building as an aim in itself. State-building was both a means to ending colonial domination and relations of exploitation, in which an exploiting feudal class was regarded as a *comprador* of the colonizer, and part of the making of a new international order. Getachew refers to the latter as "worldmaking," thus: "This anticolonial worldmaking envisioned sovereignty beyond the nation-state—it considered self-determination as a combination of state-building and worldmaking."[66]

The political formula for achieving nondomination at the local and international levels was a strong state and a loose federation of states around principles of joint economic development and equal exchange. The strong state was deemed necessary to restructure the colonial state apparatus and expand the state's territorial authority. A federation was required to unite the new, radically re-formed states around common interests and aspirations of equality and nondomination and end the economic dependence (after ending political dependence), as well as fratricidal conflicts.[67] While state-building and international cooperation were important for addressing the political and economic dimension of colonialism and uneven development, a third and cultural dimension of national liberation struggles in the 1960s and 70s should also be mentioned. The ideal of a pan-ethnic unity was advanced in many of these struggles.[68]

This anticolonial conception of worldmaking seems to have disappeared from our political consciousness.[69] This can be analyzed as the result of a threefold failure: first, strong states that had to function as the means to social transformation turned increasingly authoritarian; second, there was little development of an alternative international sphere to that based on unequal relations and exchange; and third, nationalist ideologies were adopted that tried to suppress ethnic and cultural diversity.[70]

The PKK took this perceived failure of national liberation struggles as a prompt for a critical self-investigation. At the time of the formation of the party in the 1970s, it had taken revolutionary struggles elsewhere as a relevant horizon for its own orientation. The October Revolution in Russia, the revolution in China, and the resistances in Vietnam, Angola, Mozambique, Eritrea, and other countries and regions around the world were all looked upon as part of a common heritage of the oppressed.[71] Socialist and liberation movements had not fulfilled their promise of moving toward a world free of domination, and when, toward the end of the 1980s, the self-declared socialist alternative, the Soviet Union, collapsed, PKK leader Abdullah Öcalan began a search for a way in which he could link his critical evaluations of the past experiences to a positive vision for the future.

This review had begun at a meeting of the central committee in 1984 when Öcalan pointed toward the problem of the state in real existing socialism: it was supposed to disappear but instead became more powerful.[72] Yet it was not until its fifth Congress, held from January 8 to 27, 1995, that the PKK was able to properly distance itself from the (old) Soviet Union, declaring it a deviation from socialism.[73] At the congress, Öcalan criticized the "fetishization of the state" and named this as a main reason for the failure of socialism and the liberation struggle. Öcalan's critique originated in his 1980s' speeches on socialism,[74] in which the PKK leader argued that the development of a "bureaucratic state" under "real existing socialism" had resulted in alienation and subjugation.[75] By the end of the 1980s and early 1990s, Öcalan was proposing a "new socialism" based on a societal transformation from below.

A development of this new vision followed Öcalan's abduction, trial, and imprisonment in 1999. In his defense, Öcalan neither justified himself nor made a political statement of the type expected by his followers and Kurdish communities. Instead, rejecting claims for an independent state, Öcalan proposed a new, "truly" democratic republic and a project he referred to as "democratic confederalism," "democratic autonomy," and "democratic nation." He was quickly accused of selling out, yet in his defense, Öcalan indicated he was not retreating from the struggle but searching for a re-establishment of the liberation struggle. From prison, Öcalan started to elaborate on the earlier critique of the state, including its socialist experiments, arguing that liberation cannot be achieved by means of nation-state building but rather by the deepening of self-organization. This was referred to as "radical democracy," in the sense that it aims to develop the concept of democracy beyond nation and state.[76]

In the work of Murray Bookchin, Öcalan found the ideas through which he could give a critique of the way socialist and national liberation movements generally had tried to develop their alternatives.[77] This offered him a perspective to imagine liberation, or the project of emancipation, beyond the state—namely, through the development of a new understanding of self-determination based on societal empowerment. Revolving around the ideas of *democratic autonomy* and *democratic confederalism*, two concepts Öcalan borrowed from Bookchin, the idea of politics, the struggle for liberation was separated from the idea of the state as an institution of order that tends to become an instrument of oppression.

Democratic autonomy implies a re-grounding of the political status of people based on self-administration and relations of people with one another rather than their relations with the state. It seeks to create an institutional framework in which communities develop the capacities to govern their own affairs.[78] Democratic confederalism, meanwhile, refers to the interconnected form that this takes, strengthening local administrative capacities through a confederal weaving of councils at the levels of village, neighborhood, district, city, and region. This makes the multilayered network of assemblies "confederate structures."[79] Although defined as a nonsecessionist understanding of self-determination,[80] these "confederate structures" neither accept nor question existing borders;[81] rather, with the development of confederal structures, national borders lose their meaning.[82] The democratic nation is a community in the making through self-organization. As people can participate in more than one project of community-building through self-organization, the democratic nation is pluralist.[83] And in this understanding, the nation is not organic, not an onion, and not an artichoke, but rather a *meze*, referring to an assortment and defined by its pluralism.

In short, the ideological and political transformation of the PKK can be understood as a response to the failure of the struggle for self-determination in the 1960s and 1970s to constitute a postcapitalist and postimperial world order in the twentieth century.[84] In its operationalization as state-formation, it facilitated the emergence of authoritarian forms of government, while the idea of federation as a politically decentralizing fix for economic dependence never materialized. Moreover, anticolonial nationalism, instead of accommodating social plurality, had tried to replace it with singularity, suppressing group particularity except one.[85] This is the logic behind the attempt to define a politics beyond the state and to plurify the concept of the nation.

Conclusions

The transformation of old anational and uncentralized empires into national and central states marked the beginning of the Kurdish issue as a "national question." It was the making of sovereign ethnic selves[86] that came with a politics of erasure of those perceived as ethnic others. The destruction of Kurdish identity through assimilation became perceived as necessary for the making of the Turkish nation in Anatolia.[87] As a response, and in defense, Kurdish nationalists, too, started to claim a state of their own.

When Kurdish political actors first laid claim to the right to self-determination, the concept had an exclusive character. Wilson's "right" was proclaimed against the background of the reconstruction of Europe and desire to maintain the colonial order outside Europe, as self-determination was the exclusive right of the Western, civilized world. The United Nation's "right" to self-determination was conceived in the context of ending western colonial rule, so bilateral relations between European powers (especially Britain and France) and their colonies. Both these approaches to self-determination were exclusive.

The Marxist approach to self-determination had a more inclusive character, and the call for a new world order had strong appeal, in particular in the 1960s and 1970s, when Kurdish nationalist resurgence developed. Yet, the Marxist orthodox theorem, in which the colonial status of Kurdistan was denied and class was defined as the main parameter of liberation struggle, crippled the Kurdish struggle, too. The PKK was one of the few leftist political parties to emerge at the time relatively unaffected by Marxist orthodoxy, able to view revolutions and resistances across the world as products of their own circumstances as well as part of a common heritage of the oppressed.

At its establishment, the PKK had the foundation of a Kurdistan state as a principal objective. This formation of a state was seen as a prerequisite for ending socioeconomically and politically exploitive and colonizing relations. Yet the establishment of a state was supposed to be followed by regional unity, socialist solidarity, and national liberation movement alliances. This anticolonial account of self-determination through state formation was based on the ideal dominant in the 1960s and 1970s envisaging a postimperial world on the basis of nondomination.[88] National independence was considered a condition for the making of another international order, a meaningful step toward the fulfillment of a "reworlding" political project based on nondomination.[89]

However, with the failure of liberation movements to deliver on their promises of equity and the collapse of the Soviet Union, a latent state critique became articulated with the formulation of a positive alternative: the development of a networked polity referred to by such terms as "democratic autonomy," "democratic confederalism," and "democratic nation." In so doing, the PKK revitalized and gave a new direction to the political imaginary of self-determination. Decolonization was no longer seen as a transition to nation-state[90] but as a transition *beyond* it. Paraphrasing Getachew,[91] the redefinition of self-determination beyond the state in the form of democratic confederalism and democratic autonomy thus marks a radical break with the state model of international society and reestablishes equality and nondomination as a central ideal in the world.

Notes

1. Z. Bauman, *Modernity and the Holocaust* (Cambridge: Polity Press, 1989).

2. Bauman, *Modernity and the Holocaust*, 92.

3. J. Jongerden, *Elite Encounters of a Violent Kind: Milli Ibrahim Pasa, Ziya Gökalp and Political Struggle in Diyarbekir at the end of the 20th century. Social Relations in Ottoman Diyarbekir, 1870–1915* (Leiden: Brill, 2012), 55–84.

4. Seventeen of these "population exchanges" were arranged and conducted in the period 1912–1924. Those considered not to be part of the new nation-states—Turkey, Greece, and the Balkan countries—then being established were permanently expelled from their homelands. One of the most expansive of these enforced migrations, the Greco-Turkish arrangement effected between 1922 and 1924, involved the "exchange" of about 1,250,000 "Greeks" in Turkey for about 400,000 "Turks" in Greece; see S. P. Lados, *The Exchange of Minorities: Bulgaria, Greece, and Turkey* (New York: MacMillan Company, 1932); and K. Ari, *Büyük Mübadele Türkiye'ye Zorunlu Göç 1923–1925* (İstanbul: Tarih Vakfi Yurt Yayinlari, 1995).

5. U. U. Ungor, *The Making of Modern Turkey: Nation and State in Eastern Anatolia, 1913–1950* (Oxford: Oxford University Press, 2012).

Self-Determination and National Liberation for Kurdistan | 223

6. R. Olson, *The Emergence of Kurdish Nationalism and the Sheikh Said Rebellion, 1880–1925* (Austin: University of Texas Press, 1989); C. Houston, *Crafting National Selves* (Oxford: Berg Publishers, 2008); C. Gunes, *The Kurdish National Movement in Turkey: From Protest to Resistance* (London: Routledge, 2012); A. Vali, *The Forgotten Years of Kurdish Nationalism in Iran* (Cham: Palgrave MacMillan, 2020).

7. Houston, *Crafting National Selves*.

8. S. Hoffmann, *Obstinate or Obsolete? The Fate of the Nation-State and the Case of Western Europe. International Regionalism* (Boston: Little Brown, 1968), 177–230; U. Ozkirimli, "The Nation as an Artichoke? A Critique of Ethnosymbolist Interpretations of Nationalism," *Nations and Nationalism* 9, no. 3 (2003): 339–355, L. Piper, "Return to the Organic Onions, Artichokes and 'The Debate' on the Nation and Modernity: A Critical Introduction by Umut Özkrimili: Understanding Nationalism by Montserrat Guibernau and John Hutchinson," *Theoria: A Journal of Social and Political Theory* 103 (2004): 122–140.

9. E. Hobsbawn, *Nations and Nationalism since 1780* (Cambridge: Cambridge University Press, 1990).

10. A. Giddens, *The Nation-State and Violence* (Cambridge: Polity, 1985); P. J. Taylor, *Political Geography, World Economy, Nation-State, and Locality* (London: Longman, 1985).

11. P. Clastres, *Of Ethnocide: Archeology of Violence* (Los Angeles: Semiotext(e), 2010), 101–111.

12. E. Gellner, *Nations and Nationalism* (Ithaca, NY: Cornell University Press, 1983).

13. Gellner, *Nations and Nationalism*, 56.

14. Ozkirimli, "The Nation as an Artichoke?"; Piper, *Return to the Organic Onions*.

15. A. Smith, *The Ethnic Origins of Nations* (Oxford: Basil Blackwell, 1986).

16. Piper, *Return to the Organic Onions*.

17. [7] H. Özoğlu, "Does Kurdish Nationalism Have a Navel?" in *Symbiotic Antagonisms: Competing Nationalisms in Turkey*, eds. F. Keyman and A. Kadioglu (Salt Lake City: University of Utah Press, 2011).

18. A. Hassanpour, *The Making of Kurdish Identity: Pre-20th Century Historical and Linguistic Disourses*, in *The Origins of Kurdish Nationalism*, ed. A. Vali (Costa Meza: Mazda Publishers, 2003), 106–162.

19. Özoğlu, "Does Kurdish Nationalism Have a Navel?"

20. A. Vali, *The Origins of Kurdish Nationalism* (Costa Mesa: Mazda Publishers, 2003).

21. Özoğlu, "Does Kurdish Nationalism Have a Navel?"

22. F. Ibrahim, *The Kurdish National Movement and the Struggle for National Autonomy. Nationalism, Ethnic Conflict, and Self-Determination in the 20th Century* (Philadelphia, PA: Temple University Press, 1995), 36–60.

23. B. James, "The Rise and Fall of the Kurdish Emirates (Eighteenth to Nineteenth Centuries)," in *The Cambridge History of The Kurds*, eds. H. Bozarslan,

C. Gunes, and V. Yadirgi (Cambridge, Cambridge University Press, 2021), 25–44.

24. H. Bozarslan, C. Gunes, and V. Yadirgi, *The Cambridge History of The Kurds* (Cambridge: Cambridge University Press, 2021).

25. S. Ates, "The End of Kurdish Autonomy: The Destruction of the Kurdish Emirates in the Ottoman Empire," in *The Cambridge History of the Kurds*, eds. H. Bozarslan, C. Gunes, and V. Yadirgi (Cambridge: Cambridge University Press, 2021), 73–103.

26. M. v. Bruinessen, *Agha, Shaikh and State: On the Social and Political Organization of Kurdistan* (Utrecht: Proefschrift, 1978).

27. H. J. Barkey and G. E. Fuller, *Turkey's Kurdish Question* (Oxford: Rowman and Littlefield Publishers, 1998); M. Yegen, "Prospective-Turks or Pseudo-Citizens: Kurds in Turkey," *Middle East Journal* 63, no. 4 (2009): 597–615.

28. A. Vali, *Kurds and the State in Iran: The Making of Kurdish Identity* (London: I.B. Taurus, 2011).

29. J. Tejel, *Syria's Kurds: History, Politics and Society* (London: Routledge, 2009).

30. A. Balci, *The PKK–Kurdistan Workers' Party's Regional Politics* (New York: Palgrave MacMillan, 2017).

31. R. Olson, *The Emergence of Kurdish Nationalism and the Sheikh Said Rebellion, 1880–1925* (Austin: University of Texas Press, 1989).

32. H. Bozarslan, "Kurdish Nationalism in Turkey: From Tacit Contract to Rebellion (1919–1925)," in *The Origins of Kurdish* Nationalism, ed. A. Vali (Costa Meza: Mazda Publishers, 2003), 106–162.

33. H. Özoğlu, "Nationalism and Kurdish Notables in the Late Ottoman–Early Republican Era," *International Journal of Middle East Studies* 33, no. 3 (2001): 383–409.

34. Bozarslan, "Kurdish Nationalism in Turkey."

35. Bajalan argues that Kurdish activists before World War I had sought to reconcile a Kurdish identity with Ottomanism, describing them as "Ottoman Nationalists with Kurdish colours" (Bajalan 2009). During the "war of independence" (1929–1923), Turkish nationalists had invited Kurdish notables and tribal leaders to their congresses, where they were promised equal rights (Strohmeier 2003). However, Kurdish nationalists had become rather suspicious of the Kemalists, fearing they were determined to crush Kurdish nationalism (Özoğlu 2001, 2004). After 1925, earlier references to the "peoples of Turkey" were completely abandoned and the subjects of the state had to adopt a Turkish identity (Ergil 2000).

36. D. Natali, "Ottoman Kurds and Emergent Kurdish Nationalism," *Critical Middle Eastern Studies* 13, no. 3 (2004): 383–387.

37. P. W. Wilson, "President Wilson's Address to Congress, Analyzing German and Austrian Peace Utterances." Delivered in Joint Session, February 11, 1918.

38. Ibrahim, *The Kurdish National Movement*.

39. The inclusion of the oil-rich Southern Kurdistan/Mosul in Iraq would make the new state pay dearly for the costs of its occupation by the British, which itself saw imperial resources drained (Terry 2008).

40. M. Strohmeier, *Crucial Images in the Presentation of a Kurdish National Identity: Heroes and Patriots, Traitors and Foes* (Leiden: Brill, 2003).

41. Strohmeier, *Crucial Images*, 101–103.

42. See Wilson's Fourteen Points at https://theworldwar-prod.s3.amazonaws.com/prod/s3fs-public/1982.170.18_excerpt.jpg and the history of the UN and decolonization at www.un.org/dppa/decolonization/en/about

43. A. Getachew, *Worldmaking after Empire The Rise and Fall of Self-Determination* (Princeton, NJ: Princeton University Press, 2019).

44. E. Harsch, *Revolution and Nation-Building in Burkina Faso. Beyond Nationalism and the Nation-State: Radical Approaches to Nation*. Edited by I. Corut and J. Jongerden (London: Routledge, 2021), 177–197.

45. Harsch, *Revolution and Nation-Building*, 46.

46. See www.ohchr.org/EN/ProfessionalInterest/Pages/Independence.aspx

47. C. J. Edmonds, "Nationalism and Separatism," *Journal of Contemporary History* 6, no. 1 (1971): 87–107.

48. B. Park, J. Jongerden, F. Owtram, and A. Yoshioka, "On the Independence Referendum in the Kurdistan Region of Iraq and Disputed Territories in 2017," *Kurdish Studies* 5, no. 2 (2017): 199–214.

49. M. v. Bruinessen, "Kurdish Nationalism and Competing Ethnic Loyalties." Utrecht University Repository, 1994. http://dspace.library.uu.nl/handle/1874/20671

50. J. V. Stalin, "Marxism and the National Question" (1913). www.marxists.org/reference/archive/stalin/works/1913/03a.htm.

51. V. I. Lenin, *The Right of Nations to Self-Determination* (1914).

52. Stalin, "Marxism and the National Question." www.marxists.org/reference/archive/stalin/works/1913/03a.htm

53. See the treatment of this issue by Abdul Rahman Ghassemlou in his (1965) work *Kurdistan and the Kurds*, published by the Czechoslovakian Academy of Sciences.

54. H. Bozarslan, "Kurds and the Turkish State," in *Turkey in the Modern World*, ed. R. Kasaba (Cambridge: Cambridge University Press, 2008), 4: 333–356.

55. A. Z. Gundogan, "Space, State Making and Contentious Kurdish Politics," in *The Kurdish Issue in Turkey, A Spatial Perspective*, eds. Z. Gambetti and J. Jongerden (London: Routledge, 2015), 27–62.

56. I. Beşikci, *Cezaevinden Mektuplar* (Istanbul: İsmail Beşikci Vakfı Yayınları, 2014).

57. J. Jongerden and A. H. Akkaya, "The Kurdistan Workers Party and a New Left in Turkey: Analysis of the Revolutionary Movement in Turkey through the PKK's Memorial Text on Haki Karer," *European Journal of Turkish Studies* 14 (2012).

58. Jongerden and Akkaya, "The Kurdistan Workers Party"; Vali, *The Forgotten Years*.

59. Stalin (1913). "Marxism and the National Question." www.marxists.org/reference/archive/stalin/works/1913/03a.htm

60. A. Balci, *The PKK–Kurdistan Workers' Party's Regional Politics* (London: Palgrave MacMillan, 2017).

61. Vali, *The Forgotten Years*.

62. Vali, *The Forgotten Years*.

63. The Three Worlds Theory, as developed by Mao Zedong, basically distinguished three worlds—the First World, composed of the two super-powers, the imperialist USA and socialist-imperialist USSR, the Second World, composed of Europe, Japan, and other developed countries, and the Third World, assembling the underdeveloped—and called for solidarity within the Third World, against the threat(s) of the First (and Second) World(s). This implied that Maoist parties in the Third World had to focus on the major contradiction—between their country and the USA/USSR—and, if necessary, put aside the minor internal contradictions. See Jongerden and Akkaya (2019).

64. Ibid.

65. *Kurdistan Devrimcileri* 1978, 20–24.

66. Getachew, *Worldmaking after Empire*.

67. Harsch, *Revolution and Nation-Building*.

68. The political project of Thomas Sankara (1983–1987) in Burkina Faso is relevant here as it was based on a unity in (ethnic, cultural) diversity. This was a form of nation-building that did not aim at an identity hegemony but placed a Burkina Faso national identity on top of other identities (Harsch 2021, 159). This is similar to proposals made by the Kurdish movement during the 2000s, in which "*Türkiyeli*" as an overarching civilian denominator on top of existing identities as Kurds, Turk, Circassian, Laz, and Alevi had to replace that of the ethnic qualifier "*Türk*."

69. Getachew, *Worldmaking after Empire*.

70. Getachew, *Worldmaking after Empire*; Harsch, *Revolution and Nation-Building in Burkina Faso*.

71. J. Jongerden, "Learning from Defeat: Development and Contestation of the "New Paradigm" within Kurdistan Workers' Party (PKK)," *Kurdish Sudies* 7, no. 1 (2019): 72–92.

72. Jongerden, "Learning from Defeat."

73. A. Balci, *The PKK-Kurdistan Workers' Party's Regional Politics* (London: Palgrave MacMillan, 2017).

74. A. H. Akkaya, "The Kurdistan Workers' Party (PKK): National Liberation, Insurgency and Radical Democracy beyond Borders." PhD dissertation, Political and Social Sciences, Ghent University, 2016.

75. A. Öcalan, *Sosyalizme de Israr Insan Olmakta Israr* (Istanbul: Aram, 1999).

76. M. Karasu, *Radikal Demokrasi* (Neus: Wesanen Mezopotamya, 2009).

77. Jongerden, "Learning from Defeat."

78. C. Gunes, "Unpacking the 'Democratic Confederalism' and 'Democratic Autonomy': Proposals of Turkey's Kurdish Movement," in Minority Self-Government

in Europe and the Middle East, eds. O. Akbulut and E. Aktoprak (Leiden: Brill Nijhoff, 2019), 246–267.

79. A. Öcalan, *War and Peace in Kurdistan* (London: Transmedia Publishing, 2014).

80. N. Bezwan, "Addressing the Kurdish Self-Determination Confict: Democratic Autonomy and Authoritarianism in Turkey," in *Democratic Representation in Plurinational States: The Kurds in Turkey*, eds. E. Nimni and E. Aktoprak (Cham: Palgrave MacMillan, 2018), 59–82.

81. Öcalan, *War and Peace in Kurdistan*.

82. Karasu, *Radikal Demokrasi*.

83. A. Öcalan, *Democratic Nation* (Neus: Mesopotamian Publishers, 2016).

84. Getachew, *Worldmaking after Empire*.

85. J. Cocks, *Passion and Paradox: Intellectuals Confront the National Question* (Princeton, NJ: Princeton University Press, 2002).

86. Houston, *Crafting National Selves*.

87. M. H.Yavuz, "Five Stages of the Construction of Kurdish Nationalism in Turkey," *Nationalism and Ethnic Politics* 7, no. 3 (2001): 1–24.

88. Getachew, *Worldmaking after Empire*.

89. Sandipto Dasgupta, "Review of Adom Getachew's Worldmaking after Empire." *Millenium: Journal of International Studies* 48, no. 3 (2020): 351–359.

90. Getachew, *Worldmaking after Empire*.

91. Getachew, *Worldmaking after Empire*.

References

Akkaya, A. H. (2016). "The Kurdistan Workers' Party (PKK): 'National Liberation, Insurgency and Radical Democracy beyond Borders,'" PhD dissertation, Political and Social Sciences Ghent University.

Ari, K. (1995). Büyük Mübadele Türkiye'ye Zorunlu Göç, 1923–1925. İstanbul: Tarih Vakfi Yurt Yayinlari.

Ates, S. (2021). "The End of Kurdish Autonomy: The Destruction of the Kurdish Emirates in the Ottoman Empire." In *The Cambridge History of the Kurds*, eds. H. Bozarslan, C. Gunes, and V. Yadirgi. Cambridge: Cambridge University Press.

Bajalan, D. R. (2009). "Kurds for the Empire: 'Young Kurds' (1898–1914)." Master's Thesis, Istanbul Bilgi University, Social Sciences Institute.

Balci, A. (2017). *The PKK-Kurdistan Workers' Party's Regional Politics*. London: Palgrave MacMillan.

Barkey, H. J., and G. E. Fuller (1998). *Turkey's Kurdish Question*. Oxford: Rowman and Littlefield Publishers.

Bauman, Z. (1989). *Modernity and the Holocaust*. Cambridge: Polity Press.

Beşikci, İ. (2014). *Cezaevinden Mektuplar*. Istanbul: İsmail Beşikci Vakfı Yayınları.

Bezwan, N. (2018). "Addressing the Kurdish Self-Determination Conflict: Democratic Autonomy and Authoritarianism in Turkey." In *Democratic Representation in Plurinational States: The Kurds in Turkey*, eds. E. Nimni and a. E. Aktoprak. Cham: Palgrave MacMillan.

Bozarslan, H. (2003). "Kurdish Nationalism in Turkey: From Tacit Contract to Rebellion (1919–1925)." In *The Origins of Kurdish Nationalism*, ed. A. Vali. Costa Meza: Mazda Publishers.

Bozarslan, H. (2008). "Kurds and the Turkish State." In *Turkey in the Modern World*, ed. R. Kasaba. Cambridge: Cambridge University Press.

Bozarslan, H., C. Gunes, and V. Yadirgi (2021). *The Cambridge History of The Kurds*. Cambridge: Cambridge University Press.

Bruinessen, M. v. (1978). *Agha, Shaikh and State: On the Social and Political Organization of Kurdistan*. Utrecht: Proefschrift.

Bruinessen, M. v. (1994). "Kurdish Nationalism and Competing Ethnic Loyalties." Utrecht University Repository. http://dspace.library.uu.nl/handle/1874/20671

Clastres, P. (2010). "Of Ethnocide." In *Archeology of Violence*, ed. P. Clastres. Los Angeles: Semiotext(e).

Cocks, J. (2002). *Passion and Paradox: Intellectuals Confront the National Question*. Princeton, NJ: Princeton University Press.

Edmonds, C. J. (1971). "Nationalism and Separatism." *Journal of Contemporary History* 6, no. 1: 87–107.

Ergil, D. (2000). "The Kurdish Question in Turkey." *Journal of Democracy* 11, no. 3: 122–135.

Gellner, E. (1983). *Nations and Nationalism*. Ithaca, NY: Cornell University Press.

Getachew, A. (2019). *Worldmaking after Empire The Rise and Fall of Self-Determination*. Princeton, NJ: Princeton University Press.

Giddens, A. (1985). *The Nation-State and Violence*. Cambridge: Polity.

Gundogan, A. Z. (2015). *Space, State Making and Contentious Kurdish Politics. The Kurdish Issue in Turkey, A Spatial Perspective*. Edited by Z. Gambetti and J. Jongerden. London: Routledge: 27–62.

Gunes, C. (2012). *The Kurdish National Movement in Turkey: From Protest to Resistance*. London: Routledge.

Gunes, C. (2019). "Unpacking the 'Democratic Confederalism' and 'Democratic Autonomy': Proposals of Turkey's Kurdish Movement." In *Minority Self-Government in Europe and the Middle East*, eds. O. Akbulut and E. Aktoprak. Leiden: Brill Nijhoff.

Harsch, E. (2021). *Revolution and Nation-Building in Burkina Faso. Beyond Nationalism and the Nation-State: Radical Approaches to Nation*. Edited by I. Corut and J. Jongerden. London: Routledge: 177–197.

Hassanpour, A. (2003). "The Making of Kurdish Identity: Pre–20th Century Historical and Linguistic Disourses." In *The Origins of Kurdish Nationalism*, ed. A. Vali. Costa Meza: Mazda Publishers.

Hobsbawn, E. (1990). *Nations and Nationalism since 1780*. Cambridge: Cambridge University Press.
Hoffmann, S. (1968). "Obstinate or Obsolete? The Fate of the Nation-State and the Case of Western Europe." In *International Regionalism*, ed. J. S. Nye. Boston: Little Brown.
Houston, C. (2008). *Crafting of National Selves*. Oxford: Berg.
Ibrahim, F. (1995). *The Kurdish National Movement and the Struggle for National Autonomy. Nationalism, Ethnic Conflict, and Self-Determination in the 20th Century*. Edited by B. Berberoglu. Philadelphia, PA: Temple University Press.
James, B. (2021). "The Rise and Fall of the Kurdish Emirates (Eighteenth to Nineteenth Centuries)." In *The Cambridge History of The Kurds*, eds. H. Bozarslan, C. Gunes, and V. Yadirgi. Cambridge: Cambridge University Press.
Jongerden, J. (2012). "Elite Encounters of a Violent Kind: Milli Ibrahim Pasa, Ziya Gökalp and Political Struggle in Diyarbekir at the end of the 20th century." In *Social Relations in Ottoman Diyarbekir, 1870–1915*, eds. J. Jongerden and J. Verheij. Leiden: Brill.
Jongerden, J. (2019). "Learning from Defeat: Development and Contestation of the "New Paradigm" within Kurdistan Workers' Party (PKK)." *Kurdish Studies* 7, no. 1: 72–92.
Jongerden, J., and A. H. Akkaya (2012). "The Kurdistan Workers Party and a New Left in Turkey: Analysis of the Revolutionary Movement in Turkey through the PKK's Memorial Text on Haki Karer." *European Journal of Turkish Studies* 14.
Jongerden, J., and A. H. Akkaya. *The Kurdistan Workers Party (PKK) and Kurdish Political Parties in the 1970s* (London: Routledge, 2019).
Jwaideh, W. (2006). *The Kurdish National Movement: Its Origins and Development*. Syracuse, NY: Syracuse University Press.
Karasu, M. (2009). *Radikal Demokrasi*. Neus: Wesanen Mezopotamya.
Kyramargiou, E. (2022). "Refugees of the 1923 Population Exchange between Turkey and Greece: Greek Efforts for Integration and Assimilation." In *The Routledge Handbook on Contemporary Turkey*, ed. J. Jongerden. London: Routledge.
Lados, S. P. (1932). *The Exchange of Minorities: Bulgaria, Greece, and Turkey*. New York: MacMillan Company.
Lenin, V. I. (1914). *The Right of Nations to Self-Determination*. Publisher Unknown.
Natali, D. (2004). "Ottoman Kurds and Emergent Kurdish Nationalism." *Critical Middle Eastern Studies* 13, no. 3: 383–387.
Öcalan, A. (1999). *Sosyalizme de Israr Insan Olmakta Israr*. Istanbul: Aram.
Öcalan, A. (2014). *War and Peace in Kurdistan*. London: Transmedia Publishing.
Öcalan, A. (2016). *Democratic Nation*. Neus: Mesopotamian Publishers.
Olson, R. (1989). *The Emergence of Kurdish Nationalism and the Sheikh Said Rebellion, 1880–1925*. Austin: University of Texas Press.
Ozkirimli, U. (2003). "The Nation as an Artichoke? A Critique of Ethnosymbolist Interpretations of Nationalism." *Nations and Nationalism* 9, no. 3: 339–355.

Özoğlu, H. (2001). "Nationalism and Kurdish Notables in the Late Ottoman–Early Republican Era." *International Journal of Middle East Studies* 33, no. 3: 383–409.

Özoğlu, H. (2004). *Kurdish Notables and the Ottoman State: Evolving Identities, Competing Loyalties, and Shifting Boundaries*. Albany, NY: SUNY Press.

Özoğlu, H. (2011). "Does Kurdish Nationalism Have a Navel?" In *Symbiotic Antagonisms: Competing Nationalisms in Turkey*, eds. F. Keyman and A. Kadioglu. Salt Lake City: University of Utah Press.

Park, B., J. Jongerden, F. Owtram, and A. Yoshioka (2017). "On the Independence Referendum in the Kurdistan Region of Iraq and Disputed Territories in 2017." *Kurdish Studies* 5, no. 2: 199–214.

Piper, L. (2004). "Return to the Organic Onions, Artichokes and 'The Debate' on the Nation and Modernity: A Critical Introduction by Umut Özkrimili: Understanding Nationalism by Montserrat Guibernau and John Hutchinson." *Theoria: A Journal of Social and Political Theory* 103: 122–140.

Romano, D. (2006). *The Kurdish Nationalist Movement: Opportunity, Mobilization and Identity*. Cambridge: Cambridge University Press.

Sandipto Dasgupta (2020). "Review of Adom Getachew's Worldmaking after Empire." *Millenium: Journal of International Studies* 48, no. 3: 351–359.

Smith, A. (1986). *The Ethnic Origins of Nations*. Oxford: Basil Blackwell.

Stalin, J. V. (1913). "Marxism and the National Question." www.marxists.org/reference/archive/stalin/works/1913/03a.htm

Strohmeier, M. (2003). *Crucial Images in the Presentation of a Kurdish National Identity: Heroes and Patriots, Traitors and Foes*. Leiden: Brill.

Taylor, P. J. (1985). *Political Geography, World Economy, Nation-State, and Locality*. London: Longman.

Tejel, J. (2009). *Syria's Kurds: History, Politics and Society*. London: Routledge.

Terry, J. D. (2008). "The Forty Thieves: Churchill, the Cairo Conference, and the Policy Debate over Strategies of Colonial Control in British Mandatory Iraq, 1918–1924. Master's thesis, University of North Carolina at Chapel Hill, Department of History.

Ungor, U. U. (2012). *The Making of Modern Turkey: Nation and State in Eastern Anatolia, 1913–1950*. Oxford: Oxford University Press.

Vali, A., ed (2003). *The Origins of Kurdish Nationalism*. Costa Mesa: Mazda Publishers.

Vali, A. (2011). *Kurds and the State in Iran: The Making of Kurdish Identity*. London: I.B. Taurus.

Vali, A. (2020). *The Forgotten Years of Kurdish Nationalism in Iran*. Cham: Palgrave MacMillan.

Wilson, P. W. (1918). "President Wilson's Address to Congress, Analyzing German and Austrian Peace Utterances." Delivered in Joint Session, February 11, 1918.

Yavuz, M. H. (2001). "Five Stages of the Construction of Kurdish Nationalism in Turkey." *Nationalism and Ethnic Politics* 7, no. 3: 1–24.

Yegen, M. (2009). ""Prospective-Turks" or 'Pseudo-Citizens': Kurds in Turkey." *Middle East Journal* 63, no. 4: 597–615.

10

The Biafra Separatist Movement and Resurgence of Igbo Nationalism in Nigeria

Bernard Ugochukwu Nwosu and Kenneth Omeje

Introduction

This chapter explores the resurgence of separatist agitation and ethnic nationalism among large sections of the Ibo ethnic community in south-eastern Nigeria, especially the youth population, since the onset of the fourth civilian republic in 1999. This seemingly popular separatist nationalism is anchored in the quest for sovereign statehood known as Biafra, a throwback to the defunct Republic of Biafra of 1967 to 1970, unilaterally declared by the Igbo-dominated South-eastern region of Nigeria in their bid to secede from the federation, which resulted in a civil war that ultimately ended in favor of the Nigerian federal state. Since the contemporary revival of the Igbo separatist nationalism, the campaign has been championed in two successive phases by "new generation" activists who did not experience the defunct Biafra secessionist war, the most prominent being the Movement for the Actualization of the Sovereign State of Biafra (MASSOB) during the first phase of the campaign, and the Indigenous People of Biafra (IPOB) in the present second phase.

Nationalism can be understood as a form of identity politics that also includes a specific definition of collective national interests and claims for self-determination in the form of various degrees of territorial autonomy. It also has to do with the political framing and reframing of collective interests that political actors define in territorial national terms in the context of nationalism.[1] In considering nationalism in Catalan, Scotland, and Quebec, Beland and Lecours confined their work to the civil actions of politicians in nationalism struggles. However, African experiences of such struggles are somewhat different because they are more assertive, with potentials for conflictive explosion, as well as being driven by movements that are different from political parties as in the cases of the Ambazonia secessionist movement in Cameroon, the Azawad secessionist movement in Mali, and the neo-Biafran movements in Nigeria.

Based on their own focus, Beland and Lecours noted that nationalist politicians seek to garner popular support for achieving greater autonomy within the state or outright independence. In this regard, politicians pursue three strategies for political advantage—namely, credit-claiming for things considered well done, blame-avoiding for wrong policies, as well as blame-generating and mobilization of citizens for the kind of interest that appeal to them, usually greater autonomy. These ways of seeking political advantage can also apply to political actors to varying extents and with different frames of reference depending on their history and/or social contexts. In cases of nationalist movements that are not in mainstream politics and usually in conflict with sitting governments, they resort more to blame-generating behaviors against the government.

In the Nigerian context, nationalist movements of the secessionist variants do not operate through political parties as in Catalona, Quebec, and Scotland. Rather, they form their own organizations to mount separatist tension against the state. Although some politicians in Nigeria demonstrate a measure of sympathy for nationalist groups, they rarely articulate any ideological position in that regard or pursue it as one of the goals of their party.

Ethnic nationalism in Nigeria according to Nnoli[2] has a history that goes back to colonial days. In that regard, the emergence of urban townships and new forms of livelihoods brought about by colonialism was a major factor in population movements. Seekers of colonial job opportunities moved to urban places, and in that process folks from one linguistic group could easily migrate into the domain of another and peacefully coexist with them. Over time, migrants grew in population and socioeconomic competition increased, migrants and the host population organizing themselves along communal lines. Communal associations such as Yoruba Union, Igbo State Union, and Urhobo Renascent Convention sprang up in the colonial urban settlements.

These associations were points of recourse for members who had problems, including new migrants seeking to be assisted in settling in the new urban area. Too often, when members of a groups gained access to lucrative jobs and other resources, they used their positions to find jobs or opportunities for members of their group. Those who lost out in the socioeconomic competition blamed their plight on the advantages enjoyed by other communal groups, thus laying a foundation for the gestation of animosity sometimes expressed in open communal or ethnic clashes. In its fully mature form, ethnic nationalism became a practice for differential inclusion of the members of a communal group and exclusion of others in all spaces of value allocation and competition.

A more direct tracing of ethnic nationalism to colonialism has to do with the myth and propaganda spread by British colonial authorities that the colonial people were "separated from one another by great distances, by differences of history and traditions and by ethnological, racial, tribal, political, social and religious barriers."[3] These identities and individualities were consciously preserved with official policies. In Zaria, for instance, three categories of settlements were created for the inhabitants: (1) the walled city for the Indigenous people; (2) *Tudun Wada* for Northerners who were not indigenous to the town; and (c) *Sabon gari* for native foreigners who were mostly migrants from Southern Nigeria.

As the state continued to evolve along these polarized communal lines and competition also grew, material scarcity offered opportunity for the manipulation of silent communal resentments. For instance, in 1945, a general strike by Nigerian workers affected the supplies of food to the North by rail, leading to a severe food shortage. For several weeks, people could not get their daily ration of grains distributed by the District Officer. With hunger and anxiety mounting, the British blamed the general strike and the hardship it occasioned on the leading anticolonialist of the time, Nnamdi Azikiwe of the Igbo ethnic stock. They urged the Northerners to boycott the strike and also incited them against the Igbo, which led to the Jos communal riot of 1945.[4]

The political development of the country unduly emphasized communal differences, which increasingly made political mobilization take a communal trajectory. Major political parties became identified with specific ethnic communities. The National Convention of Nigerian Citizens (NCNC), which had a national outlook at the beginning, eventually degenerated to a largely ethnic Igbo party, the Action Group (AG) party clearly started as an ethnic party of the Yoruba while the Northern People's Congress (NPC) was mainly associated with the Hausa/Fulani group. Consequently, the distribution of political power focused more on what communal groups have received in relation to other communal groups.

The petty bourgeois politicians presented and masked their interest as broadly representing those of their groups. Indeed, this is part of why the January 15, 1966, coup was viewed in ethnic terms and its reprisals were made a collective ethnic punishment for the Igbo because the leader of the coup was Igbo. Also, the Igbo in contemporary Nigeria perceive themselves to be collective victims of the consequences of a power play that resulted in a civil war that they lost. Thus, their collective nationalism in Nigerian politics has been primarily in response to this notion and incidents of collective victimhood.

Most works on new Igbo nationalism focus on the post-military political struggle of the Igbo since 1999, especially the secessionist agitation. These works are accused of being monodimensional by Ibeanu, Orji, and Iwuamadi (2016) due to their limited emphasis on events of the Nigerian fourth republic.[5] However, after the Biafran War of 1967 to 1970, the most contemporary expression of Igbo nationalism with uncommon vibrancy or militancy has only occurred during the present fourth civilian republic that commenced in 1999. It is expressed mostly in the form of assertive secessionist politics. Centrally, the agitational politics is a contestation of a deeply felt sense of exclusion, real or imagined, by the Igbo regarding the distribution of public office appointments, major rent-related contracts, and development infrastructures by the federal government.

This tendency is aggravated by the fact that Nigeria is a rentier state founded on the distribution of oil largesse by the federal state, which holds a disproportionately greater share of the state's oil revenues in what many critics have dubbed a fake federal structure. The 1970s witnessed the emergence of an oil-centered rentier state through the assertive nationalism of the hegemonic postcolonial elites, based on two strategies adopted by the federal state.[6] The first was to acquire a dominant federal share and control of the oil economy hitherto dominated by the Transnational Oil Companies (TNOCs). The second was to ensure a decisive centralization of power and resources in the federal state through systematic disempowerment of the subnational space. This strategic game plan of the federal state has more or less remained a salient feature of rentier politics in Nigeria since the early 1970s, and it is a feature that many in the ethnic minority-dominated oil-bearing states of the Niger Delta region and the Igbo states of the South-East perceive as working to the advantage of the political elites from the larger ethnic groups that have mostly dominated the state apparatuses since independence, notably the northern Fulani/Hausa group.

The collective grievance of the Igbo is further linked to a history that commenced immediately after the Biafran separatist war, fought largely (but not exclusively) by the Igbo ethnic community of south-eastern Nigeria, in the aftermath of which they lost their pre–civil war prominence in Nigerian politics. It is remarkable that had Biafra won the civil war, Nigeria would have lost more than 75 percent of its oil resources, a reality that dawned on the federal military government in the wake of the separatist campaign, and which has contributed to the emergence in the early 1970s of the oil rent dispensation and the new rentier elite that thrive on it.[7]

The Igbo demands for self-determination and the forceful crackdown on the agitation by the state continually generate new research frontiers that call for detailed investigation to enrich our understanding of the politics of ethnic nationalism in contemporary Nigeria and Africa. In this chapter, we explore first why Igbo nationalism and the agitation for Biafra not only resurfaced in the present fourth civilian republic but also tends to have progressively spiraled in momentum. Second, we examine why this separatist campaign has evolved through two distinct phases led by rival and openly antagonistic groups. We are particularly interested in understanding whether there are any observable shifts in paradigm across the two successive phases of the campaign. Third, we study the *modus operandi* of the separatist campaigners and the effectiveness of their strategies. Fourth, our research is interested in finding out the impact of this separatist campaign on both the Igbo community and the Nigerian state. Finally, beyond secessionism and sovereign statehood, our study investigates whether there are any less radical demands of the neo-Biafra movement that if fulfilled could sufficiently appease campaigners to end their separatist agitation and accept a common destiny under the framework of a coherent Nigerian federation.

Sovereign Reincarnation?
Biafran Struggle as the New Igbo Nationalism

The defunct state of Biafra was declared in 1967 by the subnational government of the former Eastern region of Nigeria as a protest of the massacre of Easterners in the northern part of the country in the aftermath of the July 29, 1966, counter-coup. The counter-coup was a brutal reaction to the abortive January 15, 1966, military coup led by a team of young army officers that abruptly terminated the first civilian republic. General Johnson Aguyi-Ironsi of Igbo ethnic origin led the Nigerian military to stop the army officers from seizing power, and consequently became the head of state.

The coup was controversially perceived as an Igbo coup, which resulted in the killing of a few prominent leaders from the Northern and Western regions of the country, including Prime Minister Abubakar Tafawa Balewa, Premier of the northern region Sir Ahmadu Bello, and Premier of the western region Samuel Ladoke Akintola. The counter-coup of July 1966 was plotted by another team of young officers mainly from the Northern region, which resulted in the abduction and killing of the Igbo head of state General Aguyi-Ironsi together with his host at the time of the coup, Col. Adekunle Fajuyi, military governor of the western region. The counter-coup was followed by an organized pogrom against military personnel and people of Igbo origin residing in the Northern and Western regions of the country. Over fifty thousand people were killed in the roughly one-year pogrom. Efforts to find a peaceful solution to the pogrom and the political crisis provoked by the counter-coup failed, resulting in a civil war fought between the federal government forces and the separatist Biafran side for roughly three years (July 1967 to January 1970). Biafra's commanders surrendered to the Nigerian authorities on January 12, 1970.

The war settlement did not result in conventional demands for reparation. Instead, the post-conflict transitional justice principle of "no victor no vanquished" rhetorically proclaimed by the military head of state General Yakubu Gowon was the principle on which the war ended. The Igbo community have felt a collective sense of the existence of a glass ceiling and being generally unwanted as a group in Nigeria since the end of the civil war.[8] However, in the first three decades following the civil war the major approach of the Igbo to their perceived marginalization had been the pathway of a negotiated reintegration into the mainstream of the country's political and social life. This approach dominated Igbo politics during the second civilian republic (1979–1983) and the abortive third republic (1992–1993), as well as during the different military interregnums.

From the standpoint of the Igbo, given the despotic nature of military rule, it would probably have been imprudent to contemplate agitation and protests for primordial group justice as the military would in all probability have crushed such a campaign with maximum force. Besides, if such an agitation had come from the Igbo, some elements who were displeased that the Igbo were not given tough reprisals by the General Gowon's regime at the end of the war,⁹ would probably have taken advantage of any popular agitation by the Igbo to revive and intensify their collective persecution.

The end of military rule and return of democratic rule in Nigeria in 1999 was a change from a wholly closed political space that permitted virtually no chance of separate and assertive identity demands by aggrieved national groups. Of course, during the era of military rule, pockets of environmental justice movements had started with the most vocal being the Movement for the Survival of Ogoni People (MOSOP) founded by Ken Saro Wiwa whose leadership popularized the group's agitation by anchoring it on environmentalism. His stinging protest was to attract an extreme consequence of execution by hanging in 1995 by the military regime of General Abacha.¹⁰ Perhaps out of fear of consequences or out of need for a more opportune moment no other such group came up until the commencement of the fourth civilian republic in May 1999.

Upon the inauguration of Olusegun Obasanjo as the first civilian President of Nigeria's fourth republic, an Indian trained lawyer, Ralph Uwazurike founded an organization to revive the defunct state of Biafra called Movement for the Actualization of the Sovereign State of Biafra (MASSOB). According to the founder, his reason for establishing the movement was that in 1999 he reflected on the circumstance of the Igbo and recalled how the Aburi Accord was not implemented by Gowon's regime as a step that could have prevented the civil war. A few years after the civil war, the federal government's postwar transitional justice policy code named the 3Rs—"reconciliation, reconstruction, and rehabilitation"—was hurriedly abandoned. Besides, when President Obasanjo assumed power as civilian president, he continued the postwar refusal to appoint any Igbo senior officer as one of the military service chiefs, irrespective of the massive support of the Igbo community to his political victory. On these grounds, Uwazurike concluded that the Igbo were not wanted in Nigeria and he therefore set up MASSOB to revive the agitation for a Biafra Republic, thereby heralding the resurgence of Igbo nationalism.¹¹

While the agitation by MASSOB remains ongoing since 1999, another group called the Indigenous People of Biafra (IPOB) also entered the arena of secessionist agitation. IPOB became an alternative to MASSOB members who felt disenchanted with the leadership of the movement based on an allegation that Uwazurike had sabotaged the struggle for Biafran independence by accepting a bribe from the government and caused a split in the ranks of his group.¹² Furthermore, the breakaway faction accused Uwazurike of embezzling about US$ 500,000 of MASSOB's funds and initially attempted to expel him. Since 2014, the splinter group IPOB has grown to become the more visible and militant agitator for the restoration of Biafra. Under the leadership of Mazi Nnamdi Kanu, the organization elevated the tempo and public knowledge of their struggle through the mechanism of radio broadcasting. In addition, other neo-Biafran groups have also risen and have been engaged in the politics of Biafran revival. Some of the organizations include the Biafran Youth Congress (BYC), Biafran Liberation Council (BZM), Biafran Liberation Council (BLC), and the Coalition of Biafran Liberation Groups (COBLIG).[13]

The most important intersection of the struggles of these organizations is their politics of Igbo nationalism, which in recent years has been chiefly driven by IPOB and their contestations with the federal and state governments. One uniting element for MASSOB, IPOB, and other neo-Biafran groups is their collective hate for the conservative Igbo politicians who for reasons of populist opportunism also articulate their politics around pro-Igbo nationalist sentiments. The neo-Biafran groups believe that such politics is based on negotiation of incremental political reintegration of the Igbo into Nigeria. To the separatist agitators, the approach of the Igbo politicians achieves only a token of privilege that the elite enjoys to the exclusion of the masses.

With its avowed opposition to the seemingly self-serving approach of the Igbo politicians, the resurgence of Igbo nationalism in the post-military era is seen by Nwangwu, Onuoha, Nwosu, and Ezeibe (2020) to represent the second generation of Igbo nationalism.[14] According to them, this second generation is a successor to the first generation that started in 1970 after the civil war, championed and dominated by the conservative Igbo petty bourgeoisie (notably the top civil servants and public office holders at both the national and subnational levels as well as their business associates).

The first generation of Igbo nationalism provided a platform for the promotion of the interests of the Igbo petty bourgeoisie, and they focused on issues related to value allocation such as distribution of political appointments and sensitive policy positions and infrastructure. They apply tact and diplomacy in engaging with the elites of other Nigerian groups, especially the majority ethnic groups. These first-generation Igbo nationalists believe that a gradual dialogic approach and negotiation would lead to the reintegration of the Igbo into the mainstream of Nigerian politics in which they had played key roles in the pre–civil war years. Nonetheless, this group of Igbo nationalists are seen by the younger generation activists to be disconnected from the masses. The new generation of young people consider their approach as both selfish and conspiratorial because the positions they negotiate in the name of the Igbo merely serve the elitist interest of the petty bourgeois elements.

To be sure, the Igbo elite in national politics tend to engage in political dealings and alliances seen to amount to treachery to the overall interest of the Igbo.[15] In this connection, they are accused of engaging in horse trading that ultimately betrays Igbo interests. For instance, they have publicly declared a felt need for an Igbo to emerge as Nigerian president through democratic election, but their politics in the central Igbo sociocultural group called Ohanaeze as well as the dictates of their personal political interest made them renege on the strategic need to commit their efforts toward campaigning and ensuring the emergence of a Nigerian president of Igbo extraction.[16] From the standpoint of campaigners, the underpinning philosophy of a Nigerian president of Igbo ethnic origin is to guarantee full Igbo reintegration in Nigeria following the civil war they lost more than fifty years ago. The second important reason for aspiring to have a Nigerian president of Igbo extraction is that the Nigerian presidency wields enormous powers in the distribution of public goods. The 1999 constitution assigns far-reaching responsibilities to the central government, and the president is decisive in determining who gets what. Thus, the Igbo pursuit of the presidency is a pursuit of an interest to apply such powers in remedying what they perceive as the neglect of infrastructural development in their region. While this seems to be part of the declared interest of the first generation of Igbo nationalists, their self-serving politics gives them away as not being sincerely committed to it.

It is the thinking of the militant second-generation Igbo nationalists that the first generation of Igbo nationalists are self-serving groups and do not represent the masses and protect their interests before the Nigerian state that led to the rise of what Nwangwu et al. (2020) refer to as the second generation of Igbo nationalists.[17] This second generation represents the contemporary resurgence of Igbo nationalism, which articulates its nationalist agenda in a demand for Igbo emancipation from the Nigerian state believed to suppress and marginalize the Igbo community. The conviction of these groups is that the deprivations of the Igbo nation that are inflicted in the Nigerian state will come to an end with the establishment of a sovereign state of Biafra.

In the early days of the neo-Biafra movement, its Diaspora arm undertook some watershed events related to their struggle, including the opening of the Biafra House in Washington, DC, on September 23, 2001, with the late former leader of Biafra Emeka Odumegwu Ojukwu in attendance. They also established shortwave radio broadcasting, Voice of Biafra International (VOBI). In addition, they convened the first international conference on Biafra in Greenbelt, Maryland, on October 18, 2003, all facilitated by the Washington-based Biafra Foundation and BAF. This conference was important in articulating the core idea behind the resurgence of Biafra struggles in Nigeria as part of its communique concluding that "the conditions that led to the Biafra-Nigeria war are still present and worse, that the persecution of Ndi-Igbo in Nigeria continues to dictate the overall and specific policies of federal government." Accordingly, the conference warned governments in the Eastern region (Igbo-dominated part of Nigeria) to desist from collaborating with the agencies of the federal government of Nigeria in the harassment and murder of the citizens of Eastern Nigeria, particularly MASSOB members.[18]

Several Nigerian authors share the perspective of the neo-Biafran conference of 2003 that the federal government did less than a proper reintegration of the Igbo after the civil war.[19] Proponents see the government policy lines toward the Igbo as a vendetta for fighting the civil war. For instance, the carving out of parts of Egbema clan in Imo State (populated by the ethnic Igbo) and joining them to Rivers State (populated by a group of ethnic minority groups) was one instance that such notion of vendetta was felt by the Igbo.[20] Another indicative grievance is that Igbo oil-rich states have been progressively excluded from benefitting from revenues accruing to oil-producing areas. In 2006, Imo and Abia States (two ethnic Igbo States) were excluded from the Consolidated Council on Social and Economic Development of Coastal States of the Niger Delta (CCSEDSC) by the federal government. Thus, Igbo nationalism as Onuoha (2008) argues[21] has focused on situations, policies, and actions that produce grievances and the overwhelming feeling of deprivation of nationhood.

It is pertinent to mention that the defunct Republic of Biafra in 1967 included some of the Eastern ethnic minorities, which presently form part of what is known as the South–South region of the federation. In the resurgence of the Biafra struggle, not a lot of reference is made to how the federal government treats minorities. In many instances, the minorities of the defunct Eastern region of Nigeria's first republic reject being included as part of the territorial claims that secessionist agitators are making, either out of fear of punishment from the federal government or fear of being dominated by the Igbo should they become allies and successfully achieve Biafra. Thus, the post–civil war resurgence of Biafra captures the Igbo nationalist resurgence in the Nigerian project. For instance, in the first application of sit-at-home protest as a form of civil disobedience on August 26, 2004, MASSOB leader Ralph Uwazurike said it was to protest the intimidation and marginalization of the Igbo and the Nigerian occupation of the Biafran territory for more than thirty-nine years.[22]

Further, the new Igbo nationalism is portrayed by campaigners as a struggle for all Igbo territorial communities, despite their location in Nigeria. This is because there are groups that share Igbo ancestry but are geographically carved into states where they are clear minorities, outlying states surrounding the core Igbo states such as Benue, Rivers, Delta, and Cross-River States. Non-Igbo cultural groups in these states have declared on many occasions that they do not associate with the Biafran struggle due to lack of trust between them and the Igbo.[23] In a large sense, therefore, the resurgent Biafra struggle is nebulous about how to deal with this geo-cultural puzzle. It therefore seems more like an Igbo variant of *Zionism*, a veritable agitation for an equitable political space, perhaps in a dreamland of Biafra. This thinking is captured in what some analysts tag as Biafra not of territory but of the mind.[24] In this regard, Biafra is viewed as a metaphor that represents a struggle for equity or justice in the distribution of public good in Nigeria.

Evidently, in the Biafran struggle, the Igbo tend to respond to the very character of postcolonial Nigeria in which configurations of power render the citizen marginal in social contract relations.[25] Given the marginality of the citizen, the ethnic group materializes as a transactional agency that serves as an interlocutor between the citizen and the state. Members of any ethnic group that feels short-changed in value allocation prefer to unite around primordial interests in interfacing with the state rather than citizens contesting such limitations of the state as a matter of their rights. Therefore, it sometimes appears there is a sense of confusion about whether the neo-Biafran activists are struggling for a totally different sovereign state or for the restoration of equal standing of the Igbo with other majority ethnic groups in Nigeria with which it had shared such status prior to the Biafran War.

The seeming lack of clarity about whether the neo-Biafran groups are fighting for a new sovereign state or a better deal for the Igbo within Nigeria came up in MASSOB, when its leader was accused by a breakaway faction of the organization of betraying their objective. The purported betrayal was in connection with an allegation that MASSOB leader Uwazurike was making guarantees to the police high command that MASSOB did not aim to break

Nigeria or create crisis for the Buhari administration. His accusers mentioned that Uwazurike also informed the police that he signed a Memorandum of Understanding in 2013 with retired Major Al Mustapha, the former chief security officer to the Late Head of State; General Sanni Abacha; Alhaji Asari Dokubo, who leads an ethnic Ijaw militant group in the Niger Delta region of Nigeria; the late Dr. Frederick Faseun, former leader of the Oodua People's Congress (OPC) in southwest Nigeria; and Alhaji Yerima Sani of northern Nigeria to refrain from activities that would affect the oneness of Nigeria.[26] The factionalization of MASSOB and consequent decline in the confidence and influence wielded by its leadership led to the popular ascendancy of IPOB, which is currently the main anchor of neo-Biafran nationalism. Thus, the decline of MASSOB and rise of IPOB represent two major phases of contemporary Igbo nationalism to which we now turn.

The Two Phases of Neo-Biafran Nationalism

The first major phase of the neo-Biafran Igbo nationalism in the fourth republic is the one represented by the rise of MASSOB. The rise of a crisis of confidence in MASSOB leadership led some of its former members to explore alternative platforms for the furtherance of their Igbo nationalist struggle manifestly couched in the neo-Biafran separatist ideology. One of the earliest members to decamp from MASSOB to IPOB is Mazi Nnamdi Kanu.

According to Emeka Emekesiri, who claims to be the founder of IPOB, he considered the United Nations Declaration in 2007 on the rights of Indigenous People and filed a case against the federal government of Nigeria at the Federal High Court in Owerri, the capital of Imo State in Nigeria. The suit sought the relief that the Igbo who were persecuted and hunted down but not consumed by the civil war be seen as the Indigenous People of Biafra with a right of self-determination. According to him, IPOB was meant to be the name for remnants of Biafra and not an organization similar to the one that Nnamdi Kanu registered as a limited liability company in the UK. Kanu had attended a meeting of IPOB and narrated stories of how Mr. Uwazurike started Radio Biafra in London in 2009 but stopped financing the five persons who were running the radio. The five equally joined IPOB from MASSOB after the suit filed against the federal government on behalf of IPOB. After joining IPOB, Kanu and his group interviewed some founding "elders" and protagonists of IPOB and aired their views worldwide through Radio Biafra. This convinced the protagonists that Nnamdi Kanu and those he came with from MASSOB are good for the media needs of IPOB.

At the time, the leader of IPOB was the late Justice Eze Ozobu. His deputy was the late Dr. Dozie Ikedife, while the secretary was Col. Joe Achuzia. Suddenly, Kanu used Radio Biafra to attack IPOB leadership by announcing that the elders had become traitors and saboteurs. He broadcast disparaging remarks about the elders and used his media instrument to start damaging the good relationships built with foreign countries like Britain, America, France, and Germany. Consequently, on May 12, 2014, Kanu was ostracized from IPOB, and this was published in the newspapers. Nnamdi Kanu decided to unilaterally register IPOB in the UK as a limited liability company. It was the IPOB faction he registered in 2014 that was proscribed by the federal government in 2017.[27]

What is clear from this narrative is that as the driving platforms for the pro-Biafra nationalist movement experiences cracks and shifts, feeling of nationalism itself continues to wax. When MASSOB provided its brand of leadership, it stood out strong among its followers until it suffered a trust challenge. The trust crises led to the transfer of loyalty to IPOB as the new platform. In all unfolding vicissitudes, the fervor around Igbo nationalism was sustained despite the cracks, which also happened in IPOB. Thus, when Nnamdi Kanu carved a different trajectory for his own IPOB, the strength of the message he communicated through the radio waves spread fast in influence, attracting followership among the Igbo, especially the young generation, most of whom never experienced the first declaration of Biafra in 1967 and the civil war that followed. But even as the nationalist sentiments continue to grow, the paradox is that the organizations that drive the process lack mutual trust. While factions of MASSOB and IPOB have lampooned the Ralph Uwazurike–led faction of MASSOB, the latter has no kind words for IPOB, which they charge with spreading disinformation about the Biafran struggle. According to Uwazurike, the MASSOB leader, he went to London, set up Radio Biafra, and appointed Nnamdi Kanu as the director. However, Mr. Kanu deployed the radio in blackmailing him.[28] Since 2015, the most politically visible face of the Biafran struggle has been the Kanu's faction of IPOB.

Despite the mutual recriminations between the groups, they share similar positions on issues affecting the Igbo. In some cases, they issue statements dealing with the same matters, such as their collective unwillingness to accept any special land allocation to the Fulani for cattle business in Igboland.[29] MASSOB had issued supportive statements for an unconditional release of Nnamdi Kanu during his detention in the first term of Buhari's presidency.[30] Accordingly, the major institutional drivers of neo-Biafra Igbo nationalism have altered, but the focus appears intact while the tempo of activities continues to grow.

During the first phase of the neo-Biafra struggle, dominated by MASSOB, the approach was more peaceful, mostly involving sit-at-home protests and peaceful demonstrations across Nigerian major cities like Onitsha, Aba, Enugu, and Lagos. In the second phase, led by IPOB, the movement has become more militant, added more verve to their radio broadcasting, evolved an armed wing called the Eastern Security Network (ESN), and has turned increasingly confrontational. The confrontations of IPOB go beyond the major target of their resistance struggle, the Nigerian state. They also berate Igbo elites, impose sit-at-home orders, and enforce the same. Accordingly, the struggle has not shifted in paradigm, although shifts had occurred in the platforms for coordinating it. Generally, it is a part of the emerging "new nationalisms" across the globe, which in the context of the neo-Biafra movement has been consistently committed to advancing the Igbo interest in Nigeria despite the convoluted endogenous and exogenous challenges the movement has faced.

Strategies of the Neo-Biafran Movement and Effects on the Nigerian State and the Igbo Society

In pursuit of their radical demands for a separate statehood, the neo-Biafran Igbo nationalists have deployed strategies that range from peaceful protests and public rallies in the past to more recently adopting threats toward and violent engagements with the Nigerian state. This study had noted that among the three core strategies adopted by the pro-Biafra activists is the blame-generating strategy highlighting and amplifying the contradictions in the Nigerian federation designed to disadvantage the Igbo community. They generally deploy this strategy to demonstrate the various facets of national life where the Igbo are sorted to the margins via-a-vis other ethnic groups. Such incidences of marginalization include the neglect of infrastructural development of Igboland, the excision and transfer of mineral-rich Igbo communities to non-Igbo states, a disproportionate number of states to the Igbo-speaking south-eastern part of Nigeria relative to their population in the federation, and nonappointment of the Igbo in crucial decision-making political positions in the country.[31] It needs to be noted that Igbo national-

The Biafra Separatist Movement and Resurgence of Igbo Nationalism | 245

ists who belong to the conservative wing of the Igbo elites also deploy this blaming strategy to demand broader opportunities for the Igbo. But the neo-Biafran nationalists apply the same logic for the purpose of discrediting the federal state and instigating rejection sentiments against it among the Igbo.

Among the several instruments used for the furtherance of the strategy of blame generation included radio broadcasting. MASSOB pioneered the Voice of Biafra International. Presently, IPOB uses Radio Biafra. There is also the generalized use of the internet and social media for the purposes of the organization. With these electronic media, they disseminate information about the fringe or inequitable position of the Igbo in Nigerian politics. In their information dissemination, they apply "provocative messages laced with misinformation, hate speech and anti-Nigerian derision."[32] An extreme example of this verbal propaganda is the spread of the fake information that Buhari died in London when he was sick, while the cloned version of Mr. Buhari that purports to be the president of Nigeria is one Mr. Jubril from Sudan.[33] The hate speech and abuses in question also include Igbo politicians, whom they portray as collaborationist stooges working with the Nigerian state.

Physical attack and threats on Igbo leaders and politicians were also an attention-seeking strategy of IPOB at some point. The leadership of IPOB ordered that some Igbo leaders be attacked on sight. Specifically, they recommended stoning for the serving leader of Ohanaeze Ndi-Igbo, the umbrella sociocultural union of the Igbo nation.[34] Following a physical attack in Germany on a Nigerian Igbo Senator by members of IPOB, the leader of the organization called for similar attacks and even placed a prize on information regarding oversea travels itinerary of any of the South-East governors whom he warned never to travel outside Nigeria.[35]

Another strategy has been the forceful enforcement of the observation of Biafra Day memorials observed on May 30 every year. People are directed to sit at home to commemorate those who were killed during the Biafran War. All neo-Biafran activists join in this event, and it attracts massive public compliance. Markets, offices, and transport systems are totally shut down on such days. There were initial voluntary responses by the Igbo in the South-East and parts of the South-South region, but IPOB now enforces compliance for the memorial and threatens physical repercussions for those who do not observe it by sitting-at-home on such days.

The sit-at-home strategy of celebrating the Biafra Day had been extended to other issues such as protesting the recent federal government's abduction, deportation, and detention of the leader of IPOB Mazi Nnamdi

Kanu from Kenya on the June 27, 2021. IPOB ordered that with effect from August 9, 2012, everybody must compulsorily sit-at-home once a week (every Monday) in the entire five states of South-East, Nigeria in protest, until Mr Kanu was released. This style of protest, which is comparable the 'ghost town' strategy used in Cameroon by Ambazonia separatists, is also ordered to be observed on any day that Mr Kanu is to be arraigned in court.

IPOB is unable to maintain its avowed peaceful strategy for the establishment of Biafra. The organization now has an armed wing called the Eastern Security Network (ESN). This wing of IPOB is purported to have been created to resist the incursion of violent Fulani pastoralists that invaded farmlands and attacked communities in the South-East and other parts of Nigeria. They have had confrontations with both Fulani herdsmen and Nigerian security forces.[36]

This militant dimension in the neo-Biafran struggle, though tied to the ravages of Fulani herdsmen in the South-East, seems like a fulfilment of a remote strategic vision of IPOB. Nnamdi Kanu had a few years prior to the formation of the Eastern Security Network, attended the World Igbo Congress in the United States and solicited for arms for the Biafran struggle.[37] Despite the long-term strategic vision of being armed as a group, their rapid drift towards armed militancy is a likely product of several unprovoked attacks and killings of unarmed pro-Biafran activists in different parts of the South-East by government security forces. About 150 unarmed protesters were killed across South-East between 2015 and 2016.[38] Twenty-one IPOB members were also killed in Enugu on August 23, 2020, with forty-seven arrested. In that incident, two government security personnel lost their lives. Such incidence and similar events in the past would have given impetus to the quick establishment of an armed wing for the Biafran struggles. It is believed that the hard-nosed use of force by the government against the Biafran activists not only popularized IPOB and their dead members as martyrs for the Igbo cause but also pushed them into greater resilience and contentiousness.

Spinoffs and Possible Trajectories

Spinoffs

The neo-Biafran Igbo nationalism occasions significant spinoffs around politics, economy, and society, not only in the South-East but across Nigeria.

The Biafra Separatist Movement and Resurgence of Igbo Nationalism | 247

Among the Igbo, it has created an awakening of consciousness of their ethnic identity and collective victimization. This sentiment is also reinforced by the political actions and pronouncements of the current Nigerian President Muhammadu Buhari. For instance, in a conversation at the United States Institute for Peace after the 2015 elections, Buhari declared that he would prioritize the areas that gave him 97 percent of the votes against places whose votes added up to 5 percent, an allusion to the insignificant votes he received from the Igbo states of the South-East region. In the 2015 presidential elections, Buhari scored an insignificant 198,248 votes in the South-East out of his total polled votes of 15,424,921. His prioritization game plan suggestion tends to point to a deliberate decision to neglect the South-East. As well, in his maiden media chat on December 30, 2015, Buhari demanded to know how the Igbo are marginalized in Nigeria and what they want, which many neo-Biafra campaigners saw as insensitivity on the part of the President. The most recent example was Buhari's perceived ethnic slur directed at the Igbo via his twitter handle in which he referred Biafran agitators to the carnage of the civil war and threatened to speak to them in the language they understand. In the words of the President: "Many of those misbehaving today are too young to be aware of the destruction and loss of lives that occurred during the Nigerian Civil War. Those of us in the fields for 30 months, who went through the war, will treat them in the language they understand."[39] The Igbo interpretation that President Buhari hates them builds on these expressions and attitude complex. Its net effect is the reinforcement of Igbo nationalism through the Biafran struggle.

In a 2018 survey by the Global Igbo Alliance dealing with whether the Igbo wanted the Republic of Biafra, regional autonomy akin to the first republic, or one united Nigeria. The outcome showed that 80.45 percent wanted Biafra, 17.99 percent preferred regional autonomy, and 1.57 percent wanted to remain in Nigeria as presently constituted.[40] The growth in the tempo of Igbo nationalism and an increasing widening of the desire for Biafra within a regime in which the Igbo clearly point at markers of exclusion suggests a causal link in the data. Essentially, the quality of politics and national leadership determines the nature of integration in a deeply divided society and Buhari's speeches and actions are not seen to promote political integration.

Biafran agitation and the rise of forceful implementation of their orders have created fears among the residents of South-East Nigeria. A mere pronouncement by IPOB that people must stay at home any day attracts high-level compliance not out of support for the order but for fear of consequences. Even the counter-orders by state governments do not persuade the citizens to flout the sit-at-home injunction because they doubt that the government could protect them from IPOB reprisals. Indeed, the governors have confessed helplessness in dealing with the crisis because they do not control the security forces, the federal government does.[41] Ultimately, public indifference to government has spiraled while neo-Biafran agitation gains momentum and acceptance.

In terms of economic effects of this conflict, the weekly shut-down of activities in the South-East is estimated to cost the region a total of 50 billion Naira (equivalent to US$121,654,501.22) over a period of one month. The private sector accounts for 60 percent of these losses (Independent, 2021). The impact would be more far-reaching except for the fact that the South-East economy depends largely on sole proprietorship trading and artisanal activities. The obvious implication of this is that both the individual and overall GDP of states within the region would logically decline, as well as the quality-of-life indicators. Of course, slightly different but related to the economy is that schools are shut down on such days, with obvious adverse implications for dropout levels and human resource development.

The increase in political agitation and clashes with security forces have equally paved the way for criminals to take advantage of the atmosphere created by neo-Biafran activists to step up robbery, assassinations, and other criminal activities in the Igbo states. Conflict Database of the Nextier SPD (2021) reported 124 violent incidents in South-East Nigeria from October 1, 2020, to September 30, 2021. The number of casualties of security personnel is 73, and civilian casualties 263. Injured persons is 51, kidnapped 46. Some of the landmark incidents included an attack of a prison in Owerri in Imo State that resulted in the escape of 1,844 inmates, kidnapping, serial killing of civilians, policemen and other security personnel in the South-East.[42]

IPOB is accused by the federal authorities of being responsible for the insecurity across the South-East while they deny responsibility and claim that the insecurity is a deliberate ploy to vilify and victimize IPOB. Some state governors have suggested that most of the attackers in the South-East are not of Igbo origin; for example, 70 percent of those arrested for violent attacks in Imo State were, according to the governor of the state, found not to be Igbo.[43] By implication, dangerous criminals tend to have built on the foundation of fear and threat laid by IPOB to carry out criminal activities. Overall, this questions the entire neo-Biafran campaign and the *raison d'être* of contemporary Igbo nationalism because it has appeared rather difficult to see whose interest it serves.

Possible Trajectories

The future direction of Igbo nationalism based on the neo-Biafran approach and the nature of demands depends on the role of both domestic and external forces. The domestic forces include the inclination of other ethnic groups in Nigeria and their disposition to lend support to the neo-Biafran cause, or perhaps maintain indifference or outright hostility to Igbo nationalism. The beginning of the neo-Biafran struggle in the fourth republic, for instance, attracted scathing comments against the separatists and the Igbo in general from other ethnic groups in the north and south of Nigeria. The federal government's jackboot approach in responding to the agitators was considered appropriate. This attitude lingered through the regimes of Olusegun Obasanjo, the late Umaru Musa Yar Adua, and Goodluck Jonathan. However, a major shift in that attitude appears to have occurred since the emergence of the Buhari regime. Opinions tend to have shifted from considering the separatists as enemies of an indivisible Nigeria to perceiving them as Indigenous people with rights of self-determination that must be respected.

A few factors account for this shift in attitudes. First is the rise of aggressive herdsmen, mostly of the Fulani ethnic stock, who migrate to different parts of the country, graze their cattle on people's farmlands, and attack sedentary communities that own such farms when they complain. This became rife in the north central states, especially in Benue and Plateau States. In a specific incident in Benue State, the Fulani herdsmen killed seventy-three persons in one day (Ogundipe, 2018a). Elsewhere, in Enugu State in South-East Nigeria, the nomadic herdsmen killed forty-six individuals in one attack in 2017.[44] Similar attacks were also common in most states in the South-West and South-South parts of the country.

In all the attacks by the herdsmen of Fulani origin, the ethnic group of the Nigerian president, none of the attackers was ever arrested or prosecuted, as security forces seemed helpless and constrained from taking action against the violence. Indeed, T. Y. Danjuma, a retired army general and former defense minister, had accused the army of aiding the herdsmen in their violent attacks across Nigeria.[45] Equally, new territorial claims were made by members of a Fulani sociocultural group called *Miyetti Allah Kautal Hore*, and even a cartel of Fulani cattle breeders, Miyetti Allah Cattle Breeders Association (MACBAN), claimed to have rights over every part of the Nigerian territory. This claim and the indifference of the security forces in moving against the main actors in agrarian violence in Nigeria irked other Nigerian ethnic communities. As a result, the ethnic communities who feared being overrun by the Fulani herders resorted to ethnic nationalism and resistance as one effective strategy to contain the perceived expansionist ambitions of the Fulani.

The common victimhood suffered by several ethnic communities in the face of the threat posed by Fulani herdsmen helped in correcting the misperceptions that many ethnic communities hitherto held about the Igbo nationalism and the Biafran struggle for self-determination. Separatist agitation akin to the neo-Biafra movement emerged elsewhere in the Yoruba-dominated South-West region of Nigeria under the leadership of Sunday Igboho, demanding a sovereign state for the Yoruba nation. In the South-South region, pockets of alliances had been brokered between the Igbo groups and the Niger Delta militant group fronted by Alhaji Asari Dokubo, who leads the Niger Delta People Volunteer Force. Similarly, some elites from the north central states of Nigeria have openly apologized to the Igbo and expressed reckoning for the political suppression they are subjected to in Nigeria. Remarkably, a group led by the late Mr. Obadiah Mailafia announced on May 19, 2021, that they regretted the role of the north central region (also known as the Middle Belt region) in the Biafran War because they, not the Fulani, were the main fighting force of the Nigeria army in the civil war.[46]

These domestic factors, especially the common consciousness of the southern states and the Middle Belt region, appear likely to generate the push that would compel the entrenched interest in the Nigerian state to concede to pressure for the restructuring of Nigeria by substantial devolution of powers and resources from the center to the constituent subnational states or regions in a political arrangement akin to the first civilian republic. In a restructured Nigeria, constituent groups are expected to become autonomous and be able to determine their development pathways and substantially independent of the central government. It is likely that should the federal authorities continue to resist the growing demand for restructuring, separatist agitators who could resort to armed struggles will grow further in strength and determination. This could be a recipe for disaster. The resort to armed conflict would be costly in terms of human and material resources, and from all indications an implosive centrifugal war in Nigeria will produce far-reaching regional destabilization and a completely failed state comparable to war-torn Somalia.

Presently, early warning signals are sufficient for the international community and African regional institutions to step in to help mediate a constructive reinvention of Nigeria to avert a major conflagration. If Nigeria slides into an implosive armed struggle—a scenario we will never advocate—the possible settlement after a probable carnage may include the option of referendum for the Igbo and indeed a few other ethno-regional groups to determine whether they want to remain in Nigeria.

Conclusion

The resurgence of Igbo nationalism in the present fourth republic has been marked by militant neo-Biafran agitation. This comes in the form of demands for sovereign statehood. The persistent use of military force to suppress the separatist agitation tends to reinforce the resolve of campaigners and fuel their demand for a new state. While previous governments since the inception of the fourth republic have reasonably countered the Biafran agitation, the Buhari regime, which has pursued more divisive policies than previous governments, is evidently contending with a more determined resistance against the Nigerian state. To a large extent, the Igbo nationalists and neo-Biafran agitators consider Buhari's regime hostile to the Igbo community. Thus, the intensity of Igbo ethnic nationalism appears driven by the character of the political regime in question.

Igbo nationalism in the fourth civilian republic has moved from a peaceful separatist agitation phase when MASSOB was the leading campaigner for the sovereign state of Biafra to the second and militant phase under championed by IPOB. Remarkably, IPOB was peaceful at the beginning, but later adopted an armed struggle strategy when under the President Buhari's regime the emboldened Fulani herdsmen began to violently attack unarmed Igbo communities in the South-East. The federal government's deployment of security personnel to crack down on IPOB members is another factor that prompted IPOB to resort to armed violence. Presently, IPOB operates an armed wing called the Eastern Security Network, but the latter has been overwhelmingly clamped down if not decimated by state security forces. Other strategies of the struggle include radio broadcasting, use of internet (social media platforms) to disseminate information, and imposition of compulsory sit-at-home demonstrations in the entire South-East.

It is our view that the coercive suppression approach adopted by the state to neutralize the neo-Biafra movement could result in two alternative trajectories. The first is that the growing solidarity of ethnic communities and states in the entire southern Nigeria and the Middle Belt region may compel the entrenched political interests in the country to seek the alternative pathway of devolutionary restructuring to stave off the disintegration of Nigeria. This is by far a preferred and more proactive scenario. The second alternative, should the current hard power strategy of the federal government continue, would be that separatist agitators may be forced to acquire more arms to confront the state, thereby exacerbating the conflict with more deadly consequences, including the scary prospect of Nigeria becoming a totally failed and ultimately dismembered state.

Notes

1. Daniel Beland and Andre Lecours, "Nationalism and the Politics of Austerity: Comparing Catalonia, Scotland, and Quebec." *National Identities* (2019). 10.1080/14608944.2019.1660312

2. Okwudiba Nnoli, *Ethnic Politics in Nigeria* (Enugu: Pan African Centre for Research on Peace and Conflict Resolution, 2008).

3. Ibid., 143.

4. Ibid.

5. O. Ibeanu, N. Orji, and K. Iwuamadi, "Biafra Separatism: Causes, Consequences, and Remedies" (2016). www.researchgate.net/publication/312129707_Biafra_Separatism_Causes_ Consequences_and_Remedies

6. Kenneth Omeje, "The Rentier State: Oil-related Legislation and Conflict in the Niger Delta, Nigeria," *Conflict, Security and Development* 6, no. 2 (2006): 211–230.

7. Ibid., 217. See also Ike Okonta, "The Lingering Crisis in Nigeria's Niger Delta and Suggestions for a Peaceful Resolution," CDD Working Paper, No. 1. Centre for Democracy and Development, London, 2000.

8. Jideofor Adibe, "Biafran Separatist Agitations in Nigeria: Causes and Trajectories" (2017). www.brookings.edu/blog/africa-in-focus/2017/07/12/separatist-agitations-in-nigeria-causes-and-trajectories

9. See Max Siollun, *Oil, Politics, and Violence: Nigeria's Military Coup Culture (1966–1976)* (New York: Algora Publishing, 2009).

10. Karl Maier, *This House Has Fallen* (London: Penguin, 2000).

11. Chidi Nkwopara, "Why I founded MASSOB." *Vanguard* (6 January 2020). www.vanguardngr.com/2020/01/why-i-founded-massob-%E2%80%95-uwazuruike

12. Vincent Ujumadu, "MASSOB Accuses Uwazurike of Sabotage, Vow to Probe Him" (2015). www.vanguardngr.com/2015/09/16th-anniversary-massob-accuses-uwazurike-of-sabotage-vows-to-probe-him/

13. Godwin Onuoha, "Memory, Reconciliation, and Peacebuilding in Post–Civil War South-eastern Nigeria." African Peacebuilding Network, APN Working Papers, No. 19 (2018).

14. C. Nwangwu, F. Onuoha, B. Nwosu, and C. Ezeibe, "Political Economy of Igbo Biafra Separatism and Post-War Igbo Nationalism," *African Affairs* 119, no. 4 (2020): 1–26.

15. Godwin Onuoha, "Contemporary Igbo Nationalism and the Crisis of Self-Determination in the Nigerian Public Sphere." CODESRIA, 12th General Assembly, Dakar, Senegal, 2008.

16. Ibid.

17. Nwangwu et al., op. cit.

18. K. Omeje, "Enyimba Enyi: The Comeback of Ibo Nationalism in Nigeria," *Review of African Political Economy* 32, no. 106 (2005): 630–636.

19. See P. W. Effiong, "40+ Years Later . . . the War Hasn't Ended . . ." In Chima J. Korieh (ed.), *The Nigerian-Biafra War* (New York: Cambria Press, 2012), 260–276. See also Charles Ekpo, "Explaining the Resurgence of Biafra Radicalisation and Nationalism in South-East Nigeria," *African Journal on Terrorism* 8, no. 1 (2019): 92–121; and Onuoha (2008), *supra*.

20. O. Ibeanu and G. Onu, *Ethnic Groups and Conflicts in Nigeria*, vol. 2, South-East zone. Programme on Ethnic and Federal Studies, Department of Political Science (Ibadan: University of Ibadan, 2001).

21. Onuoha, "Contemporary Igbo Nationalism."

22. Omeje, op. cit.

23. Cletus Ukpong, "Why South–South Can't Be Part of Biafra," *Premium Times* (21 October 2016). www.premiumtimesng.com/news/top-news/213280-south-south-cant-part-biafra-former-nigerian-general.html; Owen Akenzua, "Delta Is Not a Part of Biafra Republic. *Guardian* (16 September 2016). https://guardian.ng/news/delta-is-not-part-of-biafra-republic

24. Vincent Ujumadu, "I Want Biafra of the Mind, Not of Land," *Vanguard* (14 May 2021). www.vanguardngr.com/2021/05/i-want-biafra-of-the-mind-not-of-land-%E2%80%95-abaribe

25. B. Nwosu, "Citizens on the Margins: Peacebuilding, National Integration and Political Restructuring in Nigeria," *African Journal for Security and Development* 2, no. 3 (2018): 116–131.

26. Ujumadu, op. cit.

27. Dennis Agbo, "Biafra Existed 500 Years before Nigeria Was Created," *Vanguard* (2020). www.vanguardngr.com/2020/11/biafra-existed-500-yrs-before-nigeria-was-created-emekesiri-original-founder-of-ipob

28. Punch, "IPOB Brought Falsehood into Biafran Struggle. *Punch* (4 February 2018). https://punchng.com/ipob-brought-falsehood-into-biafran-struggle-says-uwazurike

29. Anayo Okoli, Peter Okutu, and Chimaobi Nwaiwu, "Southern Nigeria Has No Land for Herdsmen." *Vanguard* (16 March 2021). www.vanguardngr.com/2021/03/southern-nigeria-has-no-land-for-herdsmen-ipob-massob

30. Jude Ossai, "MASSOB Rejects Conditional Release of IPOB Leader, Kanu, Others" *Nigerian Tribune* (31 July 2016). https://tribuneonlineng.com/massob-rejects-conditional-release-ipob-leader-kanu-others

31. Orji Ibeanu and Iwuamadi, op. cit.

32. International Crisis Group, "Nigeria's Biafran Separatist Upsurge" (2015). www.crisisgroup.org/africa/west-africa/nigeria/nigeria-s-biafran-separatist-upsurge

33. Chijioke Jannah, "Jubril of Sudan: Nnamdi Kanu Vows to Release More Proof of Fake Buhari in Aso Rock." *Daily Post* (8 December 2018). https://dailypost.ng/2018/12/08/jubril-sudan-nnamdi-kanu-vows-release-proof-fake-buhari-aso-rock-today

34. New Telegraph, "Nnamdi Kanu's Death Decree on Nwodo." *New Telegraph* (8 July 2020). www.newtelegraphng.com/nnamdi-kanus-death-decree-on-nwodo

35. James Eze, "Nnamdi Kanu Speaks on Ekweremadu Attack, Offers N1m for Southeast Governors' Itinerary. *Premium Times* (18 August 2019). www.premiumtimesng.com/regional/ssouth-east/347341-nnamdi-kanu-speaks-on-ekweremadu-attack-offers-n1m-for-southeast-governors-travel-itinerary.html

36. John Nwachukwu, "Eastern Security Network: Kanu Warned against Sending Youths to Confront Fulani Herdsmen without Arms." *Daily Post* (2020). https://dailypost.ng/2020/12/16/eastern-security-network-kanu-warned-against-sending-youths-to-confront-fulani-herdsmen-without-arms

37. The News, "Nnamdi Kanu Begs for Guns and Bullets." *The News* (28 October 2015). https://thenewsnigeria.com.ng/2015/10/28/video-nnamdi-kanu-begs-for-guns-and-bullets

38. Nicholas Ibekwe, "How Nigerian Security Forces Killed 150 Pro-Biafra Protesters—Amnesty International." *Premium Times* (24 November 2016). www.premiumtimesng.com/news/headlines/216166-nigerian-security-forces-killed-150-pro-biafra-protesters-amnesty-international.html

39. Peoples Gazette, "Igbo Youths Want Genocide Like the Civil War: They Will Get It from Me—Buhari." *Peoples Gazette* (1 June 2021). https://gazettengr.com/igbo-youths-want-genocide-like-nigerian-civil-war-theyll-get-it-from-me-buhari

40. Vanguard, "Opinion Says Overwhelming Igbo Majority Wants Biafra." *Vanguard* (3 March 2018). www.vanguardngr.com/2018/03/opinion-poll-shows-overwhelming-igbo-majority-wants-biafra

41. Ochogwu, Sunday, "Nnamdi Kanu, Why Governors Can't Stop IPOB's Sit-at-Home Order." *Daily Post* (11 October 2021). https://dailypost.ng/2021/10/11/nnamdi-kanu-why-southeast-govs-cant-stop-ipobs-sit-at-home-order-ikpeazu

42. B. Nwosu and N. Nwokolo, "The Inevitability of Peace Dialogue." *Nextier SPD Policy Weekly* (2021). https://nextierspd.com/the-inevitability-of-peace-dialogue

43. Vanguard, "No Fewer than 400 People Arrested over Security Threat in Imo." *Vanguard* (24 May 2021). www.vanguardngr.com/2021/05/no-fewer-than-400-people-arrested-over-security-threats-in-imo

44. Francis Igata, "Blow-by-Blow Account of How Herdsmen Killed Forty-Six Natives." *Vanguard* (30 April 2016). www.vanguardngr.com/2016/04/enugu-blow-blow-account-herdsmen-killed-46-natives

45. Samuel Ogundipe, "Military, Police Complicit in Killings across Nigeria—T.Y Danjuma" (24 March 2018). www.premiumtimesng.com/news/headlines/262959-military-police-complicit-in-killings-across-nigeria-t-y-danjuma.html

46. Chiedozie A. Ogbon, "Why Ndigbo Mourn Mailafia." *Nigerian Tribune* (23 September 2021). https://tribuneonlineng.com/why-ndigbo-mourn-mailafia

References

Adibe, Jideofor. 2017. "Biafran separatist agitations in Nigeria: Causes and trajectories." www.brookings.edu/blog/africa-in-focus/2017/07/12/separatist-agitations-in-nigeria-causes-and-trajectories

Agbo, Dennis. 2020. "Biafra existed 500 years before Nigeria was created." Vanguard. www.vanguardngr.com/2020/11/biafra-existed-500-yrs-before-nigeria-was-created-emekesiri-original-founder-of-ipob

Akenzua, Owen. 2016. "Delta is not a part of Biafra republic." Guardian (September 16). https://guardian.ng/news/delta-is-not-part-of-biafra-republic/

Beland, Daniel, and Andre Lecours. 2019. "Nationalism and the politics of austerity: Comparing Catalonia, Scotland, and Quebec." National Identities. 10.1080/14608944.2019.1660312

Effiong, P. W. 2012. "40+ Years Later . . . the War Hasn't Ended . . ." In Chima J. Korieh (ed.), *The Nigerian-Biafra War*. New York: Cambria Press.

Ekpo, Charles. 2019. "Explaining the Resurgence of Biafra Radicalisation and Nationalism in South-East Nigeria." *African Journal on Terrorism*, 8, no. 1: 92–121.

Eze, James. 2019. "Nnamdi Kanu speaks on Ekweremadu attack, offers N1m for Southeast governors' itinerary." Premium Times (August 18). www.premiumtimesng.com/regional/ssouth-east/347341-nnamdi-kanu-speaks-on-ekweremadu-attack-offers-n1m-for-southeast-governors-travel-itinerary.html

Ibeanu, O., and Onu, G. 2001. "Ethnic groups and conflicts in Nigeria vol. 2, South-East zone." Programme on Ethnic and Federal Studies, Department of Political Science. Ibadan: University of Ibadan.

Ibeanu, O., N. Orji, and K. Iwuamadi. 2016. "Biafra separatism: Causes, consequences, and remedies." www.researchgate.net/publication/312129707_Biafra_Separatism_Causes_Consequences_and_Remedies

Ibekwe, Nicholas. 2016. "How Nigerian security forces killed 150 pro-Biafra protesters—Amnesty International." Premium Times (November 24). www.premiumtimesng.com/news/headlines/216166-nigerian-security-forces-killed-150-pro-biafra-protesters-amnesty-international.html

Igata, Francis. 2016. "Blow-by-blow account of how herdsmen killed 46 natives." Vanguard (April 30). www.vanguardngr.com/2016/04/enugu-blow-blow-account-herdsmen-killed-46-natives

Independent. 2021. "South-East has lost N50 billion to sit-at-home order." Independent (September 18). https://independent.ng/ipob-south-east-has-lost-n50bn-to-sit-at-home-order-naccima

International Crisis Group. 2015. "Nigeria's Biafran separatist upsurge." www.crisisgroup.org/africa/west-africa/nigeria/nigeria-s-biafran-separatist-upsurge

Jannah, Chijioke. 2018. "Jubril of Sudan: Nnamdi Kanu vows to release more proof of fake Buhari in Aso Rock." Daily Post (December 8). https://dailypost.ng/2018/12/08/jubril-sudan-nnamdi-kanu-vows-release-proof-fake-buhari-aso-rock-today

Maier, Karl. 2000. *This House Has Fallen*. London: Penguin.

New Telegraph. 2020. "Nnamdi Kanu's death decree on Nwodo." New Telegraph (July 8). www.newtelegraphng.com/nnamdi-kanus-death-decree-on-nwodo

Nextier SPD. 2021. "Stemming the tears: A pragmatic approach to solving Nigeria's security challenges." https://nextierspd.com/stemming-the-tears-a-pragmatic-approach-to-solving-nigerias-security-challenges

Nkwopara, Chidi. 2020. "Why I founded MASSOB." Vanguard (January 6). www.vanguardngr.com/2020/01/why-i-founded-massob-%E2%80%95-uwazuruike/.

Nwachukwu, John. O. 2020. "Eastern Security Network: Kanu warned against sending youths to confront Fulani herdsmen without arms." Daily Post. https://dailypost.ng/2020/12/16/eastern-security-network-kanu-warned-against-sending-youths-to-confront-fulani-herdsmen-without-arms/

Nwangwu, C., F. Onuoha, B. Nwosu, and C. Ezeibe. 2020. "Political economy of Igbo Biafra separatism and post-war Igbo nationalism." African Affairs, 119, no. 4: 1–26.

Nwosu, B., and N. Nwokolo 2021. "The inevitability of peace dialogue. Nextier SPD Policy Weekly." https://nextierspd.com/the-inevitability-of-peace-dialogue

Nwosu, B. 2018. "Citizens on the margins: Peacebuilding, national integration and political restructuring in Nigeria." *African Journal for Security and Development* 2, no. 3: 116–131.

Ochogwu, Sunday. 2021. "Nnamdi Kanu, why governors can't stop IPOB's sit-at-home order" Daily Post (October 11). https://dailypost.ng/2021/10/11/nnamdi-kanu-why-southeast-govs-cant-stop-ipobs-sit-at-home-order-ikpeazu

Ogbon, Chiedozie, A. 2021. "Why Ndigbo mourn Mailafia. Nigerian Tribune" (September 23). https://tribuneonlineng.com/why-ndigbo-mourn-mailafia

Ogundipe, Samuel 2018b. "Military, Police complicit in killings across Nigeria—T.Y Danjuma" (March 24). www.premiumtimesng.com/news/headlines/262959-military-police-complicit-in-killings-across-nigeria-t-y-danjuma.html

Ogundipe, Samuel. 2018a. "Benue killings: Signpost blaming Fulani herdsmen for 73 deaths causes stir." Premium Times (March 12). www.premiumtimesng.com/regional/north-central/261507-benue-killings-signpost-blaming-fulani-herdsmen-73-deaths-causes-stir.html

Okoli, Anayo, Peter Okutu, and Chimaobi Nwaiwu. 2021. "Southern Nigeria has no land for herdsmen." Vanguard (March 16). www.vanguardngr.com/2021/03/southern-nigeria-has-no-land-for-herdsmen-ipob-massob

Onuoha, Godwin. 2008. "Contemporary Igbo nationalism and the crisis of self-determination in the Nigerian public sphere." CODESRIA, 12th General Assembly, Dakar, Senegal.

Onuoha, Godwin. 2018. "Memory, reconciliation, and peacebuilding in post-civil war South-eastern Nigeria." African Peacebuilding Network, APN Working Papers No 19.

Ossai, Jude. 2016. "MASSOB rejects conditional release of IPOB leader, Kanu, Others." Nigerian Tribune (July 31). https://tribuneonlineng.com/massob-rejects-conditional-release-ipob-leader-kanu-others

Peoples Gazette. 2021. "Igbo youths want genocide like the civil war: They will get it from me—Buhari." Peoples Gazette (June 1). https://gazettengr.com/igbo-youths-want-genocide-like-nigerian-civil-war-theyll-get-it-from-me-buhari

Punch. 2018. "IPOB brought falsehood into Biafran struggle." Punch (February 4). https://punchng.com/ipob-brought-falsehood-into-biafran-struggle-says-uwazurike

Siollun, Max. 2009. "Oil, politics, and violence: Nigeria's military coup culture (1966–1976)." New York: Algora Publishing.

The News. 2015. "Nnamdi Kanu begs for guns and bullets." The News (October 28). https://thenewsnigeria.com.ng/2015/10/28/video-nnamdi-kanu-begs-for-guns-and-bullets/

Ujumadu, Vincent. 2015. "MASSOB accuses Uwazurike of sabotage, vow to probe him." www.vanguardngr.com/2015/09/16th-anniversary-massob-accuses-uwazurike-of-sabotage-vows-to-probe-him/

Ujumadu, Vincent. 2021. "I want Biafra of the mind not of land." Vanguard (May 14). www.vanguardngr.com/2021/05/i-want-biafra-of-the-mind-not-of-land-%E2%80%95-abaribe/

Ukpong, Cletus. 2016. "Why South-South can't be part of Biafra. Premium Times." (October 21). www.premiumtimesng.com/news/top-news/213280-south-south-cant-part-biafra-former-nigerian-general.html.

Vanguard. 2018. "Opinion says overwhelming Igbo majority wants Biafra." Vanguard (March 3). www.vanguardngr.com/2018/03/opinion-poll-shows-overwhelming-igbo-majority-wants-biafra

Vanguard. 2021. "No fewer than 400 people arrested over security threat in Imo." Vanguard (May 24). www.vanguardngr.com/2021/05/no-fewer-than-400-people-arrested-over-security-threats-in-imo

11

Beyond a Militia

Notes on the History and Ideology of the Huthi (Ansar Allah) Movement in Yemen

Felipe Medina Gutiérrez

Introduction[1]

On January 17, 2022, Abu Dhabi was hit by drones apparently sent by the Huthi movement.[2] The United Arab Emirates responded fiercely by carrying out bombardments in Yemen, which put two elements on the international stage. First, the war in Yemen exists and remains largely ignored by the so-called "international community." Second, the Huthi movement continues to be a key player in the conflict, and there is a serious lack of knowledge about them.

The neglect of the war in Yemen leads to a short reflection on the Ukraine–Russia conflict since 2022. Starting from a message of solidarity to all the victims of such hostility, the strong attention by the media to the situation in Ukraine contrasts with little mention of what has been happening in Yemen for years. This highlights the great hypocrisy that exists among members of the so-called "international community," because we don't see the same concern or condemnation about the military operations there that have been profoundly affecting the Yemeni population.

Given the absence of information about Yemen, the lack of knowledge of its internal situation is understandable. More especially, the northern region of the country, the home of the Huthi movement, remains unknown to most Western hemisphere observers. As Brandt rightly pointed out: "The flow of information from Yemen's extreme north was further impeded by the inaccessibility of its often rugged, mountainous terrain, and of its tribal customs and traditions (often despised and denigrated by urban middle-class Yemeni intellectuals)."[3] In this context, the group is depicted as an archaic and purposeless militia. However, the reality is much more complex, and this chapter offers a deeper analysis of the Huthi movement.

To study this group, we must be aware of its origin and its evolution. Is it a product of Yemen's modern history, or is it a recently created group? Similarly, highlighting some points of their "ideology" is beneficial for developing a better understanding of the organization and of the current war. Does nationalism influence and contribute to a better understanding of this group? Are their activities similar to nationalists' discourses, or are they purely religious? And, finally, are they a group that blindly obeys Iran?

The Huthi movement has roots in the contemporary history of Yemen. While most of its members follow the religious tradition of Zaydi Islam,[4] their political agenda also responds to local factors, which are linked to a nationalist agenda. This group does not seek a caliphate, nor seek to revive the *Imāma*[5] (at the moment). It is therefore important to approach some of the elements that compose the Huthi "ideology." In the absence of an official framework, we will try to trace the presence of nationalist elements linked to religious discourse, as well. The chapter also discusses the extent of the relationship and influence between the Huthi movement and the Islamic Republic of Iran, arguing that it is not a proxy relationship, although the links between the two have grown over the years. We seek a more complex and critical approach than the usual one that states the Huthis are an archaic group empty of purpose or with demands without political significance.[6]

The Huthi (Ansar Allah) Movement: Appearing out of Nowhere?

To understand this group, we must trace its origin in the evolution of modern Yemen. Some explanations can be found in history from the end of the Islamic system of the *Imāma*, the 1962 Republican revolution, and the civil war until 1970. This had a profound impact upon the Zaydi community, as the *Imāma* ruled parts of Yemen[7] (especially the north in Sa'da) for a thousand years (late ninth century to 1962).[8] The *Imāma* has a strong tradition in parts of Yemen.

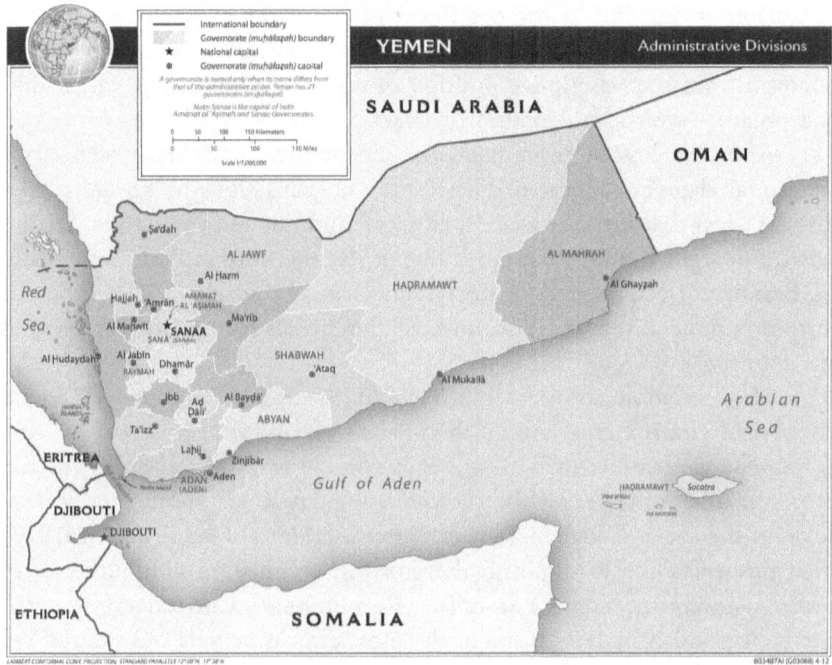

Map 11.1. Yemen: Administrative divisions.

Historical Overview: The Republican Revolution and Contemporary Yemen

When the republican era began in Yemen in 1962, many of the social and political groups that had been favored for decades faced a difficult period of readjustment. The country has a complex social structure with formal hierarchies, one of them being the *Sada* (sing. *sayyid*), the Zaydi religious aristocracy that lives mainly in Sa'da, a region in the north of Yemen inhabited by tribes of the Khawlan bin 'Amir confederation. Historically, they obtained positions of influence in society due to their knowledge of Islamic religion (e.g., Islamic law)[9] and in regions such as northern Yemen "they sit at the top of the pyramid. They control and benefit from a lot of political, religious, social, and economic privilege (by owning power, land, and real estate)."[10]

The 1962 revolution affected the political aspirations and power of the *sada*. As Brandt pointed out: "Unlike the failed coup of 1948, the 1962 Revolution did not aim at the replacement of one imam by a more just or capable imam, but at the overthrow of the imamic system as a whole. In consequence not only the imam, but also the *sādah* (adj. *sayyid*) were removed from their ascriptive position of power and influence, which they had obtained over a millennium of imamic rule."[11]

After the loss of prominence in the political and social scene, two additional elements appeared. First came the accusations by several parties inside Yemen that the *sada* were "foreigners" and not Yemeni natives. Second was the marginalization of regions like Saʿda, the northern core of Yemen. As Brandt correctly stated: "The system change after the 1960s civil war further peripheralized and disconnected the Saʿdah region from the rest of the country."[12]

This situation continued throughout the Republican period, which saw several governments. ʿAbdullah al-Sallal (1962–1967) gave way to ʿAbd al-Rahman al-Iryani (1967–1974), whose time was characterized by the rise of power and influence of the *shuyukh* (sing. *sheikh*),[13] another important actor in the social ladder of Yemen. Later, Ibrahim al-Hamdi (1974–1977) tried unsuccessfully to diminish the growing domination and authority of certain *shuyukh* through the so-called "Revolutionary Corrective Initiative," but he was killed in 1977. One of the most critical periods was that of ʿAli ʿAbdullah Saleh, of Zaydi origin, who would be president of North Yemen from 1978 to 1990, and president of the unified Republic of Yemen until 2011. His legacy shaped much of what the country was in recent years, especially with the creation of its political party, the General People's Congress (GPC), which would establish a new system of patronage and cooptation characterized by neopatrimonialism.[14]

Huthi Family, 1990s Zaydi Revivalism and Emergence of the Believing Youth Movement

It is appropriate to consider the general context of the 1970s and 1980s in the Middle East. The decline of Arab nationalism following the death of Gamal Abdel Nasser and the rise of the power of Saudi Arabia due to its petroleum industry was marked by the spread of religious conservatism and of Wahhabism, the Saudi kingdom's founding ideology. Fears of the 1979 Iranian revolution and the expansion of communism in south Yemen encouraged Riyadh to deepen its influence in Yemen, propagating the Wahhabi teachings, especially in the northern part of the country. As Weir pointed out: "Leaders of this reformist, puritanical school of Sunnī Islam propagated their beliefs through lesson circles, mosques, and colleges in their native *bilāds* [lands] in explicit opposition to Zaydism" (brackets are mine).[15] This is what Brandt called the "Sunnization of the Zaydi *madhhab*"[16] and the spread of different kinds of Sunni radicalism in the heart of the Zaydi lands.

The reply to this phenomenon was known as the "Zaydi revivalism" in Yemeni historiography, which involved activities on many fronts. The founding of the political party Hizb al-Haqq (1990) was also accompanied by the creation of the Believing Youth (1992), a proselytizing movement aimed at regaining the Zaydi tradition ground and affirming the identity of their community. In this context, the al-Huthi family[17] developed a more formal influence in the affairs of Yemen thanks to the activism of Badr ad-Dīn al-Huthi (1926–2010) and his son Hussein al-Huthi (1960–2004), both important leaders in the genesis of the movement. This period is therefore essential, as Brandt summed up: "Being promoted by the Saudi and (at times) the Yemeni government, the spread of radical Sunnism in the Zaydi heartland triggered the emergence of a Zaydi resistance movement. In the context of the Saʿdah region, the Zaydi revival had an immensely far-reaching impact, providing the basis for the emergence in the 1990s of the "Believing Youth"—an organization that transformed the theological discourse of the Zaydi renaissance into religious revival and social activism on grassroots level."[18] This event is crucial to note because it helps to contextualize the rivalry between the Zaydis linked to the Huthis against the followers of Wahhabism, both inside and outside Yemen.[19] Moreover, it is here that we will see the beginnings of something called "the Huthi movement." According to Brandt: "Factional disputes within the Zaydi revival soon escalated, ultimately leading to an internal split and the emergence of the group which, from 2001, became known as 'Houthis' (*al-Ḥūthiyyūn*) and, from 2011, as Anṣār Allah."[20]

In 1994, Yemen entered another civil war, leading to the consolidation of the Saleh GPC one-party state system, despite the existence of a "controlled opposition" with political parties such as Islah (founded in 1990), the Nasserists, and the Baathists. At that time, the influence of ʿAli Mohsen al-Ahmar in the armed forces and *sheikh* ʿAbdallah al-Ahmar (d. 2007) in parliament rose to be more prominent.

From the Saʿda Wars to the Capture of the Capital 2014

The arrival of the second millennium presented a complex context: the second *intifada* in Palestine, and the effects of the strategy and discourse of the

"War on Terror" in the wake of the attacks of September 11, 2001, which led to the U.S. invasion of Afghanistan and Iraq (2001–2003), as well as the horrors of Bagram, Guantanamo, and Abu Ghraib prisons. The Saleh government of Yemen supported the "War on Terror," gaining economic support from Washington and security cooperation agreements.

However, this led to an increase in critical voices within Yemen, including Hussein al-Huthi. His criticism through preaching and speeches (known as *malāzim*) raised awareness and popular support, especially in Sa'da, against these government relationships and alliances with the United States, but also added a central feature in the ideology of his followers. As noted by Van der Kroft: "The Houthis developed intensely anti-U.S. rhetoric, particularly after the US invasion of Iraq in 2003."[21] Al-Ahmad added: "Following the attacks on the twin towers in September 2001 and the invasion of Iraq, Hussein al Houthi developed a radical theory that combined Zaydi revivalism with an anti-imperialist, anti-U.S. agenda."[22] It is in this context that the characteristic slogan of the group would become popular: "Allah is the Greatest, Death to America, Death to Israel, a Curse Upon the Jews, Victory for Islam."[23]

All this criticism led to an open conflict with the Saleh government known in Yemeni historiography as the "Sa'da Wars" (2004–2010).[24] One of the most important events occurred on September 10, 2004, when the government announced the death of Hussein al-Huthi. According to his followers, his demise on the battlefield made him a martyr.[25] Later, the natural death of the founder of the Huthi movement, Badr al-Din al-Huthi, in 2010, gave the opportunity to his other son, 'Abdel Malik, to assume the leadership of the Huthi, which has continued to this day. The Huthi, far from being defeated, advanced from being a preaching group to being a mass movement, with military capability, which saw its influence and control spread from Sa'da to the east of the 'Amrān governorate, al-Jawf, and Ma'rib. Not all Yemenis welcomed them, as many decided to fight the Huthi expansion.

The "Sa'da Wars" showed the considerable decline of President Saleh's power that ended with the 2011 uprisings. This process demanded the fall of the system, which involved different actors, including students, peasants, professionals, and political parties and associations, the participation of woman being a key aspect. The Huthi joined the protests in Yemen, and there were pro-Huthi groups in the Change Square (*Sahat at-Taghir*) in Sana'a, one of the most important places for the protest movement. Wells described this episode: "*The Shabab al-Sumud* (literally "Steadfast Youth") tent is frequented by Zaidi youth from urban areas like Taiz and Sanaa who have limited to no experience with actual war. For them, the movement appeals to a sense of social justice; it offers one among many new outlets to express disenchantment with the regime's repressive apparatus. [. . .] the Houthis in Change Square have formed a number of coalitions with parties of diverse political bends."[26]

The period between 2012 and 2014 showed how Saleh finally yielded to popular protests in the framework of the intervention of the Gulf Cooperation Council (GCC), which in addition to securing him legal immunity elected as "interim" president 'Abd Rabbuh Mansur Hadi, who called for a National Dialogue Conference (NDC) in 2013–2014.[27] The Huthis took part, despite rejecting the GCC proposal, but ended up refusing the federal motion for affecting their regions of influence.

One of the most significant events was the sudden Huthi-Saleh alliance; despite their clear enmity, they made agreements that led to the capture of the capital Sana'a in September 2014. Three elements were key: the announcement by the Hadi government of the withdrawal of the gas subsidy, an inability to resolve crises, and the complicity of sectors of the country's armed forces loyal to Saleh that allowed the takeover.[28] The Huthi movement spread into other governorates establishing its authority, including traditionally non-Zaydi areas, which would cause them to clash with different forces. Some tribes supported them, but others began to be subdued. The civil war started and soon internationalized when Hadi fled to Aden, and then to Saudi Arabia, where he made official requests to the GCC countries, asking for a military intervention.

The Current War and Proliferation of Players (2015–present)[29]

In 2015, the military coalition led by Saudi Arabia and the United Arab Emirates (with crucial help from the U.S. and UK) launched military operations in Yemen with the aim of restoring the "legitimacy" of interim President Hadi and crushing the Huthi uprising.[30] The coalition imposed a blockade, and the war has now been going on for years, making Yemen the country with the worst humanitarian crisis in the world.

In 2016 Ansar Allah formed the Supreme Political Council, which absorbed power from the Supreme Revolutionary Committee. That same year, they established the National Salvation Government. A year later, the Huthi-Saleh alliance fractured, and the former president was killed, probably by Ansar Allah, amid accusations that he wanted to negotiate with the Saudi-led coalition. As a result, the Huthi lost support from the GPC, which fractured. Individuals such as Tareq Saleh became opponents of the Huthis.[31]

The 2018–2020 period witnessed several critical moments. The conflict in al-Hudeida port between the Huthi and the Saudi/UAE-led coalition was stopped by the mediation process of the United Nations in order to avoid a humanitarian catastrophe. In September 2019, the Huthi movement showed a stunning military drone capability with attacks on oil-processing facilities operated by ARAMCO company at Abqaiq and Khurais in Saudi Arabia. One month later, the Southern Transitional Council (STC) took control of Aden, where the Hadi government was located.[32] As a result, the same year, the so-called Riyadh Agreement was established, an "initiative" of Saudi Arabia for the Hadi and the STC to share power, something that became official in December 2020 with the announcement of a unity cabinet. The year ended with the Aden airport terrorist attack that showed the cruelty of the war.

Important developments in the conflict have occurred recently. Internationally, U.S. President Joe Biden's announcement that Washington would end military support to Saudi Arabia sparked false hope by encouraging the belief that the war would end. It did not, as logistical support continued, and when Biden visited Saudi Arabia in July 2022, the war in Yemen was not a vital issue. However, his administration revoked the designation of the Huthis as a terrorist group, a classification set by former Secretary of State Mike Pompeo. Internally, the Covid-19 pandemic caused extensive damage to the health infrastructure. Clashes are ongoing in many regions, such as in Shabwa, Ma'rib, Taiz, and Hudeida. The leading role of the Giant Brigades, backed by the UAE, in their struggle against the Huthi is also significant. Importantly, Ansar Allah and the UN signed an agreement in March 2022 to address the FSO *Safer* oil tanker crisis. A month later, Yemen's exiled president Hadi and Vice President Al-Ahmar transferred their powers to the new eight-member Presidential Leadership Council (PLC), chaired by Rashad al-Alimi. Since then, the PLC has tried to negotiate with the Huthis, thus far without success. The diversity of interests makes it difficult to achieve the Council's objectives. Ansar Allah has also engaged in UN-brokered ceasefires with the warring parties, but renewing truce deals is always a major challenge. Finally, in April 2023, Saudi officials held talks with the Huthi movement in Sana'a, with Oman as mediator and as an effect of improved diplomatic relations between Saudi Arabia and Iran. A potential deal to end the war between Saudi Arabia and the Huthi is a positive step toward stopping the general war in Yemen.[33]

A Broader View of Islam or Yemeni Nationalists? Notes on the "Ideology" of the Huthi (Ansar Allah) Movement

There are two premises to approaching an understanding of the "ideology" of the Huthi movement. First, there is no official and unified ideological framework of the group.[34] Second, they are still involved in a transformation of "their ideology," so it would be a mistake to study it in absolute and monolithic terms. Salmoni, Loidolt, and Wells noted this problem: "The Huthi organism has yet to identify itself or act in terms of what it *seeks* rather than solely what it *opposes*."[35]

Another challenge is to establish who belongs to the Huthi movement. It is often stated that it is confined to the Zaydi community in Yemen, which constitutes approximately 35 percent of the population.[36] However, there is a range of membership that exceeds the religious dimension, which oscillates between family, militancy, pragmatism (e.g., armed forces, tribes), and a much broader base of sympathizers that cannot be reduced to the Zaydi population. We are dealing with a mass movement, young, trained, efficient, and with military capacity. Authors such as Haykel highlighted that "the Houthis are the best organized and ideologically motivated group in Yemen."[37]

An Imagined Religious Community?

The "ideology" of the Huthis is deeply linked to the religion that projects an identity of a homogeneous community, or using the words of Anderson: "a religiously imagined community."[38] To do this, they present themselves as an Indigenous actor and, like any nationalist movement, they take advantage of the cultural wealth inherited historically, tracing their origin from an Islamic legacy, and stressing a Yemeni Arab identity. As Anderson stated: "The nations to which they give political expression always loom out of an immemorial past."[39]

Furthermore, Anderson explained the Dynastic Realm whose legitimacy "derives from divinity, not from populations, who, after all, are subjects, not citizens,"[40] and the same applies for the Huthi. This "religiously imagined community" belongs to the line of descendants of the Prophet Muhammad (*sada* Hashemites). This implies the presence of a favored group, including the Huthi family, superior to other citizens and seen as "an elite, privileged class within society" (Shujaa al-Deen, quoted in Dashela) and as a nationalist vanguard.[41] As Nagi has noted, this has benefited them enormously: "Through making this connection and adopting the Hashemites' identity, the movement gained the respect accorded to Hashemites and took advantage of their presence and networks outside areas of Houthi influence. This was a clear first step toward the Houthis moving beyond their religious identity to having an overtly political one."[42]

Since 2014, the *sada* have to some degree regained their importance. As Weissenburger pointed out: "Thus empowered, the *sādah* made a comeback to leading positions in many sectors of public life (Lackner 2018, 165), a new head mufti was installed (Yemen Press, 2017), school books seem to have been changed in accordance with the movement's religious ideas (al-Yaman Today, 2017) and books on social issues such as on the role of women in Islamic society ('Abd al-Malik al-Ḥūthī, 2018) were published."[43] However, the Huthi movement also embodies a political organization. Today, some elements of the Zaydi tradition do not appear to be among their priorities. Such is the case of the imamate, a pillar of Zaydi belief, whose restoration they have not explicitly called for.[44] This issue merits further discussion.

Ansar Allah Movement: Anti-Republicans Who Want to Restore Al-Imāma?

Since the 2014 context, the debate about the Huthi wanting to establish an imamate, destroy the republic, and ensure that Hashimis rule has re-emerged as a discursive narrative product. However, it has been under analysis since the Saʿda Wars, so it is not by chance that today we see this same argument. As Salmoni, Loidolt, and Wells have noted: "Houthis are thus portrayed as foreign-inspired elements seeking to sunder hard-won republican unity through brutal actions that oppress the Yemeni people in hopes of returning the country to the dark ages of the imamate according to interpretations of Zaydism that are fundamentally incorrect or out of step with the spirit of the times."[45] This speech was useful for the government both in terms of Yemeni internal opinion and in the international arena. Brandt described this strategy: "The government tried to shift the focus of the conflict by accusing the Houthis of seeking to re-establish an imamate and positioning itself as the defender of the Republic. This only distracted a receptive public from the anti-US narrative but allowed Sana'a to integrate the fight against the Houthis into the international 'War on Terror.'"[46]

It is true that ideologically they claim descent from the imamate before the 1962 revolution.[47] However, there is no record of Ansar Allah saying they want to restore the *imāma*, and no one has declared himself *imām*. Recent pronouncements attempt to show an apparent desire to maintain the republic. In 2014, 'Ali al-Bukhayti spoke of a "participatory state" (*dawla al-sharaka al-wataniyya*), or "second republic" (*al-jumhuriyya al-thaniya*). His exact words were: "The "second republic" was neither the Imamate of the sayyids nor the shaykhs' republic that has governed Sa'da in recent decades, but rather a republic which ensures participation and representation of all people and groups."[48] Likewise, Mohammed al-Huthi, head of the Supreme Revolutionary Committee of Ansar Allah, in the context of the al-Hudaida crisis and reiterating the words of the spokesman of the movement Muhammad 'Abdel Salam, said: "I think that the government during the transition will be consensual because post-war Yemen will need consensus to allow it to prepare for elections. We welcome the holding of serious elections that can reshape the House of Representatives and other electoral boards in the Republic of Yemen."[49]

However, it is important to mention that, for the Huthis, maintaining the republican facade helps to avoid criticism, especially for the historical reasons mentioned above. They did not overthrow state institutions (when they could have done so) but rather made a pragmatic use of them to benefit of their political project of hegemony. As Schmitz suggested: "They want to claim at least the mantle of the Yemeni republicanism despite their actions that belie a lack of adherence to the substance of the ideals of Yemeni republican government." Accordingly, he provides a good example: "The Huthi leader Abd al-Malek is the real source of power, but not in a formal position of government." His power "outside state institutions destroys the integrity of state institutions."[50]

If the Huthi movement were to opt out of the republican model it would face problems with its non-Zaydi supporters and even with those Zaydi that renounced the *Imāma* in the November 1990 document.[51] As Brandt acknowledged: "To date, the Houthis' position on the question of governance is still based on this understanding as formulated by Badr al-Dīn: *sayyid* rule is recommended, but not an absolute necessity."[52] Johnston et al. also acknowledge that "while some Houthis do call for 'a return to the rule of the Zaydi Imam,' their objectives are not primarily religious or internationally focused."[53]

Of course, the absence of an official position leads to doubts, and thus to the convenience of some actors to keep the narrative of the Huthi as antirepublicans.[54] It should be also stressed that some focus more on the anti-republican Huthi debate than the open desire of secessionism and independence of al-Hirak and the STC in the areas of southern Yemen, which would also fracture the republic.[55] Part of this also leads us to think of the usual practice of many analysts to read everything in a religious way and not to consider other elements such as nationalist rhetoric.

Huthis and the Nationalist Discourse

The different practices the Huthis have taken in recent years show the use of nationalist discourse to help bring about their political projects and to raise more supporters of their cause in Yemen. We can identify five activities that contribute to this debate.

Espousing a Rhetoric of Struggle against the Enemy and Injustice

One of the things the nation-state needs to legitimize and cohere is the "common enemy identified," so establishing an army and evoking a war is essential for the nationalistic discourse. As Anderson said: "Indeed, one might go so far as to say that the state imagined its local adversaries, as in an ominous dream, well before they came into historical existence."[56] In the confrontation with the coalition, besides the other players of the conflict, the response of the movement is not at the group level, but at the national level, repudiating the aggression on Yemeni soil and presenting themselves as defenders of the country. This has been an advantage for the Huthi: "One reason for the success of the Houthis is the disunity and infighting among the several Yemeni factions arrayed against them. Another is the superior fighting spirit and ideological motivation of the Houthis. They have framed the war as one against foreign domination, appealing to a strong sense of Yemeni nationalism."[57]

Creating an enemy in national terms and from a geopolitical perspective to develop cohesion and legitimize the regime is not a new approach.[58] That legitimacy aims to reach a larger audience for the Huthi, who in fact had tried this strategy with their name, Ansar Allah.[59] Heinze recalled that: "Not all Huthi sympathizers, however, were staunch defenders of Huthism; many of them were simply frustrated by the transitional government's inactivity."[60] In fact, many people joined because they see the Huthi movement as the "lesser evil."[61]

The response to this aggression articulated a propaganda organized by the state influenced by a strong militarism and territorial expansion that claimed the "Yemeni" national territory.[62] Intrinsic elements of nationalism and the nation-state are present such as the reference to the flag, the act of "dying for your country," as well as the issue of boundaries.[63]

Finally, the Huthi stress a defense of the "faith" to reject "extremism" in Yemen, referring to groups linked to the Wahhabi tradition such as Al-Qaida, the Islamic State, and some groups close to Islah: "They used their Zaidi identity to affirm their opposition to Salafi-jihadi groups, at a time when the government was fighting al-Qaeda in the Arabian Peninsula. This enabled them to appeal to an even broader cross-section of Yemeni groups. The Houthis again depicted such actions as combating extremism, an attractive slogan that resonated with those worried about terrorist groups in Yemen."[64]

Anti-Imperialism and the Slogan (or the Cry al-Sarkha)

Much of the ideological basis of the movement originated in the activism of Hussein al-Huthi, the "War on Terror," and the illegal invasions of Afghanistan and Iraq, as well as the confrontation during the Sa'da Wars. The defense of the territory is an interesting dimension of the Huthi mentality and it is from here that one can understand the "anti-imperialist" references recurrent in the movement such as the slogan (or the cry *al-Sarkha*) characteristic of the group since 2003, but clearly inspired by the 1979 revolution in Iran: "Allah is the Greatest, Death to America, Death to Israel, a Curse Upon the Jews, Victory for Islam."

There are different interpretations of the slogan. Haykel, for example, links it to the religious aspect: "Houthi's ideology consists of a combination of anti-imperialist and anti-American rhetoric ("Death to America, Death to Israel") with a radical Islamist vision of a world ruled by a descendant of the Prophet."[65] Authors like Dorlian "see the initial anti-government stance of Hussein al-Houthi's group as more politically than religiously motivated; a political opposition that found its expression in the "anti-imperialists" Houthi slogan."[66] Finally, regarding Israel and the mention of the Jews, the group should clarify if it refers to anti-Jewish racism or anti-Zionism (an ideology distinguished from the Jewish community itself). Their antagonistic stance with the State of Israel is seen in every opportunity to show solidarity (at least in words) with Palestine.[67]

The Zamil: Identity, Propaganda, and Recruitment[68]

The *zamil* is common tribal oral poetry in the Arabian Peninsula and, as Steven Caton has noted, can be persuasive rhetoric.[69] The Huthi have been employing *zamil* in recent years, and this undoubtedly contributes to the identity of the group, with an effect on society and on the course of the war.

From the perspective of Summer, "the *zāmil* [is] a nationalistic practice; as a cultural form that suits the listener; and as an affective force." Although religious speech is central to the Huthi *zawamil*, it is framed in a nationalist discourse because it tries to create a sense of identity. The *zamil* then "is a speech act where social groups index specific identities in order to place those in the conflict in a shared social world in which agreement is conceivable." In her study, Summer further notes that "because the *zāmil* expresses group sentiment, it is particularly amenable to nationalism. Nationalism often depends upon conceiving 'many as one'; the nation presents as a single body with one culture, history and set of traditions."[70] It is important to remember that the strategic use of a cultural practice for the production of a specific identity or ideology, such as nationalism, is well known in the Middle East and elsewhere, known as invented traditions.[71]

The Huthi movement developed a style of *zamil* used as a powerful tool of identity, propaganda, and recruitment.[72] As Summer pointed out, by "entrenching their religious ideology within language typical of the *zamil* and disseminating their poems far and wide, the Huthis create a finely tuned media and recruitment tool."[73] Porter also emphasized the power of *zamil*: "Possibly the most versatile and beloved form of Houthi propaganda is their poetry. Their *zawamil* and *anasheed* are commonly described as war poems or anthems, but their subject matter ranges from international politics and religious tradition to social issues and praise of leaders. Houthi *zawamil* frequently include threats to Saudi Arabia, the United Arab Emirates, Israel, and the United States, and are intended to inspire followers and intimidate rivals."[74] The *zamil* is thus integrated into a range of instruments linked to nationalism in order to project a specific cause. Summer rightly highlighted: "Namely, the consistent presence of the Yemeni flag, invocations of the Yemeni Republic and the performance of the *barʿa* and *zāmil*, which coalesce to claim that Ḥuthī acts of violence are, in fact, performances of nationalism on behalf of all Yemenis."[75]

Since the Huthi don't represent most of the population, there can be criticism of the relationship between the nationalist discourse, the Huthi, and their use of *zamil*. In this regard, Summer leaves us an interesting thought on the feasibility of this analysis: "One may consider the relationship between nationalism and the Huthi *zāmil* as illogical, in light of the armed group's descent on Sanaa without the will of the people, and the religious ideology they propagate, which does not represent all Yemenis. On the other hand, inserting national symbols, imagery, and discourse into their poetry to evoke nationalist sentiments links their group to the national narrative, regardless of whether or not the nationalism presented is ideal."[76]

Education, Speeches, and Media

Educational institutions have always been an important aspect for the consolidation of the nationalist discourse. After the takeover of the Ministries of Education and Higher Education, the propaganda work of the Huthi movement is complemented by the dissemination activities in schools, universities, and summer camps. This includes changes to the educational national curriculum more akin to their political and religious perspectives, particularly in public school system and own schools.[77] The same applies to the mosques, something common in the region, especially in the Friday sermon (known as *khutba*).[78]

In the same context, the media and social networks are a point *par excellence* of political propagation and nation-building. Ansar Allah sees them as tools for the "psychological warfare" or "soft power." Thus, Huthi media productions weave together themes of national pride and self-reliance, armed resistance, divine legitimacy, praise of martyrs, and a wealth of Yemeni cultural and social themes.[79] 'Abdel Malek, current leader, takes full advantage of different platforms to communicate diverse contents with the public, thanks to official media outlets such as al-Masira TV, YouTube, Twitter, Telegram, and websites such as "Ansarollah.com."

The Huthi media continues to expand and adapt to new contexts. However, it is important to stress that "modern technology ensures that the Huthi's grip is not absolute, since all platforms and sources of information cannot be blocked or censored. They face alternative and adversarial narratives from other war actors."[80]

Tribes: Join Us![81]

The Huthi are composed of tribes, with a dynamic relationship among them. Some in the north, mainly Hashid and Bakil, have joined their cause; with other tribes agreements have been made, but others have been subdued due to military expansion. Although religious discourse is central to the Houthi, Dashela reveals that part of the explanation for the support of tribal sectors is also due to "the use of populist rhetoric portraying it as confronting an external aggressor, again winning over the tribes." This also shows the importance of the use of a nationalist discourse: "Coalition behavior in areas that did not witness direct conflict with the Houthi movement, such as Socotra Island in the Arabian Sea, Mayun Island at Bab al-Mandab Strait, as well as Al-Mahra governorate, also helped encourage tribesmen to join the war from a nationalist perspective."[82]

Cultural practices such as the *zamil* have an impact on tribes as well. As Summer emphasized: "The Huthi ideology, as exemplified in the *zamil*, intertwines with tribal and nationalist discourse to interpellate the Huthi fighter." In this sense: "Activating Yemeni nationalism and tribal genealogy in a single line, the poem positions the tribesmen as warriors of glorious heritage, united against those who could threaten Yemen." It "works to persuade the tribesmen that rallying behind the Huthis is akin to pledging allegiance to God and is inextricably linked to their identities as honorable tribesmen, pious Muslims, and Yemeni citizens."[83] As mentioned, the reader must bear in mind the important dynamic facing the fragmentation of the tribes.[84]

Problems in Governing, New Enemies

The major challenge for the Huthi movement is that it has been unable to obtain the support of most of the Yemeni population. Today, there are important opposition fronts, and it is relevant to consider the views of a large part of the country's citizenship, especially woman and young people.[85] The transit of religious organization, then resistance group and insurgency, and now of political authority in power reflects weaknesses.

As a movement that has survived as opposition to the government, but not been prepared to rule, the Huthis have shown a lack of experience in solving the daily issues of citizenship such as health, work (salary payments), and provision of public services, although they have shown some ability to maintain them and even benefit from domestic petroleum supplies, public revenues, taxes, and telecommunications.

Daily reports of human rights violations are also frequent.[86] The Huthi are involved with dissident or opposition violence. There are charges of torture, enforced disappearance, and military coercion, as well as reports of enforced conscription for young men in areas under their control, including child recruitment.[87] Charges of violence against women,[88] as well as kidnapping, have also been made.

The Huthi Movement and the Islamic Republic of Iran Debate

Part of the debate about ideology and nationalism involves the relationship with Iran. It is asked whether the movement has roots in Yemeni history or whether it is a group that blindly obeys Tehran to the point of some stating it is a *proxy*. This debate is not new and has been repeated for decades, even among Yemenis. Since 2010, authors such as Salmoni, Loidolt, and Wells have established a discussion around the "Houthis as foreign" topic, with special attention to the issue of the influence of Iran.[89] More recently, Brandt recalled this same rhetoric:

> Since the inception of the Sa'dah wars in 2004, Yemeni officials have accused foreign countries of supporting the Houthis; Iran, in particular, has been highlighted as a foreign state sponsor of rebellion. Until 2009, however, Iran didn't show much interest in the Houthis, and until 2011 there was virtually no hard evidence for direct Iranian involvement in Sa'dah, as it made more sense for Tehran to maintain good relations with Sana'a than to support a movement that then had little prospect of actually overthrowing the Salih regime, and would probably not be subservient to Tehran even if it did.[90]

It is also important to note that the Huthi and Iran don't belong to the same religious branch of Islam. Despite some reports that the Huthi are "Twelvers," the truth is that the majority have a Zaydi identity. As Brandt has claimed: "It depicted the Houthis as a movement backed and remote-controlled by Iran, at times even as renegades who had abandoned Zaydi Fiver Shiism in favor of Iranian Twelver Shiism, portraying them as a 'foreign' proxy group of Fifth Column of Iranian Imamism in Yemen. By depicting the Houthis as foreign agents of supported by Iran, the government raised suspicions that they were importing Iran's Islamic revolution to Yemen."[91] Van der Kroft argued: "However, the Houthis are not a direct proxy group that merely follow Iran's orders [. . .] The sectarian aspect of the Houthi-Iran alliance is often overblown—the Houthis practice the Zaidi form of Islam that, although a branch of the Shia sect, is far closer to the Sunni practices in Yemen than the Twelver Shia branch championed by the Iranian regime."[92]

Since 2014–2015, Iran has played a stronger role in the news about Yemen, and the speech of Huthi movement as a *proxy* of Tehran is framed in the "Cold War" with Saudi Arabia in the Middle East. However, the Huthi have their own agenda. For example, Iran, according to some authors, advised Ansar Allah not to take the capital in 2014, and yet it happened.[93] The risk of following the *proxy* argument is explained by several authors: "Since the Houthi conflict began to hit international headlines in 2014, it has often been defined against regional contexts, such as the Iranian-Saudi proxy war or the Sunni-Shia divide. This is not to say that these regional conflict drivers were insignificant, but they have primarily served to reduce the Houthi conflict to a catchy denominator, thereby obfuscating its local dynamics and complex nature."[94] Along the same lines, Haykel stated: "The Saudis somewhat mistakenly see the Houthis as a purely Iranian proxy akin to Hezbollah in Lebanon. The Houthis are indeed close allies of Iran and some of their ideological inspiration comes from Khomeini's revolutionary ideas. Also, they no doubt coordinate their strategy and even specific attacks on Saudi Arabia with Tehran. Yet, the Houthis are a deeply rooted social and political phenomenon of the Yemeni scene and have an agenda that is ultimately about achieving local goals."[95]

Recognizing the internal agenda is crucial to this discussion as there are different nationalisms. The Huthis don't follow the Iranian nationalism, and the Iranians don't follow the Yemeni nationalism. In fact, as Johnston et al. have noted: "At their core the Houthis are focused on domestic issues and historic grievances. They want greater influence in Yemeni political affairs and inclusion in (or dominance of) whatever new political order emerges following the war."[96]

Unfortunately, the danger of manipulation and fake news is present. Recently, the Saudi/UAE-led coalition showed a video of apparently ballistic missiles located in the al-Hodaida area as evidence of Iran's smuggling and supply of weapons to the Huthi. However, it was a video with false information as it turned out the images corresponded to the U.S.-led occupation of Iraq in 2003, which led to harsh criticism on social networks.[97]

This doesn't mean the Huthi movement and the Islamic Republic of Iran have no links or common ground. As Johnsen pointed out: "In August 2019, the Houthis appointed an ambassador to Iran. Just over a year later, in October 2020, Iran reciprocated by sending an ambassador, Hassan Irloo, to Sana'a, effectively recognizing the Houthis as the legitimate government of Yemen. Iran and the Houthis are closer than ever, largely because of the Saudi-led war in Yemen."[98]

Thus, it is much more interesting to consider the conclusions offered by the study of Johnston et al. by proposing two scenarios as a more realistic conclusion than the *proxy*: a transactional relationship versus a partnership.[99] In the future, interesting questions may arise, including: If the variable of Iran disappears from the war tomorrow, would the Huthi continue there? (Answer: surely, yes). How many of the groups supported by Saudi Arabia and UAE would survive? These questions become relevant in the framework of recent de-escalation talks between Saudi Arabia and Iran that involve this issue. Relevant negotiations are occurring between the Huthi and the Saudis that may lead to the end of hostilities (but not of the general war in Yemen) that also show the religious agenda is not relevant. The Huthi are not currently a *proxy*, but they may be on their way to becoming one.

Conclusion

The Huthi movement, a crucial actor for understanding the current war in Yemen, is in constant transformation and evolution. This chapter presented a discussion about the history and key elements in the movement. In this respect, the study yielded three important conclusions.

First, the text reviewed the historical conditions that gave rise to the Huthi movement. It is essential to be aware of past episodes, such as the end of the *Imāma* or the republican revolution, followed by the change in the social and political role of the *sada* and the Zaydi community in general, as well as the marginalization of the northern areas. The arrival of Saudi Wahhabism in the region and the consequent appearance of "Zaydi revivalism," as well as the activities of the Believing Youth, are undoubtedly episodes that help to understand the role of the Huthi family and serve as a backdrop for its origin.

In the same way, the "War on Terror" context, and specifically the Sa'da Wars episodes, transformed the Huthi family into an organized movement with military capability and experience. Later, the Huthi movement acquired more sympathizers following the 2011 uprisings, the capture of the capital in 2014, and the current war. The Huthi are not an external phenomenon to the Yemeni reality, and it is also true that Yemen is not reduced to just the Huthi.

Second, in the absence of an official ideological framework, the approach made about Huthi "ideology" yielded interesting elements for discussion. The debate about the *Imāma* and the republic in their project is tied to the presence of elements linked to nationalism and the nation-state. Thus, the construction of a common enemy and the consequent defense against foreign aggression, raised in terms not of Ansar Allah but of a Yemeni nation and people, becomes important. The Huthis' emphasis on anti-imperialism matters, but especially the slogan and the strategic use of invented traditions like the *zamil*. This nationalism is influenced by a clear religious spirit, which articulates its identity, but not exclusively.

These aspects show that although we cannot generalize that this is a purely nationalist movement, we are dealing with a group that is not archaic and rigid, much more than a militia.

Finally, it is crucial to be aware that all nationalisms end up excluding what they don't consider as part of the "nation," and the Huthis are no exception. A significant part of the population opposes this political project. Huthis also oppose other nationalisms present in Yemen, which says a lot about the "Yemeni nation" and the future of the country. Such is the case of the al-Hirak movement / Southern Transitional Council (STC) and others in southern Yemen; supporters of the Islah party and related trends; followers of the "legitimate" government; al-Qaida in the Arabian Peninsula (AQAP) as well as other armed groups.

With these thoughts, we have sought in this chapter to deepen the debate about one of the most important players in the war in Yemen: the Huthi movement. The wrong path is to continue believing they are a militia empty of purpose or with demands with no political significance. On the contrary, the movement will need to be considered, with all its differences, in articulating the future of the country and achieving a stable and lasting peace with justice for all its communities.

Notes

1. In order for the reader to read the chapter fluently, we will not use any specific method of transliteration from Arabic to English language. Quotes will keep their original form.

2. Also known as *Ansar Allah* (Supporters of Allah). The difference is that the first name is used by people outside the group to refer to them, while the second name is the way the group prefers to be called. We will use them interchangeably.

3. M. Brandt, *Tribes and Politics in Yemen: A History of the Houthi Conflict* (Oxford: Oxford University Press, 2017), 2.

4. The Huthi movement is closely related to Zaydism, one of the branches of Shia Islam (followers of Ali ibn Abi Talib). They are usually called "The Fivers" because of their believe in Zayd ibn Ali as the fifth *imam* (leader) of Islam unlike most of Shia Muslims, known as the "Twelvers" (*Ithna Ashariya*), who believe in a line of twelve imams according to which Muhammad ibn al-Hassan, called the *Mahdi*, went into occultation (*ghaybah*) and therefore await his return. For a detailed study, see A. Tabataba'i, *Shi'ite Islam* (Albany, NY: SUNY Press, 1977).

5. Also known as imamate; this is an Islamic doctrine and a belief in the *imams*.

6. This chapter is not a comprehensive survey of Yemeni history, nor of the Huthi movement as such. On the crisis since 2014–2015, in the English language there

are key analyses to read, such as the contributions of Sheila Carapico, Daniel Varisco, Helen Lackner, Marie-Christine Heinze, and Gregory D. Johnsen, as well as Think Tank reports such as those published by the Sana'a Center for Strategic Studies. As for the Huthi movement, the works of Salmoni, Loidolt, and Wells and Marieke Brandt are crucial, among other researchers. This chapter doesn't aim to replace them but rather benefits from the entire framework of contributions of these and other authors.

7. According to Weir: "The first Zaydī state in Yemen was founded over a thousand years ago by Yaḥyā b. Ḥusayn (d. 298/911), a Hijazi *sharīf* and scholar (*ʿālim*) of great learning and vaunting political ambition. [. . .] warring tribes in the area of Ṣaʿdah area invited him to mediate between them. After making peace, Yaḥyā proclaimed himself head (*imām*) of the Zaydī *dawlah*, adopting the honorific "al-Hādī ilā al-Ḥaqq" ("the guide to what is right"), and with the military support of allied tribes, defeated others which opposed him." S. Weir, *A Tribal Order. Politics and Law in the Mountains of Yemen* (Austin: University of Texas Press, 2007), 229.

8. It is often clarified that the *Imāma* did not rule all of Yemen, as at the same time there were other strong powers such as the Rasulid Sunni dynasty.

9. For more on the history and characteristics of the *sada*, see P. Dresch, *Tribes, Government, and History in Yemen* (Oxford: Clarendon Press, 1993), 140–183.

10. M. Al-Mahfali, "Anti-Black Racism in Yemen: Manifestations and Responses," *Arab Reform Initiative*, August 5, 2021. www.arab-reform.net/publication/anti-black-racism-in-yemen-manifestations-and-responses

11. Brandt, *Tribes and Politics*, 52.

12. Brandt, *Tribes and Politics*, 99.

13. The *sheikh* is a title of respect that can be used to refer to a tribal chief, an Islamic religious leader, or a royal family member (e.g., Persian Gulf countries).

14. As Phillips stated: "The Yemeni regime is neopatrimonial. In a patrimonial system, the "right to rule is ascribed to a person rather than an office." The ruler governs and maintains power through patron–client relations as opposed to law or ideology, and the clients extend their political loyalty (or at least acquiescence) to the patron in exchange for benefits. Neopatrimonialism refers to the permeation of these informal patrimonial loyalties into formal political institutions." S. Phillips, *Yemen's Democracy Experiment in Regional Perspective: Patronage and Pluralized Authoritarianism* (New York, NY: Palgrave Macmillan, 2008), 4. For more about the political system during the Saleh era, see also S. Phillips, *Yemen and the Politics of Permanent Crisis* (Abingdon: Routledge, 2011).

15. Weir, *A Tribal Order*, 296.

16. Brandt, *Tribes and Politics*, 111.

17. On the origins of the al-Huthi family, see Brandt, *Tribes and Politics*, 139, and Salmoni, Loidolt, and Wells, *Regime and Periphery in Northern Yemen*, 103.

18. Brandt, *Tribes and Politics*, 99–100.

19. A good discussion about this is presented in A. Khoshafah, "Houthi-Salafi Coexistence Agreements: Motives and Future Prospects," *Sana'a Center for Strategic Studies*, December 3, 2021. https://sanaacenter.org/publications/analysis/15839.

20. Brandt, *Tribes and Politics*, 113.

21. L. Van der Kroft, "Who are the Houthis?," *International Centre for Counter-Terrorism*, June 1, 2021, 3. www.jstor.org/stable/resrep34009.5

22. S. Al-Ahmad (Director) "The Fight for Yemen." *Frontline*. www.pbs.org/wgbh/frontline/film/fight-for-yemen/transcript

23. The local context also promoted the consolidation of the group. Inequitable distribution of wealth and marginalization was a key fact. As Brandt highlights: "The economic and political marginalization of the Sa'dah region, the uneven distribution of economic sources and political participation, and the religious discrimination against its Zaydi population provided fertile soil in which the Houthi movement could take root and blossom." Brandt, *Tribes and Politics*, 135.

24. For details of the six phases of the war, see Salmoni, Loidolt, and Wells, *Regime and Periphery in Northern Yemen*; Brandt, *Tribes and Politics*.

25. I explore in another text different hypotheses of his death. In addition, this event is important because it is the root of recent enmities between followers of the movement and people such as Saleh (although they would set up an alliance) and Ali Mohsen, vice president until 2022.

26. M. Wells, "Yemen's Houthi Movement and the Revolution," *Foreign Policy*, February 7, 2012. https://foreignpolicy.com/2012/02/27/yemens-houthi-movement-and-the-revolution

27. Hadi's government established alliances with Islah and Ali Mohsen, who before the fall of Saleh switched to the opposite side. He was appointed vice president with military influence.

28. Some authors emphasize the issue of corruption of the Hadi government: "The Houthis became a revolutionary movement, fighting against a corrupt, ineffective government and calling for reform." See A. Nagi, "Yemen's Houthis Used Multiple Identities to Advance," *Carnegie Middle East Center*, March 19, 2019. https://carnegie-mec.org/2019/03/19/yemen-s-houthis-used-multiple-identities-to-advance-pub-78623

29. The war in Yemen presents a plurality of actors, with the Huthi just one of them. See G. D. Johnsen, "Foreign Actors in Yemen: The History, the Politics and the Future," *Sana'a Center for Strategic Studies*, January 31, 2021. https://sanaacenter.org/publications/main-publications/13042 and the Matrix in E. DeLozier, "Yemen Matrix: Allies & Adversaries," *The Washington Institute for Near East Policy*, September 17, 2020. www.washingtoninstitute.org/policy-analysis/yemen-matrix-allies-adversaries

30. Kuwait and Oman had different approaches to the Yemeni crisis. Qatar was dismissed from the coalition in 2017. Egyptian support was important in the military operations in the Red Sea.

31. He began to be supported by the coalition and would be important as commander on the Red Sea. In addition, the same year, Saudi Arabia started the deployment to the region of al-Mahra near the Omani border.

32. The STC is sometimes confused with al-Hirak, originating in 2008 in southern Yemen. Today, however, the STC gathers most supporters of the secessionist

flag of the south, although there are other groups in this region that oppose the leadership of the STC.

33. This may have an effect, considering that two tracks of peace efforts failed: Hadi-Huthi talks sponsored by the United Nations (e.g., Stockholm Agreement) and Hadi-STC talks (e.g., Riyadh Agreement). The inclusion of all involved parties, such as women and armed groups (e.g., AQAP), is still lacking. Most of the negotiation processes of the UN have been unsuccessful for many reasons. One of them is that they refer to Saudi Arabia and United Arab Emirates as impartial actors and not as parties committed to support internal players in the war (the same applies to the United States).

34. The following documents, while not an ideological framework but rather Houthi views on religion, politics, and the future of Yemen, are still useful to the reader: 2012 Intellectual and Cultural Manifesto; 2014 Peace and National Inclusion; 2015 Constitutional Declaration; and 2019 National Vision. For a detailed analysis of the latter, see Schmitz, "Huthi Visions of the State: A Huthi Republic with an Unofficial Imam," in *The Huthi Movement in Yemen: Ideology, Ambition and Security in the Arab Gulf*, ed. A. Hamiddadin (London: I.B. Tauris, 2022), 199–216.

35. Salmoni, Loidolt, and Wells, *Regime and Periphery in Northern Yemen*, 234.

36. Minority Rights Group International (n.d.) *Yemen. Zaydi Shi'a*. Retrieved March 30, 2022 from https://minorityrights.org/minorities/zaydi-shias. The majority in Yemen is the Sunni community (Shafi'i) 65 percent, and there are other minorities such as Shia Ismaili (15,000 people) and a small Jewish community of fifty people.

37. See B. Haykel, "The Houthis, Saudi Arabia, and the War in Yemen," *Hoover Institution*, Issue 2131, June 15, 2021. www.hoover.org/research/houthis-saudi-arabia-and-war-yemen. It is also important to reiterate that they aren't a tribe or a clan, despite their important size and relationship with the tribes. See Salmoni, Loidolt, and Wells, *Regime and Periphery in Northern Yemen*, 45–62.

38. B. Anderson, *Imagined Communities. Reflections on the Origin and Spread of Nationalism* (London: Verso, 2006), 16.

39. Ibid., 11–12.

40. Ibid., 19.

41. See A. Dashela, "Northern Yemeni Tribes during the Eras of Ali Abdullah Saleh and the Houthi Movement: A Comparative Study," *Sana'a Center for Strategic Studies*, February 16, 2022. https://sanaacenter.org/publications/analysis/16670

42. Nagi, op. cit.

43. A. Weissenburger, "*Al-Mawaddah al-Khālidah*? The Ḥūthī Movement and the Idea of the Rule of the *Ahl al-Bayt* in Yemen's Tribal Society," in *Tribes in Modern Yemen: An Anthology*, ed. M. Brandt (Vienna: Austrian Academy of Sciences Press, 2021), 129. The impact is also seen in the proliferation of religious festivities and rituals such as al-Ghadir Day, Birthday of the Prophet, International Jerusalem Day, and Martyrs Day.

44. E. Summer, "Experiencing the Ḥūthī Zāmil," *Arabia Felix Centre for Studies*, September 4, 2021. https://arabiafelixstudies.com/en/experiencing-the-Ḥuthi-zamil

45. Salmoni, Loidolt, and Wells, op. cit., 169. Furthermore, the northern tribal areas, where the Houthi movement has a social basis, are depicted as "chaotic, endemically violent, and backwards (*mutakhallif*), with an inadequate understanding of the benefits of modern politics and republican progressivism," Ibid., 177.

46. Brandt, *Tribes and Politics*, 135.

47. See Dashela, "Northern Yemeni Tribes," op. cit.

48. M. Brandt, "The Huthi Enigma: Ansar Allah and the 'Second Republic,'" in *Yemen and the Search for Stability. Power, Politics and Society After the Arab Spring*, ed. M. C. Heinze (London & New York: I.B. Tauris, 2018), 170.

49. N. Shaker and F. Edroos, "Mohammed al-Houthi: We want a united and democratic Yemen," *Al-Jazeera English*, December 25, 2018. www.aljazeera.com/features/2018/12/25/mohammed-al-houthi-we-want-a-united-and-democratic-yemen

50. Schmitz, op. cit., 213, 202, 214.

51. "This manifesto abandoned the Hādawī *sharṭ al-baṭnayn* by denying (albeit with some obscure passages) that righteousness in the political realm is linked to the Prophet's descendant's divine right to rule." Brandt, *Tribes and Politics*, 119.

52. Ibid., 115.

53. T. Johnston, M. Lane, A. Casey, H. J, Williams, A. L, Rhoades, J, Sladden, N. Vest, J. R. Reimer, and R. Haberman, "Could the Houthis Be the Next Hizballah? Iranian Proxy Development in Yemen and the Future of the Houthi Movement," *RAND*, 2020, 7. www.rand.org/content/dam/rand/pubs/research_reports/RR2500/RR2551/RAND_RR2551.pdf

54. In the background there is also the discussion of whether there is still a republic or whether there is a Yemeni state.

55. The southern cause in Yemen is complex. Behind, lies a historical struggle against discrimination and hegemony of the north. For a detailed study, see Halliday (1990) and the different publications by Susanne Dahlgren, among others.

56. Anderson, *Imagined Communities*, xiv.

57. Haykel, op. cit.

58. We can refer to examples such as the Turkish state with the Kurds, or Israel with the Palestinians.

59. "The name was derived from a Quranic verse that would appeal to a religious Yemeni society while echoing the name Hezbollah, with all the political imagery that accompanied the Lebanese party. The Houthis also invoked the political vision and writings of Hussein al-Houthi, which reflected themes that appealed to Sunni followers of the Shafi'i school of Islamic law, such as Muslim unity, prophetic lineages, and opposition to corruption. This allowed the Houthis to mobilize not only northern Zaidi's, but also inhabitants of predominantly Shafi'i areas." Nagi, op. cit.

60. M. C. Heinze, "The Triumphant Advance of the Houthi Rebels," *Qantara* (September 24, 2014). https://en.qantara.de/content/political-upheaval-in-yemen-the-triumphant-advance-of-the-houthi-rebels

61. There are even Ethiopian warriors who have nothing to do with Zaydism, who are recruited into the army and remembered as martyrs. See al-Masdar Online, Newsroom. https://almasdaronline.com/articles/233541

62. To the north, there is constant conflict with Saudi Arabia with no operations of territorial conquest but rather skirmishes to affect their military rival. To the south, their plan was to reach Aden, the capital of southern Yemen, but this expansion has been halted by STC-Aligned forces, al-Hirak, the coalition, and other armed groups, such as AQAP. To the east and southeast, they have influence in Mahra region, and they talk about recovering the sovereignty of Socotra Island, under occupation by UAE.

63. Some people within the Huthi movement propose alternative borders. For example, Dhayf Allah al-Shami, a supposed high member of Ansar Allah, said, "The Houthis are part of the Muslim world. We can't be defined by a sect or confined by borders. Our borders are the Holy Quran and the Islamic and Arab world. We will help oppressed people all over the world." Al-Ahmad, op. cit. This is a broader Islamic identification, where the concept of *Umma* or community of believers knows no classical boundaries.

64. Nagi, op. cit.

65. Haykel, op. cit.

66. S. Dorlain, "The Sa'dah War in Yemen: Between Politics and Sectarianism," *The Muslim World* 101, 182–201, as paraphrased in Brandt, *Tribes and Politics*, 134.

67. For example, Muhammad al-Houthi rejected the Abraham Accords: "The deal was a betrayal of the Palestinian cause and of pan-Arabism." See S. Farrell, "Israel hails UAE deal but Palestinians—and settlers—dismayed," *Reuters*, August 13, 2020. www.reuters.com/article/us-israel-emirates-trump-reactions/israel-hails-uae-deal-but-palestinians-and-settlers-dismayed-idUSKCN2592R5

68. For detailed studies of the Huthi and the *zamil*, see Summer *Experiencing . . .* , op. cit., and E. Summer, "The Huthi *Zāmil*: Folk Literature or propaganda?" in *The Huthi Movement in Yemen: Ideology, Ambition and Security in the Arab Gulf*, ed. A. Hamidaddin (London: I.B. Tauris, 2022), 139–157.

69. Steven Caton, *Peaks of Yemen I Summon: Poetry as Cultural Practice in a North Yemeni Tribe* (Berkeley: University of California Press, 1990), as quoted in Summer, op. cit. It is important to emphasize that the *zamil* is not limited to the Huthi movement. It is a practice prior to the emergence of the group that symbolizes a broad literature and art practice.

70. Summer, *Experiencing*, op. cit.

71. Summer, *The Huthi Zāmil*, 162. For more on this concept, see E. Hobsbawn and T. Ranger, *The Invention of Tradition* (Cambridge & New York: Cambridge University Press, 2004).

72. The reader can watch video examples simply by searching for "Houthi *zamil*" or "Issa Allaith" on YouTube.

73. Summer, *The Huthi Zāmil*, 161.

74. H. Porter, "A Battle of Hearts and Minds: The Growing Medio Footprint of Yemen's Houthis," *Gulf International Forum*, June 1, 2020. https://gulfif.org/a-battle-of-hearts-and-minds-the-growing-media-footprint-of-yemens-houthis

75. Summer, *Experiencing*, op. cit.

76. Summer, *Experiencing*, op. cit.

77. See A. Nagi, "Education in Yemen: Turning pens into Bullets," *Carnegie Middle East Center*, November 15, 2021. https://carnegie-mec.org/2021/11/15/education-in-yemen-turning-pens-into-bullets-pub-85777

78. It is important to consider the work of the Committee to Guide Religious Discourse. As Khoshafah pointed out: "The functions of this committee, which is overseen by the Ministry of Religious Endowments in Sana'a as well as the coordinating committee, is to guide religious discourse in a way that does not conflict with fundamental national values and is appropriate to the Yemeni people and unifies them on a single track, while maintaining the intellectual traces of each movement." Op. cit.

79. H. Porter, "Propaganda, Creativity and Diplomacy: The Huthis Adaptive Approach to Media and Public Messaging," in *The Huthi Movement in Yemen: Ideology, Ambition and Security in the Arab Gulf*, ed. A. Hamidaddin (London: I.B. Tauris, 2022), 140.

80. Ibid., 146–147.

81. For a detailed study of tribes in Yemen, see Brandt, *Tribes in Modern Yemen*, op. cit.

82. Dashela, op. cit.

83. Summer, *The Huthi Zāmil*, 170, 172, 173.

84. Today in Yemen the tribes on the opposing side of the Huthi (government and allies) have a relative strength (due to the frailty of the government), while those on the side of the Houthi or, that have made agreements, are weak due to the power of the Huthi. Abdul Ghani al-Iryani, interview by author, 2022.

85. One aspect that deserves to be analyzed in more detail is the participation of women in the Huthi movement in the development of nationalism. See E. K. Strzelecka, "Women under the Huthi Regime: Gender, Nationalism, and Islam," in *The Huthi Movement in Yemen: Ideology, Ambition and Security in the Arab Gulf*, ed. A. Hamidaddin (London: I.B. Tauris, 2022), 93–111.

86. The Yemeni organization *Mwatana for Human Rights* often publishes reports of Human Rights violations of all parties.

87. A report by the UNSC Secretary General (2021) estimates that between 2019 and 2020, a total of 861 children were recruited. Attributed to the Houthis (605), Yemeni Armed Forces (171), and Security Belt Forces (52), among others. See Security Council—United Nations, "Children and Armed Conflict in Yemen—Report of the Secretary General," August 27, 2021. https://reliefweb.int/sites/reliefweb.int/files/resources/S_2021_761_E.pdf

88. See Mwatana for Human Rights, "'Moments of Hell.' Ansar Allah (Houthi) Group Practices Gravely Undermine Womens Rights," March 8, 2022. https://mwatana.org/en/undermine-women

89. Salmoni, Loidolt, and Wells, op. cit. 169–171.

90. Brandt, *Tribes and Politics*, 203.

91. Brandt, *Tribes and Politics*, 204.

92. Van der Kroft, op. cit. See also H. Lackner, *Yemen in Crisis. The Road to War* (London & Brooklyn: Verso, 2019).

93. A. Watkins, R. Grim, and A. Ahmed, "Iran Warned Houthis against Yemen Takeover," *HuffPost*, April 4, 2015. www.huffpost.com/entry/iran-houthis-yemen_n_7101456

94. Brandt, *Tribes and Politics*, 2.

95. Haykel, op. cit. United Arab Emirates and Israel follow this thesis of Houthi as proxy of Iran.

96. Johnson et al., op. cit., 7.

97. K. Shalaby, "Saudi led coalition apologies fake Yemen video Houthi missiles," *Middle East Eye*, January 13, 2022. www.middleeasteye.net/video/saudi-led-coalition-apologises-fake-yemen-video-houthi-missiles

98. Johnsen, op. cit.

99. Johnston et al., 110–113.

References

Al-Mahfali, M. 2021. "Anti-Black Racism in Yemen: Manifestations and Responses." Arab Reform Initiative (August 5). www.arab-reform.net/publication/anti-black-racism-in-yemen-manifestations-and-responses

Anderson, B. 2006. *Imagined Communities. Reflections on the Origin and Spread of Nationalism*. Revised edition. London & New York: Verso.

Brandt, M., ed. 2021. *Tribes in Modern Yemen: An Anthology*. Vienna: Austrian Academy of Sciences Press.

Brandt, M. 2018. "The Huthi Enigma: Ansar Allah and the 'Second Republic,'" in *Yemen and the Search for Stability. Power, Politics and Society After the Arab Spring*, ed. M. C. Heinze. London & New York: I.B. Tauris.

Brandt, M. 2017. *Tribes and Politics in Yemen: A History of the Houthi* Conflict. Oxford: University Press.

Dashela, A. 2022. "Northern Yemeni Tribes during the Eras of Ali Abdullah Saleh and the Houthi Movement: A Comparative Study," Sana'a Center for Strategic Studies, February 16, 2022. https://sanaacenter.org/publications/analysis/16670

Dresch, P. 1993. *Tribes, Government, and History in Yemen*. Oxford: Clarendon Press.

Farrell, S. 2020. "Israel hails UAE deal but Palestinians—and settlers—dismayed." Reuters, August 13, 2020. www.reuters.com/article/us-israel-emirates-trump-reactions/israel-hails-uae-deal-but-palestinians-and-settlers-dismayed-idUSKCN2592R5.

Haykel, B. 2021. "The Houthis, Saudi Arabia and the War in Yemen," Hoover Institution, Issue 2131, June 15, 2021. www.hoover.org/research/houthis-saudi-arabia-and-war-yemen

Heinze, M.C. 2014. "The triumphant advance of the Houthi rebels," Qantara. https://en.qantara.de/content/political-upheaval-in-yemen-the-triumphant-advance-of-the-houthi-rebels

Johnsen, G. D. 2021. "Foreign Actors in Yemen: The History, the Politics and the Future," Sana'a Center for Strategic Studies, January 31, 2021. https://sanaacenter.org/publications/main-publications/13042

Johnston, T., M. Lane, A. Casey, H. J. Williams, A. L. Rhoades, J. Sladden, N. Vest, J. Reimer, and R. Haberman. 2020. "Could the Houthis Be the Next Hizballah? Iranian Proxy Development in Yemen and the Future of the Houthi Movement," *RAND*, 2020. www.rand.org/content/dam/rand/pubs/research_reports/RR2500/RR2551/RAND_RR2551.pdf

Khoshafah, A. 2021. "Houthi-Salafi Coexistence Agreements: Motives and Future Prospects," Sana'a Center for Strategic Studies, December 3, 2021. https://sanaacenter.org/publications/analysis/15839

Lackner, H. 2019. *Yemen in Crisis. The Road to War*. London & Brooklyn: Verso.

Nagi. A. 2021. "Education in Yemen: Turning pens into Bullets," Carnegie Middle East Center, November 15, 2021. https://carnegie-mec.org/2021/11/15/education-in-yemen-turning-pens-into-bullets-pub-85777

Nagi, A. 2019. "Yemen's Houthis Used Multiple Identities to Advance," Carnegie Middle East Center, March 19, 2019. https://carnegie-mec.org/2019/03/19/yemen-s-houthis-used-multiple-identities-to-advance-pub-78623

Phillips, S. 2011. *Yemen and the Politics of Permanent Crisis*. Abingdon: Routledge.

Phillips, S. 2008. *Yemen's Democracy Experiment in Regional Perspective: Patronage and Pluralized Authoritarianism*. Nueva York, NY: Palgrave Macmillan.

Porter, H. 2022. "Propaganda, Creativity and Diplomacy: The Huthis Adaptive Approach to Media and Public Messaging," in *The Huthi Movement in Yemen: Ideology, Ambition and Security in the Arab Gulf*, ed. A. Hamiddadin. London: I.B. Tauris.

Porter, H. 2020. "A Battle of Hearts and Minds: The Growing Medio Footprint of Yemen's Houthis," *Gulf International Forum*. https://gulfif.org/a-battle-of-hearts-and-minds-the-growing-media-footprint-of-yemens-houthis

Salmoni, B. A., B. Loidolt, and M. Wells. 2010. *Regime and Periphery in Northern Yemen: The Huthi Phenomenon*. Santa Mónica: RAND.

Schmitz, Ch. 2022. "Huthi Visions of the State: A Huthi Republic with an Unofficial Imam," in *The Huthi Movement in Yemen: Ideology, Ambition and Security in the Arab Gulf*, ed. A. Hamiddadin. London: I.B. Tauris, 2022.

Security Council—United Nations. 2021. "Children and Armed Conflict in Yemen—Report of the Secretary General," August 27, 2021. https://reliefweb.int/sites/reliefweb.int/files/resources/S_2021_761_E.pdf

Shaker, N., and F. Edroos. 2018. "Mohammed al-Houthi: We want a united and democratic Yemen," Al-Jazeera English, December 25, 2018. www.aljazeera.com/features/2018/12/25/mohammed-al-houthi-we-want-a-united-and-democratic-yemen

Summer, E. 2022. "The Huthi *Zāmil*: Folk Literature or Propaganda?," in *The Huthi Movement in Yemen: Ideology, Ambition and Security in the Arab Gulf*, ed. A. Hamiddadin. London: I.B. Tauris, 2022.

Summer, E. 2021. "Experiencing the Ḥūthī Zāmil," Arabia Felix Centre for Studies, April 29, 2021. https://arabiafelixstudies.com/en/experiencing-the-Ḥuthi-zamil

Tabataba'i, A. 1977. *Shi'ite Islam*. Albany, NY: SUNY Press.

Van der Kroft, L. 2021. "Who are the Houthis?," *International Centre for Counter-Terrorism*, June 1, 2021. www.jstor.org/stable/resrep34009

Watkins, A., R. Grim, and A. Sh. Ahmed. 2015. "Iran warned Houthis against Yemen takeover," *HuffPost*, April 4, 2015. www.huffpost.com/entry/iran-houthis-yemen_n_7101456

Weissenburger, A. 2021. "*Al-Mawaddah al-Khālidah*? The Ḥūthī Movement and the Idea of the Rule of the *Ahl al*-Bayt in Yemen's Tribal Society," in *Tribes in Modern Yemen: An Anthology*, ed. M. Brandt. Vienna: Austrian Academy of Sciences Press.

Wells, M. 2012. "Yemen's Houthi Movement and the Revolution," Foreign Policy (February 27, 2012). https://foreignpolicy.com/2012/02/27/yemens-houthi-movement-and-the-revolution

Videos/Documentaries

Shalaby, Kh. (13 January 2022). "Saudi led coalition apologies fake Yemen video Houthi missiles." *Middle East Eye*. www.middleeasteye.net/video/saudi-led-coalition-apologises-fake-yemen-video-houthi-missiles

Al-Ahmad, S. (Dir.) (2015). "The Fight for Yemen." *Frontline*. www.pbs.org/wgbh/frontline/documentary/fight-for-yemen

Interactive Charts

DeLozier, E. (September 17, 2020). "Yemen Matrix: Allies & Adversaries." *The Washington Institute for Near East Policy*. www.washingtoninstitute.org/policy-analysis/yemen-matrix-allies-adversaries.

IV
Afterword

12

Nationalism and National Identity in the Twenty-First Century

GREGORY MAHLER

Frustrated Nationalism in Comparative Perspective

In current times we are witnessing both the *causes* that lead nationalist movements to act and the *consequences* of those actions. As this volume is in production we cannot avoid seeing evidence of Russia's quite remarkable assault on Ukraine, and the equally remarkable resistance that the vastly outmanned and outgunned Ukraine is putting up to the Russian onslaught. In this conflict, both sides, apparently, are acting in the name of nationalism, with Russia claiming that Ukraine is and has been a part of a Greater Russia, and Ukraine claiming that it is and of right ought to be an independent nation. Those of us who consider ourselves to be students of human history look on these events with a sense of wonder and ask whether it is possible that Russia's leaders have learned nothing from modern history. Observers who thought that World War II would be the last such exercise in which one nation would seek to conquer another for the purposes of expanding its national borders[1] have found themselves stunned by the actions of Vladimir Putin of Russia, but not stunned by the resistance of Ukraine.

In her recent article on the role of nationalism and ethnicity in the 2014 Russia–Ukraine crisis, Erika Harris focused on the politicization of the historical narratives in the conflict between Ukraine's desire to free itself from Russian rule and Russia's determination to control Ukraine's political future. She argued that nationalism was clearly a significant factor in the conflict, and it remains an obstacle to its resolution.[2]

The concept of "frustrated nationalism" is meant to suggest that individuals and groups that seek sovereign states of their own—the ultimate goal of nationalism—will not aways achieve their goals and will, when their goals are unmet, be frustrated. We have seen a number of case studies of this kind of frustration in this volume, moving from the French-Canadian case in Quebec to the Scots in the United Kingdom to native peoples in North America to tension in Chiapas, Mexico, to the Māori in New Zealand, to Tibetans in exile, to the Kurds in Turkey and Syria, to the Biafrans in Nigeria, and ending with the Houthi in Yemen. In all of these cases, significant groups that were minorities in a political setting sought to redraw a map and become majorities in a new nation-state in which their group had sovereignty. They were not successful.

Types of Nationalism

We have seen a variety of different nationalisms in the pages of this volume, including indigenous assertions of national identity in Canada, New Zealand, and Mexico, federal nationalisms as in the United Kingdom (despite the fact that it isn't a federal government) and Canada, nationalism under conquest (in Tibet), and failed secessionism but recently resurgent nationalism (in Biafra and Kurdistan), to name only a few categories into which we could place these scholarly essays. In all of these cases we have found the types of factors that have been the subject of study in this volume—including ethnic identity, cultural factors, religion, language, historical patterns of behavior, national myths, resource distribution, and the like—serving as motivating forces for the nationalist agendas we have met.

As we have seen, the concept of nationalism can be defined in many ways. The literature cited has characterized anticolonial nationalism, civic (or liberal) nationalism, ethnic nationalism, religious nationalism, territorial nationalism, and even most contemporaneously "pandemic nationalism,"[3] to name just some of the labels we can find in the literature. The central idea to keep in mind is that the *motivation* for the nationalist goal is often affected by perspective, and many movements that have been labeled as one kind of nationalism by one person or group (e.g., "that is an ethnic nationalist movement") can be labeled as a different kind of nationalism by others (e.g., "those revolutionaries are Marxists").

In many of the instances seen in this volume, the nationalist agendas of the organizations involved led to successful or partially successful outcomes for the minority groups in question, such as the Māori in New Zealand, the Mi'kmaw in Eastern Canada, and the Mestizaje in Mexico. In other instances, the agendas did not meet with successfully attained goals, such as the scenarios we saw with "Virtual Tibet," with the Kurds, or with the Biafran movement in Nigeria. In yet other instances, the verdict remains in doubt, although the degree of oppression and suffering being experienced by the nationalist groups are nowhere near the same as we saw with the cases of Tibet, Kurdistan, or Biafra, such as the case of Scottish nationalism in the United Kingdom (where there might be widespread disenchantment with the union with Britain, but there is not the same sense of oppression as is found in other settings) or the nationalist movement in Quebec (which has successfully negotiated some devolution of sovereignty in the past but seeks further authority).

Key Variables in the Nationalism Quest

The variables we have seen in this volume to be significant in the generation of nationalist motivations, including ethnic identity, culture, religion, language, historical patterns of behavior, national myths, resource distribution, urbanization, rise of the middle class, communication, internal environment, and the like, are variables that can be at the same time easy to identify and difficult to quantify. We saw in the chapter on the Houthi in Yemen that motivations for Houthi activity may be based on religion, may be based on pragmatic political alliances with Iran, may be based on geographic and resource management, or may be based on other factors, which may explain the Houthi view of opposing other nationalisms present in Yemen. Elsewhere, the task of working on a "virtual Tibet" is understandable under the level of Chinese oppression that exists, but that oppression makes it very difficult to measure the extent of support for the virtual Tibet among the population that exists in real Tibet. In yet another case, the Mexican government may have started to grant legal recognition to various ethnic groups extant in the political system, but the number and behavior of those ethnic groups made policymaking more difficult than it might have been.

The various sources referred to in this volume have confirmed a number of key elements of nationalism often cited in the scholarship of nationalism, including cultural elements, religious elements, ethnic elements, territorial elements, language elements, and historical elements. These six elements are almost universal in the struggles described here. In modern history they have produced nationalist movements that have been successful in achieving their goals of self-government—we have used the term "sovereignty" here—and independence. In the cases described here, however, they have not been enough, and even these key elements fail to adequately mobilize the masses and integrate key segments of the population into effective communities to create a sense of nationhood.

Xavier Coller shows us that nationalist movements "succeed in attracting people because they have been able to generate a consensus about the nature of the community, its territorial limits, its defining elements (identity domains), its history, and the like."[4] Sometimes, however, whatever the degree of enthusiasm of the nationalist groups involved the consensus simply cannot be developed, and the nationalist endeavor fails, or the consensus may exist within a specific minority group but it is not recognized by an "other" non-minority group. Several of the chapters included in this volume have described this kind of situation—perhaps the cases of Biafra and Tibet are the clearest examples—and the nationalist urges that exist in those populations has had to remain unfulfilled and frustrated. This doesn't mean they go away, of course, and history has shown us that they may await a change in governmental context that will allow them to resurface and try to achieve their goals again in the future.

The failure of Third World nationalism has been ascribed to many causes and circumstances, including ethnic, cultural, linguistic, and religious factors, as well as "the formation and consolidation of a public sphere in which citizens have the feeling of participating in the polity and of being integrated into the sphere of the state."[5] Lahouari Addi writes that the inability of many nationalisms found in the third world—including several of the cases described in this volume—calls into question "the relationship between nationalism and the nation."

Social scientists have been too quick to embrace the notion that as soon as a country becomes independent, it constitutes a nation. This may be the case, of course, but most often a nation is the result of a long historical process during which consensual values emerge to furnish grounds for national concord and civil peace. This is not the picture presented today by most Third World countries, where obedience to the central power is secured by force or the threat of force.[6]

We have seen that nationalism is an ideology that wants to align the *nation* (defined in terms of culture, ethnicity, geography, language, religion, and traditions, among other factors) with the *state* (defined in terms of power, territory, and sovereignty). It is a movement that is often ascribed to the modern political era—often said to have begun with the French Revolution in the eighteenth century—and to Western Europe, although clearly today it is much more globally extant. In today's world, the future of the nation-state is less clear than it has been in the past, primarily because of the rise of multinational corporations and international nongovernmental organizations, and modern globalism is certainly a force working to weaken nationalist forces around the world, although it must be said that there are today nationalist movements that are not yet nation-states that are aspiring to that status, including many described in this book.

The Nation-State and Multinational Corporations

In 1974, Joseph Nye wrote what would become a definitive article on multinational corporations for *Foreign Affairs* in which he addressed the growing phenomenon of large businesses operating across borders and exercising great power over governments.[7] The question addressed by Nye involved the future of the nation-state, and whether we were entering an era in which multinational corporations would dominate nation-states. He wrote:

> The odds are that both the size and political impact of multinationals will continue to grow . . . Predictions that 300 giant corporations will run the world economy tend to be based on simple projections of past ten-percent annual growth rates, and fail to take into account some of the disadvantages that appear with large size, particularly in manufacturing, when temporary monopoly advantages have been competed away. The challenge to governments will come more from global scope and mobility than from corporate size. Even smaller multinations can make crucial allocative decisions that challenge the welfare goals of governments. Corporate mobility . . . is not only a challenge to small states, but also to large states like the United States.[8]

Data from 2013 show that Walmart would have ranked as the twenty-eighth largest economy in the world, Royal Dutch Shell as the twenty-ninth, ExxonMobil the thirtieth, and Sinopec the thirty-first. "All of them with bigger revenues than the GDPs of, for example, Austria, South Africa, Thailand, Denmark, Singapore and Nigeria. A top one hundred of global economies and global corporations would include thirty-seven international businesses among its numbers."[9]

While multinationals have not replaced nation-states in the international political-economic setting, it is the case that they continue to be very significant, and the appearance of thirty-seven international businesses among the top hundred global economic actors indicates this to be the case. Modern history has shown, though, that the nation-state is not going to go away, and the existence of the nation-state—and, therefore, nationalism as a significant global ideology—is going to continue to be significant.

The Frustration of Nationalism, Again

We have seen here that actors in many different settings in the political world believe that a nation-state *should* be able to develop easily once some level of community is established based upon one (or several) of the key variables that we described above. This has not always proven to be the case, however, and it has often resulted in the kinds of protracted political violence that is described in several of the articles in this book—in greatest detail in the chapters on Biafra (chapter 10) and the Houthi (chapter 11)—as well as in outcomes of long-term uncertainty, such as described in the chapters on Tibet (chapter 8) and Kurdistan (chapter 9). Just because *some* actors in a political setting believe that their case merits the establishment of a sovereign nation-state does not mean *all* (or even *enough*) significant actors believe that, and that a sovereign nation-state is going to be successfully established. This is best illustrated by the argument of Peter Calvert of the possible existence of what he called the *reductio ad absurdum* of a nationalist movement being victorious, leading to the establishment of a sovereign and independent state, and subsequently having to face *its own* struggle with nationalist movements *within* its population that are seeking to win *their own* independence.[10]

This kind of situation leads to the frustration we have seen described again and again here and in other literature. Whether it is French-Canadians in Quebec, the Scots in the United Kingdom, the Mi'kmaw in Atlantic

Canada, the Zapatista uprising in Mexico, the Māori in New Zealand, the Tibetans in Occupied Tibet, the Kurds in Turkey and Syria, the Biafrans in Nigeria, or the Houthi in Yemen, being under the governmental control of an "other" group is not something that is desirable or, often, pleasant. As we noted in the first chapter, sovereignty is about exercising power over someone, and if you are the someone over whom power is being exercised, that exercise of power can be frustrating, at least, or oppressive, at most.

We started this chapter with a comment about the situation that we are now witnessing in Ukraine, with an aggressive Russia claiming that Ukraine was a part of its national patrimony, and an independent and sovereign Ukraine rejecting the Russian claim. Ukraine is a good illustration of the types of forces described in this book. In modern history, Ukraine first officially declared itself to be independent in 1917, and was partitioned between Poland and Bolshevik Russia at the end of World War I, with the Bolshevik-controlled portion of Ukraine becoming the Ukrainian Soviet Republic in 1918. In 1922, the Ukrainian Soviet Socialist Republic joined with several other Soviet Socialist Republics (Russia, Byelorussia, and Transcaucasia) to become part of the Soviet Union (the Union of Soviet Socialist Republics). In 1945, Ukraine was made one of the founding members of the United Nations, even though it was part of the Soviet Union and clearly under Russian domination. Following the dissolution of the Soviet Union in 1991, Ukraine became an independent state.

As Ukraine has moved toward more economic and political interactions with the West, Russia has been less and less happy with the way an independent Ukraine has been behaving. In early 2014, Russian-backed paramilitaries seized the Luhansk and Donetsk oblasts of Ukraine in the "Revolution of Dignity," and later in 2014, Russia annexed Crimea. Although the Minsk Agreements (2014, 2015) sought to stop the fighting in east and south Ukraine, the ceasefire agreements did not hold.

In recent years, Russia has been increasingly unhappy with Ukraine's openness to the West, especially with talk of Ukraine joining the North Atlantic Treaty Organization (NATO).[11] Russia demanded a formal agreement from NATO guaranteeing that Ukraine would never be a member of NATO (this following several Eastern European states joining NATO).[12] Despite its lack of excitement about Ukrainian membership, NATO would make no such agreement.[13]

In 2021, Russia began a military build-up along its borders with Ukraine, and in February of 2022 invaded Ukraine, claiming that it was governed by neo-Nazis who were persecuting the ethnic Russian minority there.[14] More than a year later, the fighting is ongoing. The conflict may end with Russia controlling all of what was Ukraine at the beginning of the twenty-first century, some of Ukraine, or none of Ukraine, but most likely it will end with one of the groups of political actors feeling frustrated at the outcome of the conflict and feeling inclined at some point in the future to revisit their nationalist agenda.

Many political scientists have written about the relationships among nationalism, state-building, and war (and other types of political violence), and have ascribed the development of nationalism to the fear of war: "External threats have such a powerful effect on nationalism because people realize in a profound manner that they are under threat because of who they are as a nation; they are forced to recognize that it is only as a nation that they can successfully defeat the threat."[15] The causal arrow may go in the other direction as well, of course, with nationalism not arising because of external threats but with nationalism *being* the external threat to other groups.

These are all questions that call for further study, and debate, and it is certain that these questions will serve as the subject of future scholarship in this area. They are questions that reflect the concerns of significant populations, and questions that affect significant populations. It is thus no surprise that nationalist movements, and *frustrated* nationalist movements as well, will continue to generate further study in the future.

Notes

1. Steve Balestrieri, "Putin Thinks All of Ukraine Is Part of Russia," 1945 (February 21, 2022). www.19fortyfive.com/2022/02/putin-thinks-all-of-ukraine-is-part-of-russia

2. See Erika Harris, "What Is the Role of Nationalism and Ethnicity in the Russia–Ukraine Crisis?" *Europe-Asia Studies* 72, no. 4 (2020): 593–613. See also Taras Kuzio, "Russia-Ukraine Crisis: The Blame Game, Geopolitics, and National Identity," *Europe-Asia Studies* 70, no. 3 (2018): 462–473.

3. Harris Mylonas and Ned Whalley, eds., "Pandemic Nationalism," *Nationalities Papers* 50: 1:3–12.

4. Xavier Coller, "Collective identities and Failed Nationalism," Pôle Sud 2:25 (2006); 107–136.

5. Lahouari Addi, "The Failure of Third World Nationalism,' *Journal of Democracy* 8, no. 4 (1997): 110.

6. Addi, 110.

7. See David Smith, "Who Runs the World?" *Reflect,* the Equatex *Magazine and Blog.* www.equatex.com/en/article/who-runs-the-world

8. Joseph S. Nye Jr., "Multinational Corporations in World Politics," *Foreign Affairs* 53, no. 1 (1974): 163.

9. Smith, "Who Runs the World," op cit.

10. Peter Calvert, "On Attaining Sovereignty," in Anthony Smith, Nationalist Movements, 135–136.

11. Gabrielle Tétrault-Farber and Tom Balmforth, "Russia Demands NATO Roll Back from East Europe and Stay Out of Ukraine." Reuters. 17 December 2021. www.reuters.com/world/russia-unveils-security-guarantees-says-western-response-not-encouraging-2021-12-17

12. Thomas S. Szayna. "The Enlargement of NATO and Central European Politics." Woodrow Wilson International Center for Scholars. 29 October 1997. www.wilsoncenter.org/publication/142-the-enlargement-nato-and-central-european-politics

13. Cassandre Coyer. "Why Is Ukraine Not in NATO and Is It Too Late to Join? Here's What Experts, NATO Say." *The Miami Herald.* 25 February 2022. www.miamiherald.com/news/nation-world/world/article258774458.html

14. "Ukraine Conflict: Russian Forces Attack after Putin's TV Declaration." BBC News. 24 February 2022. www.bbc.com/news/world-europe-60503037

15. Jeffrey Herbst, "War and the State in Africa," *International Security* 14, no. 4 (117–139).

About the Contributors

Felipe Medina Gutierrez is professor of Islamic Civilization at the Universidad del Rosario and professor of Middle East at the Faculty of Political Science and International Relations of the Pontificia Javeriana University in Colombia. He earned his MA in Asian and African Studies, specializing in the Middle East, from El Colegio de Mexico (CONACYT Scholarship). He studied Classical Arabic (basic and intermediate levels) at the Arabi Center for Arabic Studies in Alexandria, Egypt. He has visited many countries in the region of his specialty, including Morocco, Algeria, Tunisia, Egypt, Palestine, Lebanon, Jordan, Turkey, Oman, Iran, and recently, Kazakhstan and Uzbekistan. His research lines are history, politics, and conflicts in the Middle East and North Africa, as well as history, politics, culture, and law in Islam.

Neil Harvey is a professor and Head of the Department of Government at New Mexico State University. He received his BA (Honors) in Latin American Studies from Portsmouth Polytechnic (UK) in 1983, MA in Government (Latin America) from the University of Essex (UK) in 1984, and PhD in Government, also from Essex, in 1990. His main areas of research concern rural social movements and Indigenous rights in Mexico and Latin America. He has published widely on this topic, including the book *The Chiapas Rebellion: The Struggle for Land and Democracy* (1998). In collaboration with Dr. Jeremy Slack at the University of Texas-El Paso (UTEP), he currently co-directs the National Science Foundation's Research Experience for Undergraduates program on immigration policy and US-Mexico border communities.

Raffaele Iacovino is associate professor in the Department of Political Science at Carleton University. His interests include Canadian and Quebec politics, federalism, citizenship and immigration, and citizenship education.

He has also held the positions of Invited Professor of Quebec Studies at McGill University; Postdoctoral Fellow at the Canada Research Chair on Democracy and Sovereignty at l'Université du Québec À Chicoutimi; and Skelton-Clark postdoctoral fellow of Canadian Affairs in the Department of Political Studies at Queen's University. He is the co-author, with Alain-G. Gagnon, of *Federalism, Citizenship and Quebec: Debating Multinationalism* (2007), which won the 2011 edition of the Canada Publishing Award for Japan (International Council for Canadian Studies).

Joost Jongerden is an associate professor in the Rural Sociology Group at Wageningen University, the Netherlands. His work takes place at the intersection of rural sociology, political sciences, and historical sociology. He has worked on forced migration, rural development, and political and violent conflict in the Kurdistan region. His main interest is in the dynamics of dispossession, displacement, and violent conflict and the ways in which people not only respond to conditions in which they are made vulnerable but also develop alternatives. In 2012, he was a founding member of the journal *Kurdish Studies*, of which he was an editor until 2020. In 2021, he founded the journal *Commentaries*. https://wur.academia.edu/JoostJongerden

Åshild Kolås is a social anthropologist and research professor at the Peace Research Institute Oslo (PRIO), where she leads the research project "e-Topia: China, India and Biometric Borders." She has carried out fieldwork in the Tibetan exile community in India and Nepal, in the Tibetan region, and in multi-ethnic communities in China and Northeast India, and has written extensively on governance, identity politics, nationhood, and representation. Kolås is the author of *Tourism and Tibetan Culture in Transition: A Place Called Shangrila* (2008) and co-author of *On the Margins of Tibet: Cultural Survival on the Sino-Tibetan Frontier* (2005) (with Monika P. Thowsen). She is the editor of several anthologies and has co-edited two volumes on Basque nationalism with Pedro Ibarra Güell—*Sovereignty Revisited: The Basque Case* (2018) and *Basque Nationhood: Towards a Democratic Scenario* (2016).

Gregory Mahler is research professor of politics and Academic Dean *Emeritus* at Earlham College. He is the the author of a large number of book chapters and journal articles, and author or editor of over thirty volumes in the field of comparative politics. These books have focused on political institutions and political behavior, with a specialization in the area of the Middle East, more specifically Israeli politics and the Arab–Israel conflict.

His text *Comparative Politics* has been in print since 1983, and is currently in its sixth edition (2019). His text on *Politics and Government in Israel* will be appearing in its fourth edition in 2024, and a new edition of his edited volume *The Arab-Israeli Conflict* will be published in 2023. Prior to this volume, his most recent book was *Foreign Perceptions of the United States under Donald Trump* (2021).

Bernard Ugochukwu Nwosu is a senior research fellow at the Institute for Development Studies, University of Nigeria, Enugu Campus. He also holds a joint parallel position as a senior lecturer in the political science department of the same university. Ben trained for his PhD at the University of Waikato, New Zealand, and specializes in the broad area of political theory. His research centers on democratic theory and democratization, civil society, issues of power, participation, inclusiveness, and conflict. He has published several works, many of which have appeared in peer-reviewed international journals and book chapters. His most recent book is *Civil Society and Democracy in Nigeria* (2021), and he contributes to policy briefs on security/conflicts in Nigeria/Africa through the Nextier SPD Weeklies.

Tashi Nyima is a researcher at the Peace Research Institute Oslo (PRIO) in the research project "e-Topia: China, India and Biometric Borders." He holds a doctoral degree in China studies from the University of Oslo, Department of Culture and Oriental Languages (IKOS). He is also an authorized interpreter in Norway and is fluent in Tibetan, Norwegian, Chinese, and English, with basic skills in Hindi. His research focuses on Tibetan identity, language, cultural change, pastoralism, development discourse, resource management, and digital governance, with a particular focus on China's westward development drive, Chinese state development narratives, and China's policies in Tibet and beyond. He has previously worked for the Norwegian Center for Human Rights and the Evolution Institute, and has conducted fieldwork in India, Tibet, Inner Mongolia, and other parts of China, as well as the northern Sami region of Norway. His publications include *Newly Recognized Languages in Chamdo: Geography, Culture, History and Language* (2019), *Pastoralism in Tibet Today: A Study of Pastoral Policy and Practice* (2019), and *Development Discourses on the Tibetan Plateau: Urbanization and Expropriation of Farmland in Dartsedo* (2010).

Kenneth Omeje is the Vice President for Academic Affairs of Management International University (MIU) in London, and extraordinary professor,

School of Government Studies, North-West University (NWU) in South Africa. He is also a visiting professor at the Institute for Peace and Security Studies in Addis Ababa University, Ethiopia and the University for Peace (UPEACE) Africa Program in Addis Ababa. He has previously held the positions of professor of International Relations & Security Studies at the United States International University in Nairobi, Kenya, and senior research fellow at the Department of Peace Studies, University of Bradford. In addition, he has held visiting research fellowship positions at the Center for African Studies, University of Florida, Gainesville (Spring 1992); Law Department, Keele University, UK (Spring 2000); Department of International Politics, University of Wales, Aberystwyth (Spring 2001); and Georg Eckert Institute (GEI) in Braunschweig, Germany (Autumn 2014). He has over one hundred academic publications, and his most recent book is *The Failure and Feasibility of Capitalism in Africa* (2021).

Simone Poliandri is a cultural anthropologist specialized in Native American studies. He is an associate professor of anthropology and the director of the American Studies program at Bridgewater State University in Bridgewater, Massachusetts. He holds a PhD from Brown University and is an elected member of the Phi Beta Kappa Society. He has conducted ethnographic fieldwork among the Mi'kmaw people of the Canadian Maritimes since 2000, working on issues of tradition and traditionalism, Indigenous identity, and Aboriginal nationalism and nationhood. He published a monograph and an edited volume centered on Native American/First Nations identity dynamics and nation-building, as well as academic articles and chapters on topics including social science research methods, Mi'kmaw residential school experiences, contemporary Aboriginal maritime harvesting, and Native American ethnohistory. He was born and raised in Rome, Italy, and lives in Massachusetts with his wife and daughter.

David Ryan is professor of modern history at University College Cork, Ireland, and Research Fellow at the Centre for War and Diplomacy, Lancaster University, UK. He has published extensively on contemporary history and U.S. foreign policy, concentrating on interventions in the post-Vietnam era. His books include *Not Even Past: How the United States Ends Wars*, edited with David Fitzgerald and John M. Thompson (2020); *Obama, US Foreign Policy and the Dilemmas of Intervention*, coauthored with David Fitzgerald (2014); *US Foreign Policy and the Other*, edited with Michael Cullinane (2015); *Frustrated Empire: US Foreign Policy from 9/11 to Iraq* (2007); *Vietnam in*

Iraq: Tactics, Lessons, Legacies and Ghosts, edited with John Dumbrell (2007); *The United States and Europe in the Twentieth Century* (2003); *US Foreign Policy in World History* (2000); and *US-Sandinista Diplomatic Relations: Voice of Intolerance* (1995). He is also the author of numerous articles.

Dolores Trevizo is professor of sociology and Chair of the Latinx and Latin American Studies Program at Occidental College. She has published articles on various protest movements in Mexico since 1968, including those demanding human rights for political dissidents as well as for families of activists disappeared during the dirty war. Her first book, *Rural Protest in the Making of Democracy in Mexico, 1968–2000*, examines how various movements contributed to Mexico's transition to electoral democracy. This book was followed by a co-edited volume, *Democracy and Its Discontents in Latin America*. Her current research on Mexico's vigilante movements is appeared in the journal *Latin American Politics and Society* (*LAPS*) in 1922. In addition to her ongoing research on political movements in Mexico, she studies Mexican immigrants in the United States. She recently co-authored a book entitled *Neighborhood Poverty and Segregation in the (Re-) Production of Disadvantage: Mexican Immigrant Entrepreneurs in Los Angeles*.

Toon van Meijl is professor of cultural anthropology at Radboud University, Nijmegen, the Netherlands. He obtained a doctorate from the Australian National University in 1991 and has been engaged in long-term anthropological research among the Tainui Māori in Aotearoa, New Zealand, since 1982. His research concentrates on issues of cultural identity and the self, particularly among young people in multicultural societies, and on sociopolitical questions emerging from the debate about property rights, especially of Indigenous peoples. Since his appointment to the chair of cultural anthropology in 2011, he coordinates the research program of the department that focuses on the relationship between diversity and inequality, with special attention for issues of citizenship, democracy, and dialogue.

Christopher A. Whatley, OBE, is emeritus professor of Scottish history at the University of Dundee, Scotland. He is a Fellow of the Royal Society of Edinburgh. His publications include books and articles on aspects of the Industrial Revolution in Scotland, as well as popular culture, protest, and everyday life, best exemplified by his *Scottish Society, 1707–1830: Beyond Jacobitism, towards Industrialisation* (2000). Other interests include the early nineteenth-century Scottish novelist John Galt and the political and cultural legacy of Scotland's national poet Robert Burns: *Immortal Memory: Burns and the Scottish People* (2016). He is best known for his extensive work on the making of the United Kingdom. His award-winning *The Scots and the Union* (2006, 2007) was brought up to date in an extended edition for the Scottish independence referendum in 2014. He continues to write and comment on Scotland's place within the UK.

Index

Abenaki people in Canada, 108
Abkhazia, as disputed nation, 11
Aboriginal people of Canada, 106
Acheson, Dean, U.S. Secretary of State, and Vietnam, 37
Afghanistan, and nationalism, 15
Africa: nationalism, 232; and U.S. foreign policy on nationalism, 40
agricultural production and peasant consumption, Mexico, 140
Algeria, and nationalism, 14
Al-Huthi, Hussein, 264
Ansar Allah (Houthi) movement in Yemen, 19–20, 268–269. *See also* Huthi
anticolonial nationalism, 292; Kurdish nationalism in Turkey, 218–221
anti-imperialism: and Huthi, 271; nationalism and, 5
Anti-Zionism, and Huthi, 271
Aquash, Annie Mae, and Mi'kma'ki nation-building, 114–115
Arbroath Abbey, and Scottish nationalism, 80–81
Armenians and nationalism, 15
Artsakh, as disputed nation, 11
Asian nationalism, 9
Assembly of First Nations in Canada, 106

assimilation, and Québec nationalism, 62
Atlantic Charter, and U.S. foreign policy, 35–39
attributes of ethnic community, 8

Ba'ath regime and Kurdish identity, 212
Baltic states and Scottish nationalism, 94
Bannockburn, symbol of Scottish nationalism, 87
Basques, and nationalism, 14
Bengali nationalism, 9
Biafra: nationalism, 14, nationalism, 231–252, 293; radio broadcasting, 245; separatist movement in Nigeria, 19; War of 1967–1970, 234–235
Biafra Day, 244
Biafra House, Washington D.C., 240
Biafran Liberation Council, 238
Biafran Youth Congress, 238
biculturalism, in New Zealand, 169–173
Black history, U.S., and American foreign policy, 32
Bolshevik definition of self-determination, 215
Brazil, and nationalism, 16

Britain: colonialism and nationalism, 9; colonialism in Nigeria, 233; Scottish nationalism and, 17; Scottish Parliament and, 84; settler colonial power and Mi'kmaq in Canada, 108
British East India Company and Scottish trade, 85
British Empire, and Scotland, 85–86, 92
Buddhism, and Tibetan nationalism, 19

Cairo Conference (1921) and Kurdistan, 213
Canada: First Nations in, 106; Indian Act of 1876, 110; Mi'kmaq nationalism, 17; Mi'kmaw First Nation people, 105–125; Québec nationalism, 16–17; treaty rights of native peoples, 117
Catalonia and Madrid, and Scottish nationalism, 94
Celtic Revival, and Scottish nationalism, 90
Central Tibetan Administration, 192–193
centralization of native populations in Canada, 111
Charter of Rights and Freedoms of Québec, 65, 70
Chiapas, Mexico, 156; counterinsurgency in Mexico, 152–153; Indigenous nationalism in Mexico, 18; nationalism, 292
China: as disputed nation, 11; occupation of Tibet, 188; Tibet nationalism and, 18–19
Church of Scotland, and British union, 82
civic nationalism, 5, 292; in Québec, 59
Coalition of Biafran Liberation Groups, 238

Cold War: European political decolonization, 36; U.S. foreign policy, 38, 41–43
collective identity: national identity and, 8; in Québec, 64
colonialism, and ethnic nationalism in Nigeria, 233; colonialism and nationalism, 9; British colonialism in Nigeria, 233; U.S. foreign policy, 34
Commission of Inquiry, Québec, 63–65
communalism, and nationalism, 14–15
communication and nationalism, 293
community, ethnic, attributes, 8
Confederacy of Mainland Mi'kmaq, 119
conflicts to watch, and nationalism, 15–16
consequences of nationalism, 291
Consortium of European Social Science Data Archives, 10
constitution (draft) for "virtual" Tibet, 190–191
constitution, Mexican, and national integration, 137–138
contextual nationhood among Mi'kmaq, 106, 112–114
Criollos, Mexican elites of 19th Century, 135
Cuba, and U.S. foreign policy, 42–43
culture: assimilation of Mi'kmaqs in Canada, 110; autonomy, resurgence of, in Scotland, 93; in exile, Tibet, 189–194; Mi'kmaq nationhood, 113; Mexican revolution, 156; nationalism, 2, 4, 5, 293; New Zealand, 171–173; Scottish nationalism, 86–87
Cyprus, as disputed nation, 11

Dalai Lama: and Tibetan nationalism, 19; Tibet political institutions, 190–194; "virtual" Tibet, 185–201

De Gaulle, Charles, and Québec, 5
Declaration of Arbroath, Scotland, 80–81
decolonization: global fragmentation in Cold War, 38; source of new nations, 8; United States and, 28
democratic Tibet, 189–194
Department of Indian Affairs, Canada, 111
Department of Information and International Relations, Tibet, 193
dialect and language and Scottish nationalism, 87–88
digital communication, and Tibetan nationalism, 186
diplomatic history, U.S., and American Indians, 31
disputed nations, 10–12
Dumbarton Oaks, and U.S. foreign policy, 40
Dutch colonialism and nationalism, 9

East India Company, and Scottish trade with Britain, 85
Eastern Security Network, in Biafra, 246
economic costs of Biafran conflict, 248
economic development and indigenous people, Mexico, 145
education: and Huthi, 273; and Young Māori Party in New Zealand, 170; initiatives, Mexico, 144
England and Wales, and Scottish nationalism, 17
ethnic groups, 2; Biafran conflict and, 250; disputed nations and, 10; Igbo conflict and, 247; nationalism and, 2, 5, 7–8, 10, 13, 291–292, 293; Nigeria and, 232–233, 240–241; Québec and, 59
European political decolonization, 36

expansionism, U.S., and foreign policy, 27

faith, and Huthi rhetoric in Yemen, 270–271
fascism, and nationalism, 5
federal nationalism, 292
First Nation people of Canada, 105–125; centralization of populations, 111; Mi'kmaw in Canada, 105–106
foreign policy, U.S., and nationalism, 30–31
Fourteen Points, and Woodrow Wilson: Kurdistan and, 213; nationalism and, 35
France: colonialism and nationalism, 9; colonial power and Mi'kmaq in Canada, 108; option of union with Scotland, 81–84
Francophone majority in Québec, 61–62; and Québec nationalism, 16–17
French Revolution, and nationalism, 9, 295
French-Canadian nationalism, 292
Fulani and Igbo conflict, 243, 246, 249–250

George, Lloyd, and nationalism, 14
Government-in-exile for Tibet, 186–187, 189–194
Gowon, Yakubu, Nigeria, 236
Great Britain, and Scottish nationalism, 79–95
Guatemala, and U.S. foreign policy, 42
Gulf, and nationalism, 16

Hadi, Abd Rabbuh Mansur, President of Yemen, 265–266
health services, Mexico, 144–145
historical memories, and national identity, 8

Hitler, and nationalism, 14
homeland, and national identity, 8
Huthi: anti-imperialism, 271; Anti-Zionism, 271; education, 273; ideology, 267–270; Iran, 274–275; Islamic group, 260; nationalism in Yemen, 19–20, 259–278, 293; nation-building, 5; poetry, 271–273; propaganda, 271–273; republicanism, 269; rhetoric in Yemen, 270–273; Zaydi community, 267

Ibo. *See* Igbo
Iceland as nation-state, 4
identity: ethnic, and nationalism, 293; Mexican, and land reform, 141; myth, nationalism as, 3; Québec, 57–58
ideology: nationalism, 5; Huthi, 267–270; nationalism as, 6; U.S. and self-determination, 27–33
Igbo: ethnic identity, 247; nationalism in Nigeria, 19, 234–242, 249–250; territories, 241
immigration: New Zealand, and Māori, 166; Québec, 60
imperial anticolonialism, and U.S. foreign policy, 30, 32
Import Substitution Industrialization, Mexico, 138
independence and nationalism, 294; Québec, 57
India, and Tibetans in the diaspora, 185–187
Indian Act of 1876 in Canada, 110
Indians, American, and nationalism, 31
indigenous autonomy, Mexico, 151–155
indigenous population: culture and Mexican nationalism, 148; Māori struggle in New Zealand, 18; Mexico, 17–18, 143, 146–149; Nigeria, 242; sovereignty, New Zealand, 167–179
Indochina, and U.S. foreign policy, 37
integration, national, Canada, and Québec, 58, 64
interculturalism in Québec, 60–66, 69–70
international economy, and nationalism, and U.S. foreign policy, 33, 40
internationalism, Woodrow Wilson and, 34–35
Iran: Huthi in Yemen, 274–275; Kurdistan Democratic Party, 217; Kurdistan national liberation, 19, 213
Iraq, and nationalism, 16
Iron Curtain, United States foreign policy and, 28
irredentism, and nationalism, 14–15
Israel, as disputed nation, 11
Italy, and fascism, 5

Jacobites, and Scottish independence in 1707, 83–84
Japan: fascism, 5; nationalism, 9

Korean nationalism, 9
Kosovo, as disputed nation, 11
Kulturnation, 4
Kurdistan: anticolonialism, 218–221; Cairo Conference (1921), 213; "Fourteen Points" of Woodrow Wilson, 213; Iraq and, 213; Marxism, 215–218; national liberation in, 19, 207–222; 292, 293; Ottoman Empire and, 209–212; self-determination, 213–215; Syria and, 212, 214; Treaty of Sèvres, 213; Turkey, 218–221

Kurdistan Democracy Party: in Iran, 217; in Turkey, 216

land reform in Mexico, 18, 139–145; indigenous rights, 146–147; Mexican revolution, 155–156
language: Māori, New Zealand, 177–178; nationalism, 2, 5, 10, 293; Tibetan, and nationalism, 18–19
location and nationalism, 5
Louis XIV, and Scotland, option for union with Britain, 81

majoritarian identity, Québec, 58–60, 66, 71
Maliseet people in Canada, 108
Māori: culture, 164; grievances, 174–176; identity, 168–169; Indigenous rights, 18; nationalism, 171–173, 292; Parliament, 167–168; population decline, 167; renaissance, 177–178; rights, New Zealand, 163–179; sovereignty, 165–166
Māoritanga, separatism, in New Zealand, 169–173
Marshall case, and treaty rights in Canada, 117
Marshall Plan, and U.S. foreign policy, 38
Marxism, and Kurdish national liberation, 215–218
Membertou First Nation, 124
Mestizaje in Mexico, 135, 293; ideology of, 151–155; indigenous rights in Mexico, 146–149; nationalism in Mexico, 135–157; racial group, Mexico, 141–142
Mexico: constitution and national integration, 137–138; health services, 144–145; ideology of Mestizaje, 151–155; indigenous peoples, 17–18, 135–157; indigenous rights, 143, 146–149; land reform in, 139–145; multiculturalism, 149–151; oil industry, 138; Woodrow Wilson's views on, 34–35; Zapatista uprising, 146–149, 151
Mi'kmaq people in Canada, 105–125, 293; identity and medical challenges, 110; nationalism, 17; nationhood and treaty rights, 112–113, 118; powwows, 113; relations with British settlers, 108; rights initiative, 120–121; territory, 106
Mi'kmaq-Nova Scotia-Canada Consultation Terms of Reference, 121–122
Miawpukek First Nation in Canada, 108
military rule, Nigeria, 237
minorities: Québec nationalism, 58; and sovereign power, 12
Monroe Doctrine, and U.S. foreign policy, 29–30, 32–33
Movement for the Actualization of the Sovereign State of Biafra, 237–238
Movement for the Survival of Ogoni People, 237
Mozambique, and nationalism, 15
multiculturalism, Mexico, 149–151
multinational corporations and nationalism, 13, 295–296
Muslims in North India, and nationalism, 15
Myanmar, and nationalism, 15
myths and nationalism, 293

Napoleon, and nationalism, 14
Nasser, Gamal Abdel, death of, 262
nation, 1–2, 4; distinct from state, 3–4
National Association for the Vindication of Scottish Rights, 88–89
national consciousness and nationalism, 2

National Convention of Nigerian Citizens, 233
National Council of Indigenous Peoples, Mexico, 146
national identity, 3; Mi'kmaq and, 114; Québec and, 63
National Indian Brotherhood in Canada, 106
national integration, Canada, and Québec, 58
national liberation in Kurdistan, 19
National Party of Scotland, 90
nationalism: American Indians, 31; anticolonialism, 292; Biafra, 232, 235–242; Chiapas, 292; civic, 292; communication, 293; conflict, 13–15; culture, 293; defined, 2, 231–232; ethnic identity, 292–293; fascism, 5; French Revolution, 295; French-Canadian, 292; Houthi, 293; ideology, 6; Igbo, 235–242; independence movements, 294; indigenous groups, New Zealand, 164–165; key variables, 293–295; Kurdish, 292; language, 293; Māori, 292; Mexico, 135–157; Mikmaw, 106; modern phenomenon, 9; multinational corporations, 295–296; nation-state, 2, 12–13; oil in Nigeria, 234; pandemic, 292; prior to nationhood, 9; Québec, 57–72; regional tribes, Canada, 109; religion, 292–293; resource distribution, 293; revolutionary nationalism in Mexico, 135–139; Scottish nationalism, 93, 292–293; secessionism, 292; territorial, 292; Third World, 294; Tibet, 292, 293; types of, 5; U.S. foreign policy, 28–33; urbanization, 293
nationalization of oil industry, Mexico, 138

nation-building, 6–7; ethics of, 5–6; Mexico, 1910, 137; Mi'kmaq and Nova Scotia government, 120–121
nationhood, 5; ethnic identity, 7–8; Mi'kmaq, 112–113
nation-state: defined, 1, 3, 12–13; and nationalism, 12–13
Nazi Germany, and fascism, 5
Negroes in the American South and nationalism, 15
Nehru, Jawaharlal, and Indian nationalism, 35, 36
Neo-Biafran nationalism, 242–244
neoliberal multiculturalism, Mexico, 149–155
New Zealand: biculturalism, 169–173; cultural nationalism, 171–173; immigration, 166; indigenous rights in, 18, 163–179; Māori identity, 168–169; Māori language and culture, 177–178; Māori nationalism, 165–166, 171–173; Māori Parliament, 167–168; Māori population decline, 167; Māori rights, 173–174; Māori sovereignty, 164–165; Māoritanga, 169–173; pan-tribal unity, 166–168; Waitangi Tribunal, 173–174; Young Māori Party, 168–169
Nicaragua, and U.S. foreign policy, 43
Nigeria: Biafran separatist movement, 19; colonialism in, 233; ethnic minorities, 240–241; ethnic nationalism in, 232–233; Fulani in, 243, 246; military rule, 237; nationalism, 232–233
North Korea, as disputed nation, 11
Northern Cyprus, as disputed nation, 11

Obasanjo, Olusegun, President of Nigeria, 237

Index | 313

Öcalan, Abdullah, and Kurdish nationalism in Turkey, 219–220
oil: Mexico, 138; nationalism, Nigeria, 234; Yemen, 266
Open-Door policies, United States and, 27
Ottoman Empire and Kurdish nationalism, 209–212

Pale of Settlement, and nationalism, 15
Palestine, as disputed nation, 11
pandemic nationalism, 292
pan-tribal unity, New Zealand, 166–168
parliament, Tibetan, 193, 195–196
Passamaquoddy people in Canada, 108
patriotism, and nationalism, 2
Pearson, Lester, Canadian Prime Minister, 5
PEMEX, and Mexican nationalism, 138
Penobscot people in Canada, 108
poetry, and Huthi, 271–273
pogroms against Jews and nationalism, 15
politics and religion in "virtual" Tibet, 188–189
popular support, Huthi, 274
postcolonial empire, United States as, 16, 27, 28, 29
powwows as cultural activity for Mi'kmaq, 113
propaganda, Huthi, 271–273
Putin, Vladimir, invasion of Ukraine, 291

Qalipu First Nation in Canada, 108
Québec: assimilation in, 62; Charles De Gaulle and, 5; Charter of Rights and Freedoms, 65, 70; collective identity in, 64; Commission of Inquiry, 63–65; ethnic nationalism in, 59; Francophone majority in, 61–62; immigration to, 60; independence movement of, 57; integrative pluralism in, 64; interculturalism in, 60–66, 69–70; majoritarian identity, 66, 71; majority culture, 58–60; nation, 4; national identity in, 63; national integration, 58; nationalism, 16–17, 57–72; Quiet Revolution, in Quebec, 58, 59, 60; "Reasonable Accommodations" in, 63–64; religious accommodation in, 64–65; secularism in, 64–68; secularism, 57; Sovereignty-Association, 60–61

racial mixing, Mexico, 141
radio broadcasting, in Biafran conflict, 245
rallies, in Biafran strategy, 244–245
realism, and U.S. foreign policy, 43–44
"reasonable accommodations" in Québec, 63–64
redistribution of land ownership, Mexico, 139–145
refugees from Tibet, 187, 194–196
region and representation in virtual Tibet, 195–196
religion and nationalism, 2, 5, 10, 92, 293; in "virtual" Tibet, 188–189
religious accommodation in Québec, 64–65
relocation of Mi'kmaq to urban areas in 1950s, 112
representation in "virtual" Tibet, 186–187, 194–196
reserves and Mi'kmaq nationhood, 118
residential schools for native peoples in Canada, 110–111, 114, 115, 116
resource distribution and nationalism, 293
revolutionary nationalism in Mexico, 135–139

rhetoric and Huthi, 271–273
Robert the Bruce, and Scottish nationalism, 87
Roosevelt, Franklin, and U.S. views on decolonization, 36
Russia as state, 4; invasion of Ukraine, 291, 297–298

Sa'da Wars, Yemen, 264–265
Sahrawi Arab Democratic Republic, as disputed nation, 11
Saleh, Ali Abdullah, of Yemen, 262, 264, 265
San Andrés Accords on Indigenous Rights and Cultures, Mexico, 152
Saudi Arabia: Houthi movement in Yemen, 19–20, 266; Iran, 274–275
Scotland: Bannockburn as symbol, 87; Celtic Revival movement, 90; culture and Scottish nationalism, 86–87; disintegration of British Empire, 92; economic attractions to Britain, 85; Enlightenment, and Scottish identity, 86; ethnic identity, 7; Great Britain and, 79, 85–86; Home Rule Association, 89–90; identity and Scottish Enlightenment, 86; nation, 80; National Party, 80, 91; nationalism, 17, 79–95, 292–293; option of union with France, 81–84; Parliament, and union in Britain, 84; Parliament, lack of power to hold referendum on independence, 95; public opinion against incorporation in 1706, 82; reasons for union in Britain, 81–82; referendum on leaving the United Kingdom in 2014, 93; Scots language, 87–88; Scots National League, 90; unhappiness with British links, 80; withdrawal from United Kingdom, 93–94

Scots National League, and Scottish nationalism, 90
Scott, Sir Walter, and Scottish nationalism, 88
secession and nationalism, 14–15, 292
Second World, United States foreign policy and, 28
secularism in Québec, 57, 64–68
self-determination: Biafran, 235; Kurdistan, 19, 213–215; U.S. ideology, 28–33
separatism, in New Zealand, 169–173
Sèvres, Treaty of, and Kurdistan, 213
Singhalese nationalism, 9
social nation, 2; Mi'kmaq nationhood, 113
solidarity, and national identity, 8
Somaliland, as disputed nation, 11
Sons-of-the-soil, and nationalism, 14–15
South Caucasus and nationalism, 15
South Korea, as disputed nation, 11
South Ossetia, as disputed nation, 11
Southern Transitional Council, Yemen, 266
sovereignty, 12: in indigenous groups, New Zealand, 164–166; nation-building, 6–7, 10, 12; part of nationalism, 2
Sovereignty-Association in Québec, 60–61
Special People's Congress, Tibet, 191
Staatsnation, 4
Stalin, Josef, and concept of self-determination, 214
state, distinct from nation, 3–4; nationalism and, 13
statelessness, 3
Sudan, and nationalism, 15
Supreme Justice Commission and Tibetan Parliament in Exile, 192, 197–198

Syria and Kurdish nationalism, 19, 212, 214

Taiwan, as disputed nation, 11
Taliban, and nationalism, 15
Tamil nationalism, 9
territory: Igbo in Nigeria, 241; Mi'kmaq, 106, 112–113, 118; nationalism, 3, 292
Thai nationalism, 9
Third World nationalism, 294; and U.S. foreign policy, 28, 41–43
Tibet: Buddhism, and China, 18–19; Central Tibetan Administration, 192–193; Chinese occupation of, 188; culture in exile, 189–194; democracy, 189–194; digital communication, 186; government-in-exile, 186–187, 189–194; nationalism, 14, 185–201, 292–293; Parliament-in-Exile and Supreme Justice Commission, 193, 195–196, 197–198; parliamentary representation, 194–196; political institutions and Dalai Lama, 190–194; politics and religion in, 188–189; refugees, 187, 194–196; Special People's Congress, 191; struggle with China, 18–19; Supreme Justice Commission, 192; virtual government, 188; welfare associations in diaspora, 196
Transnistria, as disputed nation, 11
Treaty of Sèvres and Kurdistan, 213
Treaty of Waitangi, New Zealand, 164–166
treaty rights, native people in Canada, 117
Turkey: Kurdistan Democracy Party, 216; Kurdish nationalism, 19, 207–222
types of nationalism, 292–293

U.S. foreign policy, 27–44: economic integration and, 29–33; expansionism, 27; nationalism, 16; Vietnam, 37–38
Ukraine: nationalism, 15; Russian invasion, 259, 291, 297–298
United Arab Emirates, and Huthi, 274–275
United Nations, and disputed nations, 10–11
United States. *See* U.S.
urbanization and nationalism, 293

Vietnam: nationalism, 9; and U.S. foreign policy, 30, 37; Woodrow Wilson and, 35
"Virtual Tibet": communication, 186; constitution, 190–191; politics and religion, 188–189; representation in Tibet, 194–196; Tibetans, 199–200
Voice of Biafra International, 240

Wabanaki Confederacy in Canada, 108
Wahhabism, and Houthi movement in Yemen, 19–20
Waitangi Tribunal, Māori rights in New Zealand, 173–174
Wales and England, and Scottish nationalism, 17
Wallace, William, and Scottish nationalism, 89
war and nationalism, 13–16
welfare associations in Tibetan diaspora, 196
Welsh ethnic identity, 7
Wilson, Woodrow: colonialism and, 34–35; concept of "self-determination," 213; internationalism, 35; nationalism and, 13–14; U.S. foreign policy, 28–33; Vietnam and, 35

women's history and American foreign policy, 32
World War I, and nationalism, 14
World War II, U.S. foreign policy and, 38

Yemen: 1962 revolution, 261–262; 1994 civil war, 263; evolution of, 260–262; Houthi movement in, 19–20, 259–278; oil, 266; Sa'da Wars, 264–265; Saudi Arabia, 266; Southern Transitional Council, 266
Young Māori Party, New Zealand, 168–169

Zapatista uprising, Mexico, 17–18, 146–149, 149–151, 151–156
Zaydi community and Huthi movement, 262–263, 267

www.ingramcontent.com/pod-product-compliance
Lightning Source LLC
Chambersburg PA
CBHW031706230426
43668CB00006B/123